# SEXUAL DISORIENTATIONS

# TRANSDISCIPLINARY THEOLOGICAL COLLOQUIA

Theology has hovered for two millennia between scriptural metaphor and philosophical thinking; it takes flesh in its symbolic, communal, and ethical practices. With the gift of this history and in the spirit of its unrealized potential, the Transdisciplinary Theological Colloquia intensify movement between and beyond the fields of religion. A multivocal discourse of theology takes place in the interstices, at once self-deconstructive in its pluralism and constructive in its affirmations.

Hosted annually by Drew University's Theological School, the colloquia provide a matrix for such conversations, while Fordham University Press serves as the midwife for their publication. Committed to the slow transformation of religio-cultural symbolism, the colloquia continue Drew's long history of engaging historical, biblical, and philosophical hermeneutics, practices of social justice, and experiments in theopoetics.

Catherine Keller, *Director*

# SEXUAL DISORIENTATIONS

## Queer Temporalities, Affects, Theologies

KENT L. BRINTNALL,
JOSEPH A. MARCHAL,
AND STEPHEN D. MOORE

EDITORS

FORDHAM UNIVERSITY PRESS • NEW YORK • 2018

Fordham University Press also publishes its books in a variety of electronic formats. Some content that appears in print may not be available in electronic books.

Visit us online at www.fordhampress.com.

Library of Congress Cataloging-in-Publication Data available online at https://catalog.loc.gov.

Printed in the United States of America

20 19 18   5 4 3 2 1

First edition

CONTENTS

# SEXUAL DISORIENTATIONS

# Introduction
# Queer Disorientations: Four Turns and a Twist

STEPHEN D. MOORE, KENT L. BRINTNALL, AND JOSEPH A. MARCHAL

*In order to be become orientated, you might suppose that we must first experience disorientation.*
—SARA AHMED, *Queer Phenomenology*

*If one wants to . . . consider sexual politics during this time, a certain problem arises. . . . We already have more than one time at work in this time. . . . The way in which debates within sexual politics are framed is already imbued with the problem of time, of progress in particular, and in certain notions of what it means to unfold a future of freedom in time.*
—JUDITH BUTLER, "Sexual Politics, Torture, and Secular Time"

It's about time. This book is principally about time—queer time, to be precise. But it's also about time that a book on queer theologies tackled queer temporalities, together with queer affects.[1] Like the colloquium out of which it emerged, this volume seeks to engage with certain field-reorienting—and field-disorienting—inflections of queer theory whose origins lie in the mid- to late 1990s but which have been oddly underremarked even by those in the theological disciplines most invested in all matters queer. The literature by biblical scholars, theologians, and church historians that has been assembled incrementally under the patchwork queer banner is by now a sprawling, endnote-defying corpus.[2] Yet the prominent developments in queer theory surveyed in this introduction do not feature significantly or at all in that corpus. Symptomatically, one searches in vain for mention of them in the field-consolidating works of queer biblical criticism and queer theology that have appeared even since 2005, whether multiauthored works such as *The Queer Bible Commentary* (2006), *Bible Trouble* (2011), and *Queer Theology* (2007),[3] or singly authored works such as Patrick Cheng's cartographically ambitious *Radical*

*Love: An Introduction to Queer Theology* (2011) and Susannah Cornwall's theoretically nuanced *Controversies in Queer Theology* (2011). The present volume presupposes these previous, altogether indispensable volumes, along with other similar studies too numerous to name. What motivates, indeed necessitates, this volume, however, is not a mere reflexive desire to fill a gap or occupy a supplemental space. The volume instead emerges from the conviction, shared by the editors and, we suspect, by many of the contributors, that the theological fields have much to offer the cross-disciplinary enterprise of queer studies, a conviction elaborated in the final section of this introduction.

This collection seeks to blaze a new trail, then, to strike out from a heavily trodden path. The trajectories of queer theory with which it aims to intersect will be sketched summarily and then mapped more thoroughly in the pages that follow. Our introduction attempts to orient the reader to certain disorientations that have occurred in queer theory since the mid-1990s: *sexual* disorientations, needless to say, but also *temporal* disorientations and disorienting *feelings*. We begin with the summative sketch, our (no doubt delusional) attempt to transcend the disorienting scene and describe what we see from on high.

## ECSTATIC OVERVIEW

> We know time through the field of the affective, and affect is tightly bound to temporality. But let us take ecstasy together, as the Magnetic Fields request.
>
> —JOSÉ ESTEBAN MUÑOZ, *Cruising Utopia*

Some of the most significant, most discussed works in queer theory have interrogated time. They have questioned, reframed, and reimagined how we enact our relations to the past and the future. This timely body of work *on* time seeks to replace reliance on logics of repetition, linearity, periodicity, and teleology with counterlogics of hauntological historiography, erotohistoriography, and queer temporal drag; anachronisms and proximities; contaminations and caresses across temporal gulfs. Such work includes Carolyn Dinshaw's time-folding reconception of historiography as a practice enabling queer touches across time; Carla Freccero's reconception of it as a practice of becoming ghostly in relation to a past by which one is perpetually haunted; Madhavi Menon's counterheterotemporal historiography without historical chronology, historical periods, or historical method; Judith Halberstam's and Elizabeth Freeman's counterchrononormative imaginings of alternative temporalities unregulated by the paradigmatic markers of heteronormative life experience, most of all marriage and reproduction; Lee Edelman's antisocial insistence that certain forms of commitment to certain forms of futurity serve to eradicate queers and queerness; José Esteban Muñoz's utopian insistence that queerness is of value only when viewed on the glimmering horizon of the future; and Heather Love's unsettling redirection of the queer gaze backward to a dark, disavowed past. Just as the foundational works of queer theory revealed that gender, sexuality, and race/ethnicity are not natural or inevitable but social and conventional—and hence ethical and political—these time-(dis)oriented works of queer theory demonstrate that even seemingly commonsensical categories such as past, present, and future are no less culturally constructed and no less intimately bound up with the (il)logics of desire and power.

This body of work influences and is extended by several essays in this collection. For example, Joseph Marchal's engagement with the Corinthian women, the apostle Paul, and their respective interpreters helps us think about our complex relation to history and our competing understandings of time. The alternative temporality of the Corinthian women impels us to interrogate certain of the oppositions within contemporary queer debates about time, while these debates dissonantly feed back into queering disidentifications with long dead but haunting figures who persist partially while posing prophetic possibilities. Examining another Pauline text, James Hoke asks how time and empire are bound together—and how they might become unbound—in the Letter to the Romans. Drawing on Elizabeth Freeman's concepts of chrononormativity and erotohistoriography (more on which below), Hoke shows how the Roman Empire bound time by setting itself up as the eternal "end of history" and argues that the wo/men of the early Christian assemblies invite us to share with them pleasurably queer sensations at a tempo that is out of step with the sex/gender logics of Rome.

Laurel Schneider tries to move us away from biblical texts and Western theoretical frames by turning to Gerald Vizenor's notion of *survivance*, a Native American–inflected concept that acknowledges histories of violence, conquest, and devastation but also offers a much more complex future than a mere overcoming of a tragic past. Schneider draws the concept of survivance into a cross-cultural conversation with queer theology, reflecting on the queer affects and temporalities that make such theology possible, even beyond the survivable name "queer." In Jacqueline Hidalgo's contribution to the volume, there is a bridging of biblical and indigenous worlds through an engagement with Cherríe Moraga's "Codex Xerí," the conclusion to *The Last Generation* and a text that tries to recall a past that has been lost under the weight of conquest. "Codex Xerí" sets the biblical book of Revelation alongside the many glyphs of Latinx revelation, be they written on barrio walls or are present in bodily assemblies, thereby becoming competing scriptures as objects of temporal refraction. In her essay Karmen MacKendrick poetically and provocatively explores what it means to remember at all, what it *feels like* to have the past occupy the present in a manner that might transform the future. Via

Augustine and Judith Butler, MacKendrick evokes a God who haunts and argues that such a haunting ties an immemorial past to a future of possibility. If the remembered God is the possible, the open, then all time is queer, always open to being other than it is.

Some of the most significant, most discussed works in queer theory have also analyzed feelings, emotions, inchoate sensations, and other bodily reactions to sensory stimuli; in other words, or in a word, they have analyzed affect. The emergence and development of affect theory has been intimately bound up with queer theory. And that intimate interconnectivity has been evident in explorations of queer temporality; Carolyn Dinshaw, Carla Freccero, Elizabeth Freeman, and Heather Love all model affective modes of queer historiography. But the fusion of temporality and affectivity has extended well beyond their work. As Sara Ahmed, Lauren Berlant, Ann Cvetkovich, Judith Halberstam, and Eve Kosofsky Sedgwick have variously taught us, it is not just how we *think* about time but also how we *feel* about time that matters: the traumas of the past, the fragility of the present, the seductiveness of the future. Temporality is a politically and ethically charged category because its affective resonances are incalculably consequential. Past, present, and future are the interflowing, ever-shifting sites where happiness, joy, shame, loss, mourning, disgust, despair, hope, pride, and victory are experienced and processed. It is in the boundary-eroding current of time that longing and love, identification and connection, pleasure and desire collect, coalesce, and circulate. Our affective orientation to the world, like our temporal one, is entangled with complex social and cultural processes that clamor for careful analytical attention.

Several authors in the present volume try to take the reader into these new ways of feeling and experiencing time. Both Karen Bray's concept of bipolar time and Linn Marie Tonstad's concept of entrepreneurial subjectivity seek to name, describe, and transcribe the set of feelings that characterizes life in late capitalism. For both authors, experiences of fragmentation, dissolution, and shattering are part of the dominant cultural order, which requires us to rethink the queer or countercultural potential of such experiences of time. Specifically, Bray asks how post-Fordist temporalities *feel*, and argues that the post-Fordist moment is a Holy Saturday moment—a day lived in the wake of crucifixion and the shadow of an uncertain resurrection. Bray's bipolar time is a moment of protest and potentiality from within this shadow, a dialectic between the soul-deadening effects of capitalism and the "mad" feeling that things might be otherwise. Tonstad, meanwhile, asks how time can become a site of nonreproduction of heterosexual and heterosocial sameness, and argues that the various temporalities of late and financialized capitalism have introduced new forms of reproduction and new forms of discontinuity. Tonstad employs the temporality of entrepreneurial subjectivity to pose questions to some influential theological and queer-theoretical strategies for countering capitalism's rapacity.

Ann Pellegrini reckons with feelings that belong as much to the queer as to the religious and are bound up with the temporal. She argues that psychoanalysis may provide us with conceptual tools for thinking about strange experiences of time, since it has always been interested in odd and unsettling temporal conjunctions. The secular aspirations of psychoanalysis sometimes result in a tension in the ways it tells time. On the one hand, psychoanalysis frequently submits to a developmentalist imperative. On the other hand, this chrononormativity is at profound odds with its capacity to cause past and present to coexist in ways that confound secular time's forward march. Maia Kotrosits, too, is concerned with the relationship of present to past, linking the contemporary and ongoing trauma of AIDS to the ancient traumas that inform the Gospel of Mark in an effort to think about the ways that we strive and fail to manage traumatic interruptions of time. She extends Tim Dean's reflections on the anxiety of temporal suspense and the challenge of living with inconclusiveness to Mark's apocalyptic tale of waiting for the end of everything. Mark's Gospel emerges from a sense of doomed inevitability and a terrifying lack of resolution, while attesting to the queerness of time and the problem of history. In his essay Mark Jordan ruminates on how—perhaps whether—we can actually write the complex feelings of time that queer theories and queer theologies call to our attention. For Jordan, thinking with Foucault, whatever queer theology has managed to do, it has not yet been able to sustain new forms for speech about bodily pleasures in lived time. The episodes, the claims, the passions of queer theology encircle us, waiting for us to recognize that we must learn to write differently about them. Jordan writes his own longing to recover the desires that first animated queer theology, desires now lost in time or frustrated by the absorption of queer theology into the academic mainstream.

## THE ANTINORMATIVE TURN

> What immortality was to the Greeks, . . . what faith was to the martyrs, . . . what glamour is to drag queens, normalcy is to the contemporary American.
>
> —MICHAEL WARNER, *The Trouble with Normal*

Let us begin again and turn our cursory sketch into a more serviceable map. Queer theory's origins—the tensive relationship between early academic and early activist deployments of the term "queer," the fateful coining of the term "queer theory," the field-constituting identification of a queer theory canon composed of iconic specimen texts and iconic precursor texts—have been recounted many times and do not require another recital.[4] What concerns us here is a certain thickening of the plot, a complexification of what queer theory became beyond what it was initially thought to be, that presumed identity being the poststructuralist analysis of sex and sexuality.

This "beyond" may be narrated in term of four turns or swerves within queer theory: an antinormative turn, an antisocial turn, a temporal turn, and an affective turn. These assorted swerves were not discrete developments. The temporal turn and the affective turn were interlinked, as already demonstrated. And the antinormative turn, the antisocial turn, and the temporal turn were yet more thoroughly intertwined. The antisocial turn in particular may be regarded as an instance both of the antinormative and the temporal turns, a further contortion within those two turns—even though the antisocial turn predates the temporal turn, strictly speaking, but temporal paradox is partly what the temporal turn is all about.

In 1993, a mere three years after the term "queer theory" was coined,[5] Eve Sedgwick could already report in "Queer and Now," the opening essay in her *Tendencies* collection, "A lot of the most exciting recent work around 'queer' spins the term outward along dimensions that can't be subsumed under gender and sexuality at all,"[6] while Michael Warner, introducing *Fear of a Queer Planet* the same year, could write, "In different ways queer politics might . . . have implications for any area of social life."[7] It was becoming particularly apparent that queer theory could be extended, elasticized, so as to wrap around normality—or "normativity," as one soon learned to say—in any of its hydra-headed forms and subject it to defamiliarizing and destabilizing analysis.[8]

Warner's own critical voyage into the tepid waters of normativity—his much-discussed book *The Trouble with Normal* (1999)[9]—tacked close to the sexual shore, as did the queer of color critique associated with Cathy J. Cohen, José Esteban Muñoz, Siobhan B. Somerville, Roderick A. Ferguson, and other scholars for whom a queering of gender and sexuality always needed a concomitant consideration of race and ethnicity, those other towering pillars of exclusionary normativity.[10] But other queer explorations ventured farther from the sexual shore. Robert McRuer, introducing his own book *Crip Theory* (2006), quoted from *The Trouble with Normal* but added: "A critique of normalcy has similarly been central to the disability rights movement and to disability studies."[11] In a particularly striking decoupling of queer theory from sexuality, McRuer proposed a concept of "compulsory able-bodiedness" in counterpoint to Adrienne Rich's proto-queer-theoretical concept of "compulsory heterosexuality,"[12] noting that "able-bodiedness, even more than heterosexuality, still largely masquerades as a nonidentity, as the natural order of things," as the very face and form of the normal.[13] Jasbir Puar's *Terrorist Assemblages: Homonationalism in Queer Times* (2007), meanwhile, declared as its theme "the proliferation, occupation, and suppression of queernesses in relation to patriotism, war, torture, security, death, terror, terrorism, detention, and deportation, themes usually imagined as devoid of connection to sexual politics in general and queer politics in particular"[14]—but the dark backdrop for "the surprising but not fully unexpected flowering of new normativities in these queer times."[15] Many other such examples could be cited.

Many authors in this collection examine the complex inflections of queerness across race, nation, and ethnicity. Eric Thomas engages the book of Revelation in conversation with African and African American readers, fully conversant with experiences of colonization, slavery, violence, and dehumanization, in an effort to work through what it means for queers in such communities to find hope. The threats of not being listed in the lamb's book of life, not being one of the 144,000 who have not defiled themselves with women, or being cast into the "hell" of the lake that burns with fire and sulfur are empty for queer people of color throughout the African Diaspora who experience Armageddon as the everyday. Thomas proposes that a revisioned apocalyptic epilogue can become a prologue for the articulation of Africana queer utopian futures outside of Christo-heteronormativity. Jacqueline Hidalgo, whose essay has already been introduced in brief, outlines the specific practices of reading, the specific acts of creativity, and the specific strategies of resistance that inform Cherríe Moraga's production of a canon that takes seriously the experience of an indigenous people overwhelmed, but never fully sundered, by colonial imperialism. Laurel Schneider's examination of Gerald Vizenor's concept of *survivance* shows that any simple or straightforward conception of hope is not adequate for understanding the way that colonized peoples have lived through the devastation, if not the eradication, of their lives and communities.

Such work strategically strays from overly narrow notions of the sexual. The conception of queer theory as possessing a formidable extrasexual reach—a reach exceeding heteronormativity and homonormativity to encompass normativity as such—has long been disseminated. In consequence, desexualized definitions of queer theory, and queer studies in general, such as that offered by Kath Browne and Catherine J. Nash in their introduction to *Queer Methods and Methodologies* (2010) have long been commonplace: "Queer scholarship . . . in its contemporary form is anti-normative and seeks to subvert, challenge and critique a host of taken for granted 'stabilities' in our social lives."[16]

The unsexing of the queer has, however, also occasioned periodic (self-) questioning among queer theorists. "What's Queer about Queer Studies Now?" inquired a 2005 thematic issue of the journal *Social Text*.[17] A retrospective volume on queer theory from 2011, with a who's who list of contributors, was titled *After Sex?* and its introduction began, "What has queer theory become . . . ? What, if anything, does it not include within its purview?"[18] More pointedly, it asked: "Can work be regarded as queer if it's not explicitly 'about' sexuality?"[19] And, inevitably perhaps—it was surely only a matter of time—a collection from 2015, this time a thematic issue of the journal *differences*, was titled "Queer Theory without Antinormativity." Its editors, Robyn Wiegman and Elizabeth A. Wilson, begin by noting how queer theory has, since its inception, been thoroughly marked by opposition to the tyranny of normativity—"heteronormativity, homonormativity, whiteness, family values, marriage, monogamy, Christmas: all have been objects of sustained critique"—so much so that such critique is commonly thought to "[mark] the spot where *queer* and *theory* meet."[20] That norm in turn becomes the target of the collection: "Can queer theorizing proceed without a primary commitment to antinormativity?"[21] David V. Ruffolo had already conducted an interrogation in his monograph *Post-Queer Politics* (2012) of the queer/heteronormative binary itself, deeming it inadequate to "the contemporary complexities of neoliberal capitalism and globalization."[22] But in plummeting so precipitously into the "post-" and the "anti-," we risk imposing premature apocalyptic closure on our tale of four turns, so let's turn back.

## THE ANTISOCIAL TURN

> Dare we trace, then, the untraversable path that leads to no good and has no other end than an end to the good as such?
> —LEE EDELMAN, "Antagonism, Negativity, and the Subject of Queer Theory"

The second turn in queer theory, the antisocial turn, may be regarded as a radical inflection of the antinormative turn. The common tag for this turn is "the antisocial thesis in queer theory." Its origins are ordinarily associated with Leo Bersani's 1987 article "Is the Rectum a Grave?" and more particularly with his 1995 book *Homos*,[23] but its apogee is said to be Lee Edelman's 2004 book *No Future: Queer Theory and the Death Drive*.[24] Extraordinary claims have been made for this book. Michael O'Rourke, for example, recounting the "afterlives" of queer theory, remarks: "In the wake of Edelman's book there has been an almost universal rejection of, a resounding 'fuck you,' to the future and what has come to be called the 'anti-social thesis' now dominates the post-political, post-futural, anti-or post-relational landscape of queer studies."[25] Notwithstanding such claims, however, virtually every engagement with Edelman's book has sought to critique it, resist it, or otherwise establish distance from it. Edelman's pronouncements have often been quoted, but they have rarely been sympathetically extended or analytically deployed.

Brock Perry's turn to Edelman's work in the present volume, in an effort to understand what pleasures might be available to queer readers in the horrific scenes of hell represented in the second-century *Apocalypse of Peter*, begins to remedy this problem. Certain trademarked features of Edelman's thought, reviewed below, enable Perry to make profound queer sense of an ancient apocalyptic scenario in which gender deviants are forced by their tormentors to climb a cliff and throw themselves from it eternally. In allowing ourselves to be haunted by the queer figures inhabiting this particular hell, Perry argues, we may also be able to share in their jouissance, to experience the self-loss of their fall, and to hold open the future for others whose lives continue to be made hell by those who would leave them behind as the price of admission into paradise. Similarly, Kent Brintnall's Edelmanian analysis of pro-LGBT exegeses of the Sodom and Gomorrah story also tries to show the value of Edelman's ideas for queer interpreters of religious texts and traditions. Pro-LGBT interpretations of Sodom and Gomorrah illustrate the dynamics Edelman traces in *No Future*: They seek to displace queerness onto other bodies without recognizing the violence of that gesture, all the while denouncing homophobia. At issue, for Brintnall, is the structural antagonism, the implacable violence, that structures the social and that seems to characterize the divine in its most excessive moments.

"Should a homosexual be a good citizen?" Bersani inquired in *Homos*, adding: "It would be difficult to imagine a less gay-affirmative question at a time when gay men and lesbians have been strenuously trying to persuade straight society that they can be good parents, good soldiers, good priests."[26] Yet the radical incommensurability of homosexuality with "the good" as socially defined, with "the social" itself as heteronormatively conceived, was precisely what Bersani wanted to affirm—and what he held that homophobes had, in fact, recognized. In "Is the Rectum a Grave?," indeed, he had gone so far as to say, "It is perhaps necessary to accept the pain of embracing, at least provisionally, a homophobic representation of homosexuality."[27]

Edelman adopts the same counterintuitive strategy in *No Future*: "We should listen to, and perhaps even be instructed by, the readings of queer sexualities produced by the forces of reaction."[28] What the right has gotten right, for Edelman—more right than the left—is that queerness threatens "the wholesale rupturing of the social fabric."[29] This is because the warp and woof of the social, for Edelman, is "the logic of reproductive futurism,"[30] meaning that the telos of the social is its propagation and protection so that it may be preserved and handed down to "the Child," a figure that validates the sacrifices of the present and secures the promise of the future. This figural Child demarcates "the perpetual horizon of every acknowledged politics" and is "the fantasmatic beneficiary of every political intervention"[31] but should never "be confused with . . . any historical children."[32] The Child may, in fact, inflict harm on children, according to Edelman, demanding their sacrifice along with that of the adults conscripted to protect them. Reproductive futurism imposes an absolute "ideological limit on political discourse as such, preserving in the process the absolute privilege of heteronormativity," by anathematizing its opposite, expelling it from the political arena, rendering it unthinkable.[33] "Impossibly," however, "against all reason," Edelman's project is enacted in the very space that heterogenital politics renders all but ineffable[34]—all of which leads to the most infamous passage in the book:

> Queers must respond to the violent force of such constant provocations not only by insisting on our equal right to the social order's prerogatives, not only by avowing our capacity to promote that order's coherence and integrity, but also by saying explicitly what Law and the Pope and the whole of the Symbolic order for which they stand hear anyway in each and every expression or manifestation of queer sexuality: Fuck the social order and the Child in whose name we're collectively terrorized; fuck Annie; fuck the waif from *Les Mis*; fuck the poor, innocent kid on the Net; fuck Laws both with capital ls and with small; fuck the whole network of Symbolic relations and the future that serves as its prop.[35]

Significantly for religious studies, Edelman seems to see reproductive futurism as a kind of unofficial state religion: The Child is "the prop of the secular theology on which our social reality rests: the secular theology that shapes at once the meaning of our collective narratives and our collective narratives of meaning."[36] In Edelman's article "Antagonism, Negativity, and the Subject of Queer Theory" (2006) reproductive futurism becomes "the universal empire of the Futurch"[37]—a neologism Edelman declines to decode but which appears to be an amalgam of "Future" and "Church." Outside the towering walls of the Futurch, but also unsettlingly within it, stands the *sinthom*osexual, another Edelmanian neologism, this one crafted from Jacques Lacan's late concept of the *sinthome*, that disruptive yet indispensable (non-)place of meaninglessness within the Symbolic Order (which, for Lacan, is the domain of language, law, and culture).[38] But *sinthom*osexuality also evokes the "sin" of homosexuality, and this sin makes the *sinthom*osexual "into something of a s(a)in(t)."[39] "To embrace the impossibility, the inhumanity of the *sinthom*osexual: that," for Edelman, "is the ethical task for which queers are singled out."[40] And yet the *sinthom*osexual is more a sinner than a saint all told, who "won't offer a blessed thing by way of salvation, won't promise any transcendence or grant us a vision of something to come," who is neither a martyr nor a "proponent of martyrdom for the sake of a cause," who "forsakes all causes, all social action, all responsibility for a better tomorrow," who in place of activism "performs, instead, an act," that "of repudiating the social, of stepping, or trying to step . . . beyond compulsory compassion, beyond the future and the snare of images keeping us always in its thrall."[41]

The queer strategy of principled negativity that achieved its most radical expression in Edelman's *No Future*—for the antisocial turn in queer theory is also the negative turn—found alternative expression in Judith Halberstam's *The Queer Art of Failure* (2011), a calculated bathetic descent into "ways of being and knowing that stand outside of conventional understandings of success," success "in a heteronormative, capitalist society" equating all too easily with "specific forms of reproductive maturity combined with wealth accumulation."[42] It is with José Esteban Muñoz's *Cruising Utopia: The Then and There of Queer Futurity* (2009), however, that Edelman's book is most commonly associated and with which it is most commonly contrasted.

Muñoz frames his book as a critical response to "the antirelational turn" (what we have been calling the antisocial turn) in queer studies as epitomized by the work of Bersani and above all Edelman.[43] In particular, Muñoz responds to Edelman's argument "that the future is the province of the child and therefore not for the queers" by counterarguing "that queerness is primarily about futurity" and even about hope.[44] In what is probably the most quoted sentence of the book, Muñoz asserts: "I contend that if queerness is to have any value whatsoever, it must be viewed as being visible only in the horizon."[45] The book's opening statements lyrically illuminate this claim:

> Queerness is not yet here. Queerness is an ideality. Put another way, we are not yet queer. We may never touch queerness, but we can feel it as the warm illumination of a horizon imbued with potentiality. We have never been queer, yet queerness exists for us as an ideality that can be distilled from the past and used to imagine a future. The future is queerness's domain.[46]

The present, meanwhile, is a "quagmire" and "the here and now is a prison house," a "totalizing rendering of reality."[47]

Muñoz's musings on queerness are occasionally marked by a quasi-religious resonance. In the book's opening statement, for instance, we read, "Queerness is the thing that lets us feel that this world is not enough, that indeed something is missing,"[48] and a later passage cleverly segues from the "step[ping] out of the here and now or straight time" enabled by the drug ecstasy to the ecstatic mystical transports epitomized by Saint Teresa of Ávila.[49] Yet it is not to religion but to aesthetics that Muñoz explicitly appeals for guidance: "The aesthetic, especially the queer aesthetic, frequently contains blueprints and schemata of a forward-dawning futurity. Both the ornamental and the quotidian can contain a map of the utopia that is queerness."[50] That Muñoz employs the term *utopia* in apposition with his queerness-to-come is significant. This is, indeed, a book about utopia—utopia as politicized through the thought of Theodor Adorno, Walter Benjamin, Herbert Marcuse, and above all Ernst Bloch (who, ostensibly at least, is as much Muñoz's muse in *Cruising Utopia* as Lacan is Edelman's in *No Future*),[51] and pressed through the dual wringers of queer art and queer theory. In his concluding reflections Muñoz states: "Utopia in this book has been about an insistence on something else, something better, something dawning. I offer this book as a resource for the political imagination. This text is meant to serve as something of a flight plan for a collective political becoming."[52]

Although Muñoz sees his book as "replacing a faltering antirelational mode of queer theory"—one epitomized by Edelman's *No Future*—"with a queer utopianism,"[53] Muñoz's concept of the queer might not be as far removed from Edelman's as might first appear. For Muñoz, the queer is never quite here. For Edelman, the queer is equally evasive of present pinning down: "For queerness can never define an identity; it can only ever disturb one," Edelman states.[54] Muñoz's and Edelman's relative closeness, notwithstanding the real differences that separate them, renders them both vulnerable to the charge brought against their brand of queer theory by, say, the editors of *Queer Futures* (2013), namely, that it "testifies to the desire to reach out to an ever elusive, always already other place that queer has come to signify," an endeavor that, however, threatens to alienate queer from the mundane details of LGBTIQ existence.[55] This is a sobering critique, although one could readily imagine Edelman and Muñoz each arguing out of his own theoretical armature that the regulated details of day-to-day existence are precisely the bars that either lock queer in or lock it out.[56]

In the present collection, Brandy Daniels, bringing the theologian Sarah Coakley into conversation with Muñoz, with a specific interest in the question of how ritual practices can create new subjectivities, new relations to future possibility, and new experiences of hope, underscores the theological potential of Muñoz's ideas. Daniels argues that Coakley's theology forecloses openness to the other by adhering to what Muñoz calls "straight time's choke hold." For Daniels, Muñoz's account of the future in the present as something to be enacted in and through affective and other excesses is imperative for a theological imagination that is truly liberative. Karen Bray and Linn Marie Tonstad, in different ways, also find Muñoz a generative conversation partner in trying to understand the challenges created by neoliberal capitalism. For both authors, securing a sense of possibility is absolutely vital; for neither author are these possibilities clear or certain. Muñoz, then, opens up a different conception of the hope that so many religious discourses promise.

With Edelman's challenging concept of reproductive futurism and Muñoz's answering concept of queer futurity we are already immersed in queer temporalities. But let us wade out of this particular stream to situate the temporal turn in queer theory more broadly.

## THE TEMPORAL TURN

> And lately, time is the "asexual" domain I've been working on, though I can't say that this feels like a departure from, or a beyond to, queer theory.
>
> —ELIZABETH FREEMAN, "Still After," in *After Sex?* edited by Janet E. Halley and Andrew Parker

The turn to temporality in queer theory is related to the turn to antinormativity to the extent that it is a further deployment of the "queer" in spheres that are not simply coextensive with the sexual or the gendered. This temporal turn has taken several interrelated forms. The differently calibrated but equally time-attuned work of Edelman and Muñoz may be regarded as one manifestation of it. A second manifestation entails an extension of the interrogation of normativity to reimaginings of normal or straight time: time marked by such life experiences as marriage, reproduction, and child rearing. "Queer subcultures," as Judith Halberstam notes in the introduction to *In a Queer Time and Place* (2005), "produce alternative temporalities by allowing their participants to believe that their futures can be imagined according to logics that lie outside of those paradigmatic markers of life experience—namely, birth, marriage, reproduction, and death."[57] Halberstam parses out the "logic of reproductive temporality" as follows:

> The time of reproduction is ruled by a biological clock for women and by strict bourgeois rules of respectability and scheduling for married couples. Obviously, not all people who have children keep or even are able to keep reproductive time, but many and possibly most people believe that the scheduling of repro-time is natural and desirable. Family time refers to the normative scheduling of daily life (early to bed, early to rise) that accompanies the practice of child rearing. The time of inheritance refers to an overview of generational time within which values, wealth, goods, and morals are passed through family ties from one generation to the next. It also connects the family to the historical past of the nation, and glances ahead to connect the family to the future of both familial and national stability.[58]

The parallels with Edelman's concept of reproductive futurism are obvious, although Halberstam's thoughts on queer time seem to have developed independently of it.[59] For Halberstam, however—whose *In a Queer Time and*

*Place* is, after all, subtitled *Transgender Bodies, Subcultural Lives*—"the transgender body functions in relation to time and space as a rich site for fantasies of futurity and anachronism."[60] Why this is so is not hard to see. The discontinuous life narratives of trans folk particularly epitomize the alternative temporalities of which Halberstam writes, the imagining and embodying of futures that fall altogether outside the paradigmatic markers of normative life "progression"—even as the normalizing medical scripts extract an alternative progress narrative from the trans person ("All through my childhood, I was a girl trapped in a boy's body . . .").[61]

For Halberstam, however, queer time, is not the sole preserve of LGBTIQ folk, for "all kinds of people" elect or are obliged to live outside of repro-time "as well as on the edges of logics of labor and production," such as "ravers, club kids, HIV-positive barebackers,[62] rent boys, sex workers, homeless people, drug dealers, and the unemployed," and "perhaps such people could productively be called 'queer subjects' in terms of the ways they live (deliberately, accidentally, or of necessity) during the hours when others sleep and in the spaces (physical, metaphysical, and economic) that others have abandoned."[63] Conversely, as Halberstam hints, many LGBTIQ folk are wedded to repro-time, to domesticity and consumption.[64] Subsequently, in "Theorizing Queer Temporalities: A Roundtable Discussion" (2007), Halberstam will explain that queer time is "a way of being in the world and a critique of the careful social scripts that usher even the most queer among us through major markers of individual development and into normativity."[65] Contrary to understandings of psychoanalysis that emphasize its passion for teleological developmental schemes, Ann Pellegrini in the present volume reminds us of Freud's sensitivities to the various ways that normal development can veer off the tracks. Maia Kotrosits, through an engagement with Tim Dean's ruminations on barebacking, highlights the allure of a certain end—a definitive conclusion to one's narrative—juxtaposing that desire with the traumas of history that belie it. Turning once again to Augustine, among others, Karmen MacKendrick helps us see how memory—an act that seems to be only and always about the past—compels us to rethink any simple notion of development and temporal passage because of the way it constantly reorders present, past, and future.

Much of Halberstam's delineation of queer time, it may be noted, applies, mutatis mutandis, to the ancient Mediterranean world and the place of Jesus and his movement within it, as represented particularly but not only in the Synoptic Gospels. The Synoptic Jesuses, and even the Johannine Jesus, might be said to inhabit queer time in Halberstam's sense of the term, their lives apparently unscripted by the ancient Mediterranean institutions of marriage, biological progeny, conventional labor, or material inheritance. Neither does

Paul seem to run on Roman time, least of all in 1 Corinthians 7, declaring "it is well for a man not to touch a woman" (7:1), "to the unmarried and the widows I say that it is well for them to remain unmarried as I am" (7:8), "concerning virgins . . . I think that, in view of the impending crisis, it is well for you to remain as you are" (7:25–26), and other antinormative injunctions—not that Paul can simply be assimilated with the queer in its most radical forms, and similar counterarguments could be leveled against the Synoptic Jesuses or any Jesus. But it is interesting to note that queer time is not entirely out of joint with the charter documents of Christian theology.

Another signal work on queer time is Elizabeth Freeman's *Time Binds* (2010). As the book's subtitle *Queer Temporalities, Queer Histories* suggests, it concerns the translation of queer time into queer history: "Throughout this book, I try to think against the dominant arrangement of time and history."[66] In effect, Freeman's musings on time take up where Halberstam's left off. Freeman's arguments coalesce around certain fruitful neologisms. *Chrononormativity* names the process whereby "naked flesh is bound into socially meaningful embodiment through temporal regulation," the goal being "maximum productivity."[67] For Freeman, temporal regulation and economic regulation are inextricably intertwined. Under chrononormativity, reproduction is subordinated to production. Under capitalism, sexuality is both teleologically regulated by, and thoroughly assimilated to, economics:

> In the United States, for instance, states now license, register, or certify birth (and thus citizenship, eventually encrypted in a Social Security ID for taxpaying purposes), marriage or domestic partnership (which privatizes caretaking and regulates the distribution of private property), and death (which terminates the identities linked to state benefits, redistributing these benefits through familial channels). . . . In the eyes of the state, this sequence of socioeconomically "productive" moments is what it means to have a life at all.[68]

If Freeman's concept of chrononormativity is about temporal regulation, her concept of *temporal drag* is about temporal dislocation. The latter concept is inspired by "the classically queer practice of drag performance,"[69] as famously interpreted by Judith Butler,[70] but now reinterpreted by Freeman with reference to the temporal connotations of drag: "retrogression, delay, and the pull of the past on the present."[71] Freeman aims to "reenvision the meaning of drag for queer theory." She asks: "What is the *time* of queer performativity?"[72] Temporal drag, for Freeman, is less about "the psychic time of the individual than . . . the movement time of collective political fantasy."[73] And what temporal drag queers is not so much the signifiers "woman" or "man" as the signifier "history."[74] It is "a way of forcing the present to touch its own disavowed past or seemingly outlandish possible futures."[75] It is a "performance of anachrony,"[76] a "practice of archiving culture's throwaway objects, including the outmoded masculinities and femininities from which usable pasts may be extracted."[77] As one recent example of temporal drag, Freeman cites "the gravitational pull that 'lesbian,' and even more so 'lesbian feminist,' sometimes seems to exert on 'queer.'" In many queered classrooms and even in certain works of queer theory, "the lesbian feminist seems cast as the big drag," fated to necromantically conjure up "essentialized bodies, normative visions of women's sexuality, and single-issue identity politics that exclude people of color, the working class, and the transgendered."[78]

In an exchange about temporal drag in "Theorizing Queer Temporalities," a roundtable discussion in which Freeman participated, Carolyn Dinshaw adduces a rather different instance of the phenomenon: "The evangelical Christian movement in the United States . . . works off people's feeling out of step with contemporary mores," which Dinshaw styles a "felt experience of asynchrony" that can "be exploited for social and political reasons."[79] One might argue further, adapting Freeman's language, that the collective performance of temporal drag that is Christian evangelicalism entails a reclaiming of "culture's throwaway objects, including the outmoded masculinities and femininities from which usable pasts may be extracted":[80] "Wives, be subject to your husbands as you are to the Lord. . . . Just as the church is subject to Christ, so also wives ought to be, in everything, to their husbands" (Eph 5:22–24).[81]

The third key concept around which Freeman's arguments in *Time Binds* pivot is *erotohistoriography*. A mode of historiography that refuses both the assumption that "history should be understood rather than felt" and that historiography and fiction are "clearly separable," erotohistoriography "uses the body as a tool to effect, figure, or perform" an encounter with the past as "already in the present."[82] Erotohistoriography recognizes "that contact with historical materials can be precipitated by particular bodily dispositions, and that these connections may elicit bodily responses, even pleasurable ones, that are themselves a form of understanding. It sees the body as a method, and historical consciousness as something intimately involved with corporeal sensations."[83] We are fully into the realm of affective historiography here.[84] But before exploring this realm further, let us ponder how other theorists have queered history and historiography.

"Temporality has inflected queer theory from its outset," as Freeman notes.[85] This should not surprise us. The earliest "precursor" text of queer theory, and the most influential, was, after all, a work of historiography, Michel Foucault's introduction to his *History of Sexuality* (1976).[86] But the queer swerve within historiography is more commonly associated with a certain body of work within medieval and early modern studies, notably, Louise Fradenburg and Carla Freccero's introduction to *Premodern Sexualities* (1996), Carolyn Dinshaw's *Getting Medieval* (1999), Jonathan Goldberg and Madhavi Menon's "Queering History" (2005), Freccero's *Queer/Early/Modern* (2006), and Menon's *Unhistorical Shakespeare* (2008).[87] Emerging from the earliest phases of such work was a historiographical distinction between "alteritism," on the one hand—simply put, the conviction that the past is truly another country, altogether alien to "ours," structured by cultural assumptions utterly different from ours—and "continuism," on the other hand—the countervailing conviction that profound cultural continuities bridge past and present.[88]

Dinshaw would trouble that dichotomy. "Our choices as queer historians," she insists in *Getting Medieval*, "are not limited simply to mimetic identification with the past or blanket alteritism."[89] In "Theorizing Queer Temporalities," Dinshaw waxes autobiographical about the writing of *Getting Medieval*, which originated as her doctoral dissertation, "an agon played out between these two positions" of alteritism and continuism.[90] As "a lesbian graduate student in that desert of normativity, Princeton," and subject to "the scholarly imperative . . . to view the past as other," she had "stowed away, not just as scholarly resource but also as token of affirmation and desire, [John] Boswell's *Christianity, Social Tolerance, and Homosexuality*."[91] Boswell's thoroughly untrendy essentialism, his appeal to a transhistorical constancy of homosexuality, to an endless parade of "gay people" from the first century to the fourteenth, spoke to Dinshaw. Boswell's desire for transhistorical queer community kindled her own "queer desire for history."[92] In *Getting Medieval*, Dinshaw explored the possibility of "collapsing time through affective contact between marginalized people now and then,"[93] the present and the past, even the remote past. Her wager was that "queers can make new relations, new identifications, new communities with past figures who elude resemblance to us but with whom we can be connected partially by virtue of shared marginality, queer positionality."[94] In particular, Dinshaw called for "a touch across time," a recurrent metaphor in *Getting Medieval*.[95] "This book turns out to be in many ways about touch," she remarks.[96] And the metaphor has seized the imaginations of many scholars, including certain scholars of religion[97]—hardly surprising, given that the history *Getting Medieval* queers is, much of the time, "church history," communities such as the Lollards and individuals such as Margery Kempe looming large in it.[98]

The note struck by Dinshaw in *Getting Medieval* is sounded still more insistently in Goldberg and Madhavi's manifesto-like article "Queering History."

"We need to question the premise of a historicism that privileges difference over similarity," they write,

> recognizing that it is the peculiarity of our current historical moment that such a privileging takes place at all. Why has it come to pass that we apprehend the past in the mode of difference? How has "history" come to equal "alterity"? . . . In opposition to a historicism that proposes to know the definitive difference between the past and the present, we venture that queering requires what we might term "unhistoricism." Far from being ahistorical—or somehow outside history—unhistoricism would acknowledge that history as it is hegemonically understood today is inadequate to housing the project of queering. *In opposition to a history based on hetero difference, we propose homohistory.* Instead of being the history of homos, this history would be invested in suspending determinate sexual and chronological differences while expanding the possibilities of the nonhetero, with all its connotations of sameness, similarity, proximity, and anachronism.[99]

In effect, Menon's *Unhistorical Shakespeare* is the practical implementation of Goldberg and Menon's concept of unhistoricism as outlined in this quotation.[100] In *Unhistorical Shakespeare*, homohistory acquires its antonym: *heterotemporality*. The academic historian's embrace of (hetero) difference "for relating past and present produces a compulsory heterotemporality," claims Menon.[101] In the counterhistoricist project that is Menon's homohistory, "desires always exceed identitarian categories and resist being corralled into heterotemporal camps."[102]

What Menon's work demonstrates even more than Dinshaw's is that the opposite of continuism in the history of sexuality—the continuism commonly said to be epitomized by Boswell's *Christianity, Social Tolerance, and Homosexuality*—is not only alteritism, with its insistence that premodern or even early modern sex cannot be assimilated to modern sexual identitarian categories such as homosexual or heterosexual.[103] The opposite of continuism in the identitarian mode is also continuism in the anti-identitarian mode. Teetering on the outermost anti-identitarian edge of the continuist spectrum, Menon declares: "A homosexuality that is posited as chronologically and sexually identifiable adheres to the strictures of heterohistoricism and is therefore not, according to the logic of my argument, queer at all."[104] This is queer theory at its most pitilessly poststructuralist translated into queer historiography.[105] But queer theory has also assumed post-poststructuralist forms, as we are about to see.

## THE AFFECTIVE TURN

> I would not want to suggest that work on "affect" comes after queer theory or is separate from sexuality. . . . Indeed, affect and sexuality are not merely analogous categories but coextensive ones with shared histories.
> —ANN CVETKOVICH, "Public Feelings," in *After Sex?*
> edited by Janet E. Halley and Andrew Parker

With Freeman and Dinshaw, we have already arrived at the affective turn in queer theory. Dinshaw retrospectively styled *Getting Medieval* a work of affective historiography and implied that its affectivity was what made it a work of queer historiography:

> Developing queer history through the concept of affective connection—a touch across time—and through the intentional collapse of conventional historical time, I wanted in *Getting Medieval* to help queer studies respond to [the] desire [for history that many queers feel]. In fact, I intended to make affect central to the project of queer history writing; this would, I contended, further the aim . . . of transforming history altogether. It would *queer* historiography.[106]

Heather Love in *Feeling Backward* (2007), her own experiment in queer affective historiography, incisively frames the affective turn in lesbian and gay histories as a swerve "from discussions of the stability of sexual categories over time to explorations of the relation between queer historians" and their historical subjects.[107] The question for affect-attuned queer historians is less "Were there gay people in the past?" than "Why do we care so much if there were gay people in the past?" or "What relation with these figures do we hope to cultivate?"[108] Love writes: "Exploring the vagaries of cross-historical desires and the queer impulse to forge communities between the living and the dead, this work has made explicit the affective stakes of debates on method and knowledge."[109]

Love, however, is critical of what she sees as an idealizing tendency in queer affective histories: "Friendship and love have served as the most significant models for thinking about how contemporary critics reach out to the ones they study."[110] Dinshaw would exemplify this tendency, although Love does not single her out. Love, unlike Dinshaw, prefers to "focus on the negative affects . . . that characterize the relation between past and present."[111] Many queers attest or assume

> that since Stonewall the worst difficulties of queer life are behind us. Yet the discomfort that contemporary queer subjects continue to feel in

> response to the most harrowing representations from the past attests to their continuing relevance. The experience of queer historical subjects is not at a safe distance from contemporary experience; rather, their social marginality and abjection mirror our own. The relation to the queer past is suffused not only by feelings of regret, despair, and loss but also by the shame of identification.[112]

Carla Freccero's work constitutes an especially influential example of queer affective historiography, one that appears to circumvent the pitfall of idealization that Love has pinpointed. In her essay "Queer Spectrality" (2007), for instance, Freccero argues that "as queer historicism registers the affective investments of the present in the past . . . it harbors within itself not only pleasure, but also pain, a traumatic pain whose ethical insistence is to 'live and tell' through complex and circuitous processes of working through."[113] The historical analyses contained in Freccero's monograph *Queer/Early/Modern* (2006) "proceed otherwise than according to . . . a presumed logic of the 'done-ness' of the past, since queer time is haunted by the persistence of affect and ethical imperatives in and across time."[114] If "touching" is Dinshaw's metaphor of choice for how past and present intersect, "haunting" is Freccero's, together with its associated terms: "ghost," "specter," "spectrality," "hauntology." Freccero is here channeling Jacques Derrida, specifically his *Specters of Marx*.[115] Freccero adapts the Derridean concept of "spectrality" so that it conjures up "a mode of historical attentiveness" to the ways in which the past and the future, those no longer living and those not yet living, press upon us in the present with ethical insistence, thereby rendering the present "porous" and "permeable" in relation to past and future, so that the present becomes "suffused with affect," enabling us "to mourn and also to hope."[116]

In her essay "Queer Times" (2011), Freccero notes that "what most resist[s] queering" in her home field of Renaissance studies is a certain "version of historicism" that insists "on the past's difference from the present in the arena of sexual and gender identity"—in a word, alteritism.[117] If anything, this is even truer of such theological fields as biblical studies and church history. Freccero's challenge to her own field, then,[118] is also a challenge to these theological fields. She calls historians of Christianity to recognize that their—let's just say our—historiographical investments are inevitably infused with intense affective attachments and identifications, queer desires and fantasies; and rather than imagining that such "anachronistic" elements can be exorcised from our historiographical practices, we ought to acknowledge them instead, to allow ourselves to be openly haunted by them and by the long dead subjects who continue to make spectral—and ethical—claims on us from beyond the grave. At issue ultimately, for Freccero, is "the force of affect in history."[119] Queer affective historiography would, among other things, entail "theoriz[ing] affect's persistence across time and its force as that which compels past-, present-, and future-directed desires and longings."[120] Such a historiography might be styled a canny continuism, a continuism strategically transgressive of the alteritist protocols of traditional historiographical propriety, and an exorcising of the specter of "anachronism" in order to commune with other specters, other ghosts, future as well as past.[121]

Freccero's primary theoretical resource for her queer affective historiography is Derrida's *Specters of Marx*, as we noted, although neither queerness nor affectivity are explicitly thematized in that work. Queerness, affectivity, and historiography all converge more noticeably in Foucault's first volume of his *History of Sexuality*. Indeed, it would be hard to adduce a better textual example of the elusive category of "queer affectivity" than Foucault's account of the psychiatric medicalization of the sexual—most of all "the sexually peculiar"—in the nineteenth century.[122] This scopic mode of power engendered "an interplay of intense sensations."[123] It "set about contacting bodies, caressing them with its eyes, intensifying areas, electrifying surfaces, dramatizing troubled moments. It wrapped the sexual body in its embrace."[124] It entailed "a sensualization of power and a gain of pleasure"—a spiral of pleasure, indeed: "An emotion rewarded the overseeing control . . . ; the intensity of the confession renewed the questioner's curiosity; the pleasure discovered fed back to the power that encircled it. . . . Pleasure spread to the power that harried it; power anchored the pleasure it uncovered"—and so on.[125] Intense sensations, sensualized surfaces, contagious pleasures, powerful or abject emotions—students of affect theory will cathect here to a cluster of familiar terms and themes, even though Foucault is not ordinarily seen as a progenitor of affect theory.

But Eve Sedgwick is. Even as poststructuralist queer theory was approaching its zenith in the mid-1990s and Sedgwick was being hailed as one of its inventors,[126] she coauthored an essay with Adam Frank, "Shame in the Cybernetic Fold" (1995), that asked impertinent questions about poststructuralism and would be seen retrospectively as a foundational text for affect theory.[127] The essay begins: "Here are a few things theory knows today."[128] What theory "knows," Sedgwick and Frank explain, includes such things as that language is all-important whereas biology is not important at all.[129] Indeed, "'theory' has become almost simply coextensive with the claim (you can't say it often enough) *It's not natural*," a stance Sedgwick and Frank dub "reflexive antibiologism."[130] Flying in the face of everything theory teaches us, Sedgwick and Frank devote their essay to "a figure not presently well known, the U.S. psychologist Silvan Tomkins (1911–1991),"[131] not a poststructuralist, nor even a structuralist, but a thinker—and writer—with whom they have nonetheless fallen in love. ("What does it mean to fall in love with a writer?" they muse.)[132] Tomkins's biologically based research distinguishes nine affects (such as enjoyment-joy, distress-anguish, shame-humiliation), each generating its own drives and responses, each influencing consciousness and cognition.[133] Sedgwick and Frank remark: "You don't have to be long out of theory kindergarten to make mincemeat of, let's say, a psychology that depends on the separate existence of eight (only sometimes it's nine) distinct affects hardwired into the human biological system."[134] And yet this biopsychology or psychobiology is, in Sedgwick and Frank's view, calibrated to take the precise measure of affect in situations in which classic poststructuralist theory would be a clumsy tool at best. Although such theory is an exquisitely refined instrument when it comes to the dissection of, say, literary language, it is all but incapable when it comes to affect. "There is no theoretical room for any difference between being, say, amused, disgusted, ashamed, and enraged," Sedgwick and Frank claim.[135]

But what is queer about any of this? Not a whole lot, strictly speaking. "I'm rather abashed that *Touching Feeling* includes so little sex," Sedgwick confessed in her introduction to it.[136] And yet the example of a revered queer theorist stepping to the side of poststructuralism the better to grapple with affect proved highly influential. And in the work of other theorists and critics, some impelled by Sedgwick's example, others pursuing trajectories parallel to it, affect and emotion, feeling and sensation merged with sex and sexuality and even with queerness. Such work included that of Lauren Berlant on the U.S. political sphere as an affective public space of intimacy and sentimentality; on the "cruel optimism" that characterizes the affective state of the contemporary U.S. moment; and on desire, love, and romance in the modern notion of what a person is or should be; Ann Cvetkovich on how trauma catalyzes the creation of cultural archives and political communities, including lesbian public cultures; and on depression as a public feeling, a political feeling, and a social and cultural phenomenon; Sara Ahmed on the cultural politics of emotion, including queer affectivity; and on the moral order imposed by the cultural injunction to be happy and on those who challenge it, including "the unhappy queer"—together with other examples too numerous to mention.[137] Gregory J. Seigworth and Melissa Gregg in the extraordinarily expansive taxonomy of eight analytic approaches to affect that is the centerpiece of their introduction to *The Affect Theory Reader* (2010) delineate this diverse, soft-bordered body of work as follows:

> The fifth [approach] is found in the regularly hidden-in-plain-sight politically engaged work—perhaps most often undertaken by feminists, queer theorists, disability activists, and subaltern peoples living under the thumb of a normativizing power—that attends to the hard and fast materialities, as well as the fleeting and flowing ephemera, of the daily

> and the workaday, of everyday and every-night life, and of "experience" (understood in ways far more collective and "external" rather than individual and "interior"), where persistent, repetitious practices of power can simultaneously provide a body (or, better, collectivized bodies) with predicaments and potentials for realizing a world that subsists within and exceeds the horizons and boundaries of the norm.[138]

It should not, however, be imagined that the biopsychology of Silvan Tomkins is driving much of the work in queer affect theory or in affect theory generally. Sedgwick's infatuation with Tomkins has impelled many theorists to dip into his work—to live "a theoretical moment not one's own," as she puts it[139]—but relatively few have lingered long there. Far more consequential for affect theory has been the para-poststructuralist oeuvre of Gilles Deleuze,[140] including Deleuze's exhilarating thought experiments with Félix Guattari, and their mediation and further elaboration by Brian Massumi.[141] Affect in the Deleuzoguattarian-Massumian mode is the ineffable, preprocessed, visceral, visual, aural, tactile, olfactory, kinetic, rhythmic, chaotic encounter with the material world prior to structured sensory perception, prior to conscious cognition, prior to linguistic representation—and even prior to emotion or feeling.[142]

Yet this implacably austere, ostensibly inhospitable concept of affect implicitly permeates Seigworth and Gregg's introduction to *The Affect Theory Reader*, and explicitly permeates Patricia Ticineto Clough's pivotal collection *The Affective Turn* (2007), while affect theorists as prominent as Lauren Berlant and Kathleen Stewart also work with concepts of affect that are essentially Deleuzian.[143] Also relevant here is Jasbir Puar's much-discussed book, *Terrorist Assemblages: Homonationalism in Queer Times* (2007), which argues that the heteronormativity essential to U.S. nation-state formation is now supplemented by homonormativity as homonationalism, while Orientalized "terrorist" bodies have become the anathematized repositories of sexual perversion.[144] Although Deleuze's name is invoked sparingly in Puar's book, its analysis both of "the machinic assemblage that is American patriotism"[145] and of "the assemblage of the monster-terrorist-fag"[146] is essentially Deleuzian or, more precisely, Deleuzoguattarian, "assemblage" being a fundamental concept for Deleuze and Guattari.[147]

Chrysanthi Nigianni and Merl Storr's edited collection *Deleuze and Queer Theory* (2009) and David V. Ruffolo's *Post-Queer Politics* (2009) attempt to extend the Deleuzian trajectory of queer affect theory to its logical limit.[148] (Early) Butler is the specific foil of the introduction to *Deleuze and Queer Theory*[149] and several of its essays, although poststructuralist theories of language and representation are its general foil. The editors, for example, opine: "What strikes and troubles one in the field known as 'Queer Theory' is primarily an insistence on performativity. . . . Is . . . the heterosexual matrix of imposed naturalized performances the only reality we can imagine? Is language the only air we can breathe? Is text the only land we can inhabit? Is parody the only resistance we can imagine?"[150] They call for a "return" of the "real" body and "real" matter, a body "whose forces and potentialities cannot be reduced to its cultural representations and the norms of gender[,] a matter that is no longer seen as static and passive."[151] Claire Colebrook in "On the Very Possibility of Queer Theory," her contribution to *Deleuze and Queer Theory*, notes that, in literary studies at least, "the queer theory industry has been mobilized around a re-reading of the canon's images of heterosexual desire to show moments of instability, deviation, and mobility."[152] Colebrook claims, however, that Deleuze offers a markedly different model of reading with considerable potential for queer theory. "Against a critical reading," which would analyze how "art or literature queers the pitch of the normal," Deleuze models "a positive reading in which temporality in its pure state"—which is also a state of pure virtuality that precedes and exceeds the habitual repetitions that organize a body and constitute a self—"can be intuited and given form as queer, as a power to create relations, to make a difference, to repeat a power beyond its actual and already constituted forms."[153]

The essays in *Deleuze and Queer Theory* do not speak with a single voice, but certain resounding notes do recur, and they are also heard in Ruffolo's *Post-Queer Politics*. Ruffolo observes how language has "served as the primary means to account for all human experience" in classic poststructuralist thought, how the body has frequently been a casualty of such theory, and how queer theory has been fully implicated in these tendencies.[154] Ruffolo claims to find in the work of such representative queer theorists as Butler, Sedgwick, Halberstam, and Muñoz a common propensity to "position bodies as *effects* of power,"[155] which for him places artificial limits on the immense capacities of bodies as Deleuze and Guattari conceive of them. The elaboration of these capacities occupies dozens of pages of Ruffolo's book, but the following sentence will relay the gist of them (and note that Butler is once again the implicit foil): "I will differentiate performative bodies as *copies* from dialogical bodies as *quotes* where the body is not something exclusively given—it does not strictly reiterate existing norms—but is instead always something given *and* something created: something new is always produced through dialogical-becomings as creative potentials."[156]

To claim, however, that the Deleuzian trajectory in queer theory represents a post-Butlerian trajectory would be facile, Butler's own work already having taken a "post-Butlerian" turn with *Bodies That Matter* (1993), the book that came immediately after *Gender Trouble*, and that attempted to answer the question, "What about the materiality of the body, *Judy*?"[157] Queer theory in the Deleuzian mode is better understood as a retroactive attempt to lay different foundations for queer theory altogether, and also to expand its reach into the nonhuman. As Jeffrey J. Cohen and Todd R. Ramlow suggest in their "Pink Vectors of Deleuze" (2005–6), Deleuze's most significant challenge to queer theory resides in his conviction "that the entire world constitutes a non-anthropomorphic, infinitely connective machinery of desire. There is a capaciousness to Deleuze and Guattari's exuberant conception of sexuality," Cohen and Ramlow argue, "a boundary-breaking that cannot be reduced to the merely human frame" within which queer theory has generally been content to amble. "Throughout [Deleuze's] philosophical opus assemblages proliferate by means of which the human disaggregates, scattered across a molecular field of animals, objects, intensities in ceaseless movement."[158] This too is queer, perhaps the most disorienting queering of all.[159]

## THE THEOLOGICAL TWIST

> We have for some time been collaboratively compiling a dossier on a feeling or attitude we call "divinity." The presiding figure for these meditations has been, naturally, Divine, the late star of many John Waters films.
>
> —EVE KOSOFSKY SEDGWICK AND MICHAEL MOON, "Divinity: A Dossier, a Performance Piece, a Little-Understood Emotion," in Sedgwick, *Tendencies*

Several of the authors in the present collection attempt to capture the uncanny affects that imbue our lives but resist being summoned to consciousness. MacKendrick makes the work of memory unfamiliar, and by doing so troubles our conception—and thereby our feeling—of time and also of God. Kotrosits invites us to be haunted by death, by catastrophe, by traumatic loss, by a messiah who forever fails to appear. Bray, Pellegrini, and Tonstad provide thick descriptions of the often unassimilable stimuli that saturate life under capitalism and that blur any neat distinctions between the religious and the secular.

Most of the authors worry, in one way or another, about our relation to, our fascination with, our negotiation of the past. Marchal probes what is at stake theoretically and politically in the competing conceptions of time held by the various constituencies refracted in Paul's letters. Relatedly, Hoke ponders the ways in which Paul's conception of time is bound up with his understanding of empire. Kotrosits's meditation on the traumas that permeate the Gospel of Mark is also a meditation on the ways in which historical events form, deform, dissolve, and reshape our capacity to narrate history. Perry wonders why certain scenes of astonishing violence against queer bodies, such as those he considers in the *Apocalypse of Peter*, continue to pull us back into histories we have supposedly left behind. Hidalgo, Schneider, and Thomas engage from different angles histories of colonial and imperial violence, pondering a range of practices and strategies for finding—or constructing—a history when one was, perhaps, never intended to survive into the present moment in the first place. Bray, Pellegrini, and Tonstad variously call attention to the ways in which history matters for any assessment of our present situation, precisely because our present situation—the way it forces us to experience time, experience our selves, and experience *experience*—is the product of very specific histories and very specific times.

As stated at the outset of this introduction, this volume emerges from the conviction that the theological fields have much to offer the cross-disciplinary enterprise of queer studies. Specifically, whereas queer theorists of temporality and affect have plumbed the ethical and political import of their work, the theological, or paratheological, resonances of their questions have been less often explored or even acknowledged. Discourses of memory and hope (variously engaged and enacted by Hidalgo, Hoke, MacKendrick, Schneider, and Thomas in the present collection), ineffability and self-dissolution (Brintnall, Perry, Tonstad), transcendence and immanence (Daniels), loss and recovery (Jordan), trauma and healing (Bray, Kotrosits), death and persistence (Marchal)—all connect to perennial and fundamental theological tropes. Religious thinkers and practitioners through the ages and around the planet have pondered questions that would not be unfamiliar to queer theorists of temporality and affect: questions about the nature of time (also engaged by Hoke and Marchal in the present volume), the seductions of emotion (Bray), the traumas of violence (Brintnall, Kotrosits, Pellegrini, Perry), the viability of hope (Daniels, Hidalgo, Schneider, Thomas, Tonstad), and the possibility of restoration (Jordan). Sacred texts from a variety of traditions derive their enthralling power from images of creation and devastation, paradisal origin and utopian horizon, apocalyptic transformation and eschatological destination (Hidalgo, Hoke, Kotrosits, Marchal, Perry, Thomas)—images and themes also refracted in much queer theoretical discourse.

The theoretical torquing of the term "queer" by Edelman, Muñoz, and other critics too numerous to name has also had the effect of turning queerness itself into a paratheological concept, an all but ineffable concept, an almost apophatic concept. What David Halperin once scathingly described as the altogether improbable scenario whereby a term formerly understood to mean "odd," "abnormal," or "sick" "now intimates possibilities so complex and rarified that entire volumes are devoted to spelling them out," while to define the term "is to limit its potential, its magical power to usher in a new age,"[160] becomes a made-in-heaven opportunity for theologians, always adept at locating the ineffable in the quotidian. But Edelman, at least, would insist that the resulting theology—or, better perhaps, atheology—would be austere in the extreme: "That's what makes queerness intolerable, even to those who call themselves queer: a nonteleological negativity that refuses the leavening of piety and with it the dollop of sweetness afforded by messianic hope."[161] Less chance, then, of the theological collaring of queerness, of its domestication, its defanging, against which fate Jordan warns in his contribution to this volume.

Apophatic and apocalyptic, utopian and eschatological ideas, images, and (dis)orientations pervade queer theorizing about time and history, affect and desire. These intriguing and suggestive overlappings are both the pretext for this volume and what has made it possible.

## NOTES

1. The epigraphs are from Sara Ahmed, *Queer Phenomenology: Orientations, Objects, Others* (Durham, N.C.: Duke University Press, 2006), 5, and Judith Butler, "Sexual Politics, Torture, and Secular Time," *British Journal of Sociology* 59, no. 1 (2008): 1.
2. Primers, monographs, and collections have included Robert E. Goss, *Jesus ACTED UP: A Gay and Lesbian Manifesto* (San Francisco: HarperSanFrancisco, 1993); idem, *Queering Christ: Beyond Jesus Acted Up* (Cleveland: Pilgrim Press, 2002); Robert E. Goss and Mona West, eds., *Take Back the Word: A Queer Reading of the Bible* (Cleveland: Pilgrim Press, 2000); Nancy L. Wilson, *Our Tribe: Queer Folks, God, Jesus, and the Bible* (New York: HarperCollins, 1995); idem, *Outing the Bible: Queer Folks, God, Jesus, and the Christian Scriptures* (Indianapolis: LifeJourney Press, 2013); Mark D. Jordan, *The Invention of Sodomy in Christian Theology*, Chicago Series on Sexuality, History, and Society (Chicago: University of Chicago Press, 1997); idem, *Blessing Same-Sex Unions: The Perils of Queer Romance and the Confusions of Christian Marriage* (Chicago: University of Chicago Press, 2005); idem, *Recruiting Young Love: How Christians Talk about Homosexuality* (Chicago: University of Chicago Press, 2011); idem, *Convulsing Bodies: Religion and Resistance in Foucault* (Stanford, Calif.: Stanford University Press, 2015); Elizabeth Stuart et al., *Religion Is a Queer Thing: A Guide to the Christian Faith for Lesbian, Gay, Bisexual and Transgendered People* (Cleveland: Pilgrim Press, 1997); Elizabeth Stuart, *Gay and Lesbian Theologies: Repetitions with Critical Difference* (Farnham, UK: Ashgate, 2003); idem, *Exploding Mystery: A Queer Science of the Sacraments*, Queering Theology (New York: T&T Clark International, 2005); Marcella Althaus-Reid, *Indecent Theology: Theological Perversions in Sex, Gender, and Politics* (New York: Routledge, 2000); idem, *The Queer God* (New York: Routledge, 2003); Marcella Althaus-Reid and Lisa Isherwood, eds., *The Sexual Theologian: Essays on Sex, God and Politics*, Queering Theology (New York: T&T Clark International, 2004); Stephen D. Moore, *God's Beauty Parlor: And Other Queer Spaces in and around the Bible*, Jews and Other Differences (Stanford, Calif.: Stanford University Press, 2001); Virginia Burrus, *The Sex Lives of Saints: An Erotics of Ancient Hagiography*, Divinations: Rereading Late Ancient Religion (Philadelphia: University of Pennsylvania

Press, 2004); Virginia Burrus, Mark D. Jordan, and Karmen MacKendrick, *Seducing Augustine: Bodies, Desires, Confessions* (New York: Fordham University Press, 2010); Theodore W. Jennings Jr., *The Man Jesus Loved: Homoerotic Narratives from the New Testament* (Cleveland: Pilgrim Press, 2003); idem, *Jacob's Wound: Homoerotic Narrative in the Literature of Ancient Israel* (New York: T&T Clark International, 2005); idem, *An Ethic of Queer Sex: Principles and Improvisations* (Chicago: Exploration Press, 2013); Deryn Guest, *When Deborah Met Jael: Lesbian Biblical Hermeneutics* (London: SCM Press, 2005); idem, *Beyond Feminist Biblical Studies*, The Bible in the Modern World 47 (Sheffield, UK: Sheffield Phoenix Press, 2012); Ken Stone, *Practicing Safer Texts: Food, Sex and Bible in Queer Perspective*, Queering Theology (New York: T&T Clark International, 2005); Ken Stone, ed., *Queer Commentary and the Hebrew Bible* (Sheffield, UK: Sheffield Academic Press, 2001); Ellen T. Armour and Susan M. St. Ville, eds., *Bodily Citations: Religion and Judith Butler* (New York: Columbia University Press, 2006); Deryn Guest, Robert E. Goss, Mona West, and Thomas Bohache, eds., *The Queer Bible Commentary* (London: SCM Press, 2006); Lisa Isherwood, *The Power of Erotic Celibacy: Queering Heteropatriarchy*, Queering Theology (New York: T&T Clark International, 2006); Lisa Isherwood and Mark D. Jordan, eds., *Dancing Theology in Fetish Boots: Essays in Honor of Marcella Althaus-Reid* (London: SCM Press, 2010); Dale B. Martin, *Sex and the Single Savior: Gender and Sexuality in Biblical Interpretation* (Louisville, Ky.: Westminster John Knox Press, 2006); Gerard Loughlin, ed., *Queer Theology: Rethinking the Western Body* (Oxford, UK: Blackwell, 2007); Donald L. Boisvert and Jay Emerson Johnson, eds., *Queer Religion*; Vol. 1: *Homosexuality in Modern Religious History*; Vol. 2: *LGBT Movements and Queering Religion* (Santa Barbara, Calif.: Praeger, 2011); Kent L. Brintnall, *Ecce Homo: The Male-Body-in-Pain as Redemptive Figure* (Chicago: University of Chicago Press, 2011); Patrick S. Cheng, *Radical Love: An Introduction to Queer Theology* (New York: Seabury Books, 2011); idem, *From Sin to Amazing Grace: Discovering the Queer Christ* (New York: Seabury Books, 2012); idem, *Rainbow Theology: Bridging Race, Sexuality, and Spirit* (New York: Seabury Books, 2013); Susannah Cornwall, *Controversies in Queer Theology*, Controversies in Contextual Theology (London: SCM Press, 2011); idem, *Sex and Uncertainty in the Body of Christ: Intersex Conditions and Christian Theology*, Gender, Theology, and Spirituality (New York: Routledge, 2014); idem, ed., *Intersex, Theology, and the Bible: Troubling Bodies in Church, Text, and Society* (New York: Palgrave Macmillan, 2015); Anthony Heacock, *Jonathan Loved David: Manly Love in the Bible and the Hermeneutics of Sex*, The Bible in the Modern World 22 (Sheffield, UK: Sheffield Phoenix Press, 2011); Teresa J. Hornsby and Ken Stone, eds., *Bible Trouble: Queer Reading at the Boundaries of Biblical Scholarship*, Semeia Studies 67 (Atlanta: Society of Biblical Literature, 2011); Stuart Macwilliam, *Queer Theory and the Prophetic Marriage Metaphor in the Hebrew Bible*, BibleWorld (London: Equinox, 2011); Manuel Mendoza Villalobos, *Abject Bodies in the Gospel of Mark*, The Bible in the Modern World 45 (Sheffield, UK: Sheffield Phoenix Press, 2012); Sean D. Burke, *Queering the Ethiopian Eunuch: Strategies of Ambiguity in Acts*, Emerging Scholars (Minneapolis: Fortress Press, 2013); E. L. Kornegay Jr., *A Queering of Black Theology: James Baldwin's Blues Project and Gospel Prose* (New York: Palgrave Macmillan,

2013); Jay Emerson Johnson, *Peculiar Faith: Queer Theology for Christian Witness* (New York: Seabury Books, 2014); Andy Buechel, *That We Might Become God: The Queerness of Creedal Christianity* (Eugene, Ore.: Cascade Books, 2015); Pamela R. Lightsey, *Our Lives Matter: A Womanist Queer Theology* (Eugene, Ore.: Pickwick Publications, 2015); Kathleen T. Talvacchia, Michael F. Pettinger, and Mark Larrimore, eds., *Queer Christianities: Lived Religion in Transgressive Forms* (New York: New York University Press, 2015); Linn Tonstad, *God and Difference: The Trinity, Sexuality, and the Transformation of Finitude*, Gender, Theology, and Spirituality (New York: Routledge, 2015). This already copious list would, of course, be many times longer if one were to factor in articles and book chapters.

3. Guest et al., *Queer Bible Commentary*; Hornsby and Stone, *Bible Trouble*; Loughlin, *Queer Theology*.
4. All three of the present authors are among the throngs who have already told the tale. See Kent L. Brintnall, "Queer Studies and Religion," *Critical Research on Religion* 1, no. 1 (2013): 51–61; Joseph A. Marchal, "Queer Approaches: Improper Relations with Pauline Letters," in *Studying Paul's Letters: Contemporary Perspectives and Methods*, ed. idem (Minneapolis: Fortress Press, 2012), 209–28; idem, "Homosexual/Queer," in *The Oxford Encyclopedia of the Bible and Gender Studies*, ed. Julia M. O'Brien (Oxford: Oxford University Press, 2014), 336–44; Moore, *God's Beauty Parlor*, 7–18; idem, "Queer Theory," in *The Oxford Handbook of Gender and Sexuality in the New Testament*, ed. Benjamin Dunning (Oxford: Oxford University Press, forthcoming).
5. It was coined by Teresa de Lauretis, who organized a conference titled "Queer Theory: Lesbian and Gay Sexualities," which was held at the University of California, Santa Cruz, in February 1990. The conference proceedings were published in *differences* 3, no. 2 (1991), and prefaced by a manifesto-like introduction by de Lauretis (iii–xviii).
6. Eve Kosofsky Sedgwick, *Tendencies* (Durham, N.C.: Duke University Press, 1993), 8–9. She illustrates her claim as follows: "The ways that race, ethnicity, postcolonial nationality criss-cross with these [gendered and sexual dimensions] *and other* identity-constituting, identity-fracturing discourses, for example. Intellectuals and artists of color whose sexual self-definition includes 'queer'—I think of an Isaac Julien, a Gloria Anzaldúa, a Richard Fung—are using the leverage of 'queer' to do a new kind of justice to the fractal intricacies of language, skin, migration, state. Thereby, the gravity (I mean the *gravitas*, the meaning, but also the *center* of gravity) of the term 'queer' itself deepens and shifts" (9). Judith Butler, too, taking her lead from such feminists of color as Cherríe Moraga, Chandra Mohanty, Hortense Spillers, and Gayatri Chakravorty Spivak, insists more than once in her "Against Proper Objects" that "the analysis of racialization and class is at least equally important in the thinking of sexuality as either gender or homosexuality, and these last two are not separable from more complex and complicitous formations of power" (*differences* 6, nos. 2–3 [1994]: 21). The conclusion of Butler's *Gender Trouble: Feminism and the Subversion of Identity* (New York: Routledge, 1990), which is titled "From Parody to Politics," set the stage for the antinormativities to come in queer

theory with its speculations on the "open[ing] up [of] other configurations, not only of genders and bodies, but of politics itself" (142).

7. Michael Warner, Introduction to *Fear of a Queer Planet: Queer Politics and Social Theory*, ed. Michael Warner, Cultural Politics 6 (Minneapolis: University of Minnesota Press, 1993), vii. He acknowledges that "the energies of queer studies have come more from rethinking the subjective meaning of sexuality than from rethinking the social," but he adds: "The major theoretical debate over constructionism seems exhausted" (x). He sees the essays in the volume he is introducing as staging an extension of queer theory from the sexual to the social, an extension rendered necessary because "the sexual order blends with a wide range of institutions and social ideology, so that to challenge the sexual order is sooner or later to encounter those other institutions as problems" (x–xi).

8. For a later but particularly cogent exercise in such defamiliarization and destabilization, see Karma Lochrie's chapter "Have We Ever Been Normal?" in her *Heterosyncrasies: Female Sexuality When Normal Wasn't* (Minneapolis: University of Minnesota Press, 2005), 1–25.

9. Michael Warner, *The Trouble with Normal: Sex, Politics, and the Ethics of Queer Life* (New York: Free Press, 1999).

10. Cathy J. Cohen, "Punks, Bulldaggers, and Welfare Queens: The Radical Potential of Queer Politics," *GLQ: A Journal of Lesbian and Gay Studies* 3, no. 4 (1997): 437–65; José Esteban Muñoz, *Disidentifications: Queers of Color and the Performance of Politics*, Cultural Studies of the Americas 2 (Minneapolis: University of Minnesota Press, 1999); Siobhan B. Somerville, *Queering the Color Line: Race and the Invention of Homosexuality in American Culture* (Durham, N.C.: Duke University Press, 2000); Roderick A. Ferguson, *Aberrations in Black: Toward a Queer of Color Critique*, Critical American Studies (Minneapolis: University of Minnesota Press, 2003). See also Juana María Rodríguez, *Queer Latinidad: Identity Practices, Discursive Spaces*, Sexual Cultures (New York: New York University Press, 2003); Ian Bernard, *Queer Race: Cultural Interventions in the Racial Politics of Queer Theory*, Gender, Sexuality, and Culture 3 (New York: Peter Lang, 2004); Dwight A. McBride, *Why I Hate Abercrombie and Fitch: Essays on Race and Sexuality* (New York: New York University Press, 2005); E. Patrick Johnson and Mae G. Henderson, eds., *Black Queer Studies: A Critical Anthology* (Durham, N.C.: Duke University Press, 2005)—to list only early work in this mode. But this "early" work in turn regularly gestured back to still earlier work and queer precursors separate from the white triumvirate of Foucault, Butler, and Sedgwick, precursors that included Barbara Smith (*Toward a Black Feminism Criticism* [New York: Out & Out Books, 1977]), Cherríe Moraga (*Loving in the War Years*: Lo Que Nunca Pasó por Sus Labios [Boston: South End Press, 1983]), Audre Lorde (*Sister Outsider: Essays and Speeches* [Berkeley, Calif.: Crossing Press, 1984]), Gloria Anzaldúa (*Borderlands*/La Frontera: *The New Mestiza* [San Francisco: Aunt Lute Books, 1987]), and Hortense Spillers ("Mama's Baby, Papa's Maybe: An American Grammar Book," *Diacritics* 17, no. 2 [1987]: 65–81).

11. Robert McRuer, *Crip Theory: Cultural Signs of Queerness and Disability*, Cultural Front (New York: New York University Press, 2006), 7.

12. Ibid., 2; cf. Adrienne Rich, "Compulsory Heterosexuality and Lesbian Experience," *Signs* 5, no. 4 (1980): 631–60.

13. McRuer, *Crip Theory*, 1. McRuer was taking his lead from Alison Kafer, "Compulsory Bodies: Reflections on Heterosexuality and Able-bodiedness," *Journal of Women's History* 15, no. 3 (2003): 77–89. See also idem, *Feminist Queer Crip* (Bloomington: Indiana University Press, 2013), and, for a coupling of crip theory and sexuality, Robert McRuer and Anna Mollow, eds., *Sex and Disability* (Durham, N.C.: Duke University Press, 2012).

14. Jasbir Puar, *Terrorist Assemblages: Homonationalism in Queer Times* (Durham, N.C.: Duke University Press, 2007), xii.

15. Ibid., xiii.

16. Kath Browne and Catherine J. Nash, "Queer Methods and Methodologies: An Introduction," in *Queer Methods and Methodologies: Intersecting Queer Theories and Social Science Research*, ed. Kath Brown and Catherine J. Nash (Farnham, UK: Ashgate, 2010), 7.

17. David L. Eng, Judith Halberstam, and José Esteban Muñoz, eds., "What's Queer about Queer Studies Now?" (thematic double issue) *Social Text* 23, nos. 3–4 (2005). The introduction to the collection, however, never quite answers the question it raises. On the one hand, it calls for an almost boundless intersectionality: "What does queer studies have to say about empire, globalization, neoliberalism, sovereignty, and terrorism? What does queer studies tell us about immigration, citizenship, prisons, welfare, mourning, and human rights? (Eng, Halberstam, and Muñoz, Introduction, 2)—and so on for many more sentences. On the other hand, it neglects to address the question of whether the "queer" in a "queer studies" so colossally distended is in danger of popping and leaking all of its meaning.

18. Janet Halley and Andrew Parker, Introduction to *After Sex? On Writing since Queer Theory*, ed. Janet Halley and Andrew Parker, Series Q (Durham, N.C.: Duke University Press, 2011), 1. At least one of the contributors to this collection, Elizabeth Freeman, had already questioned the evacuation of the term "queer" in queer theory, arguing that "what makes queer theory *queer* as opposed to simply deconstructionist is also its insistence on risking a certain vulgar referentiality, its understanding of the sexual encounter as precisely the body and ego's undoing" (*Time Binds: Queer Temporalities, Queer Histories*, Perverse Modernities (Durham, N.C.: Duke University Press, 2010), 11; cf. xxi.

19. Ibid., 2.

20. Robyn Wiegman and Elizabeth A. Wilson, "Introduction: Antinormativity's Queer Conventions," *differences* 26, no. 1 (2015): 1.

21. Ibid.

22. David V. Ruffolo, *Post-Queer Politics*, Queer Interventions (Farnham, UK: Ashgate, 2012), 4. This book represents an attempt to uncouple the queer theory train from its Foucauldian-Butlerian engine and hitch it to a Deleuzoguattarian engine instead—an attempt not limited to Ruffolo, however, and one to which we shall return.

23. Leo Bersani, "Is the Rectum a Grave?" *October* 43 (Winter 1987): 197–222, reprinted in idem, *Is the Rectum a Grave? and Other Essays* (Chicago: University of Chicago

Press, 2010), 3–30. Bersani, it should be noted, did not and does not identify as a queer theorist; see "Rigorously Speculating: An Interview with Leo Bersani," in *Leo Bersani: Queer Theory and Beyond*, ed. Mikko Tuhkanen (Albany: State University of New York Press, 2014), 279. Moreover, the notion that the antisocial thesis originated with Bersani has been contested, notably by Tim Dean who argues that it properly began with French philosopher and novelist Guy Hocquenghem, specifically with his Deleuzoguattarian reading of Freud in *Homosexual Desire*, trans. Daniella Dangoor, Series Q (Durham, N.C.: Duke University Press, 1993; French original 1972). See Tim Dean, "The Antisocial Homosexual," *PMLA: Publications of the Modern Language Association of America* 121, no. 3 (2006): 827. Hocquenghem's book is regularly overlooked in genealogies of queer theory. For a recent book-length, frequently critical engagement with the antisocial thesis—a book that accords a significant role to Hocquenghem, as it happens—see Lorenzo Bernini, *Queer Apocalypses: Elements of Antisocial Theory*, trans. Julia Heim (New York: Palgrave Macmillan, 2017).

24. Lee Edelman, *No Future: Queer Theory and the Death Drive* (Durham, N.C.: Duke University Press, 2004.

25. Michael O'Rourke, "The Afterlives of Queer Theory," *Continent* 1, no. 2 (2011): 132. James Penney ascribes equal importance to the antisocial thesis (even while rejecting it) in his scene-setting survey of recent developments in queer theory. Apart from the antisocial thesis, argues Penney, "recent queer textual production" consists almost entirely of "two moribund categories: introductions and textbooks that repeat old mantras from the 1990s, and a range of largely untheorized studies of cultural phenomena featuring non-normative sexual content, otherwise fully conventional in scope and aim" (*After Queer Theory: The Limits of Sexual Politics* [London: Pluto Press, 2014], 2). Penney does not accord sufficient weight to the developments in queer theory we shall be considering under the rubrics of temporality and affectivity.

26. Bersani, *Homos*, 113.

27. Bersani, *Is the Rectum a Grave?* 15.

28. Edelman, *No Future*, 16.

29. Ibid., 14. Cf. ibid., 4: "Rather than rejecting, with liberal discourse, this ascription of negativity to the queer, we might, as I argue, do better to consider accepting and even embracing it."

30. Ibid., 17.

31. Ibid., 3. Edelman's arguments concerning the Child are anticipated in part by certain observations made by Gayle Rubin in her proto-queer-theory manifesto, "Thinking Sex: Notes for a Radical Theory of the Politics of Sexuality," in *Pleasure and Danger: Exploring Female Sexuality*, ed. Carole S. Vance (Boston: Routledge and Kegan Paul, 1984), 143–78. For example: "For over a century, no tactic for stirring up erotic hysteria has been as reliable as the appeal to protect children" (146; see also 158–59). Earlier she had argued: "Sex as we know it—gender identity, sexual desire and fantasy, *concepts of childhood*—is itself a social product" ("The Traffic in Women: Notes on the Political Economy of Sex," in *Toward an Anthropology of*

*Women*, ed. Rayna R. Reiter [New York: Monthly Review Press, 1975], 166, emphasis added).

32. Edelman, *No Future*, 11.
33. Ibid., 2.
34. Ibid., 3.
35. Ibid. 29. The word "Law" in the phrase "Law and the Pope" has a felicitous double meaning, as Edelman has just quoted Bernard Law, former cardinal of Boston. Edelman's appeal to "the Symbolic order" adds further resonance to the word. The Symbolic order is Jacques Lacan's term for the realm of language, law, and culture that preexists every human subject "and in accordance with which he has to structure himself" (*Écrits: The First Complete Edition in English*, trans. Bruce Fink [New York: W. W. Norton, 2006], 497). Lacan looms very large in Edelman's book, far larger than our brief précis of it can adequately indicate. Throughout the book, Edelman elaborates the relation of the queer to the social in Lacanian terms. For a critique of Edelman's Lacan, see Tim Dean, "An Impossible Embrace: Queerness, Futurity, and the Death Drive," in *A Time for the Humanities: Futurity and the Limits of Autonomy*, ed. James J. Bono, Tim Dean, and Ewa Plonowska Ziarek (New York: Fordham University Press, 2008), 122–40.
36. Edelman, *No Future*, 12.
37. Lee Edelman, "Antagonism, Negativity, and the Subject of Queer Theory," *PMLA: Publications of the Modern Language Association of America* 121, no. 3 (2006): 822. The article was part of a thematic section titled "The Antisocial Thesis in Queer Theory," which also included articles by Robert L. Caserio, Judith Halberstam, José Esteban Muñoz, and Tim Dean.
38. Edelman, *No Future*, 33–66, a chapter titled "*Sinthom*osexuality." Cf. Jacques Lacan, *Le séminaire livre XXIII: Le sinthome*, ed. Jacques-Alain Miller, Champ Freudien (Paris: Seuil, 2005); ET: *The Sinthome: The Seminar of Jacques Lacan, Book XXIII*, ed. Jacques-Alain Miller; trans. anon. (Malden, Mass.: Polity Press, 2016).
39. Edelman, *No Future*, 38–39.
40. Ibid., 109.
41. Ibid., 101.
42. Judith Halberstam, *The Queer Art of Failure* (Durham, N.C.: Duke University Press, 2011), 2. Halberstam is critical of Edelman's brand of negativity; see Halberstam's "The Politics of Negativity in Recent Queer Theory," *PMLA: Publications of the Modern Language Association of America* 121, no. 3 (2006): 823–24. But Edelman is even more scathingly critical of Halberstam's brand of negativity in return; see his "Antagonism, Negativity, and the Subject of Queer Theory." For Edelman, "Halberstam strikes the *pose* of negativity while evacuating its force" (822).
43. José Esteban Muñoz, *Cruising Utopia: The Then and There of Queer Futurity* (New York: New York University Press, 2009), 11.
44. Ibid.
45. Ibid.
46. Ibid., 1.
47. Ibid.

48. Ibid.

49. Ibid., 185–86.

50. Ibid., 1.

51. See Ernst Bloch, *The Principle of Hope*, trans. Neville Plaice, Stephen Plaice, and Paul Knight, 3 vols. (Cambridge, Mass.: MIT Press, 1995). Bloch is regularly invoked by Muñoz in *Cruising Utopia*; arguably, however, Bloch does not contribute as much to Muñoz's theoretical armature or interpretive strategies as that frequent invocation might lead us to expect.

52. Muñoz, *Cruising Utopia*, 189.

53. Ibid., 10.

54. Edelman, *No Future*, 17. This could also serve as a dictum for the antinormative strain of queer theory.

55. Elahe Haschemi Yekani, Eveline Kilian, and Beatrice Michaelis, "Introducing Queer Futures," in *Queer Futures: Reconsidering Ethics, Activism, and the Political*, ed. Elahe Haschemi Yekani, Eveline Kilian, and Beatrice Michaelis (Farnham, UK: Ashgate, 2013), 12.

56. Edelman in particular attempts to forestall such critiques: "There are many types of resistance for which, in writing a book like this, it is best to be prepared. One will be the defiantly 'political' rejection of what some will read as an 'apolitical' formalism, an insufficiently 'historicized' intervention in the materiality of politics as we know it. That such versions of politics and history represent the compulsory norm this book is challenging will not, of course, prevent those espousing them from asserting their 'radical' bona fides"—and so on for many more sentences (*No Future*, 157n19).

57. Judith Halberstam, *In a Queer Time and Place: Transgender Bodies, Subcultural Lives*, Sexual Cultures (New York: New York University Press, 2005), 2.

58. Ibid., 5.

59. Halberstam does not seem to have had access to *No Future* when writing *In a Queer Time*, only to Edelman's "The Future Is Kid Stuff: Queer Theory, Disidentification, and the Death Drive" (*Narrative* 6 [1998]: 18–30), which is referenced once in passing (*In a Queer Time and Space*, 2).

60. Halberstam, *In a Queer Time and Space*, 15.

61. For trans theory, see, in addition to Halberstam, *In a Queer Time and Place*, 22–124, Kate Bornstein, *Gender Outlaw: On Men, Women, and the Rest of Us* (New York: Routledge, 1994); Pat Califia, *Sex Changes: The Politics of Transgenderism* (San Francisco: Cleis Press, 1997); Judith Halberstam, *Female Masculinity* (Durham, N.C.: Duke University Press, 1998), esp. 141–74; Judith Butler, *Undoing Gender* (New York: Routledge, 2004), 57–101; Susan Stryker and Stephen Whittle, eds., *The Transgender Studies Reader* (New York: Routledge, 2006); David Valentine, *Imagining Transgender: An Ethnography of a Category* (Durham, N.C.: Duke University Press, 2007); Susan Stryker and Aren Z. Aizura, eds., *The Transgender Studies Reader 2* (New York: Routledge, 2013); Paisley Currah and Susan Stryker, eds., "Postposttranssexual: Key Concepts for a 21st Century Transgender Studies" (thematic double issue), *TSQ: Transgender Studies Quarterly* 1, nos. 1–2 (2014). For biblical scholarly and theological reflection,

see Virginia Ramey Mollenkott, *Omnigender: A Trans-Religious Approach* (Cleveland: Pilgrim Press, 2001); Justin Edward Tanis, *Trans-Gendered: Theology, Ministry, and Communities of Faith* (Cleveland: Pilgrim Press, 2003); Tricia Sheffield, "Performing Jesus: A Queer Counternarrative of Embodied Transgression," *Theology and Sexuality* 14, no. 3 (2008): 233–58; Marcella Althaus-Reid and Lisa Isherwood, eds., *Trans/formations: Controversies in Contextual Theology* (London: SCM Press, 2009); Tat-siong Benny Liew, "Queering Closets and Perverting Desires: Cross-Examining John's Engendering and Transgendering Word across Different Worlds," in *They Were All Together in One Place? Toward Minority Biblical Criticism*, ed. Randall C. Bailey, Tat-siong Benny Liew, and Fernando F. Segovia, Semeia Studies 57 (Atlanta: Society of Biblical Literature, 2009), 251–88; Joseph A. Marchal, "Bodies Bound for Circumcision and Baptism: An Intersex Critique and the Interpretation of Galatians," *Theology & Sexuality* 16, no. 2 (2010): 163–82; idem, "The Corinthian Women Prophets and Trans Activism," in *Bible Trouble*, ed. Hornsby and Stone, 223 46; Susannah Cornwall, *Sex and Uncertainty in the Body of Christ: Intersex Conditions and Christian Theology*, Gender, Theology, and Spirituality (New York: Routledge, 2014); idem, ed., *Intersex, Theology, and the Bible: Troubling Bodies in Church, Text, and Society* (New York: Palgrave Macmillan, 2015); Megan K. DeFranza, *Sex Difference in Christian Theology: Male, Female, and Intersex in the Image of God* (Grand Rapids, Mich.: Eerdmans, 2015); Christina Beardsley and Michelle O'Brien, eds., *This Is My Body: Hearing the Theology of Transgender Christians* (London: Darton, Longman, and Todd, 2016); Teresa J. Hornsby and Deryn Guest, *Transgender, Intersex, and Biblical Interpretation*, Semeia Studies 83 (Atlanta: SBL Press, 2016). It should, however, be noted that there are political tensions within this body of scholarly literature. In particular, some forms of intersex scholarship and activism draw on queer and trans trajectories, but others, quite pointedly, do not. Susannah Cornwall articulates what is often at stake here: "Making a person 'mean' concepts with which they may not wish to be associated—as when an intersexed individual is held up as necessarily queering heterosexual gender-mapping even if they themselves would not wish to be aligned with such a project—risks distorting and misrepresenting them" ("The Kenosis of Unambiguous Sex in the Body of Christ: Intersex, Theology, and Existing 'for the Other,'" *Theology and Sexuality* 14, no. 2 [2008]: 186). See also DeFranza, *Sex Difference in Christian Theology*, esp. 7.

62. In effect, Tim Dean's *Unlimited Intimacy: Reflections on the Subculture of Barebacking* (Chicago: University of Chicago Press, 2009) and his "Bareback Time" (in *Queer Times, Queer Becomings*, ed. E. L. McCallum and Mikko Tuhkanen [Albany: State University of New York Press, 2011], 75–100) constitute a profound case study of one type of person "who lives outside of repro-time." See further Maia Kotrosits's essay in the present volume.
63. Halberstam, *In a Queer Time and Space*, 10.
64. Ibid., 19.
65. Dinshaw et al., "Theorizing Queer Temporalities," 182.
66. Freeman, *Time Binds*, xi.
67. Ibid., 3.

68. Ibid., 4–5.
69. Ibid., xxiii.
70. Butler, *Gender Trouble*, 134–41. In these pages, Butler singles out drag as illustrative, indeed exemplary, of gender performativity—her theory that gender identity is the product of a socially performed set of scripted, stylized, and repetitive actions. See *Time Binds*, 62–65, in which Freeman engages in a time-attuned critique of Butler's theory of gender performativity and particularly her take on drag. Butler had by then nuanced her own earlier pronouncements on drag, writing in *Undoing Gender*, 282: "*Drag* was [in *Gender Trouble*] a way of exemplifying how reality-effects can be plausibly produced through reiterated performances, but it was never meant to be the primary example or norm for gender subversion. Of course, it makes sense that it was taken up that way, but it has never had that particular place for me. It was meant to elucidate a structure that is at work in everyday performances of gender, and so make this reiterative production of reality-effects legible as a repeated practice in so-called ordinary social life."
71. Freeman, *Time Binds*, 62.
72. Ibid.
73. Ibid., 65.
74. Ibid., 62.
75. Ibid., 78.
76. Ibid., 95.
77. Ibid., xxiii.
78. Ibid., 62. Sam McBean acknowledges *Time Binds* as "one of the few works that . . . bring[s] together feminism with queer time," and attempts to extend its trajectory in her own book. See Sam McBean, *Feminism's Queer Temporalities*, Transformations: Thinking through Feminism (New York: Routledge, 2016), 13.
79. Dinshaw et al., "Theorizing Queer Temporalities," 190.
80. Freeman, *Time Binds*, xxiii.
81. For just such a consideration, see Lynne Gerber, "The Opposite of Gay: Nature, Creation, and Queerish Ex-gay Experiments," *Novo Religio* 11, no. 4 (2008): 8–30.
82. Freeman, *Time Binds*, 95.
83. Ibid., 95–96.
84. A term Freeman herself uses only once in passing (ibid., 11). She also refers, relatedly, to "*haptic* historiography, ways of negotiating with the past and producing historical knowledge through visceral sensations" (ibid., 123).
85. Ibid., xii.
86. Michel Foucault, *Histoire de la sexualité*, vol. 1: *La volonté de savoir* (Paris: Éditions Gallimard, 1976); ET: *The History of Sexuality*, Vol. 1: *An Introduction*, trans. Robert Hurley (New York: Pantheon Books, 1978). Lynne Huffer, however, has argued that the true Foucauldian precursor text of queer theory is not Foucault's *History of Sexuality* but rather his *Folie et déraison: Histoire de la folie à l'âge classique* (Paris: Librarie Plon, 1961); ET: *History of Madness*, trans. Jonathan Murphy and Jean Khalfa (New York: Routledge, 2006). See Lynne Huffer, *Mad for Foucault: Rethinking the Foundations of Queer Theory*, Gender and Culture (New York: Columbia University

Press, 2010). Relatedly, as many readers of Butler's *Gender Trouble* have noted, the Foucauldian text that catalyzes her thinking when she begins to formulate her theory of gender performativity is not *History of Sexuality* (much less *Madness and Civilization*) but rather *Discipline and Punish: The Birth of the Prison*, trans. Alan Sheridan (New York: Pantheon Books, 1977; French original 1975). See *Gender Trouble*, 134–35, a pivotal moment in Butler's argument and one dependent on *Discipline and Punish*. Like Huffer but from a different angle, Mark Jordan has in his *Convulsing Bodies* also questioned the orthodox reading of Foucault, arguing that religion is central to Foucault's thought, especially as it pertains to human bodies—even when Foucault is not discoursing centrally on religion.

87. Louise Fradenburg and Carla Freccero, "Introduction: Caxton, Foucault, and the Pleasures of History," in *Premodern Sexualities*, ed. Louise Fradenburg and Carla Freccero (New York: Routledge, 1996), xiii–xxiv; Carolyn Dinshaw, *Getting Medieval: Sexualities and Communities, Pre- and Postmodern*, Series Q (Durham, N.C.: Duke University Press, 1999); Jonathan Goldberg and Madhavi Menon, "Queering History," *PMLA: Publications of the Modern Language Association of America* 120, no. 5 (2005): 1608–17; Carla Freccero, *Queer/Early/Modern*, Series Q (Durham, N.C.: Duke University Press, 2006); Madhavi Menon, *Unhistorical Shakespeare: Queer Theory in Shakespearean Literature and Film* (New York: Palgrave, 2008).
88. For an early appeal to this distinction, see Fradenburg and Freccero, "Introduction," xv, xix.
89. Dinshaw, *Getting Medieval*, 34. See also Freccero, *Queer/Early/Modern*, 4–5.
90. Dinshaw et al., "Theorizing Queer Temporalities," 178.
91. Ibid. See John Boswell, *Christianity, Social Tolerance, and Homosexuality: Gay People in Western Europe from the Beginning of the Christian Era to the Fourteenth Century* (Chicago: University of Chicago Press, 1980).
92. Dinshaw et al., "Theorizing Queer Temporalities," 178.
93. Ibid.
94. Dinshaw, *Getting Medieval*, 39.
95. See especially ibid., 3, 12, 21.
96. Ibid., 39.
97. Mark D. Jordan's "Touching and Acting, or The Closet of Abjection" (*Journal of the History of Sexuality* 10, no. 2 [2001]: 180–84) begins: "The most beautiful image in Carolyn Dinshaw's *Getting Medieval*, a book with many beauties, is the image of the touch across time. It refers, of course, to the touches that pass between the queer historian and the medieval bodies of her concern, but also to the touches that pass between the historian and her queer readers, who are linked to the past and to the author and—this is the hope—to each other" (180). Jordan's article is one of seven that make up "A Forum on Carolyn Dinshaw's *Getting Medieval*" in this issue of the *Journal of the History of Sexuality*, most of them by scholars of religion. See also Joseph A. Marchal, "'Making History' Queerly: Touches across Time through a Biblical Behind," *Biblical Interpretation* 19, nos. 4–5 (2011): 373–95.
98. Kempe also crops up in Dinshaw's *How Soon Is Now? Medieval Texts, Amateur Readers, and the Queerness of Time* (Durham, N.C.: Duke University Press, 2012),

or rather her book does—*The Book of Margery Kempe*—together with *The Book of John Mandeville*, *The King's Book*, medieval Rip van Winkle tales, and assorted other texts. The common theme is "*asynchrony*: different time frames or temporal systems colliding in a single moment of *now*. Such medieval texts are especially interesting in this regard because there were numerous powerful temporal systems operant in the Middle Ages: agrarian, genealogical, sacral or biblical, and historical. . . . Medieval Christianity provides the framework for heterogeneous and asynchronous temporalities on the macro scale—in all of world history—as well as on the micro scale, such as in the operations of the individual human mind" (ibid., 5–6).

99. Goldberg and Madhavi, "Queering History," 1609, emphasis added. Certain of the article's ideas are anticipated in Jonathan Goldberg, "The History That Will Be," *GLQ: A Journal of Lesbian and Gay Studies* 1, no. 4 (1995): 385–403.

100. Valerie Traub settles on "unhistoricism" as a general label for the influential anti-alteritist tendency in queer historiography. See her "The New Unhistoricism in Queer Studies," *PMLA: Publications of the Modern Language Association of America* 128, no. 1 (2013): 21–39. Further on queer (un)historicism, see Susan McCabe's review article, "To Be and to Have: The Rise of Queer Historicism," *GLQ: A Journal of Lesbian and Gay Studies* 11, no. 1 (2005): 119–34.

101. Menon, *Unhistorical Shakespeare*, 1.

102. Ibid., 1–2.

103. The same claim is sometimes made by biblical scholars for ancient sex—that is, that it cannot, and should not, be assimilated to homosexuality or heterosexuality. See, for example, Martti Nissinen, *Homoeroticism in the Biblical World: A Historical Perspective* (Minneapolis: Fortress Press, 1998); Moore, *God's Beauty Parlor*, 133–72; Martin, *Sex and the Single Savior*, especially 37–50; William Loader, *Making Sense of Sex: Attitudes towards Sexuality in Early Jewish and Christian Literature* (Grand Rapids, Mich.: Eerdmans, 2013), esp. 8. For the continuist tendency in biblical studies, see especially Robert A. J. Gagnon, *The Bible and Homosexual Practice: Texts and Hermeneutics* (Nashville: Abingdon Press, 2002). For more nuanced continuisms, see Bernadette J. Brooten, *Love between Women: Early Christian Responses to Female Homoeroticism*, Chicago Series on Sexuality, History, and Society (Chicago: University of Chicago Press, 1998); Guest, *When Deborah Met Jael*. For an extended critical appraisal of continuism and alteritism in New Testament studies, see Luis Menéndez Antuña, "Is There Room for Queer Desires in the House of Biblical Scholarship? A Methodological Reflection on Queer Desires in the Context of Contemporary New Testament Studies," *Biblical Interpretation* 23, no. 3 (2015): 399–427. He concludes: "Queer historiography, at least in the version for which I am advocating, does not blatantly discard any or both approaches, but it forewarns against their attempts to capture and picture the present in univocal terms. . . . Our reading of the past cannot be an excuse to misrepresent the present" (426). Here he appears to tack close to Eve Kosofsky Sedgwick's "Axiom 5" from her remarkable introduction to *Epistemology of the Closet* (Berkeley: University of California Press, 1990): "*The historical search for a Great Paradigm Shift may obscure the present conditions of sexual identity*" (44), not least the conditions of homosexuality: "'homo-

sexuality as we conceive of it today' . . . comprises [less] a coherent definitional field . . . than a space of overlapping, contradictory, and conflictual definitional forces" (45).

104. Menon, *Unhistorical Shakespeare*, 25. See further Madhavi Menon, "Period Cramps," in *Queer Renaissance Historiography*, ed. Vin Nardizzi, Stephen Guy-Bray, and Will Stockton (Farnham, UK: Ashgate, 2009), 229–35; idem, "Introduction: Queer Shakes," in *Shakesqueer: A Queer Companion to the Complete Works of Shakespeare*, ed. Madhavi Menon (Durham, N.C.: Duke University Press, 2011), 1–27.

105. Further recent work on queer temporalities that space constraints prevent us from reviewing in this section includes Dustin Bradley Goltz, *Queer Temporalities in Gay Male Representation: Tragedy, Normativity, and Futurity*, Routledge Studies in Rhetoric and Communication 2 (New York: Routledge, 2010); McBean, *Feminism's Queer Temporalities*.

106. Carolyn Dinshaw, "Got Medieval?" *Journal of the History of Sexuality* 10, no. 2 (2001): 203.

107. Heather Love, *Feeling Backward: Loss and the Politics of Queer History* (Cambridge, Mass.: Harvard University Press, 2007), 31.

108. Ibid.

109. Ibid. If Love's experiment in queer anachrony is a "feeling backward," Kathryn Bond Stockton's is a "growing sideways"—less as a queer take on history, however, than on individual development. Growing sideways, for Stockton, is a queer refusal of the linear trajectory of "growing up" with its requisite stages of marriage, reproduction, and the renunciation of childishness. See Kathryn Bond Stockton, *The Queer Child, or Growing Sideways in the Twentieth Century*, Series Q (Durham, N.C.: Duke University Press, 2009).

110. Love, *Feeling Backward*, 31.

111. Ibid., 31–32.

112. Ibid., 32.

113. Carla Freccero, "Queer Spectrality: Haunting the Past," in *A Companion to Lesbian, Gay, Bisexual, Transgender, and Queer Studies*, ed. George E. Haggerty and Molly McGarry, Blackwell Companions in Cultural Studies (Oxford: Blackwell, 2007), 194.

114. Freccero, *Queer/Early/Modern*, 5.

115. Jacques Derrida, *Specters of Marx: The State of the Debt, the Work of Mourning, and the New International*, trans. Peggy Kamuf (New York: Routledge, 1994; French original 1993). "Hauntology" is a Derridean neologism, a play on "ontology," the uncanny figure of the specter being, for Derrida, a ghost in the ontological machine, one that is neither fully present nor fully absent, neither fully dead nor fully alive. Hauntology haunts ontology. More precisely, "Ontology opposes [hauntology] only in a movement of exorcism. Ontology is a conjuration" (ibid., 161).

116. Freccero, *Queer/Early/Modern*, 69–70.

117. Carla Freccero, "Queer Times," in *After Sex?* ed. Halley and Parker, 17–18.

118. Ibid., 20–24.

119. Ibid., 20.

120. Ibid., 20–21.

121. Such a historiography comes to partial expression in biblical studies in Denise Kimber Buell, "God's Own People: Specters of Race, Ethnicity, and Gender in Early Christian Studies," in *Prejudice and Christian Beginnings: Investigating Race, Gender, and Ethnicity in Early Christian Studies*, ed. Elisabeth Schüssler Fiorenza and Laura Nasrallah (Minneapolis: Fortress Press, 2009), 159–90; idem, "Cyborg Memories: An Impure History of Jesus," *Biblical Interpretation* 18, no. 4 (2010): 313–41; and idem, "Hauntology Meets Posthumanism: Some Payoffs for Biblical Studies," in *The Bible and Posthumanism*, ed. Jennifer L. Koosed, Semeia Studies 74 (Atlanta: Society of Biblical Literature, 2014), 29–56, as well as in Benjamin H. Dunning, *Specters of Paul: Sexual Difference in Early Christian Thought*, Divinations: Rereading Late Ancient Religion (Philadelphia: University of Pennsylvania Press, 2011), which is also cannily continuist in its leanings (see esp. 3–5). It comes to more thoroughgoing expression in Maia Kotrosits, *Rethinking Early Christian Identity* (Minneapolis: Fortress Press, 2015), an altogether affective, frequently queer (see esp. 47–83) experiment in historiography. Kotrosits writes: "It has been a long-running modern and postmodern mistake to think that critical thinking is best represented by hyper-rational modes of analysis; or that this thinking should (or even can) be distinguished from the deep recesses and wide resonances of affect—ever tangled, social, and subjective. What would happen if we could no longer separate knowing or the work of history from their impressionistic foundations, their affective bases? This book is one answer to that question" (20).
122. Foucault, *History of Sexuality*, 44. Cf. ibid., 43: "all those minor perverts whom nineteenth-century psychiatrists entomologized."
123. Ibid., 44.
124. Ibid.
125. Ibid., 44–45. He concludes: "Capture and seduction, confrontation and mutual reinforcement: parents and children, adults and adolescents, educators and students, doctors and patients, the psychiatrist with his hysteric and his perverts, all have played this game continually since the nineteenth century" (45).
126. Primarily on the basis of her *Epistemology of the Closet*.
127. Eve Kosofsky Sedgwick and Adam Frank, "Shame in the Cybernetic Fold: Reading Silvan Tomkins," in *Shame and Its Sisters: A Silvan Tomkins Reader*, ed. Eve Kosofsky Sedgwick and Adam Frank (Durham, N.C.: Duke University Press, 1995), 1–28. Enormously important, too, for contemporary affect theory, has been Sedgwick's *Touching Feeling: Affect, Pedagogy, Performativity* (Durham, N.C.: Duke University Press, 2003), which reprints "Shame in the Cybernetic Fold" but also includes at least one other game-changing essay, "Paranoid Reading and Reparative Reading, or, You're So Paranoid, You Probably Think This Essay Is About You" (123–52). For two biblical studies articles that take their lead from the latter essay, see Jennifer Knust, "Who's Afraid of Canaan's Curse? Genesis 9:18–29 and the Challenge of Reparative Reading," *Biblical Interpretation* 22, nos. 4–5 (2014): 388–413; Maia Kotrosits, "Seeing Is Feeling: Revelation's Enthroned Lamb and Ancient Visual Affects," *Biblical Interpretation* 22, nos. 4–5 (2014): 473–502.
128. Sedgwick, *Touching Feeling*, 93. "Theory" is shorthand here for poststructuralist theories.

129. Ibid.
130. Ibid., 109.
131. Ibid., 94.
132. Ibid., 117.
133. Silvan Tomkins, *Affect, Imagery, Consciousness*, vol. 1: *The Positive Affects*; vol. 2: *The Negative Affects* (New York: Springer, 1962–63). The term "affect theory" itself was coined by Tomkins (although it has since come to mean many things that he could not have foreseen—post-poststructuralist things, for example). For a work in early Christian studies that frequently draws on Tomkins, see Virginia Burrus, *Saving Shame: Martyrs, Saints, and Other Abject Subjects*, Divinations: Rereading Late Ancient Religion (Philadelphia: University of Pennsylvania Press, 2008).
134. Sedgwick, *Touching Feeling*, 94.
135. Ibid., 110.
136. Ibid., 13.
137. See Lauren Berlant, *The Queen of America Goes to Washington City: Essays on Sex and Citizenship*, Series Q (Durham, N.C.: Duke University Press, 1997); idem, *The Female Complaint: The Unfinished Business of Sentimentality in American Culture* (Durham, N.C.: Duke University Press, 2008); idem, *Cruel Optimism* (Durham, N.C.: Duke University Press, 2011); idem, *Desire/Love* (New York: Dead Letter Office, 2012); Ann Cvetkovich, *An Archive of Feelings: Trauma, Sexuality, and Lesbian Public Cultures* (Series Q; Durham, N.C.: Duke University Press, 2003); idem, *Depression: A Public Feeling* (Durham, N.C.: Duke University Press, 2012); Sara Ahmed, *The Cultural Politics of Emotion* (New York: Routledge, 2004); idem, *The Promise of Happiness* (Durham, N.C. : Duke University Press, 2010). See also Lauren Berlant, ed., *Intimacy* (A Critical Inquiry Book; Chicago: University of Chicago Press, 2000); idem, ed., *Compassion: The Culture and Politics of an Emotion* (Essays from the English Institute; New York: Routledge, 2004); Lauren Berlant and Lee Edelman, *Sex, or the Unbearable* (Theory Q; Durham, N.C.: Duke University Press, 2014); Ann Cvetkovich, *Mixed Feelings: Feminism, Mass Culture, and Victorian Sensationalism* (New Brunswick, N.J.: Rutgers University Press, 1992); Janet Staiger, Ann Cvetkovich, and Ann Reynolds, eds., *Political Emotions* (New Agendas in Communication; New York: Routledge, 2010); Sara Ahmed, *Queer Phenomenology: Orientations, Objects, Others* (Durham, N.C.: Duke University Press, 2006).
138. Gregory J. Seigworth and Melissa Gregg, "An Inventory of Shimmers," in *The Affect Theory Reader*, ed. Melissa Gregg and Gregory J. Seigworth (Durham, N.C.: Duke University Press, 2010), 7.
139. Sedgwick, *Touching Feeling*, 117.
140. (Too) simply put, what set Deleuze to the side of structuralism and poststructuralism alike was that he was less a philosopher of language than a philosopher of sensation. Unlike Silvan Tomkins, however, Deleuze thought and wrote in intimate proximity to structuralism and what would later be labeled poststructuralism, and his work interlaces with "classic" poststructuralism in intricate ways.
141. Affect was of central importance for Deleuze. He drew the concept from Spinoza and developed it through much of his oeuvre, including his collaborative work with

Guattari. The concept of affect saturates in particular his most ambitious work with Guattari, *A Thousand Plateaus: Capitalism and Schizophrenia*, trans. Brian Massumi (Minneapolis: University of Minnesota Press, 1987; French original 1980), although the only sustained definition of affect in the book is that provided in Massumi's "Notes on the Translation," xvi: "affect/affection. Neither word denotes a personal feeling (*sentiment* in Deleuze and Guattari). *L'affect* (Spinoza's *affectus*) is an ability to affect and be affected. It is a prepersonal intensity corresponding to the passage from one experiential state of the body to another and implying an augmentation or diminution in that body's capacity to act. *L'affection* (Spinoza's *affectio*) is each such state considered as an encounter between the affected body and a second, affecting, body (with body taken in its broadest possible sense to include 'mental' or ideal bodies)." For Deleuze and Guattari's own exposition of affect, see their *What Is Philosophy?* trans. Hugh Tomlinson and Graham Burchell, European Perspectives (New York: Columbia University Press, 1994; French original 1991), 163–200. For an exceptional essay on Deleuzian affect, see Gregory J. Seigworth, "From Affection to Soul," in *Gilles Deleuze: Key Concepts*, ed. Charles J. Stivale, 2nd ed. (New York: Routledge, 2014), 181–91. For Massumi's extension of Deleuzian thought, see *Parables for the Virtual: Movement, Affect, Sensation*, Post-Contemporary Interventions (Durham, N.C.: Duke University Press, 2002), which has also been of central importance for affect theory.

142. Massumi's much-quoted distinction between emotion and affect (or "intensity," as he regularly styles it) runs as follows: "An emotion is a subjective content, the sociolinguistic fixing of the quality of an experience which is from that point onward defined as personal. Emotion is qualified intensity, the conventional, consensual point of insertion of intensity into semantically and semiotically formed progressions, into narrativizable action-reaction circuits, into function and meaning. It is intensity owned and recognized. It is crucial to theorize the difference between affect and emotion" (*Parables for the Virtual*, 28).

143. See Patricia Ticineto Clough with Jean Halley, eds., *The Affective Turn: Theorizing the Social* (Durham, N.C.: Duke University Press, 2007); Kathleen Stewart, *Ordinary Affects* (Durham, N.C.: Duke University Press, 2007).

144. For religious studies engagements with Puar's arguments, see "*Terrorist Assemblages* Meets the Study of Religion: Rethinking Queer Studies," a thematic section of *Culture and Religion* 15, no. 2 (2014), edited by Melissa M. Wilcox, with articles by Rosemary R. Corbett, Maia Kotrosits, Joseph A. Marchal, and Brock Perry, and a response by Puar.

145. Puar, *Terrorist Assemblages*, 112.

146. Ibid., 173.

147. Most of all in *A Thousand Plateaus*, in which the term "assemblage" (*agancement*) occurs on almost every page. An assemblage is a complex configuration of heterogeneous elements—such as bodies, actions, passions, expressions, territories—that enter into temporary relations with one another and produce affects, effects, and entire realities. For a sustained elucidation of the term, see esp. ibid., 88–90.

148. Chrysanthi Nigianni and Merl Storr, eds., *Deleuze and Queer Theory*, Deleuze Connections (Edinburgh, UK: Edinburgh University Press, 2009); for Ruffolo's

book see note 21 above. Both volumes were preceded by Michael O'Rourke, ed., "The Becoming-Deleuzoguattarian of Queer Studies," *Rhizomes* 11/12 (Fall 2005/Spring 2006), a collection of fifteen articles. See also Torkild Thanem and Louise Wallenberg, "Buggering Freud and Deleuze: Towards a Queer Theory of Masochism," *Journal of Aesthetics and Culture* 2 (January 2010): http://www.aestheticsandculture.net/index.php/jac/article/view/4642; Nick Davis, *The Desiring-Image: Gilles Deleuze and Contemporary Queer Cinema* (Oxford: Oxford University Press, 2013); and several of the essays in Noreen Giffney and Myra J. Hird, *Queering the Non/Human*, Queer Interventions (Farnham, UK: Ashgate, 2008).

149. Butler is, indeed, a favorite foil for revisionist works of queer theory generally. Lynne Huffer and Annamarie Jagose, for example, take her to task as a bad reader of Foucault, and Lee Edelman and Tim Dean take her to task as a bad reader of Lacan. See Huffer, *Mad for Foucault*; Annamarie Jagose, "The Trouble with Antinormativity," *differences* 26, no. 1 (2015): 26–47; Edelman, *No Future*; and Tim Dean, *Beyond Sexuality* (Chicago: University of Chicago Press, 2000).

150. Chrysanthi Nigianni and Merl Storr, "Introduction," in *Deleuze and Queer Theory*, 3.

151. Ibid., 5.

152. Claire Colebrook, "On the Very Possibility of Queer Theory," in *Deleuze and Queer Theory*, 21.

153. Ibid., 23.

154. Ruffolo, *Post-Queer Politics*, 27.

155. Ibid., 29.

156. Ibid., 35.

157. Judith Butler, *Bodies That Matter: On the Discursive Limits of "Sex"* (New York: Routledge, 1993), ix, her emphasis. She remarks: "I took it that the addition of 'Judy' [by the unnamed questioners] was an effort to dislodge me from the more formal 'Judith' and to recall me to a bodily life that could not be theorized away" (ibid.). *Bodies That Matter* might also be read as Butler's answer in advance to Karen Barad's "Posthumanist Performativity: Toward an Understanding of How Matter Comes to Matter" (*Signs* 28, no. 3 [2003]: 801–31), her new-materialist critique of poststructuralist performativity, including Butlerian performativity—but an answer that Barad has already weighed and found wanting (see especially 808n8; 821–22n26).

158. Jeffrey J. Cohen and Todd R. Ramlow, "Pink Vectors of Deleuze: Queer Theory and Inhumanism," *Rhizomes* 11/12 (Fall 2005/2006): http://www.rhizomes.net/issue11/cohenramlow.html. For a parallel, yet more elaborate argument, one equally indebted to Deleuze and Guattari, see Claire Colebrook, "How Queer Can You Go? Theory, Normality and Normativity," in *Queering the Non/Human*, ed. Giffney and Hird, 17–34.

159. Richard Grusin, introducing his edited collection, *The Nonhuman Turn* (Minneapolis: University of Minnesota Press, 2015), lists among the "intellectual and theoretical developments" that have catalyzed the nonhuman turn: "*Affect theory*, both in its philosophical and psychological manifestations and as it has been mobilized by queer theory" (viii, his emphasis). Affect, and by extension queer affectivity, pertains to the nonhuman in two ways. It "operate[s] autonomously and automatically,

independent of . . . cognition, emotion, will, desire, purpose, intention, or belief—all conventional attributes of the traditional liberal humanist subject. Second, it is also the case that affectivity belongs to nonhuman animals as well as to nonhuman plants or inanimate objects, technical or natural" (xvii). Grusin goes on to note that "the nonhuman turn often invokes resistance or opposition from participants in liberatory scholarly projects. . . . For scholars . . . who have labored so hard to rescue or protect the human from dehumanization or objectification, the nonhuman turn can seem regressive, reactionary, or worse" (xviii). "But this does not have to be the case," counters Grusin. "The question of political or social change" should be "a question of changing our relations not only to other humans but to nonhumans as well. To extend our academic and critical concern to include nonhuman animals and the nonhuman environment" should also be seen as "a politically liberatory project" (xviii–xix).

160. David M. Halperin, "The Normalization of Queer Theory," *Journal of Homosexuality* 45, nos. 2–4 (2003): 339.

161. Dinshaw et al., "Theorizing Queer Temporalities," 195. Edelman's comment stands as the final one in this extended exchange. Edelman also waxes apophatic in his "Queer Theory: Unstating Desire," *GLQ: A Journal of Lesbian and Gay Studies* 2, no. 4 (1995): 343–46.

# ↫ How Soon Is (This Apocalypse) Now? Queer Velocities after a Corinthian Already and a Pauline Not Yet

JOSEPH A. MARCHAL

These times justify impatience. Is it the end? Or was *that* the end? Well, when exactly do you mean?[1] Has it already taken too long? If so, in which ways and in what directions have these ends or these pauses turned us, even dragged us? Ultimately, why should those of us who want (at least some) things to change care? One way to address such questions, such *feelings*, about time is to attend to a range of strange temporalities bubbling up out of an ancient letter and more recent missives in queer studies. The downright eschatological mood of late in the latter pairs nicely, albeit unexpectedly, with Paul's first letter to the Corinthians, since temporality, relationality, even directionality are lively issues in the letter and those who received it: its first (first-century) audience (a community often called "church" but better addressed as an "assembly"). Among and between Paul and these other assembled people, dynamics of gender, sexuality, and embodiment were moving in time along overlapping and mutually conditioning and delimiting trajectories with (at least two) apocalypticisms. Attending to these sorts of temporalities could be important because apocalyptically tinged argumentation is used to target all kinds of marginalized and stigmatized people, including but not limited to LGBTIQ people, those most commonly called queer in a time like now.[2] The search for an alternative social and political vision can lead in different directions, to strange places and times.

The letter presents Paul's own particular apocalypticism, but I turn to the arguments in 1 Corinthians not to determine Paul's position, but to trace those Corinthians addressed by these arguments, especially the prophetic women in that community (most explicitly, though not exclusively, addressed in 1 Cor 11:1–16). These arguments, then, present glimpses of yet another apocalyptic mode of situating temporal and relational ideas and practices. For the most part these Corinthian women prophets have been marginalized or ignored in scholarly conversations about ancient apocalypticisms for at least two reasons.

First, given persistent patterns of identification, scholars tend to treat these letters primarily to get Paul's perspective (to them, authoritative), a tendency that seems only to strengthen when considering Paul as apocalyptic.[3] Second, even when the people addressed by Paul's arguments are considered, these Corinthians have been predominantly associated with other modes, including wisdom and prophecy, modes often imagined in (fraught) contradistinction to the apocalyptic.[4] However, the Corinthian women prophets indicate still other ways of gathering, mixing, and moving in time that were also apocalyptically conditioned. Their alternative temporality complicates and challenges the one Paul presents, particularly since their apocalyptic orientation reflects differences not only of time, but also of speed and direction: traveling along other vectors and at different velocities. In another time, some time around now, these apocalyptic Corinthians can help us move in different directions, presenting one alternative route for approaching Paul's letters, touching another time strangely, anachronistically, even queerly.

## QUEER POSSIBILITIES: JUST IN TIME

What would this differently timed, not-exactly-corresponding-to-Pauline apocalypticism look like? And how might it not-exactly-correspond to other strange relations to time currently agitating under the sign of queer temporalities? In such efforts to make these materials touch, the frame of my project draws most explicitly on the evocative work of Carolyn Dinshaw.[5] A medievalist among the thoroughly modern set of scholars (re)considering queer temporalities, Dinshaw is working on and within a space-time that is "distanced" from and yet also "close(r)" to the biblical.[6] Dinshaw puzzles provocatively over our relations to apparently distant historical figures as neither completely different from nor identical to "us" (and/or/as "now"), but as more desirable relations with the past, a "touch across time." Asking after and about historical figures need not be an either-or affair of "Are they like us or not?"[7] As respondents such as Ann Pellegrini helpfully recognize, Dinshaw would rather ask and answer such queries as "What other kinds of relations to the past are possible? Must we choose between the comforts—the pleasures—of identification and the cold, hard facts of difference, if that is what they are?"[8]

Thus Dinshaw proposes, "Queers can make new relations, new identifications, new communities with past figures who elude resemblance to us but with whom we can be connected partially by virtue of shared marginality, queer positionality."[9] According to Dinshaw, this queer positionality (which makes possible queer crossing and coalitioning) cannot be anticipated: "Queerness, further, is not a hard and fast quality that I know in advance, but is a relation to a norm, and both the norm and the particular queer lack of fit will vary according to specific circumstances."[10] Dinshaw's queer historical desire, then, is "an impulse toward making connections across time between, on the one hand, lives, texts, and other cultural phenomena left out of sexual categories back then and, on the other, those left out of current sexual categories now."[11] In a manner not unlike this impulse, I wonder who these (other) apocalyptic Corinthians might be, and, further "How can we know them? And thinking we know them, what do we know?"[12] Such contingent queries open up the possibilities for that elusive touch across time, a not-exactly-corresponding correspondence between people positioned queerly in, by, and perhaps partially against arguments that stigmatize, marginalize, oppress, or otherwise obscure them.

In her own contingent conversations with Dinshaw, Elizabeth Freeman has generated a number of concepts for reconsidering the binds of time, with an accent on their effects on the present. Freeman coined the term "temporal drag" as one way to reconsider our potential relations with the past, to reflect "the pull of the past on the present" in all its ambivalent qualities.[13] Freeman notes how the past exerts pressure on the present; the past drags us to look and even feel backward, but the present also reflects how the past drags on, continues, keeps showing up, even in surprising fashion.[14] Reflecting the potentially energizing functions of the past, temporal drag can be a process of queer performativity that explains the coexistence of different chronologies or temporalities.[15] Thus Freeman also asks: "Might some bodies, in registering on their very surfaces the co-presence of several historically-specific events, movements, and collective pleasures, complicate or displace the centrality of *gender*-transitive drag to queer performativity?"[16]

Freeman's conceptualization imagines a kind of embodied performativity that differs from Judith Butler's conceptualization, since temporal drag can act as "a way of connecting queer performativity to disavowed political histories."[17] Freeman suggests a different time for performativity: Rather than relying on the promise of (some future) repetition, she wonders about the disruptive pleasures of encountering "the genuine *past*-ness of the past" and our embarrassing identifications with this past.[18] Instead of casting queers as always ahead, as the vanguard, one can seek what has been presently left behind "in the fading light of whatever has been declared useless."[19] This other queer mode involves "mining the present for signs of undetonated energy from past revolutions," a kind of retroactivism "that aims to awaken the dissident and minor future once hoped for in the past."[20] Such attachments, even uses of the past in the present admit the retrospective pleasures and possibilities of interesting failures and embarrassing attempts.

Of course, people hailed as queer have often, even primarily, been characterized as those living in disjointed, out-of-sync ways, according to different life schedules or eccentric social and economic practices (including, but not limited to sexual ones).[21] As Jack Halberstam has described it, then, queer time reflects "the potentiality of a life unscripted by the conventions of family, inheritance, and child rearing."[22] Untethered to either the precedents of the past or the demand for a reproductive futurism, queer then can signify a certain concentration on the present. This is only strengthened in the eschatological crisis of a constantly diminishing future during the AIDS epidemic, with "a new emphasis on the here, the present, the now, and while the threat of no future hovers overhead like a storm cloud, the urgency of being also expands the potential of the moment and . . . squeezes new possibilities out of the time at hand."[23] Instead of securing a particular relation between past, present, and future, Halberstam argues that queer culture refuses not only reproduction and family, but also adulthood, maturity, development, longevity, and responsibility (cast in a heteronormative frame).[24] Instead of growing up and moving on, queer cultures create "sideways" relations, rupturing the heterofuturity figured as (and projected onto) the child.[25]

No scholar is more identified with this critique of reproductive futurity than Lee Edelman.[26] At the heart of his polemic is "a simple provocation: that *queerness* names the side of those *not* 'fighting for the children,' the side outside the consensus by which all politics confirms the absolute value of reproductive futurism."[27] Rather than resisting or qualifying this structural positioning, the queer should accede to his or her figural status as resistant to the cult of the Child. In Edelman's conceptualization, the power of such politics rises to biblical proportions, as "the figure of this Child seems to shimmer with the iridescent promise of Noah's rainbow, serving like the rainbow as the pledge of a covenant that shields us against the persistent threat of apocalypse now—or later."[28] Thus arrayed against the figural Child, the queer figures this apocalypse, a role that can signify only disturbance or disruption. Indeed, Edelman argues, "Queerness can never define an identity; it can only ever disturb one."[29] This constant disruption or deferral of coherence indicates, to Edelman, that queerness functions in a way akin to irony "as one of the names for the force of that unthought remainder" within signification.[30]

Unlike Edelman, José Esteban Muñoz argues that "queerness is primarily about futurity and hope. . . . Queerness is always in the horizon."[31] Indeed, as an ideality, queerness is "not yet here" or, alternately, "we are not yet queer."[32] Although he shares in a critique of "straight time" that could correspond with both Halberstam's and Edelman's projects, Muñoz adopts a critical utopianism in an attempt to imagine a future potentiality beyond what is circumscribed within the current here and now of reproductive majoritarian heterosexuality.[33] To combat a very present-day, homonormative effort to get neoliberal LGBT citizens more money, more military, and more marriage, though, Muñoz cruises the posterior, reaching around to squeeze the behind of different moments and spaces.[34] Highlighting the performativity of even the past (and following Freeman and, to a certain extent, Dinshaw), Muñoz persistently looks for an anticipatory moment or movement, "a critical deployment of the past for the purpose of engaging the present and imagining the future."[35] In this vein, punk and other modes of performance art are both apocalyptic and futuristic, a prophetic avant-garde performance "that enacts a critique of sexual normativities allowing us to bear witness to a new formation, a future in the present."[36]

## APPA(U)LLING APOCALYPSE (SOON)

These different, even queerly skewed trajectories on temporality can help alter the angles of our approach to Paul's arguments and audiences. Such an approach can be accelerated if one recognizes, with Pamela Eisenbaum, that "Paul did not convert from Judaism to Christianity, but he *did change his mind about what time it was in history*."[37] In Galatians, for instance, Paul claims that it was an *apokalypsis*, a revelation or unveiling (1:12, 16), that provided him a different vantage point, changing the trajectory of his life (1:11–17).[38] Paul ties this revelation to his claims about his own unique calling to the non-Jewish nations, the Gentiles (Gal 1:16; 2:7).[39]

The Corinthians would be among those (non-Jewish) nations to which Paul stakes an apostolic claim. Though it might seem less evident in letters such as 1 Corinthians, this apocalyptically altered worldview about the present and the future is rhetorically deployed, even from the start of this letter. Paul argues that the Corinthian assembly members are themselves waiting on an *apokalypsis* (1:7), one that will come at the end, the day of the lord Jesus Christ (1:8). In what follows, Paul juxtaposes the wisdom (1:19, 20, 26; 2:1, 4–6, 13; 3:18–20) and rulers (2:6, 8) of this world (1:20, 21, 26–28; 2:1, 5, 12; 3:19) and this age (1:20; 2:6, 8; 3:18) that are doomed (2:6; cf. 3:18), to the counterintuitive wisdom of God (1:21–25, 30), secret and hidden (2:7), but already revealed (*apokalyptō*) to some of Paul's "us" (2:10). One's efforts in this spatially and temporally topsy-turvy order will become visible on "the day," another occasion of revealing or unveiling (again, the verbal form *apokalyptō*), only now with fire (3:13).[40]

Paul's conception of this change in the temporal order interacts in distinctive ways with his arguments about conduct within the Corinthian assembly community, potentially scrambling practices of gender, sexuality, and embodiment.[41] On the one hand, conforming to the temporal and communal vision Paul prescribes would require changes from these Corinthians, dissociating themselves from those of this world (spatial) and this age (temporal), who will not inherit the coming kingdom. These other figures are associated with a range of vices (5:11–12; 6:9–10), including sexual ones—*porneia* (sexual impropriety), *moicheia* (adultery), *malakia* (softness), *arsenokōitia* (whatever that might be)—vices Paul claims that even some of the assembly members previously practiced (6:11)! On the other hand, Paul only argued for *certain* changes in the lives of his addressees; his (apparent) conviction that he was living in an apocalyptic age inspires urgency in only some facets of the social order. Although he wishes that all could be unmarried like he is (7:7–8), he argued against the separation of spouses (7:2–4, 9–16, 25–27).[42] Within this discussion of celibacy and marriage (and slavery!), he argues against (most) any other changes, repeatedly advocating for the Corinthians to remain in the situation in which they were called (7:17, 20, 24). According to Paul's argument the reason it is good for someone to stay the way they are is "because of the imminent distress (or bodily pain)" (*anagkē*, 7:26). Indeed, moments later Paul will breathlessly note that time (*kairos*) has significantly contracted (7:29), so it is really just best to live "as though not" married or mourning or rejoicing, for "the form of this world is passing away" (7:31). This apocalyptic praxis "for now" not only conditions these oft-cited passages that purport to give Paul's "stance" on matters of gender and sexuality, but it also persists in other arguments about the imminent future: when prophecies, tongues, and knowledge will all pass away (13:8), where the Corinthians (should) currently stand and hold fast (15:1–2, 58; 16:13). Of course the two are not entirely separate, since Paul's final admonition to stand firm is supported by a call to "be courageous/manly" (*andrizesthe*, 16:13). Paul also tries to differentiate which roles and activities are beneficial in the assembly (14:1–40) by reintroducing revelation (*apokalypsis*)—a gift he explicitly claims he already has, but the Corinthians do not (yet)—as one option for clarifying detrimental practices like speaking in tongues (14:6).

Significant aspects of Paul's argumentation seem oddly compatible with several of the more recent queer critiques of reproductive futurity. Paul imagines a constantly diminishing future, one in which he proves quite disinterested in a life organized around the predominant Roman imperial expectations for family, inheritance, and child rearing.[43] In Paul's extensive reflections on marriage, celibacy, and widowhood, children are hardly mentioned at all, only once in passing (7:14), and really just as incidental effects of a man and a woman being on two different sides of the imminent apocalyptic divide (the "real" issue). Paul does not believe that children are our future, as imperatives of procreation or potency are nowhere in sight. Paul accedes to a role which would most certainly be viewed as disruptive to the social order (of that time or even, for many, this time). Paul even dwells on the meaning of death for an uncomfortably long portion of the letter (15:12–57), dramatically claiming a rather different, perpetually necropolitical status: "I die every day!" (15:31).

What anachronistic juxtaposition can bring together, queer touches can also make contingent, highlighting the not-exactly-corresponding correspondences between the apocalyptic temporalities of the first and twenty-first centuries. Indeed, importantly for Paul, there is still some time left (though not much). Although some apocalypses are already unveiled for him, the day is still coming, remains (in the letter) only on the horizon, most especially for the Corinthian assembly members. Paul depicts them as babes in Christ-land (3:1): not yet (*oupō*) ready for the spiritual solid food his eschatological stomach can already digest, rather, stressing a second time that even now they are not yet ready (3:2; cf. 13:11; 14:20). Later, Paul argues that if anyone (besides himself) thinks they know something, they do not yet (*oupō*) know what they should (8:2). Perhaps, then, Paul more-closely-not-exactly corresponds with Muñoz's utopian futurity than Edelman's critique of futurity. Certainly, Paul persistently hopes for the imminent future day (1:7–8; 6:14; 9:10; 13:8; 15:19). Though he briefly even figures death himself (15:31), he hardly persists in embracing death, imagining as he does the resurrection and the destruction of even death itself (15:24–26; cf. 15:51–54).[44]

This letter also reflects the redeployment of other times, the drag of the past or the inbreaking of the future in the present. The vision Paul aims to produce and prescribe, for instance, alludes to an apocalyptic scenario unveiled to him in a relatively recent past, a scenario that should shape his (and their) present-day understanding of the primordial past and a rather imminent future. This vision hinges on his explanation of resurrection through Christ as the last, or second, Adam (15:21–22, 45–49). Resurrection as an event is in some ways already happening, since Christ is the first fruits (already risen), but for Paul the rest of humanity are still living in an almost, but not yet, moment, just before the *parousia* and the end (15:22–23). Paul's rhetorical proof contrasts a first human of dust (from Gn 2:7)[45] and the heavenly human, whose image Paul's "we" will eventually bear (15:49).[46] Instead of already being created in the image of God (as in the first creation story, see Gn 1:27), a resurrected humanity will only be in the image of a spiritual and heavenly Christ in a time still to come.

## ANOTHER APOCALYPSE (NOW)

Of course, this is not the first time Paul's arguments have combined these two different accounts of primordial events and, thus, qualified how people have been in the image of the divine. This issue of image matters a great deal to Paul's arguments about women covering their heads while praying and prophesying (1 Cor 11:1–16). In a relatively short span of time, he introduces a number of arguments for such coverings. He proposes that man is the "head" of woman (11:2), and poses an analogy between uncovered activities and the dishonor of a shaved head (11:4–6). He alludes to the potential presence of angels (11:10) and the apparent testimony of nature (11:13–15). But Paul also attempts to alter how women are already praying and prophesying in the Corinthian assembly community, unveiled (11:1–16), by citing two different creation stories. In one case he claims that only men are in the image of God (11:7, referencing Gn 1:27), and in another that women were made from and even for man (11:8, 9, referencing the latter, "dusty man-field" version, Gn 2:22–23). However, when Paul alludes to or cites this tradition (in 11:7) by appealing to man made "in the image of God," he (purposefully) excludes that these humans were made "male and female" in this divine image (Gn 1:27).[47] Antoinette Clark Wire (among other feminist scholars) has noted that this elision is probably Paul's response to the Corinthian women's own citation of this exact same tradition and of a baptismal formula that also cites this Genesis tradition (found in Gal 3:28), emphasizing that creation is reordered in this assembly community, where they are no longer male and female.[48] The first letter to the Corinthians re-cites this formula from Galatians 3:28 but tried to run away from the "male and female" pair, probably because of its use in the assembly community. Yet this baptismal formula calls up a poetic story about a primordial past, in order to claim that this ritual initiates a new creation.[49] The baptized body's relation to its present (and future) time is reorganized by the formula's own negating citation of another, primordial time—not male and female.

Paul's concept of temporal copresence is clashing with another concept of temporal copresence within his audience. Among the prophetic females, then, some of the uncovered surfaces of their bodies register different ways of relating to a past, of connecting their prophetic activities to a primordial time resituated through baptism. Paul's rhetorical efforts reflect one attempt to disavow an alternate citation of the past. The layered meanings of drag come to the fore here, not only because Paul is concerned about the clothing practices of these women, but also because their embodied practices reflect a different estimation of where and *when* they are in an(other) apocalyptic temporality. Throughout the letter Paul works to establish that the Corinthians are dwelling in an "almost, but not yet" place, between what was unveiled (to Paul) about and through Christ's crucifixion and resurrection and what is yet to come, albeit soon, in the imminent future. However, it appears that at least some Corinthian women are focused on the events of their baptisms in relation to an already new, or altered, creation. The significance of their baptism into a no longer male and female state is then reflected in their own revelatory and thus unveiling practices (*akatakalyptō*, 11:5, 13) of prayer and prophecy.[50] The copresence of these moments on such bodies comes to constitute the difference of this community, a difference that cannot be reduced to dynamics of gendered embodiment alone. Temporal drag helps one register the simultaneous copresence of different timelines here, so far including two different takes on the primordial past, reflecting two different practices of the

Corinthians (and implicitly our own present reflections, citations, even imitations of the past).

From the start Paul seems to be counteracting this other vision by juxtaposing and resituating the terminologies of wisdom they were likely using, often associating it with this world and age.[51] He addresses the Corinthians (at least) three times as if they were childlike or immature, not yet ready (3:2; 13:11; 14:20), in contrast to those who are mature, who will receive a wisdom that is "not a wisdom of this age or of the rulers of this age" (2:6). Paul's defensive postponement curdles into cutting ironies, even sarcasms at several points in the letter, including shortly after this exhortation, when he jabs: "Already you are filled! Already you are enriched! Without us you are ruling!" (4:8). Later, he will sarcastically exclaim and ask specifically about the women's communal speaking abilities, "What! Did the word of God originate with you, or are you the only ones it has reached?" (14:36).[52] Reflecting differing conceptions of the apocalyptic age and its impact, their practices of prayer, prophecy, and even speaking in tongues are expressions of their already altered lives, an already risen life; the apocalyptic reordering is not imminent, but immanent; the future of the Corinthian women prophets has already broken into the Corinthian women's present.[53]

The differences in the lives of the Corinthian assembly members are manifest enough that even Paul concedes as much at the opening of the letter. They do not lack any spiritual gift (1:7), since Paul argued about their already (in their own proximate) past: "You have been enriched in every way in him [Christ], with all speech and all knowledge" (1:5). This would be quite a difference from their before, since at the time of their own calling, not many of them were wise, powerful, or nobly born (1:26). Further, in this before, they also apparently engaged in practices Paul cast as antisocial vices, including sexual impropriety, adultery, immoderation or unmasculine "softness" (6:9–11). If their position in the world is meant to be evoked in the earlier descriptions of the foolish, weak, low, and despised (1:27–28), then their marginalization or stigmatization might even recall (or preface) the persistently oppositional, or negative, definition of queerness. Though this difference among them apparently cannot be denied, Paul works hard in the face of their vision of a realized glory to qualify their new qualities, to temper their apocalyptic temporality. This is why (despite moments like the opening in 1:4–7) Paul will try to reserve certain spiritual gifts, argue for a resurrection still to come, or insist that there still remains a secret and hidden wisdom, even from them. Where they act out of a realized and already living new/now order, Paul argued for a deferred completion and resurrection.

Their different position peeks through in many places where Paul seeks to counteract them. In contrast to Paul's vision of his own semi-exclusive knowledge of the *apokalypsis*, the Corinthians asserted that "all of us have knowledge" (8:1) and "all things are in my own power" (or, "possible for me," *exestin*, 6:12; cf. 10:23). These slogans extend into discussions of gendered and sexual behavior in this now / new age, as the Corinthians declared: "It is good for a man not to touch a woman" (7:1). Wire even suggests that these last two slogans "may have been combined in a third, 'The woman has authority over her own body' (7:4)."[54] Although Paul admits that his own unmarried status is good (7:8) and thus preferable (even superior), he works to persuade or even prescribe that women should give up this good in their changed lives, whether they were married, widowed, or betrothed. Thus, in their own dedication to withdrawing from sexual contact with men, the Corinthian women appear as even stronger candidates for living out an ancient, anticipatory critique of reproductive futurity!

Paul's prescriptions and concessions about these principles and practices point in still other directions beyond his own, toppling into inconsistencies, even contradictions. On the one hand, Paul is willing to concede that married members can refuse the other sexually, for a short period of time, "a season" (*kairos*), for praying (7:5), indicating what gains in time and practice women might be losing by themselves conceding to a marriage. On the other hand, as he notes later in the very same chapter, all of this is passing away. This very time (*kairos*) has shortened so much that he exhorts: "Let those [males] who have women (wives) live as though they did not have one" (7:29). Paul's anticipation unveils more than just his androcentric perspective (here addressing males, not females in the community). After all, if this duration of time (*kairos*) that is fast contracting is the same season (*kairos*) when members can refuse sexual overtures, then why pressure marriages in the first place? If Corinthian women have already withdrawn from these relations, and if it is both good for a man not to touch a woman (7:1) *and* good for someone to stay the way they are (7:26), then why should the situation of the Corinthians change upon receiving Paul's letter?

This effort to proscribe certain sexual activities and particularly gendered expectations resonates with the other passages where Paul specifically attempts to qualify and constrict how and when (and ultimately whether) women should pray and prophesy (11:1–16; 14:26–40). Again, if time is so short, then why is it important for these Corinthians to change these practices, when elsewhere Paul claims that he has ordered that all should stay the way they are in all of the assemblies (7:17, 20, 24, 26)? If one set of embodied practice—women's prayer and prophecy—is a reflection or even extension of another set—withdrawal from sex and marriage (with men)—practices that Paul alternatingly approves and constrains (for others), then it becomes clear that at least some Corinthian women were already drawing different conclusions about some overlapping practices with Paul. Their views of gender, sexuality, and embodiment reflect a slightly different apocalyptic temporality: Their physical unveiling signifies an already ongoing unveiling that they orally convey through their prayers and prophecies. A future has already broken into a present, invalidating the need for sex or marriage (with men), and further revealing the new temporal arrangement through a range of communal practices that transgress the ostensible divide between divine and human: prophecy, prayer, and even speaking in tongues.

## UNVEILED VELOCITIES

This examination of the different temporalities of these two apocalypticisms makes it possible to recognize that these temporalities also differ on the basis of their velocities.[55] Paul and the Corinthian women prophets differ not only on *when* they were in the series of apocalyptic events (not yet versus already; anticipated versus actualized), but *where* they were. Velocity helps us emphasize the movement and directionality of the Corinthian women prophets' alternative trajectory, on what vector they are traveling, since velocity refers to more than just speed, but the rate at which they have changed position. The differences between these apocalyptic views underscore the importance of keeping track of the different directions they take from their revelations.

In Paul's apocalyptic vision, most in this movement of assembly communities are (or should be) dwelling in an almost, but not yet here moment. A new age is about to be initiated, due to a prior, but yet not entirely complete, event of resurrection (working through Christ's crucifixion). Because the ultimate destruction of death is still to come, Paul's praxis for now reflects the anticipation of this imminent future, promoting a velocity in this direction without arriving, a rate that entails some change, but a rather minimal change in position for many in the community.[56] By way of contrast, at least some of the Corinthians, including the prophetic females, appear to be embodying and arguing out of a nonterminal velocity. Their practices of prayer, prophecy, and tongues confirm (to them) that they are already living a new life, in which the decisive transformation has already occurred through Christ's rising. Their rising status in this more vital velocity was reflected through their prior baptism as a new creation.[57] In a relatively short time their position has changed rather drastically. Their actions potentially indicate their efforts to maximize the change in direction their lives were taking. Even if they seem to agree with Paul about the general apocalyptic direction of the time, Paul's arguments indicate a desire to slow the rate and minimize the change in position for them. This difference could be attributed to their different starting points: If the Corinthian women prophets have already experienced their apocalyptic movement as a greater change (starting from a point further from this place than Paul), then it might be less surprising that they seek to continue a greater rate and change in position than Paul (who could have experienced an *apokalypsis* as less drastic, socially or otherwise). Their trajectories might have overlapped at times, but they were moving at different velocities.

This also explains how Paul and the Corinthian women prophets can come to such different conclusions about the same kinds of sexual practices. If velocity is a way to measure the rate of change of a body's position in a certain direction over time, Paul seeks minimal changes from anyone unless they have already moved their bodies from the sphere of a male's influence. Paul exhorts (nearly) everyone to stay the way they are because things will be changing soon enough. Meanwhile, the embodied actions of (at least some) Corinthian women—their prayer, prophecy, and withdrawing from social expectations around sex, marriage, and children—register significant changes in a relatively short period of time. Though once they were neither wise nor powerful nor wellborn, they are enriched with all manner of gifts and thus already living out an apocalyptic time that Paul still anticipates. They cite some of the same primordial pasts to account for this, but view their current sociopolitical significance in rather different ways than Paul. The age has changed for both Paul and the Corinthian women prophets; their apocalyptic trajectories at times coincide, but their starting points and velocities differ.

However, from another vantage point, if the Corinthian women prophets have already arrived at this realized glory in a new creation, then their velocities (over time) could almost reflect an apocalyptic stutter-step. After all, their alternative, zoetic temporal state was already achieved via an apocalyptic acceleration and direction past the necrotic, not yet temporal state and place presented and prescribed by Paul, who seemed to be arguing: Hold up, slow down, stand firm, stay there, not yet, not yet, not yet! But if this trajectory and velocity has carried them to this already risen point, and they are not pushing for any further changes in position, they are in a new place, a now place, with no current velocity at all. Thus, if (and perhaps only if) Paul is traveling on the same trajectory, it is Paul's velocity that "now" (in that past, mid-first century moment, at the time of composition or initial reception) runs a greater rate and, given enough of that precious time, he too could arrive at the same point through an albeit differently vital velocity. Traveling through apocalyptic time and space can be a rather complicated affair.[58]

At any rate, back in the twenty-first century, those interested in more recently queer temporalities have long underscored the complications of both the touches and the binds of time. Indeed, complication or messiness is precisely the basis of one of the critiques of the starkest conception of queer temporality found in Edelman's *No Future*. In response to his positioning of queerness in terms of "pure negativity," Freeman worries that his conceptualization "risks evacuating the messiest thing about being queer: the actual meeting of bodies with other bodies and with objects."[59] Of course, thinking of the Corinthians, people meeting and assembling for communal prayer and prophecy, embodying and / or calling for significant changes, including the withdrawal of their bodies from (some) sexual meetings, would have also been rather messy, especially for females or for other feminized subjects in ancient imperial contexts, those most expected to be receptive.

Yet risking a differently vulgar referent,[60] the prophesying females *and males* in the Corinthian assembly would have appeared to embrace another sort of receptivity, since many ancient texts and traditions presumed prophetic speech was a product of a divine penetration.[61] Furthermore, that anyone else—in the Corinthian assembly "then" or among more recent audiences "now"—did and still might accept their words and actions as (somehow) prophetic indicates a potential proliferation of receptive figures, those accepting penetrating prophecies. For queerly historical projects, this suggests what Carla Freccero has described, intrasubjectively, as a "penetrative reciprocity," or what Freeman calls a "bottomy historiography."[62] This provides a potential, if still only glancing point of potential connection or correspondence between the Corinthians in this ancient assembly and those of us still considering them centuries later; their and our acceptance, interest, and even transmission of prophecy can be reframed in terms of a series (even a sequence) of reciprocal receptivities. Freeman indicates another way of looking at this first-century situation, as well as the twenty-first-century encounter with it, given "the potential for collective queer time—even queer history—to be structured as an uneven transmission of receptivity rather than authority or custom, of a certain enjoyably porous relation to unpredictable futures or to new configurations of the past."[63]

• • •

In choosing to focus on the Corinthian women prophets, to (re)imagine a porous, or uneven, relationship to or among them, many in biblical studies would characterize my approach as outdated and even out of fashion, caught in the bad romance of feminist historical reconstructions.[64] In a (somewhat) parallel fashion, many in queer studies seek to dissociate their work from (both) feminist pasts (and presents), characterizing them primarily in terms of embarrassing mistakes or unfortunate attachments to now passé principles.[65] Yet *even if* they are failures (about which I am not yet entirely convinced), I propose that these kinds of projects are interesting, illuminating, even *unveiling* failures. They are the kinds of lost, dismissed, or disavowed pasts toward which many in queer studies are now turning, even feeling backward, seeking undetonated energies or useless visions of the past's alternative futures.[66]

The exchange between Paul and the Corinthians is stuffed with these alternative futures of the past. And if one is looking for embarrassing mistakes or interesting failures, then one need look no further than his imminent apocalyptic expectations or their immanent assemblages of an already unveiled existence! If they were wrong about only one thing, then they were wrong about what time it was (even as they read, or felt, the apocalyptic "clocks" differently). It seems important, first of all, to simply let their visions be mistakes! The temporal claims of Jesus and Paul and even these Corinthian women prophets were wrong; so our first scholarly impulse should not be to recuperate them or to straighten their tangled and twisted ideas into triumphant success stories.

Yet I still want to linger over the potentially radical vision and practice of those Corinthian women prophets (and those gathered around them).[67] I notice their faint correspondences to recent modes of radical politics, among those who are unreasonable, who ask for "too much" and "too soon," attempting to live into the world as it should be.[68] Paul's sarcastic cracks of "already you are" sound then like skeptical responses to activist impatience, to those who make demands for significant change now, not the promise of a still deferred future, but an alternative temporality in-breaking now. To make such claims, one needs another interpretation of temporality, a different understanding of the significance of the past and its relation to a possible future.[69] Embedded in Paul's Corinthian correspondence, one can find a prophetic sort of apocalyptic praxis, marginalized and dismissed, but potentially resonating, if not exactly corresponding to other, more recently marginalized modes.[70]

This potential resonance between biblical studies and queer studies suggests more than the need for interpreters of these bodies to recognize and engage (in both directions) across these still-too-seldom-overlapping fields. The apocalyptic vision and unveiling practice of the Corinthian women prophets present interesting failures for those interested in change of any kind. They highlight that approaches to social and political transformation are tied up not only with what speed but also with what rate one aims to change conditions, positioned in particular directions, aiming for different points, over time—what velocity—we assemble, disrupt, and alter. They reflect the potential urgencies of now (not just the now that will be soon, of Paul and The Smiths), not accepting the temporal narrative presented and prescribed for them in the letter. Just as there is more than one way to critique or resist reproductive futurity, the exchange between Paul and the Corinthians present more than one way to shape gendered and sexual practice apocalyptically (ways that also critique and resist an ancient imperial protocol of penetration and potency that might just resonate with more recent reprofuturisms). Our encounter with these alternatives should temper the exceptionalism that is potentially endemic to queer studies, perhaps especially to those narratives that promote only one way of relating to temporality as queer.[71] How can you say I go about things the wrong way? It's not that my hope is gone, it just might be reflecting a different, queerly glimpsed, but not yet entirely lost, velocity.

## NOTES

1. My posing of this temporal question (like the title of this essay) is borrowed, with apologies, from both The Smiths' "How Soon Is Now?" and Carolyn Dinshaw, *How Soon Is Now? Medieval Texts, Amateur Readers, and the Queerness of Time* (Durham, N.C.: Duke University Press, 2012).
2. For some reflections on this dynamic and the biblical interpreter's accountability for grappling with such uses, see Lynn R. Huber, "Sexually Explicit? Re-reading Revelation's 144,000 Virgins as a Response to Roman Discourses," *Journal of Men, Masculinities, and Spirituality* 2, no. 1 (2008): 3–28; Huber, "Gazing at the Whore: Reading Revelation Queerly," in *Bible Trouble: Queer Reading at the Boundaries of Biblical Scholarship*, ed. Teresa J. Hornsby and Ken Stone, Semeia Studies 67 (Atlanta: Society of Biblical Literature, 2011), 301–20; Tina Pippin, *Apocalyptic Bodies: The Biblical End of the World in Text and Image* (London: Routledge, 1999); and Tina Pippin and J. Michael Clark, "Revelation/Apocalypse," in *The Queer Bible Commentary*, ed. Deryn Guest, Robert E. Goss, Mona West, and Thomas Bohache (London: SCM Press, 2006), 753–68. For a rather different, queerly sublime approach to such apocalyptic signifiers (in brief conversation with the work of Lee Edelman), see Erin Runions, *The Babylon Complex: Theopolitical Fantasies of War, Sex, and Sovereignty* (New York: Fordham University Press, 2014), 213–45.
3. On these politics of identification, see Elisabeth Schüssler Fiorenza, "Paul and the Politics of Interpretation," in *Paul and Politics: Ekklesia, Israel, Imperium, Interpretation: Essays in Honor of Krister Stendahl*, ed. Richard A. Horsley (Harrisburg, Penn.: Trinity Press International, 2000), 40–57. For a lengthy (yet oft-ignored) critique of scholarly reassurance and claims to authoritative access (for themselves) to the "real" apocalyptic Paul, see R. Barry Matlock, *Unveiling the Apocalyptic Paul: Paul's Interpreters and the Rhetoric of Criticism*, Journal for the Study of the New Testament Supplement Series 127 (Sheffield: Sheffield Academic Press, 1996). (For one sign of Matlock's marginality in these conversations, note that his work is mentioned just once, in passing, in the entire *Oxford Handbook of Apocalyptic Literature*, ed. John J. Collins [Oxford: Oxford University Press, 2014]).
4. For instance, Richard Horsley's construction of an anti-imperial Paul leans on a differentiation between a properly apocalyptic Paul and the ostensibly individualist, even elitist, wisdom seekers in Corinth. See Horsley, "Rhetoric and Empire—and 1 Corinthians," in *Paul and Politics*, 72–102; and Horsley, *1 Corinthians*, Abingdon New Testament Commentary (Nashville, Tenn.: Abingdon Press, 1998). Categories like prophecy, wisdom, and apocalyptic are obviously also fraught genre categories, particularly in studies of the Hebrew Bible and intertestamental literature. For a both/and approach, see *Conflicted Boundaries in Wisdom and Apocalypticism*, ed. Benjamin G. Wright III and Lawrence M. Wills, Society of Biblical Literature Symposium Series 35 (Atlanta: Society of Biblical Literature, 2005). (As much as Matlock wishes to rely on apocalyptic literature to define what might count as apocalyptic worldviews, there is also considerable debate about how to identify the genre of an ostensibly indisputably apocalyptic text, the Revelation/Apocalypse of John! See, for instance, Gregory L. Linton, "Reading the Apocalypse as Apocalypse:

The Limits of Genre," and David L. Barr, "Beyond Genre: The Expectations of Apocalypse," in *The Reality of Apocalypse: Rhetoric and Politics in the Book of Revelation*, ed. Barr, Society of Biblical Literature Symposium Series 39 [Atlanta: Society of Biblical Literature, 2006], 9–42, and 71–90, respectively.)

5. Although I have already alluded to her more recent work in *How Soon Is Now?*, my (re)conceptualization of a queer relation to temporality especially draws on Carolyn Dinshaw, *Getting Medieval: Sexualities and Communities, Pre- and Postmodern*, Series Q (Durham, N.C.: Duke University Press, 1999). For further reflections on this "touch across time," as it might relate to queer biblical interpretation, see Joseph A. Marchal, "'Making History' Queerly: Touches across Time through a Biblical Behind," *Biblical Interpretation* 19 (2011): 373–95.
6. Dinshaw, however, is hardly the only scholar working on this or other, less "modern" periods with queering notions of the temporal or historical. Instructive in this regard are Carla Freccero, *Queer/Early/Modern*, Series Q (Durham, N.C.: Duke University Press, 2006); and Jonathan Goldberg and Madhavi Menon, "Queering History," *PMLA* 120, no. 5 (October 2005): 1608–17. For one recent critique of this work, see Valerie Traub, "The New Unhistoricism in Queer Studies," *PMLA* 128, no. 1 (2013): 21–39.
7. Further, Dinshaw proposes: "Thus our choices as queer historians are not limited simply to mimetic identification with the past or blanket alteritism, the two mutually exclusive positions that have come to be associated with Boswell and Foucault" (*Getting Medieval*, 34).
8. Ann Pellegrini, "Touching the Past; or, Hanging Chad," *Journal of History of Sexuality* 10, no. 2 (2001): 185–94, 188.
9. Dinshaw, *Getting Medieval*, 39.
10. Ibid. By way of contrast, Muñoz frequently thinks of queer pasts as anticipatory illuminations. For just a few examples, see José Esteban Muñoz, *Cruising Utopia: The Then and There of Queer Futurity*, Sexual Cultures (New York: New York University Press, 2009), 20, 22, and 49.
11. Dinshaw, *Getting Medieval*, 1.
12. Ibid., 12.
13. Elizabeth Freeman, "Packing History, Count(er)ing Generations," *New Literary History* 31 (2000): 727–44, 728; but see also Freeman, "Time Binds, or Erotohistoriography," *Social Text* 23, no. 3–4 (2005): 57–68, 66; and *Time Binds: Queer Temporalities, Queer Histories*, Perverse Modernities (Durham, N.C.: Duke University Press, 2010), 62. More briefly, see also Freeman, "Still After," *South Atlantic Quarterly* 106, no. 3 (2007): 495–500. On such losses, see, for instance, the reflections of Heather Love: "Taking care of the past without attempting to fix it means living with bad attachments, identifying through loss, allowing ourselves to be haunted" (*Feeling Backward: Loss and the Politics of Queer History* [Cambridge, Mass.: Harvard University Press, 2007], 43).
14. Freeman, "Packing History," 729. Here, and elsewhere, Freeman's conceptualizations fit with discussions of queer spectrality or haunting, similar to how Freccero stresses the haunting ways in which the specters of the past can make demands on

us. See, for instance, the discussion in Freccero, *Queer/Early/Modern*, 69–73. For some initial reflections on both Freeman and Freccero in relation to alternative approaches to 1 Corinthians, see Joseph A. Marchal, "Female Masculinity in Corinth? Bodily Citations and the Drag of History," *Neotestamentica: Journal of the New Testament Society of Southern Africa* 48, no. 1 (2014): 93–113.

15. See Freeman, "Time Binds," 66.
16. Freeman, "Packing History," 729.
17. Ibid. For two introductions to Butler's conceptualization and its relevance for queer approaches to Paul's letters, see Marchal, "Queer Approaches: Improper Relations with Paul's Letters," in *Studying Paul's Letters: Contemporary Perspectives and Methods*, ed. Marchal (Minneapolis: Fortress, 2012), 209–27; and Joseph A. Marchal, *Philippians: Historical Problems, Hierarchical Visions, Hysterical Anxieties* (Sheffield: Sheffield Phoenix Press, 2014), 69–92.
18. Freeman, *Time Binds*, 63.
19. Ibid., xiii.
20. Ibid., xvi, 85. In the latter instance, Freeman is referencing Lucas Hilderbrand, "Retroactivism," *GLQ* 12, no. 2 (2006): 303–17.
21. This characterization of queers coheres with the mostly negative way in which queer tends to be defined. In its most convincing version (to me), queer is defined over and against regimes of normalcy (or normativity). See, for instance, Michael Warner, *The Trouble with Normal: Sex, Politics, and the Ethics of Queer Life* (Cambridge, Mass: Harvard University Press, 1999).
22. Jack Halberstam, *In a Queer Time and Place: Transgender Bodies, Subcultural Lives*, Sexual Cultures (New York: New York University Press, 2005), 2.
23. Ibid. Here Halberstam draws upon the poetry of Mark Doty, *Heaven's Coast: A Memoir* (New York: Harper, 1996).
24. For instance, Halberstam argues: "Queers use space and time in ways that challenge conventional logics of development, maturity, adulthood, and responsibility" (*In a Queer Time and Place*, 13, referencing Samuel R. Delaney, *Times Square Red, Times Square Blue*, Sexual Cultures [New York: New York University Press, 1999]).
25. Jack Halberstam, *The Queer Art of Failure*, A John Hope Franklin Center Book (Durham, N.C.: Duke University Press, 2011), 73. This notion of "growing sideways" clearly also resonates with the work of Kathryn Bond Stockton, *The Queer Child, or Growing Sideways in the Twentieth Century*, Series Q (Durham, N.C.: Duke University Press, 2009).
26. Lee Edelman, *No Future: Queer Theory and the Death Drive*, Series Q (Durham, N.C.: Duke University Press, 2004). Although Leo Bersani's work is often credited with sparking the development of "the antisocial thesis" in queer studies, in recent debates it has been Edelman's work that has functioned as a charged point of appreciation and disagreement. See Leo Bersani, *The Freudian Body: Psychoanalysis and Art* (New York: Columbia University Press, 1986), and especially Leo Bersani, *Homos* (Cambridge, Mass.: Harvard University Press, 1995); as well as this forum that considers or responds to Bersani, but mostly Edelman: "The Antisocial Thesis in Queer Theory," *PMLA* 121, no. 3 (2006): 819–28.

27. Edelman, *No Future*, 3.
28. Ibid., 18.
29. Ibid., 17. Edelman makes this claim about queer identification (as always promissory) from within a particular Lacanian frame, where signifiers can only ever indicate a kind of promissory identification (see, for instance, ibid., 8).
30. Ibid., 24.
31. Muñoz, *Cruising Utopia*, 11. Muñoz might be overstating his case when he claims (in the immediately following sentence) that "if queerness is to have any value whatsoever, it *must* be viewed as being visible *only* in the horizon" (11, emphases added).
32. Ibid., 1; cf. 12, 22. Ironically, however, this horizon at times also sounds a lot like Edelman's description of relationality and identification as promissory (see above).
33. Ibid., 22, 26. Muñoz notes throughout the influence of Ernst Bloch but (at least to this reader) never really demonstrates the especial utility of Bloch for his particular utopian project. Indeed, what Muñoz sets up in the opening chapter(s) of this work are potentially intriguing, but never quite demonstrated in the ways the following chapters claim. Parts, then, of Muñoz's theoretical framing are significantly more useful (for at least my purposes) than other sections of his work.
34. Ibid., 22. Like Freeman, Muñoz also turns to times and spaces of the more recent past, most especially pre-Stonewall practices or parties for an anticipatory illumination.
35. Ibid., 116.
36. Ibid., 62. Muñoz, like Halberstam and Freeman, is also interested in the possibilities presented by failures (see, for instance, the discussion in *Cruising Utopia*, 146–49). On another use of punk to critique Edelman's antipolitical (or apolitical) vision, see Jack Halberstam, "The Politics of Negativity in Recent Queer Theory," *PMLA* 121, no. 3 (2006): 823–25. For Edelman's initial (so inevitably incomplete) response, see Lee Edelman, "Antagonism, Negativity, and the Subject of Queer Theory," *PMLA* 121, no. 3 (2006): 821–22. Halberstam's more developed criticism (as the scholars continue to quote The Sex Pistols back and forth to each other) can be found in Halberstam, *Queer Art of Failure*, 107–10. For an earlier, slightly less combative exchange about some of these ideas, see the roundtable featuring Edelman, Halberstam, Dinshaw, Freeman, and several others (Roderick A. Ferguson, Carla Freccero, Annamarie Jagose, Christopher Nealon, and Nguyen Tan Hoang): "Theorizing Queer Temporalities: A Roundtable Discussion," *GLQ* 13, no. 2–3 (2007): 177–95.
37. Pamela Eisenbaum, "Jewish Perspectives: A *Jewish* Apostle to the Gentiles," in *Studying Paul's Letters: Contemporary Perspectives and Methods*, ed. Joseph A. Marchal (Minneapolis: Fortress Press, 2012), 135–53, 150. See also the discussion in Pamela Eisenbaum, *Paul Was Not a Christian: The Original Message of a Misunderstood Apostle* (New York: Harper One, 2009), 148–49, 197–200, 223–24, 234–35, and 250–35.
38. Galatians is important for many scholarly conversations about the "apocalyptic Paul," particularly among those who follow or are otherwise influenced by J. Louis Martyn's work, stressing the cosmically warring factions and the new creation in this letter. See J. Louis Martyn, *Theological Issues in the Letters of Paul* (Nashville, Tenn.: Abingdon, 1997); and *Galatians*, Anchor Bible (New York: Doubleday, 1997).

For some indication of Martyn's influence (within a hermeneutically, theoretically, even ideologically constrained circle), see *Apocalyptic Paul: Cosmos and Anthropos in Romans 5–8*, ed. Beverly Roberts Gaventa (Waco, Tex.: Baylor University Press, 2013); and *Apocalyptic and the Future of Theology: With and Beyond J. Louis Martyn*, ed. Joshua B. Davis and Douglas Harink (Eugene, Ore.: Cascade Books, 2012).

39. Indicating the potential overlap between prophecy and apocalyptic, Paul describes this *apokalypsis* in terms echoing a prophetic calling (in Gal 1:15; see Is 49:1; Jer 1:5), and claims that revelation (another one, or the revelatory process in general?) guides his own movements (in Gal 2:2).

40. For my purposes here, I will be operating with a potentially "loose" definition of apocalyptic that begins "tightly" with references to *apokalypsis/apokalyptō* in Greek, but moves rhetorically from there, guided by Huber's stresses on *apokalypsis* as unveiling something hidden, operating visually, and reflecting the physical activity of lifting or removing a veil. See the discussion in Lynn R. Huber, *Thinking and Seeing with Women in Revelation*, Library of New Testament Studies 475 (London: Bloomsbury, 2013), 1–2, 11–18. With this understanding I am also untroubled by the potential conceptual overlap of apocalyptic with wisdom and/or prophecy. Antoinette Clark Wire, for one, argues: "It is better not to separate the Corinthians from the apocalyptic milieu more radically than Paul does, but instead to delineate how a wisdom-oriented apocalyptic scenario may have been conceived in Corinth" (Antoinette Clark Wire, *The Corinthian Women Prophets: A Reconstruction through Paul's Rhetoric* [Minneapolis: Fortress Press, 1990], 60; contrast this view with Horsley, "Paul and Empire—and 1 Corinthians"). If this flexible or even labile working understanding of the concept threatens to bring apocalyptic into crisis, then perhaps this crisis can be productive, precisely because it is troubling or threatening. (Here, I both sympathize with and depart from the overall criticism lodged by Matlock in *Unveiling the Apocalyptic Paul*.)

41. Much of my analysis of this letter is directly influenced by or just following the insightful feminist rhetorical work of Antoinette Clark Wire and Elisabeth Schüssler Fiorenza: Wire, *Corinthian Women Prophets*; and the essays in Elisabeth Schüssler Fiorenza, *Rhetoric and Ethic: The Politics of Biblical Studies* (Minneapolis: Fortress Press, 1999).

42. For some discussion of Paul's difference in perspective (from both ancient surroundings and more recent "followers"), see Dale Martin, "Paul without Passion: On Paul's Rejection of Desire in Sex and Marriage," in *Constructing Early Christian Families: Family as Social Reality and Metaphor*, ed. Halvor Moxnes (London: Routledge, 1997), 201–15; and reprinted in *Sex and the Single Savior: Gender and Sexuality in Biblical Interpretation* (Louisville, Ky.: Westminster John Knox, 2006), 65–76, 212–14.

43. To be fair, though, many things are not long for this world in the vision reflected in this letter. For the ancient imperial politics of sexuality, see Mary Rose D'Angelo, "Early Christian Sexual Politics and Roman Imperial Family Values: Rereading Christ and Culture," in *The Papers of the Henry Luce III Fellows in Theology*, vol. 6, ed. Christopher I. Wilkins (Pittsburgh: Association of Theological Schools, 2003), 23–48.

44. For a different perspective on this passage, see Alexandra R. Brown, "Paul's Apocalyptic Cross and Philosophy: Reading 1 Corinthians with Giorgio Agamben and Alain Badiou," in *Apocalyptic and the Future of Theology*, ed. Davis and Harink, 96–117.
45. When Paul quotes the second creation story (Gn 2:7), he inserts a "first" before this human (15:45), and stresses that the human is made of dust (four times in 15:47–49).
46. For the influences and contradictions that stemmed from later theologians engaging Paul's conceptualization of Christ and Adam, see Benjamin H. Dunning, *Specters of Paul: Sexual Difference in Early Christian Thought*, Divinations: Rereading Late Ancient Religion (Philadelphia: University of Pennsylvania Press, 2011).
47. See also the similar elision of the pair "male and female" in the slightly altered repetition or citation of the baptismal formula (from Gal 3:28) in 1 Cor 12:13. For further reflections, specifically on 11:1–16 in light of gender performativity, female masculinity, and temporal drag, see Marchal, "Female Masculinity in Corinth?"
48. See the discussion in Wire, *Corinthian Women Prophets*, 119–26, among others.
49. For some discussion of how the prophetic females were defined by a new creation (that has already happened in them), see Wire, *Corinthian Women Prophets*, 125–26, 128–29, 176, and 184–86.
50. See also the use of the word for "veiled," *katakalyptō* (11:6 twice, 11:7); both sharing the same root verb with *apokalyptō*.
51. Wire argues that their use of such terms would explain the twenty-six appearances of these terms in the opening four chapters of the letter (*Corinthian Women Prophets*, 52). Horsley agrees, but to different ends ("Paul and Empire—and 1 Corinthians").
52. A third sarcastic association comes earlier when Paul tries to qualify women's speaking practices in the assembly community. The first time he mentions the Corinthian women praying and prophesying unveiled (*akatakalyptō*), he makes the (apparently) absurd claim that such behavior is the same as if the woman's head was shaved (11:5; cf. 6). Although Wire depicts this association as a "shocking aside" (*Corinthian Women Prophets*, 118), Caroline Vander Stichele and Todd Penner have argued that this claim could be the "critical lynchpin of Paul's argument in 1 Cor 11" (Caroline Vander Stichele and Todd Penner, "Paul and the Rhetoric of Gender," in *Her Master's Tools? Feminist and Postcolonial Engagements of Historical-Critical Discourse*, ed. Vander Stichele and Penner, Global Perspectives on Biblical Scholarship 9 [Atlanta: Society of Biblical Literature, 2005], 287–310, 292).
53. See, for instance, Wire's reconstruction of their perspective in *Corinthian Women Prophets*, 162–76, and 181–88.
54. Wire, *Corinthian Women Prophets*, 94. Paul is trying to limit the application of such slogans in the community, here by inserting a "not" into the potentially combined proposition, shaping sexual practice.
55. The potential import of velocity for resituating queer temporalities was suggested to me through a "Keywords on a Swerve" presentation by Jennifer Row, "At a Loss for Time: Erotic Velocities and Queer Desires" (presentation at the "Queer and Now: Rethinking Queer Theory in the Humanities" symposium, sponsored by the

Center for the Humanities, University of Wisconsin–Madison, and organized by the Sexual Politics/Sexual Poetic Collective, March 7, 2014).

56. My diction here should indicate that I intend to use the idea of "velocity" in a more gestural or even colloquial fashion, and not necessarily in a more technical or even theoretical sense, such as that associated with Gilles Deleuze.

57. From this perspective, though the letter conjures an image of competing in a race (9:24), it is Paul who is still running behind!

58. Such complications signal one place where Deleuze and Guattari's notions of deterritorialization and nomadology could prove useful for altering our encounters with Paul's letters. For some reflections on the utility of theories of space for such encounters, see Laura S. Nasrallah, "Spatial Perspectives: Space and Archaeology in Roman Philippi," in *Studying Paul's Letters*, ed. Marchal, 53–74.

59. Freeman, *Time Binds*, xxi.

60. Such vulgar referentiality is crucial to how Freeman imagines the distinctiveness of queer theory (see, for instance, ibid., 11).

61. Dale Martin, for instance, emphasizes the polluting threat of women's prophecy in his *The Corinthian Body* (New Haven, Conn.: Yale University Press, 1995), 239–49.

62. See Freccero, *Queer/Early/Modern*, 69–104, especially 101–2; and Freeman, *Time Binds*, 109. See also Kathryn Bond Stockton, *Beautiful Bottom, Beautiful Shame: Where "Black" Meets "Queer,"* Series Q (Durham, N.C.: Duke University Press, 2006).

63. Freeman, *Time Binds*, 109. Here, Freeman is referencing Ann Cvetkovich's consideration of the expansive receptivity of lesbian sex acts, in "Recasting Receptivity: Femme Sexualities," in *Lesbian Erotics*, ed. Karla Jay (New York: New York University Press, 1995), 125–46. Freeman's disposition provides an important contrast to that of Martin's, who primarily imagines a Corinthian panic about women's prophecy as always already defined as requiring containment in the face of an assaulting penetration.

64. Even explicitly feminist work on women, gender, and 1 Corinthians tends to disavow the possibilities of reconstructing people besides Paul in the Corinthian assembly community. See, for instance, Jorunn Økland, *Women in Their Place: Paul and the Corinthian Discourse of Gender and Sanctuary Space*, Journal for the Study of the New Testament Supplement Series 269 (London: T & T Clark International, 2004).

65. Freeman, for example, seems both keenly aware of and resistant to this tendency to dissociate queer pursuits from feminist pasts (or presents) (see especially her "Packing History," and *Time Binds*). I admit to being mystified by such moves of dissociation and distancing, especially since I find the most interesting sorts of queer projects to be doing specific kinds of feminist work. See, for example, Joseph A. Marchal, "Queer Studies and Critical Masculinity Studies in Feminist Biblical Studies," in *Feminist Biblical Studies in the Twentieth Century: Scholarship and Movement*, vol. 21 of *The Bible and Women: An Encyclopaedia of Exegesis and Cultural History*, ed. Elisabeth Schüssler Fiorenza (Atlanta: Society of Biblical Literature, 2014), 304–27. Many of the most important figures at the "start" of queer theory (Judith Butler, Eve Kosofsky Sedgwick, Gayle Rubin, inter alia) worked in explicitly feminist ways.

One of the most prominent queer biblical critics also notes his own clear debts to and resonances with feminist work in biblical studies. See, for instance, Ken Stone, *Practicing Safer Texts: Food, Sex, and Bible in Queer Perspective*, Queering Theology (London: T & T Clark International, 2005), especially 12–22.

66. For more on failures in sociality, see Love, *Feeling Backward*, 22–29.; as well as Halberstam, *Queer Art of Failure*; Freeman, *Time Binds*, xiii–xxi; and Muñoz, *Cruising Utopia*, 146–49.

67. In the end prophecy is far from the only activity characterized by its porosity, to either divine communication or admittedly awkward, belated, anachronistic touches. Letters like Paul's are themselves porous, reflecting the temporal, conceptual, and practical gaps between their creator and recipients. Indeed, for Paul's letters to make much sense at all, one must recognize that Paul's procedure presumes a difference in his exchanges, expects disagreement and resistance to his arguments. (On this point interpreters of Paul's letters would do well to reconsider Wire's recontextualization of the letters' rhetoric in *Corinthian Women Prophets*, 1–11). This difference makes it possible to trace an alternative apocalyptic temporality to Paul's, but it also highlights that the process of correspondence itself necessarily reflects gaps, drags, and lags in time. (This seems more widely acknowledged among literary scholars, particularly regarding the conventions of epistolary literature. See, for instance, the observations in Freeman, *Time Binds*, 96–97.) Traveling at different velocities, the composers and receivers encounter this letter in different moments and at different points on their trajectories from each other. Epistles, then, represent important objects, places, and times for reconsidering and reframing queer temporalities. Muñoz appeals to the operation of letters in performance art to expose not only gaps, but also the alterations of circuits: "A letter's standard temporality is that of the sender's present and the receiver's future. The letter no longer has a 'here to there' trajectory. It now takes on a 'here to there to there and there too' trajectory, since a piece of mail art will move between a circuit of friends and acquaintances, being altered at every point in the journey. We can call this new temporality one of queer futurity, where the future is a site of infinite and immutable potentiality" (*Cruising Utopia*, 126–27). However, this also sounds, in part, like how Paul's letters could have functioned within, between, and among the various assembly communities, with correspondingly open possibilities for how they were (or even still might be) used. If apocalyptic ideas are transmitted to the effect of disruption, the letters could also be like the "hiccup in sequential time" Freeman imagines connecting groups beyond normative structures and practices (*Time Binds*, 3).

68. For some reflections on feminist, queer, and antiracist activists as affectively and interpersonally troublesome, even willful, see Sara Ahmed, *The Promise of Happiness* (Durham, N.C.: Duke University Press, 2010); and *Willful Subjects* (Durham, N.C.: Duke University Press, 2014).

69. For me, this raises questions like: Who can afford not to have a history, or at least make historical claims? Who can afford not to imagine a future or at least a claim on future possibilities? Feminist biblical scholars have asked these sorts of ques-

tion for decades (see, for example, Schüssler Fiorenza, *Rhetoric and Ethic*). Muñoz appears to be making a similar point in one of his critiques of Edelman (*Cruising Utopia*, 94). Given my own contexts and commitments, the respective ethical and historical visions of queer scholars like Edelman and David M. Halperin often leave me cold, likely because I am differently haunted by the past and its possibilities. I admit to being under the grip of history; though I am no good at it, I cannot quite quit it. For further reflections, see Marchal, "'Making History' Queerly."

70. It is not as though the Corinthians were already queer; the prophets are not simply figures with whom we should unproblematically identify. Rather (following Dinshaw), it is our pursuit of them, our desire to make relations with those similarly positioned, yet eluding resemblance to us, that one would call queer. For one caution about identifying ancient people ("Christians") as queer, see Maia Kotrosits, "The Queer Life of Christian Exceptionalism," *Culture and Religion* 15, no. 2 (2014): 158–65. On exceptionalism as a problem for queer studies, see Jasbir K. Puar, *Terrorist Assemblages: Homonationalism in Queer Times*, Next Wave: New Directions in Women's Studies (Durham, N.C.: Duke University Press, 2007). For my own reflections on these dynamics (including how they relate to the study of Paul's letters), see "Bio-Necro-*Biblio*-Politics? Restaging Feminist Intersections and Queer Exceptions," *Culture and Religion* 15, no. 2 (2014): 166–76; and "The Exceptional Proves Who Rules: Imperial Sexual Exceptionalism in and around Paul's Letters," *Journal of Early Christian History* 5, no. 1 (2015): 87–115

71. My work here (and elsewhere) is also trying to sound a caution about focusing on single (often traditionally dominant) perspectives or presenting monocausal accounts for historical moments or, better, movements like the ones described here. As I have noted repeatedly here (and elsewhere), feminist interpreters of Paul's letters have long interrogated the idea of taking Paul's perspective for the entire historical horizon in places like Corinth. It is only somewhat recently that (a few) other scholars (including those interested in "history from below") have also considered a more polyfactorial and interactionist model for the study of these contexts and communities. On history from below, see Joseph A. Marchal, ed., *The People beside Paul: The Philippian Assembly and History from Below*, Early Christianity and Its Literature 17 (Atlanta: SBL Press, 2015). For a more "quantum" approach to such constructions, see Richard S. Ascough, "Bringing Chaos to Order: Historical Memory and the Manipulation of History," *Religion and Theology* 15 (2008): 280–303.

# Unbinding Imperial Time: Chrononormativity and Paul's Letter to the Romans

JAMES N. HOKE

The empire binds time. The idea of time being bound by institutions of power (ancient or modern) to have a normalizing effect, of course, comes from Elizabeth Freeman. She identifies such a binding as chrononormativity, "the use of time to organize individual human bodies toward maximum productivity."[1] Under a modern capitalist system, for example, a normal "workday" is arranged (including "free" time) in such a way that workers produce more labor, and thus capital, for their employers. Chrononormativity, therefore, produces the most benefit for those at the top of the socioeconomic hierarchy.

Chrononormativity's effectiveness derives especially from its routinization of habits—social, economic, bodily, and otherwise—across populations. "Chrononormativity is a mode of implantation, a technique by which institutional forces come to seem like somatic facts," writes Freeman.[2] Tempos and rhythms that seem habitual—*normal* and everyday—pace bodies in time with the beat of the institutionalized capitalist state, whose interests are dictated by those who hold massive wealth, status, and political influence. All the while, often unsuspecting bodies have these normative temporal schemes impressed upon them, structuring the various rhythms of their lives—from regular beats, to interruptions, rests, and frenzies—to support the current social order.

When chrononormativity extends its influence beyond the routinization of individual bodies to the temporal regulation of whole populations or societies, it becomes what Freeman, following Dana Luciano, calls "chronobiopolitics."[3] "In chronobiological society," writes Freeman, "the state and other institutions . . . link properly temporalized bodies to narratives of movement and change. These are teleological schemes of events or strategies for living such as marriage, accumulation of health and wealth for the future, reproduction, child rearing, and death and its attendant rituals."[4] Through these arrangements, sexuality becomes temporally structured in ways that are dictated by the capitalist state and thus function to further the interests of the state and, by extension, those with the most socioeconomic power and influence.[5] These arrangements become routine for large populations, thus extending chrononormativity's impact. Through the normalization of time in these ways, diverse bodies can be bound to a temporal flow that progresses to benefit and preserve the longevity of the modern capitalist state.

When invoking the phrase "the empire binds time" in reference to the Pauline epistles, the "empire" is, of course, Rome in the first century CE. Though power, be it political, social, economic, or sexual, was arranged differently in the ancient world, those at the top of the imperial hierarchy—mostly elite men—also arranged time in chrononormative ways. As this essay shows, Roman "chrononormativity" and "chronobiopolitics," although taking their own ancient, imperial forms, can be seen to "bind the empire" especially in the ways in which the political dominance of the empire was connected to its maintenance of a strict sociosexual hierarchy.

This imperial chrononormativity impressed its tempos on ancient bodies, keeping all Roman subjects submissive to the sociopolitical hierarchies of the empire, making the dominance of this imperial system into a "somatic fact." Such chrononormative impressions bore on "ordinary" ancient subjects across the sociopolitical and geographic span of the empire. Most notably, as I argue in this essay, Roman chrononormativity's impressions can be detected in Paul's letter to the Romans. Paul's rather famous exhortation to obey—or submit to—governing authorities in Romans 13:1–7 bears the influence of the Roman Empire's binding of time. Therefore, in the first two sections of my essay, I lay out how Rome arranged time in chrononormative patterns, first to support its imperial domination and then specifically in its regulation of sexuality. Alongside this explanation, I read Romans 13:1–7 as one example of how imperial chrononormativity comes to be reflected and repeated in the lives of less elite imperial subjects. By reading this passage with the framework of Roman chrononormativity in mind, I show how Paul's ideas here are bound, first imperially and then sexually, to Roman hierarchies and ideologies.

Finally, Freeman's identification of modern forms of chrononormativity (and the chronobiopolitics that often accompany them) serves her larger queer project that identifies fissures wherein time can begin to be unbound from capitalist chrononormative ideologies. Describing this project, she writes, "I track the ways that nonsequential forms of time . . . can also fold subjects into structures of belonging and duration that may be invisible to the historicist eye." In the first century and its history, the ancient *ekklēsia* emerges as one of these invisible "structures of belonging" that can queerly reach across temporal boundaries in order to unbind the imperial time that we found echoed in Paul's letter.[6] Although we know that the recipients of Paul's letters were of diverse backgrounds and sometimes queried or disputed Paul's words, their voices and experiences are typically lost, and only the visible and verbose apostle is obvious. However, by engaging this aspect of Freeman's queer temporal project, I suspect that it is possible to reveal some of the experiences of wo/men in the *ekklēsia* that potentially disrupted imperial chrononormativity.[7]

Therefore, in the final section of my essay, I read "beyond the heroic Paul," as suggested by Melanie Johnson-DeBaufre and Laura S. Nasrallah, and place Paul's words into a wider conversation in the *ekklēsia* that met in Rome. Engaging with traditional, feminist, and queer historiographical reconstructions of Pauline *ekklēsiai*, I rethink imperial time and Paul's letter with the wo/men in this assembly, some of whom may have had desires—political, sexual, or otherwise—that centered on mutual pleasure. This reconstruction then draws from Freeman's work on erotohistoriography to show how a disruptive use of time that seeks bodily pleasure and a hybrid past/present opens the possibility that the wo/men of the *ekklēsia* might share (with us) in pleasurably "queer" sensations at a tempo that is "out of joint" with the sexed/gendered/imperial logics of Rome.

## BOUND IMPERIALLY

Paul's letter to the *ekklēsia* in Rome was sent to a community living at the center of an empire moving toward the peak of its ascent. With the Roman state expanding territorially while consolidating power and control centrally, the stability of this empire depended on its ability to bind all subjects under its control, quelling dissent in addition to permitting the state to expand and prosper socioeconomically. Under the Pax Romana, peace was achieved not only as a result of Rome's military prowess but also through social propaganda that communicated the proper behaviors required for the longevity of the state (which, in turn, would permit stability and prosperity for all its subjects).[8] As the state bound its subjects to its imperial control, it enforced a rigid hierarchy, with the emperor and elite Roman-born citizen males at the top and slaves, foreigners, and women at the bottom.[9]

In doing this, the empire bound time—employing a form of Freeman's chrononormativity suited for an ancient context—in order to maintain its social hierarchy and keep its subjects under control. As Freeman observes, "Manipulations of time convert historically specific regimes of asymmetrical power into seemingly ordinary bodily tempos and routines, which in turn organize the value and meaning of time."[10] Although its specific chrononormative strategies were different from Freeman's modern examples, Rome similarly manipulated time in order to support its own rigid, and quite exclusive, imperial hierarchy (a "regime of asymmetrical power") so that the hierarchy—and therefore also the imperial system itself—becomes "ordinary" and "routine," binding subjects across the hierarchy to imperial time.

One way that Rome bound time can be see in its portrayal of its empire as representing the "end of history." As explained by Neil Elliott, to stand at history's end means being "confident that the future will be only a continuation of the present."[11] Living at history's end, then, the Romans portrayed their rule as both inevitable and invincible, as the result of their superior virtue and fortune.[12] Roman rhetoric, architecture, and (when necessary) military might encouraged and enforced submission from its (often conquered) subjects.[13] Such communication of this inevitability meant that those who found themselves under Roman rule (from the lowest barbarian slave to an elite senatorial family) had no option but to submit to the emperor and his regime. Presenting itself at the end of history, this ancient imperial binding of time regularizes the hierarchical structure that guarantees its political control for all foreseeable future.

Rome's purported position at the end of history presents submission to Rome as the best option. Indeed, submission is presented as inevitable: If one's alternative is to resist, Rome makes clear that such an option is futile, given its might and its treatment of traitors and rebels. Such a presentation permits Rome to convey an ethical binary wherein Rome and those who submit to its authority are good and anyone who is against Rome is therefore evil. Elliott's description of such imperial representation highlights this binary quite well: "From the imperial center, the global struggle is perceived as a combat between good and evil, virtue and tyranny."[14] From this vantage point, one is either under the empire (therefore, obedient, tax-paying subjects) or against it. The Roman Empire binds time through such binaries: One is good or evil, virtuous or tyrannous, submissive or rebellious. If one is on the wrong side of the divide, then one stands on the wrong side of history and should expect to be crushed. Presenting itself as "the end of history," Rome effectively prohibits any concept of time that does not conform to its standards, effectively maintaining Rome's power and dominance.[15]

Rome's "end of history," then, provides a masterly example of an ancient form of Freeman's chrononormativity, wherein time and history are presented in ways that normalize imperial domination. Further, as it does this, Rome exhibits the move from normalizing the tempos of individual bodies to the manipulation of time at a societal level, arranging the varying tempos of different groupings of bodies into complementary rhythms that reinforced the normalized pace of imperial domination. Such an arrangement follows what Freeman labels "chronobiopolitics." As one example, Roman marriage and procreation laws stipulated whom citizens—particularly senatorial families and other political elites—could marry and incentivized childbearing by these same citizens.[16] These laws effectively regulated and maintained the boundaries of the elite class, particularly those most likely to hold political power. By binding subjects to particular tempos and arrangements of social/household life, the empire attempted to ensure its prolonged political dominance. Such chronobiopolitical maneuvers continued Rome's arrangement of its position in time at history's end, and all of its subjects were bound and forced into submission to imperial time.

Such an idea of a submission that is bound to imperial time appears in Paul's letter to the Romans. Chapter 13 begins: "Every soul, submit to the prevailing authorities. For there is not authority except by God, and the present ones have been placed by God" (Rom 13:1).[17] The next six verses continue to encourage what today would be called the behavior of "model citizens": Do not rebel (13:2); do good and noble things (13:3); pay taxes and give fear and honor to those who deserve them (13:6–7). In these verses, Paul appears aligned with imperial goals and rhetoric as he encourages his audience to submit to living lives that are productive and beneficial to the imperial center. Certainly, as this empire (and those that followed) became "Christian," this passage was made to champion obedience to the rule and decisions of authority as the proper behavior of the Christian citizen.[18]

Paul's exhortation betrays his replication of Roman imperial chrononormativity. In encouraging submission through the reproduction of model citizen subjects (although it is unlikely that many in Paul's audience were classified as Roman citizens), Paul parrots the script of Roman imperial politics and ethics. His letter follows the beat of imperial time and encourages its readers to do likewise. In other words, in Romans 13, Paul reveals his entanglement in imperial time, whose inevitability is implanted in Paul, who likewise attempts to submit his audience to this rhythm. Such chrononormativity is "somatic"—embodied. It implies that Paul's submission to an imperial mind-set may not always be entirely intentional: He has absorbed the rhythm, and his rhetoric marches to its beat.

Along these lines, Elliott sees similarities between Rome's representation of its time as "the end of history" and Paul's rhetoric in these verses: Submission to Rome is necessary because of Rome's temporal position. Because Elliott finds evidence of a stance of resistance and critique of Roman imperial domination throughout Paul's letters, he emphasizes the disparities between these seven verses and the remainder of Paul's letter to the Romans.[19] Here, it seems, Paul accepts the idea that Rome indeed stands at the end of history. Resistance is futile—at least for the time being. Paul's exhortation to submission can be interpreted as temporary, for Paul clearly expects the Lord's imminent arrival, which should upset and overturn the current Roman order. If this new divine order is unavoidably arriving soon, resistance in the present is pointless. As Krister Stendahl quipped, "Why walk around with a little shotgun when the atomic blast is imminent?"[20] The empire binds time today, but God (the ultimate *kyrios*, or imperial lord) binds time eternally.

Regardless of Paul's stance toward Rome (in Romans 13 and more broadly), his exhortation in Romans 13:1–7 bears the marks of Roman chrononormative arrangements as it limits to two the options for present political action with respect to Rome. Both options involve different forms of *placement* with respect to Rome, presented through forms of the Greek verb *tassō*, "to place." One option is that which he seemingly emphasizes and encourages: submitting, or placing oneself under (*hypotassō*), that is, living according to Roman rule so as not to cause disruption. The alternative to this behavior, described in 13:2, is antisubmission or displacement (*antitassō*)—rebellion against Rome, in other words.[21] Whatever form this rebellion takes (violent or otherwise), Rome will respond by bearing the sword and is to be feared (13:4). Paul presents as a binary the options for one's position with respect to the (Roman) authorities: Either be placed under (submit, *hypotassō*) or place oneself against (revolt, *antitassō*). As the only two options, this presentation reinforces the binary logic that also informed the program and propaganda of Roman dominion. Thus Paul's instructions in Romans 13 demonstrate how Rome's imperial propaganda normalizes time for those living under its authority and are likewise bound to the empire's time.

## BOUND SEXUALLY

According to Freeman's queer theoretical lens, chrononormativity arranges all aspects of life, public and private; perhaps most important, it normalizes sexual lives to permit maximum benefit for those who hold power. Already we observed how Roman laws regulating marriage and childbirth bound subjects in the ongoing reproduction of the imperial hierarchy and that such examples of Roman chronobiopolitics enforced the inevitability of imperial time. Roman imperial chrononormativity, binding time at the end of history to make inevitable its rule and hierarchies, similarly extends to the broader norms that regulated Roman sexuality in the first century CE. Rome's sexual hierarchy mirrored its social and political hierarchy. As classical scholars have shown, sex and gender in Rome were arranged by an intricate hierarchy of power at which the most elite men took the top position, figuratively and literally. According to the "penetration model" of Roman sexuality, a "normal" sexual encounter involved a person of higher status (always male) penetrating a person of lower status (indiscriminate of gender).[22] Sexual acts categorized as "unnatural" were those that most egregiously defied this hierarchy. Two terms that often exemplified or represented persons or groups of persons who practiced such "unnatural" acts were *tribades* and *cinaedi*. Both terms appear in Roman texts as a form of sexual slander, which has led some to the conclusion that the terms were more rhetorical, referring to excessive deviance—an active female (*tribas*) or a passive male (*cinaedus*)—but they do not have any connotations of a sexual preference or orientation.[23] However, this does not account for all of the uses of these terms (in particular, uses of *tribas* to refer to either partner in sex between two women), and it does not eliminate the possibility that some may have taken pleasure and therefore preferred the acts designated by such slanderous designations as an ancient sexual "subculture" (a point that will be important later when considering the potential participation of these wo/men in the Roman *ekklēsia*).[24] Even so, these polemical usages by elite men certainly reinforced the establishment of a "natural" hierarchy, in which the sexual aligned with the social and political goals of the empire and its elite.

These hierarchy-enforcing sexual protocols furthered the chronobiopolitical binding of time by literally embodying the sociopolitical hierarchy in sexual acts. Through such protocols, the imperial system becomes a "somatic fact," binding the sexual lives of its subjects into replicating its form. Conquered and penetrable, those lower on the hierarchy can only accept and submit to their situation, experiencing time in its imperial arrangement. Their only hope may be that, through proper displays of submission, they might be able to eventually rise above their current social position. Accepting one's fortune (or lack thereof) at history's end means enacting a somatic submission to all aspects of the Roman hierarchy, whether sexual, social, political, or otherwise. In this way, Rome's sexual hierarchy continues the chrononormative presentation of imperial time as being at the end of history.

But in what ways was this sexual hierarchy conveyed in order to normalize its impression on the body as temporally bound somatic facts? Beyond the acts themselves and the discourse that surrounded them, the Roman sexual hierarchy was communicated through visual depiction and through the construction of space. Analyzing panels depicting nations conquered by Roman military expansion, Davina Lopez shows how these depictions spatially represent the Roman political hierarchy using sexual and gendered imagery.[25] On these panels, the male victors (who represent Rome) stand spatially over the conquered females (who represent the nations that have since submitted to Roman rule).[26] Often their swords visually penetrate the conquered bodies, reinforcing the ways in which political submission relies on the already established patterns of gendered and sexual submission in Roman culture.[27] Along similar lines, David Fredrick argues that Roman spaces, including the household (*domus*), were designed to communicate the penetrative hierarchy that informed Roman sexual (and political) relations. "Whether one walks into a house, a theater, or one of the fora, this is the bedrock of physical and spatial experience: at the apex: 'impenetrable' penetrators, elite men; at the base, the most penetrable: the least important slaves and the poor free of either gender."[28] Through such communication of these hierarchies in everyday ancient experience, imperial subjects were made subject to the imperial system and its sexual mores as part of the normal pace of ancient life.

Drawing on this conclusion, Fredrick notes that this spatial construction of the sexual hierarchy also affects a person's view of time: Those elite men at the apex of society not only inhabit more space, they also reap the benefits of normative time. From this point, he observes, "Toward the top of the apex, one is close to entering *pure time* where all one does is *a kind of history*: simultaneously an expression of one's present influence over events near and far and (connecting past and future) one's ability to be a model for others' behavior."[29] In other words, those with social and political influence and control were those who not only could enjoy the luxuries and benefits of time, they were also those who could craft themselves at history's end so that their deeds would be recorded and remembered while they and their descendants remained on top, whether that "topping" be political, social, or sexual. Again, according to their logic, the only hope for others to enter such "pure time" is to follow the chrononormative rhythm displayed for them. Extending imperial control through chronobiopolitics by carving this hierarchical and imperial temporality into the spaces of everyday life, the hierarchy of Rome's sexual protocols thus shapes space and time so that the elite control both. As they inhabit the most space, they also use time—their own and others'—to reinforce their rule. Roman rule is not just the "end of history," it is the "top of history." The inevitable "top" position of the elite male—enforced in so many aspects of Roman daily life—also makes imperial time impenetrable. It is so normative that neither the empire, its male elite, nor their time can be fucked.

So also, I argue, it is for Paul. Although scholars (such as Elliott) find Paul's language of submission in Romans 13:1–7 unique and startling, I counter that Paul's submissive stance can be found interspersed throughout this letter, explicitly in Romans 8 or implicitly in Jesus' submission to God's plan as elaborated in Romans 2–5.[30] Paul's exhortation to submission in Romans 13 is not exclusively an acceptance of Rome's political power and authority: It also involves a submission to (or, at least, unconscious acceptance of) these chrononormative structures of sexual life under Roman rule. Turning to perhaps the most infamous of Pauline sex passages, Romans 1:18–32, readers find Paul repeating the same hierarchical protocols that governed sexual behavior in wider Roman culture.[31] As Stephen Moore elaborates in his reading of Romans, Paul's theology is infused by the Greco-Roman sexual hierarchy, and right relation to God—in this case, the ultimate imperial *kyrios*—involves complete (sexual) submission.[32]

In Romans 13 Paul's explicit language of submission, here political with respect to the "prevailing authorities" (13:1), only makes sense when considered alongside his already submissive acceptance (evident yet implicit in Romans 1:18–32) of the terms of Roman imperial sexuality.[33] Ultimately (and perhaps not entirely consciously), this is an exhortation for members of the *ekklēsia* to arrange their lives according to Roman chronobiopolitics. Obey your rulers and do not rebel—but also, do good (or noble, *agathos*) things (13:3). Doing "good" means aligning daily living (including its sexual aspects, see 13:11–14) according to what are ultimately Roman values—ways of living that promote imperial longevity. Thus Paul's notions of sexual and political submission show that his theology remains trapped in Roman chrononormativity. Even after the Lord returns, Paul's notion of time still imagines an empire at the "end of history." The only difference is that history ends with God as the Lord (*kurios*) on top ("without a bottom," as Moore quips)—the ultimate "impenetrable penetrator."[34]

## UNBINDING WITH THE *EKKLĒSIA*

Interpretations of Paul's letters typically situate him and his rhetoric as the exclusive subject and center of analysis, as the prior discussion of the appearance of imperial chrononormativity in Romans has done so far. However, following Melanie Johnson-DeBaufre and Laura Nasrallah's elaboration, a decentering approach to Paul's letters *changes the subject* by considering other voices in the *ekklēsia* alongside Paul's.[35] In this way, Paul's letters and the *ekklēsiai* in which they were read and discussed become "sites of debate, contestation, and resistance" wherein Paul's (sometimes imperially aligned) views are neither authoritative for nor representative of (nor always entirely opposed to) the entire community.[36] Moving "beyond the heroic Paul," therefore, does not represent the *ekklēsia*'s response in a binary model that is either totally submissive or resistant to Paul's rhetoric and construction of authority (a move that still reifies Paul's rhetoric as that central to response). Removing Paul from the center of the conversation does not remove him from the conversation entirely; instead, Paul's voice becomes one "among others," sometimes agreeing and sometimes disagreeing with other Christ-followers in Rome.[37] Thus, the Pauline epistles are "partial inscriptions of the political visions and debates of the Christ-assemblies."[38]

So, who else might have been a participant in these conversations in the *ekklēsia* at Rome? In partial answer to this question, Romans 16 provides evidence not only of the diversity of those present in the Roman *ekklēsia* but also of the presence of other prominent voices who likely had just as much (or more) authority in the communal conversations. The greetings and list of names in Romans 16 give only a few details about the lives of the persons behind them, but analysis of the names and brief descriptions shows that those named varied in terms of social class, gender, and birthplace (i.e., from Rome or abroad).[39] Furthermore, of those named by Paul, one third are women, and women account for almost half of those who are singled out with specific terms for leadership positions or influence.[40] However, this list only mentions those of whom Paul is aware (either because he met them elsewhere in his travels or because he has heard of them secondhand, since Paul has not visited Rome himself), and, as Elisabeth Schüssler Fiorenza has emphasized, we have to assume that other, unmentioned participants were also active in the Roman *ekklēsia* and that many of these participants were women, even if they are not explicitly mentioned or included.[41] If this is the case, then how can we uncover or reveal these diverse voices when Paul's words record the only remnant of the Roman *ekklēsia*?[42]

Reconstructions of other ancient *ekklēsiai* to which Paul wrote indicate that the conversations in these assemblies reflected the diverse backgrounds of the participants. Discussions among Christ-followers produced new questions (some of which were directed to Paul, such as in Thessalonica) as well as disagreements, with one another and with Paul. In communities like those in Corinth, it is quite apparent that some (perhaps many) led the assembly in divergent directions from the path preferred by Paul and those who more or less agreed with him. From these questions or disagreements addressed by Paul, it has been possible for scholars to reconstruct historically plausible versions of "the other side" of the conversation, as it was raised by (some) followers in communities like Corinth.[43] Such reconstructions facilitate our ability, as modern readers, to hear the many different, sometimes dissenting voices, among which Paul can be included, that participated in these "*ekklēsia*-l" conversations.

Although we have evidence that the *ekklēsia* was equally diverse in Rome, Paul's letter leaves no trace of the ideas, concerns, questions, or disagreements that wo/men raised in this assembly. But, despite the fact that these wo/men may seem "invisible to the historicist eye," given the diversity of the *ekklēsia* discussed above, such conversational dynamics certainly existed in similar patterns of tension and creativity to those in the other *ekklēsiai* to which Paul wrote. Even if Paul had little first- or secondhand knowledge of the issues and questions being discussed in Rome, it is likely that the major topics of his letter touched on some (though likely not all) of them. Thus, though the actual conversations are lost, a diverse assembly and the lively, polyvocal discussions among them remain historically plausible such that we must reconstruct other plausible "positions" within this conversation and thus reframe the theopolitical stakes implied in Paul's monovocal letter.

Doing so requires a degree of historical imagination, a term normally avoided by biblical scholars for its overt blending of ancient and modern. However, despite the refusal of "imagination" to hide its inability to prove historical accuracy, the conversations such imagination re-creates, rooted in the evidence we have of ancient *ekklēsiai*, are historically plausible. Supporting such a reconstructive imagination, Joseph A. Marchal employs a queerly feminist approach to Romans 1 in order to decenter Paul and to think transtemporally about a "queer coalition" with these assemblies.[44] Marchal's approach draws on queer approaches to time and history that rethink the binary between a historiography that is neither altericist (emphasizing the historical difference between present and past, especially with regard to "sexual orientation") nor continuist (emphasizing similarities between past and present identities).[45] Instead, this approach acknowledges the historical differences while allowing for similarities between present and past to emerge, thus blending modern theoretical models of identity and society into the reconstruction of ancient ideas and structures. "Such reconstructions," Marchal observes, "do not compel unthinking acceptance or repetitions of mimetic exactitude but, rather, have their appeal in contributing to queerly non-identical identifications, unanticipatable similarities, and unconventional temporal copresences."[46] These queer contributions and cross-temporal coalitions, then, provide the theoretical framework for situating biblical texts (and Paul's letters in particular) in historically reimagined contexts. Unsettling the centrality of Paul and the biblical text—and with it, the exclusive demands of traditional historiography—such an approach employs queer touchings of ancient and modern that allow us to read in ways other than what may be dictated by the chrononormative imperial perspectives present in these texts. Queerly, this approach does not always have to be oppositional or resistant in order to unsettle these imperial perspectives. Instead, through these "unanticipatable similarities" and "unconventional temporal copresences," they allow multiple and diverse identifications across time that slowly unsettle, or decenter, the dominant voices.

With respect to the *ekklēsia* in Rome, we know that the assembly varied in terms of gender, class, and ethnicity (Romans 16). It is possible, even quite likely, that some of these persons' sexual practices were not bound to the terms of pleasure dictated by the rigid sexual/ethical hierarchy that structured imperial society. Perhaps some preferred to pursue pleasure from sexual acts that were "unnatural" for them, like those referred to as *tribades* or *cinaedi* in Roman sexual slander. As scholars such as Bernadette Brooten and Amy Richlin have argued, it is possible that persons included under these terms preferred and practiced their "unnatural" relations as "subcultures" (of sorts) outside of the elite hierarchies. Even if those pursuing such pleasures were "at the bottom" of Roman society, it is possible that they did not allow social status (or the hope of gaining it) to define pleasure for themselves and others. Through such a disruption of the chrononormative imperial arrangements of social/sexual life, it is possible that some of these wo/men imagined less hierarchical structurings in other realms. It is possible that they enacted arrangements in their homes or in the *ekklēsia* in which leadership, influence, or power were shared and/or not determined by status.

However, it is not necessarily the case that these ancient queers-of-sorts always freely (or, at least, publicly) expressed—or even were in a position to be able to express—their nonconforming sexual desires.[47] Noting the potential for queer/sexual minorities within the *ekklēsia* (such as Tryphaena and Tryphosa of Romans 16:12 as a potentially committed missionary couple, as Mary Rose D'Angelo has suggested), Marchal suggests, "While their arrangements might not always stand in contradistinction to ancient kinship structures (especially of the household), this eccentric assemblage of figures might still represent one of those ancient cases of an especial noncorrespondence to today's heteronormativity."[48] The diversity and the dynamics of these *ekklēsiai* represent a radical—and queer—space *because of* the variety of social, sexual, and political positions and views that potentially informed their assemblies. Just as other *ekklēsiai* appear to have performed radical or disruptive ideas with respect to gender, class, race, and sex whereas others seem to have disagreed with their ideas and reported such dissension to Paul (e.g., in Corinth), the participants in this assembly of Christ-followers in Rome brought their varying experiences of Roman hierarchies to bear on their new ethical and political vision that stemmed from their new theological beliefs.

The wo/men of the Roman *ekklēsia*, therefore, did not uniformly conform to Roman (or Pauline) sexual codes or structures: Some may have, but others may have sought less "natural" pleasures and preferred to live differently. Along these lines, it is possible that some found sexual pleasure outside of penetration (maybe like the female *tribades*) or by actively preferring the penetrated role (as some have posited for the *cinaedi*); or, in general, some may have focused on mutual pleasure between or among equals, as opposed to a sexual hierarchy where only the most powerful penetrator's presumed pleasure is important. Emphasizing more mutual or collective pleasures, sex can be expressed differently and more diversely, beyond an exclusive focus on domination and sociopolitical power. As a result, perhaps these more mutual experiences of sexual pleasure prompted their practitioners to consider more egalitarian conceptions of social and political power, wherein everyone's needs are communally addressed and not dictated to benefit the elite. If some of these wo/men's sexual relationships did not conform to the structures of the Roman sexual hierarchy, then other aspects of (some of) their lives also did not correspond to the chrononormative arrangements of Roman imperial culture. Such orientations could discourage submission to a political system in which one must be "placed under" governing authorities. In other words, if their sexual encounters did not always require the (penetrated) submission of a person of lower status to a more powerful penetrator, then, in similar fashion, their engagements with politics could also have centered on an emphasis on mutual participation and shared pleasures (social, sexual, economic, etc.).

Decentering what Paul says on the subject, then, we can instead read Romans 13 as representing one opinion in the context of a lively and ongoing discussion about how this diverse community negotiated *together* their theological, political, and social commitments.[49] As a result, it is most likely that these hearers of Paul's instructions in Romans 13 (and those sexual instructions beforehand) had their own opinions about when and how to submit to imperial demands and to inhabit Roman hierarchies. Furthermore, different members would have had different social positions and different experiences of imperial conquest.[50] An orientation to politics that foregrounds mutual pleasures (sexual and otherwise) exists outside of the binary between submission to or rebellion against authority figures presented in Romans 13:1–7. By *changing the subject* so that pleasure is more mutually oriented, perhaps the *polis* becomes a place of collaboration, dialogue, and enjoyment instead of a space of competition for authority. If these ideas appeared "rebellious"—placed against the imperial order—it is because those who were "above" were perhaps threatened, no longer retaining their status as the exclusive beneficiaries of a hierarchically structured social-political-sexual system.

Assuming such pleasurable perspectives on sex and politics (which likely varied and diverged from one another), it is possible that some members (though not all) of Rome's *ekklēsia* began to "un-bind" the empire's time. Those who held such views would, then, also experience time differently, not as the "end of history," determined and dictated by power and might or as something urgently and imminently ending with the coming of a new power. Time, in such a view, is not something that must be controlled, put in place under (*hypotassō*) those forces (imperial or divine) holding authority. Unbound from its perpetuation of social, sexual, and political hierarchies, time can be enjoyed as intervals in which pleasures happen: sexual experiences, conversations in an assembly, making decisions mutually and for everyone's benefit. Thinking pleasurably with modern responses to capitalist chrononormativity, we can imagine that some opted to pursue their own pleasures (traditionally deemed "unnatural") because such pursuits were unthinkable within imperial hierarchies and they produced no benefits according to the logic of imperial domination.

Such a pleasurable rendering relies on a conception of erotohistoriography, as described by Freeman. Erotohistoriography embodies and extends Marchal's temporally queer coalition by invoking an affective understanding of history—not understood but felt.[51] Through close readings of *Frankenstein* and *Orlando*, texts that make the body a central tool for historical inquiry and experience, Freeman explains that erotohistoriography emphasizes how embodied crossings of temporal and historical boundaries allow history to be "what pleasures."[52] Such an approach recognizes that we can only reconstruct the past from the vantage point (or from the feelings) of our own perspectives and experiences. Thus, as Freeman describes, "This suggests a kind of bottomy historiography: the potential for collective queer time—even queer history—to be structured as an uneven transmission of receptivity rather than authority or custom, of a certain enjoyably porous relation to unpredictable futures or to new configurations of the past."[53] Applied to our reconstruction of the ancient *ekklēsia* in Rome, erotohistoriography reveals potential connections and shared histories across temporal eras, despite the disjunctures between then and now. Although, certainly, the ancient *ekklēsia* confronted different hierarchies and discussed different solutions, it is only through such uneven, queer connections across time that we can begin to envision these situations.

Extending across this queer temporal connection, from the twenty-first century to the first, I focus my gaze on an *ekklēsia* where time flows differently from Rome's imperial chrononormativity. Instead of feeling like the "end of history" wherein every body submits to empire and its inevitable and unending power and control, perhaps these wo/men experienced time moving at different tempos, allowing the conversations, meals, and companionship to (at least occasionally) interrupt their regular progression of time dictated by Rome. Based on what we know from other *ekklēsiai*, I assume that despite agreement and comfort, some disagreements and tensions arose and unsettled, but such disturbances sometimes innovated and revealed new connections. Time in such an *ekklēsia* does not progress toward a productive end; instead, it slows and speeds, flows and bumps as different wo/men find diverse and diverging styles of being Christ-followers. In this *ekklēsia*, some experience time not only as progressing but also as regressing, dragging, or transgressing. Through this, they find fissures in a future that is no longer already determined imperially as history's end.

Further, I imagine that sexual expression for wo/men of the *ekklēsia* affected some Christ-followers' temporal and political orientations. Experiencing pleasure at (or as) the bottom, they start to unravel the normative logic of Roman sexuality that prescribed proper pleasure exclusively from being on top, in perfect imitation of its social and political hierarchy. With this unraveling, some wo/men perhaps suggested pursuing different forms of expression (sexual, social, or political), maybe even including those deemed "deviant." By realizing that sex was not limited to hierarchical expression, it is possible that a few felt that their history was not at its end, that time's progress was not inevitably fixed. Like our more "bottomy historiography," through such experiences, I suspect some of these wo/men felt new relations to imperial time, no longer something to be experienced as the "end of history" nor an anticipatory eagerness or impatience for apocalypse, a future coming when hierarchies may be overturned, and Christ-followers can finally rise to enjoy being on top. Instead of waiting submissively for such a future to come, this diverse *ekklēsia* anticipates multiple comings, of varying qualities and quantities, at many points, revealing a more porous (and pleasurable) relation to past and future. Refusing (or ignoring) the binary to submit or rebel, such sexual/temporal relations glimpse the potential, even if never fully realized, of following God/Christ as an *ekklēsia* without replicating a submissive imperial stance. Reaching across this queer time and peering into this *ekklēsia*, we engage a different kind history, one not entirely bound to linear historiographical demands and instead one that engages queer historical possibilities as it seeks the experience of some of those "structures of belonging and duration that may be invisible to the historicist eye."

Thus, if traditional historiography and interpretation relate the imperial and Pauline structuring of time-bound-to-hierarchical-sex as authoritative, an erotohistoriographical approach to Romans 13 pursues (across time) a tempo "out of joint" with Rome's chrononormativity. By reconstructing *ekklēsia*-l conversations and pleasures from this lens, new and different tempos emerge, some convergent and some divergent, but each attempting to pursue less submissive and, instead, more mutual rhythms and ways of living as an assemblage. In the ancient *ekklēsia*, these tempos could reimagine the boundaries of politics, sex, and society, such as in the ways discussed above. From the "bottom" (sexual or not), then and now, we feel a different time, one that is not exclusively bound to the pursuit of imperial domination or even the pursuit of individual pleasure at the expense of others.

Queer time is experienced as an emphasis on collective pleasure—for Romans 13, one that is centered within the full (and diverse) *ekklēsia*. Thus, instead of assuming that political opinions in the *ekklēsia* debated between the binary poles of submission or rebellion (as Romans 13:1–7 implies), we can instead posit that some voices in the conversation did not take a position on this spectrum and instead preferred to change the subject(s) of the debate, even embodying their political difference by refusing to let politics dictate pleasure. As we decenter Paul from the biblical, perhaps some of these wo/men decentered Rome from the political—imagining a God/Christ who inhabits political space differently, not as an imperial Lord but as one who pursues pleasure and inclusivity over domination and control. Alongside a feminist decentering of Paul, erotohistoriography enables a reading of Romans (here centered on chapter 13) that dislodges the authority of its chrononormative logic. Providing pleasurable alternatives to the binary logic of submission or rebellion, such an approach emphasizes the "queer" sensations (sexual, political, social, or otherwise) among the wo/men in the *ekklēsia* and therefore unbinds the empire's time.

## NOTES

1. Elizabeth Freeman, *Time Binds: Queer Temporalities, Queer Histories* (Durham, N.C.: Duke University Press, 2010), 3.
2. Ibid.
3. Ibid., 3–6. See further Dana Luciano, *Arranging Grief: Sacred Time and the Body in Nineteenth-Century America* (New York: New York University Press, 2007), 9–12.
4. Freeman, *Time Binds*, 4.
5. Luciano specifically defines chronobiopolitics as "the sexual arrangement of the time of life" (*Arranging Grief*, 9; but see also 9–12).
6. The Greek term *ekklēsia* (plural *ekklēsiai*), generally meaning an "assembly," but often translated as "church" in traditional biblical scholarship, will be left untranslated throughout. Following the work of feminist biblical scholarship, especially that of Elisabeth Schüssler Fiorenza, I use the untranslated *ekklēsia* as a reminder of the inadequacy of English translations for this Greek term, particularly as, in its ideal form, the Greek *ekklēsia* represented a radical democratic space for all participants. Schüssler Fiorenza introduces the idea of the "*ekklēsia* of wo/men" in *In Memory of Her: A Feminist Reconstruction of Christian Origins* (New York: Crossroad, 1983, repr. tenth anniversary edition, 1994). She further develops this concept of the *ekklēsia* in *Rhetoric and Ethic: The Politics of Biblical Studies* (Minneapolis: Fortress Press, 1999). See also Schüssler Fiorenza, *Power of the Word: Scripture and the Rhetoric of Empire* (Minneapolis: Fortress Press, 2007).
7. Throughout this essay, I use "wo/men" following Schüssler Fiorenza's theoretical development of this neologism. Over decades of use by Schüssler Fiorenza as well as other feminist scholars (especially those who study the Bible), the term has come to hold myriad theoretical meanings. A succinct introduction to this concept that covers many of its meanings and usages can be found in Schüssler Fiorenza, *Wisdom Ways: Introducing Feminist Biblical Interpretation* (Maryknoll, N.Y.: Orbis Books, 2001), 57–59, see also 108–9.
8. On the use of images and Augustan propaganda, see especially Paul Zanker, *The Power of Images in the Age of Augustus*, trans. Alan Shapiro (Ann Arbor: University of Michigan Press, 1990), 101–66.
9. These categories of those at the "bottom" of the Roman social hierarchy should not be seen as mutually exclusive, but it is important to note that the Roman hierarchy was structured so that persons were made "other" in terms of gender, status, sexuality, and ethnicity. Nancy Shumate's work on the "composite other" in Rome is helpful in elaborating how these various vectors interacted; see Nancy Shumate, *Nation, Empire, Decline: Studies in Rhetorical Continuity from the Roman Era to the Modern Era* (London: Duckworth, 2006), 19–54.

10. Freeman, *Time Binds*, 3.

11. Neil Elliott, *The Arrogance of Nations: Reading Romans in the Shadow of Empire* (Minneapolis: Fortress Press, 2008), 144. In this definition of standing at the "end of history," Elliott is specifically discussing the perspectives found in the writings of Plutarch and Josephus.

12. Ibid., 143–45.

13. Davina C. Lopez has demonstrated how the message of Roman superiority over its conquered nations (*ta ethnē*) was communicated and justified both visually and literarily through imperial propaganda (such as *Judea Capta* coins, the *Aeneid*, and a relief of Claudius conquering Britannia on the Sebasteion in Aphrodisias); see *Apostle to the Conquered: Reimagining Paul's Mission* (Minneapolis: Fortress Press, 2008), 26–118. Elliott discusses the "public" and "private" transcripts (based on James C. Scott's development of these terms) in Roman discourse; in so doing, he shows how the "public" discourse—typically developed under imperial auspices—promoted or aligned with imperial propaganda. Elliott then focuses on the "private" or hidden transcripts of resistance to empire than can be encoded in discourses "from below," especially as can be found in Paul's letters. See Elliott, *Arrogance of Nations*, 25–57.

14. Elliott, *Arrogance of Nations*, 146.

15. Elliott observes that once you move outside the perspective of the imperial center, it is clear that the binary lines "follow the gradient of power. Outside of those centers, the drama remains one of exploitation and misery, and virtue does not appear to be the monopoly of the powerful" (ibid., 146).

16. On Roman marriage and its regulation, see especially Susan Treggiari, *Roman Marriage*: Iusti Coniuges *from the Time of Cicero to the Time of Ulpian* (Oxford: Clarendon Press, 1991). Mary Rose D'Angelo pays particular attention to the impact of marriage regulations on nonelite bodies and their import for reading Jewish and biblical texts. See "*Eusebeia*: Roman Imperial Family Values and the Sexual Politics of 4 Maccabees and the Pastorals," *Biblical Interpretation* 11 (2003): 139–65; and "Gender and Geopolitics in the Work of Philo of Alexandria: Jewish Piety and Imperial Family Values," in *Mapping Gender in Ancient Religious Discourses*, ed. Todd Penner and Caroline Vander Stichele (Leiden: Brill, 2007), 63–88. On marriage and adultery laws and their impact on broader Roman morality, see especially Catharine Edwards, *The Politics of Immorality in Ancient Rome* (Cambridge: Cambridge University Press, 1993), 1–62.

17. Unless otherwise noted, all translations are my own.

18. By the time of the Byzantine Empire, this passage can be found in mosaics and inscriptions on public buildings (e.g., Caesarea Maritima). Today, this passage is often used in an attempt to quell Christian dissent to U.S. policies: Neil Elliott describes its appearance in debates about the second Iraq War. See Elliott, *Arrogance of Nations*, 5–6.

19. Ibid., 153. He continues to outline three of the most important explanations for these disparities on 154–55. Elliott's overall project sees Romans as a critical engagement with Rome's empire: "In Romans, I contend, we see Paul's critical engage-

ment with the claims of imperial ideology and with the corrosive effects of those claims within the Roman congregations of Christ believers" (9).

20. Krister Stendahl, "Hate, Non-retaliation, and Love: 1QS x, 17–20 and Rom. 12:19–21," *Harvard Theological Review* 55 (1962): 345. Also quoted in Gordon Zerbe, "The Politics of Paul: His Supposed Social Conservatism and the Impact of Postcolonial Readings," in *The Colonized Apostle: Paul through Postcolonial Eyes*, ed. Christopher D. Stanley (Minneapolis: Fortress Press, 2011), 62–73.

21. While literally meaning "place against," the verb *antitassō* typically has meanings of armed resistance and opposition in battle. Against Roman authority, armed opposition is tantamount to rebellion. Ultimately, the antiplacement of which Paul speaks is a displacement of God, according to the rest of the verse (for it is God who placed Rome in authority). Thus, according to Paul, what God places only God can displace.

22. Feminist scholars working in classics began to observe this in the 1980s, most especially Bernadette J. Brooten, "Paul's Views on the Nature of Women and Female Homoeroticism," in *Immaculate and Powerful: The Female in Sacred Image and Social Reality*, ed. Clarissa W. Atkinson, Constance H. Buchanan, and Margaret R. Miles (Boston: Beacon Press, 1985). See also Amy Richlin, *The Garden of Priapus: Sexuality and Aggression in Roman Humor*, rev. ed. (New York: Oxford University Press, 1992; orig. 1983); Judith P. Hallett, *Fathers and Daughters in Roman Society* (Princeton, N.J.: Princeton University Press, 1984); and Eva C. Keuls, *The Reign of the Phallus: Sexual Politics in Ancient Athens* (New York: Harper and Row, 1985). See further Bernadette J. Brooten, *Love between Women: Early Christian Responses to Female Homoeroticism* (Chicago: University of Chicago Press, 1996). The "penetrative model" as described here was popularized by Foucauldian classicists in the early 1990s, and it can be seen outlined especially in John J. Winkler, *The Constraints of Desire: The Anthropology of Sex and Gender in Ancient Greece* (New York: Routledge, 1990), 1–44, and (specifically applied to Rome) in Jonathan Walters, "Invading the Roman Body: Manliness and Impenetrability in Roman Thought," in *Roman Sexualities*, ed. Hallett and Marilyn B. Skinner (Princeton, N.J.: Princeton University Press, 1997), 29–43. Making developments along similar lines is David M. Halperin, *One Hundred Years of Homosexuality: And Other Essays on Greek Love* (New York: Routledge, 1990). See further, Stephen D. Moore, *God's Beauty Parlor: And Other Queer Spaces In and Around the Bible* (Stanford, Calif.: Stanford University Press, 2001), 135–46.

23. On the *kinaidos/cinaedus*, see especially Winkler, *Constraints of Desire*, 45–47, and Craig Williams, *Roman Homosexuality*, 2nd ed. (Oxford: Oxford University Press, 2010), 230–45. Halperin and Ann Pellegrini both stress this view with respect to the *tribas* in their responses to Brooten's *Love between Women*. See The GLQ Forum, "Lesbian Historiography before the Name?" *GLQ: A Journal of Lesbian and Gay Studies* 4 (1998): 570–72 (Halperin's response), and 581–582 (Pellegrini's response). More recently, Diana M. Swancutt has argued that the *tribas* refers specifically to gender deviance rather than sexuality, though still referring to an active female penetrator; see "*Still* before Sexuality: 'Greek' Androgyny, the Roman Imperial Politics of Masculinity, and the Roman Invention of the *Tribas*," in *Mapping Gender in Ancient*

*Religious Discourses*, ed. Todd Penner and Caroline Vander Stichele (Leiden: Brill, 2007), 11–61.

24. Brooten argues that though the term *tribas* is almost exclusively used polemically in Greco-Roman texts, the existence of the term proves that women had sexual relations with one another in antiquity. This existence makes it possible (even probable) that actual *tribades* existed and had lifelong erotic relationships or orientations that defied the antagonistic and hierarchical use of the term by elite men. See *Love between Women*, 4–9. On the *cinaedi*, Richlin makes a similar distinction between rhetoric and reality, arguing, therefore, that the *cinaedi* (or persons like them) existed outside of the imaginations of elite men and had "real-life referents in Roman cultures" that represented a "subculture" in ancient Rome. See "Not before Homosexuality: The Materiality of the *Cinaedus* and the Roman Law against Love between Men," *Journal of the History of Sexuality* 3, no.4 (1993): 523–73, esp. 554. Analyzing first-century visual representations (which include examples from "ordinary," less elite, Roman life), John R. Clarke concludes that the visual evidence supports Richlin's argument for the existence of "non-straight" sexual subcultures in ancient Roman settings, even if the evidence only hints at this existence (making a firm historical conclusion impossible). John R. Clarke, "Representations of the *Cinaedus* in Roman Art: Evidence of 'Gay' Subculture?," *Journal of Homosexuality* 49, nos. 3–4 (2005): 271–298, esp. 296–97.
25. See Lopez, *Apostle to the Conquered*, 26–55. Her examples of these panels come from the Sebasteion in Aphrodisias.
26. Ibid., 28.
27. Ibid., 42–45.
28. David Fredrick, "Mapping Penetrability in Late Republican and Early Imperial Rome" in *The Roman Gaze: Vision, Power, and the Body*, ed. David Fredrick (Baltimore: Johns Hopkins University Press, 2002), 285; see further 236–64.
29. Ibid., 258. Emphasis added. Here (like Freeman) Fredrick is working with Pierre Bourdieu.
30. My dissertation demonstrates this point at length; see James N. Hoke, "Under God? A Queer and Feminist Subversion of Submission in Romans" (PhD diss., Drew University, 2017).
31. "So startlingly congruent, indeed, are these verses with the sociosexual script that I have been fleshing out that it seems to matter very little in the end whether Paul himself was fully cognizant of what he was saying or whether he was merely a dummy on the knee of a ventriloquist culture that spoke through him to audiences that he, or it, could never have imagined—most recently ourselves." Moore, *God's Beauty Parlor*, 146.
32. "Sex in [Paul's] symbolic economy is nothing other—*can* be nothing other—than eroticized inequality. And this inequality is immeasurably productive, masculine and feminine subjects themselves being manufactured through the eroticization of dominance and submission." Ibid., 153. See also ibid., 152–56. Moore is expanding on the point already made by Brooten: "Therefore, Paul's condemnation of sexual relations between women embodies and enforces the assumptions about gender

found in nearly all the Roman-period sources on female homoeroticism." *Love between Women*, 266.

33. This sexual submission, as Moore deftly describes, also infuses Pauline theology in Romans 2–3: Jesus Christ himself submits himself fully to God, the ultimate imperial *kyrios*. See Moore, *God's Beauty Parlor*, 156–64. Moore's reading of Pauline theology draws heavily on Stanley Stowers's radical rereading of Romans, in which he asserts that—for Paul—it is because of Christ's complete trust (and therefore submission) to God's plan that he is willing to die so that the Gentiles (alongside Jews) can also be saved. See Stanley K. Stowers, *A Rereading of Romans: Justice, Jews, and Gentiles* (New Haven, Conn.: Yale University Press, 1994), especially 194–226.
34. So, writes Moore, "Within the bounds of these [Greco-Roman sexual] discourses, a 'man' is, by definition, an impenetrable penetrator, as we have seen, a body whose exits must never be used as entrances" (*God's Beauty Parlor*, 170). "Impenetrable penetrator" is originally used by Walters, "Invading the Roman Body," 30.
35. Melanie Johnson-DeBaufre and Laura S. Nasrallah, "Beyond the Heroic Paul: Toward a Feminist and Decolonizing Approach to the Letters of Paul," in *The Colonized Apostle: Paul through Postcolonial Eyes*, ed. Christopher D. Stanley (Minneapolis: Fortress Press, 2011), 173. Their approach takes seriously the fact that Paul "presents himself as one among many other apostles, teachers, and siblings who struggled together to puzzle out the meaning of being assemblies in Christ" (161). Johnson-DeBaufre and Nasrallah's approach draws from a long history of feminist biblical scholarship, particularly that of Schüssler Fiorenza, working to decenter Pauline authority, See, for example, Schüssler Fiorenza, *Power of the Word*, 69–109; Schüssler Fiorenza, "Paul and the Politics of Interpretation," in *Paul and Politics: Ekklesia, Israel, Imperium, Interpretation. Essays in Honor of Krister Stendahl*, ed. Richard A. Horsley (Harrisburg, Pa.: Trinity Press International, 2000), 40–57. In that same *Paul and Politics* volume, see also the work of Cynthia Briggs Kittredge ("Corinthian Women Prophets and Paul's Argumentation in 1 Corinthians," 103–9) and Antoinette Clark Wire ("Response: The Politics of the Assembly in Corinth," 124–29; and "Response: Paul and Those Outside Power," 224–26).
36. Johnson-DeBaufre and Nasrallah, "Beyond the Heroic Paul," 162.
37. Ibid., 162–63.
38. Ibid., 166.
39. Peter Lampe, *From Paul to Valentinus: Christians at Rome in the First Two Centuries* (Minneapolis: Fortress Press, 2003), 164–83. See also Schüssler Fiorenza, "Missionaries, Apostles, Coworkers: Romans 16 and the Reconstruction of Women's Early Christian History," *Word & World* 6, no.4 (1986): 420–33.
40. Schüssler Fiorenza, "Missionaries, Apostles, Coworkers," 427. See also Lampe, *From Paul to Valentinus*, 165–67.
41. Schüssler Fiorenza, "Missionaries, Apostles, Coworkers," 423, 427. Her essay especially emphasizes the androcentric language in Romans 16 and the androcentric assumption of historical critical scholarship as she points out that the grammatically masculine language in the biblical text almost always includes women as well as men.

42. This was also an assembly in which Paul may never have been physically present (thus we cannot be certain to what degree of completeness is his own knowledge of the dynamics and diversity within the assembly and its discussions).
43. See especially Antoinette Clark Wire, *The Corinthian Women Prophets: A Reconstruction through Paul's Rhetoric* (Minneapolis: Fortress Press, 1990); and, using archaeological remnants to supplement rhetorical analysis, Cavan W. Concannon, *"When You Were Gentiles": Specters of Ethnicity in Roman Corinth and Paul's Corinthian Correspondence* (New Haven, Conn.: Yale University Press, 2014).
44. Joseph A. Marchal, "'Making History' Queerly: Touches across Time through a Biblical Behind," *Biblical Interpretation* 19, nos. 4–5 (2011): 373–95. Specifically, he writes, "With a queer orientation to historical time, one seeks the touch of these assemblies across time in a partial connection that one might call queer coalition" (394).
45. In queer and Greco-Roman historiography, this divide is exemplified in the division seen between the work of ("altericist") Halperin and that of ("continuist") Brooten and John Boswell. See especially Halperin, *One Hundred Years of Homosexuality*; David M. Halperin, *How to Do the History of Homosexuality* (Chicago: University of Chicago Press, 2002), especially 48–80; Brooten, *Love between Women*; The GLQ Forum; and John Boswell, *Christianity, Social Tolerance, and Homosexuality: Gay People in Western Europe from the Beginning of the Christian Era to the Fourteenth Century* (Chicago: University of Chicago Press, 1980).
46. Marchal, "'Making History' Queerly," 387.
47. I use this term "queers-of-sorts" because, although they do not directly correspond to a modern queer "identity" (insofar as queer denotes identity), there is certainly an element of queerness, particularly in its antinormative impulses, present in this reconstruction. Further, the term signals the "partial connections," as described by Marchal (in "'Making History' Queerly"), between ancient and modern "queerness."
48. Ibid., 393–94. Mary Rose D'Angelo, "Women Partners in the New Testament," *Journal of Feminist Studies in Religion* 6, no. 1 (1990): 65–86, especially 72–75, 81–85. Writing about a female missionary couple who rejected marriage in favor of this female-female relationship, even if the couple cannot be proven to have been in a physical sexual relationship, D'Angelo observes, "In this context, the choice of women to work and live together rather than with a man emerges as a sexual as well as a social choice" (83). On the presence of "sexual minorities" and committed female-female missionary couples/pairs, see also Thomas Hanks, "Romans," in *The Queer Bible Commentary*, ed. Deryn Guest, Robert E. Goss, Mona West, and Thomas Bohache (London: SCM Press, 2006), 604–5. (Both D'Angelo and Hanks are cited in Marchal, "'Making History' Queerly," 393.)
49. Peter Oakes imagines a variety of different responses to Paul's letter based on different social positions in Rome, harnessing evidence from the living spaces in Pompeii to root these responses in historical reality. Oakes, however, only considers the individual ways in which each person *heard* Paul's letter. Therefore, Paul's words remain central for each hearer instead of being located within a communal con-

versation and response. See Peter Oakes, *Reading Romans in Pompeii: Paul's Letter at Ground Level* (Minneapolis: Fortress Press, 2009).

50. Often these experiences of empire would have been inflected by social position, though not always in linear ways.
51. Freeman, *Time Binds*, 95; this is in distinction to how the "winners" traditionally write history.
52. Ibid., 118. On the "body as method," see 95–96. The idea of history as "what pleasures" is in distinction to Jameson's assertion: "History is what hurts," (in Fredric Jameson, "The End of Temporality," *Critical Inquiry* 29, no. 4 [2003]: 695–718) which Freeman discusses earlier (10).
53. Freeman, *Time Binds*, 109. Here, Freeman is working with Carla Freccero, *Queer/Early/Modern* (Durham, N.C.: Duke University Press, 2006), esp. 102.

# The Futures Outside: Apocalyptic Epilogue Unveiled as Africana Queer Prologue

ERIC A. THOMAS

## THINKING AND FEELING NEW HEAVENS

> And I saw a new heaven and a new earth, for the first heaven and the first earth passed away . . .
>
> REVELATION 21:1

This essay examines the epilogue of Revelation (22:8–21)[1] as an intervention for new imaginations of, and actions toward, a new heaven and a new earth that can be realized now in the present. It names the ways that Revelation (and therefore the Bible) is used as a means to make outsiders of queer people and proposes that the author/narrator John is not the only one who can be filled with the spirit on the Lord(e)'s day in order to envision a new heaven and a new earth. This position has particular resonance for same gender loving (SGL)[2] and transgender people of African American and African descent, because Revelation is part of the theocultural bases of innumerous articulations of liberation, divine vindication, and eschatological salvation that stem from postcolonial and post-Emancipation people of African descent. But, for the most part, Africana queer experience is sealed beneath those articulations and silenced. And yet there are "those of us . . . seeking a now that can breed futures" who have decided that "it is better to speak—remembering—we were never meant to survive."[3] By foregrounding Africana queer lived experience in rereading Revelation, I disidentify with those external and internalized messages and use my own loud voice to proclaim that Revelation's apocalyptic epilogue can be an Africana queer prologue in which to think, feel, and take actions toward alternative futures that can begin now.

## DISIDENTIFYING WITH TRIBULATION AND PATIENT ENDURANCE

> I, John, your brother and co-participant in the tribulation and reign and endurance in Jesus Christ, was on the island called Patmos on account of the word of God and the testimony of Jesus.
>
> REVELATION 1:10

The theoretical grounding of this essay is constructed from queer of color critique. José Esteban Muñoz writes that "the here and now is a prison house. We must strive, in the face of the here and now's totalizing rendering of reality, to think and feel a *then and there* . . . . a doing for and toward the future."[4] As the last book of the Christian Bible, Revelation's message has been given powerful authority by believers to determine the following: the worthy and the unworthy, insiders and outsiders; those who gain a heavenly reward and those who are left behind. Consequently, it is an example of the terms set forth by Muñoz: a text that exists for the future that thinks and feels a *then and there*, but in ways that risk turning the *here and now* into a prison house. It is in its own way a totalizing rendering of reality. We can disidentify with patiently enduring abjection and persecution. Instead, we can decide that Revelation's vision of the future may also be read alternatively and, transformed via Muñoz' strategy, as an opportunity for outsiders to live into new ways of being, doing, and flourishing.

Disidentification, according to Muñoz, "permits the spectator, often a queer who has been locked out of the halls of representation or rendered a static caricature there, to imagine a world where queer lives, politics, and possibilities are representable in their complexity."[5] This re-imagining of world is enacted by cultural workers as a survival technique by which the queer subject works within and outside the dominant sphere simultaneously.[6] Disidentification is neither an argument for assimilation into an oppressive structure nor a direct counter to the structure since, for Muñoz, this sets up a binary of "good" and "bad." Rather, disidentification creates an alternative way toward "a strategy that tries to transform a cultural logic from within, always laboring to enact permanent structural change while at the same time valuing the importance of local or everyday struggles of resistance."[7]

Whereas Muñoz gives examples of disidentifications through the realm of queer performance, I apply his concepts to contextual biblical interpretation. My Africana queer reading of Revelation is inspired by the association of LGBTQ persons with heteronormative Christian-based cultural imaginations of hell—the place that according to them all queer people will surely go.[8] My alter-interpretation responds to the practice of using biblical texts to support homophobia and violence, particularly to Africana queer folk by hetero-superior people of African descent. Following Jafari S. Allen, Lyndon K. Gill, and the scholar-activists of the black/queer/diaspora project,[9] I bring the use of ethnographic and empirical data as techniques of black queer studies and queer of color critique.[10] My cultural examples are curated from lived experiences rather than literature to emphasize that actual bodies are affected by sociocultural hegemony. As Allen notes:

> This [collection of data from real life] brings us closer to providing verbs to animate the continuation of the black radical intellectual tradition, as well as a name—or more precisely, a number of names—*lesbian, transgender, bisexual, gay, batty bwoi, masisi, bulldagger, two-spirited, maricón, same gender loving, buller, zami, mati working, dress-up girls, bois, butches, femme or butch queen, gender insurgent, marimacha, branché, bugarrón*, . . . et cetera [which we] of Africa(n descent) call ourselves. Of course, some eschew explicit naming, preferring to live their verbs, as for example, simply *am, is, are, been, being, be*—or *interrupt, invent, push, question, refuse, serve*, or *shade*, in some cases.[11]

The futures I am imagining as a Black American SGL man with my fellow Africana queer folk are relative to, and therefore must be imagined and activated from, our multiple social locations throughout African diasporas—the African continent, the Caribbean, South and North Americas, and all points between and beyond.[12] The imaginative strategies I employ from my geographical and social position in the northeast United States as a biblical scholar-minister-activist will be different from that of my Black lesbian teacher in South Africa or my homeless transgender sister in Kingston.[13] However, we can recognize and gain strength from our shared histories of oppression and the potentialities for our brilliance that are as individual as they are collective. I am thinking with the idea of an Africana queer *subterranean convergence* already conjured in Edouard Glissant's imagination of diverse Caribbean histories that counteract the concrete linearity of a single (heteronormatively Western-based) history.[14]

To this concept I add the African philosophical term *Sankofa*, associated with the symbol of "a Sankofa bird that flies forward while facing backward, while holding an egg, its future offspring in its beak—a reminder that we must understand the past in order to move the present forward into a viable future."[15] In the Akan language, Sankofa gives the imperative to "return to the source, go get it and bring it here."[16] Linda Thomas writes, "As a Sankofa people, African Americans are called to remember the unadulterated abuse suffered during the days of chattel slavery, and through this act of deliberate—

and *deliberative*—retrieval live into our eschatological determination to move forward toward the *kin-dom* of God."[17] This process of returning, remembering, and re-visioning can be embodied and pleasurable. It can inspire the practice of (re)constructing erotohistoriographies.

The queer theorist and English professor Elizabeth Freeman explains erotohistoriography as the queer practice(s) of encountering and documenting a past centered on pleasure—particularly sexual pleasure—"the potential for collective queer time—even queer history—to be structured as an uneven transmission of receptivity rather than authority or custom, of a certain enjoyably porous relation to unpredictable futures or to new configurations of the past."[18] As a practice of resistance, erotohistoriography

> allows us access to a counterhistory of history itself—an antisytematic method that informs other, much later artistic productions traveling more explicitly under the sign of queer. . . . And it uses the body as a tool to effect, figure, or perform that encounter. Erotohistoriography admits that contact with historical materials can be precipitated by particular bodily dispositions, and that these connections may elicit bodily responses, even pleasurable ones, themselves a form of understanding. It sees the body as a method, and historical consciousness as something intimately involved with corporeal sensations.[19]

Connecting these terms ("Sankofa" and "erotohistoriography"), an Africana queer practice of pleasurable and embodied remembering (and re-membering) enables us to create alternative futures that include new ways of being community, practicing dignity, and making visible histories and hurts that have been hidden (or sealed).[20] We need to discover the power based on our experiences and our potential to imagine a *then and there* to change our *here and now*. I suggest this power comes from the embodiment of erotic subjectivity.

Lyndon K. Gill refers to erotic subjectivity as "at once an interpretive perspective and a mode of consciousness; it is both a way of *reading* and a way of *being* in the world."[21] It is a dissolution of the body / spirit binaries in which sexuality is "bad" and piety is "good" in preference for an integration of the two resulting in political empowerment. Informed by Audre Lorde's essay "Uses of the Erotic: The Erotic as Power,"[22] Gill writes:

> My articulation of the erotic expands beyond being mere euphemism for sexual desire and reaches simultaneously toward a political attentiveness and a spiritual consciousness. This tripartite political-sensual-spiritual awareness makes possible and desirable a more broadly and deeply conceived articulation of love. And it is this love that so often provides the

> motivation for political action, sensual intimacy, and spiritual hunger—together constitutive elements of an erotic subjecthood.[23]

Gill's political-sensual-spiritual reconstruction of erotic subjectivity is a resource for the agency to become Sankofa people (following Linda Thomas's explanation) and imagine alternative futures to change the present. In other words, Africana queer folks can become catalysts of our own flourishing, leaving neither our spirituality nor our sensuality behind. Returning to José Esteban Muñoz, erotic subjectivity is what empowers the getting from the *here and now* to a *then and there*. Gill adds the verbs *reading* and *being* to Muñoz's *doing* for the future.

Revelation 22:14–15 reads: "Highly honored (blessed) are the ones who wash their robes, so that they will have the right to the tree of life and may enter the city by the gates. Outside are the dogs and sorcerers and sexually exploited[24] and murderers and idolaters, and everyone who loves and practices deceit." The threat of being excluded from heaven (the New Jerusalem) presented by the text of Revelation and its homophobic heteronormative interpreters in the *future* are moot for Africana queer people whose lives, as the result of homo- and transphobic violence and rejection, are a living hell in the *present*. From the standpoint of "those outside" (Rv 22:15), those who absorb the brunt of the negative lived experiences of Africana queer subjects, I use my own "loud voice" to proclaim that alternative visions of the future can be imagined and embodied.[25] Throughout history and in the present, many queer people struggling to survive in contemporary African diasporas have been and are "outside" of community ("Outside [*exō*] are the dogs . . ."). We are outside of the histories of independence, social-cultural concepts of blackness, and religious acceptance, among other exclusions, in our multiple geographic locations.

In Africa more than fifty countries have anti-homosexuality laws. More than ten Caribbean countries have anti-sodomy laws which carry over the "anti-buggery" laws of British colonization. Most recently, contemporary Western tolerance of homosexuality has created the myths that homosexuality is un-African or is the result of Western European influence. This stance reifies the fallacies that all queer people and their allies are white and that all "real" Africans and people of African descent are heterosexual. In reality "one could argue that at least in some African contexts, it was not *homosexuality* that was inherited from the West but rather a more regulatory *homophobia*."[26] This regulation largely comes from the religious-industrial complex: colonial missionaries, Western televangelism, and contemporary council(s) of church(es), diaspora reconstructions of postcolonial masculinities and femininities, and the internalization of hypermasculine "dangerous Black man" tropes constructed in white and Black popular culture. In addition to being false, these myths erase, obfuscate, and eliminate Africana queer people from cultural contributions and recognition as citizens, family members, and kin.[27] Of the latter problems listed, Gaurav Desai notes, "Simon Nkoli, an important South African gay activist, suggests that for him the most difficult aspect of 'coming out' as a Black man in South Africa was the rejection that one felt from one's own ethnic community as well as the racism inherent in the white gay community."[28]

What is at stake for this critique is a means by which to unveil, on the one hand, intragroup conflicts within African diaspora based on postcolonial and neocolonial responses to normalizing factors of race, gender (particularly performance of masculinity and femininity), nationhood, and sexual orientation that put queer people in conflict with their own kinfolk. On the other hand, it critiques intragroup conflicts in LGBTQ communities in which Western (white) gay and lesbian politics and ideologies cast as "backward" the strategies for negotiating identity and sociality used by U.S. racial-ethnic LGBTQ people and queer people of color in diasporas.[29] Thus, alternative visions of the future must be imagined, subverting the apocalyptic text and contested contexts that make the here and now into a prison house. We need to envision futures that bring what is useful from our past in order to equip ourselves with the courage and hope to alter our present.

## TO THE LEGENDARY HOUSES OF LABEIJA, EXTRAVAGANZA, MUGLIER, LATEX, MIZRAHI, EBONY, AND OMNI

> Write therefore, the things you saw, and the things you are seeing, even what is about to happen after these things . . .
>
> REVELATION 1:19

Revelation is perhaps the grand narrative par excellence of eschatological time telling. It is narrated by a self-proclaimed prophet named John, who directed his message to seven churches located in the Roman province of Asia Minor,[30] around the late first century CE. Revelation tells teleological tales of "what was, is, and what is to take place after these things" (1:19). Revelation presents a vision of the (only) future in which one day God will wipe away the tears from the eyes of the faithful (21:4), and we will "walk in Jerusalem just like John."[31] In his vision John witnesses the conquering of the satanic beast and its followers by a white-horse-riding, multiple-diadem-wearing, sword-in-mouth-wielding Jesus (19:11–21). John sees a new heaven and a new earth, and a New Jerusalem, a holy city coming down out of heaven from God. There, death and mourning will be no more, for the former things have passed away (21:1–4). John's message is sent to seven churches in Asia Minor putting them on notice of what they must do in order to gain access to the new heaven, new earth, and New

Jerusalem. Entrance into the New Jerusalem is the great reward for those with ears to hear its message—"those who conquer" (2:7, 11, 17, 26; 3:5, 12, 21). However, "outside are the dogs and sorcerers and sexually exploited, and murderers and idolaters, and everyone who loves and practices deceit" (22:15).

With the possible exception of the Syrophoenician (or Canaanite) woman's reply to Jesus in the gospels of Mark and Matthew ("even the dogs under the table eat the children's crumbs"—Mk 7:25–30; Mt 15:21–28), both biblical testaments use "dogs" as a negative trope. Dogs lick open sores, eat human flesh, and scavenge for food.[32] In some interpretive circles, scholars have suggested that "dogs" is a pejorative term that early Christ followers employed to malign (other) Jewish people.[33] Dogs in the ancient world were in some cases companions for hunting as well as domesticated pets—just as in contemporary times.[34] Several biblical scholars conclude that "the dogs" (*hoi kynes*) in Revelation 22:15 refer pejoratively to homosexuals, although there is no textual evidence to support their claims.[35] Bruce Metzger, for example, calls the dogs "sodomites."[36] David Aune suggests that "dogs" is a metaphor meaning "the wicked" and links it to the fornicators and prostitutes in the long list of vices.[37] The array of unsavory character types in 22:15 is typical of many vice lists found in New Testament and other ancient writings.[38] In other words, the lists are sociorhetorical constructions strategically used by ancient writers to describe the attributes of acceptability and abjection for their respective contexts. In modern contexts, biblical vice lists seem to have spiritual authority and moral currency only when the objects of the lists are considered to be homosexuals or queer people. In most cases biblical vice lists are not invoked as polemics against murderers, drunkards, or those who are deceitful, for example. Instead, they are deployed as "clobber texts" against LGBTQ people.

The propensity of certain biblical scholars and many more nonscholarly biblical interpreters to associate the "dogs" of Revelation 22:15 with sexually and socially deviant persons may be contextualized by Zimbabwean President Robert Mugabe's numerous claims that homosexuals are "worse than pigs and dogs."[39] During a speech celebrating his eighty-eighth birthday Mugabe urged his fellow Zimbabweans to shun Western values including homosexuality. He stated: "We reject that [homosexuality] outright and say to *hell* with you."[40] In the United States the claims that "AIDS is God's curse" and "fags go to hell" are slogans on the signs of several anti-LGBT protesters reflecting how Revelation's message is (mis)appropriated to suborn hatred and violence against LGBTQ people.[41] Rather than disavowing the connection made between dogs and homosexuals, I disidentify with it. Instead, thinking with the "dogs outside" (22:15), I imagine New Jerusalem as a kind of queer failure and rationale for radical erotic subjectivity from the margins.[42] It could be the New Jerusalem that John envisions is not a place Africana queers should ascribe to.

Looking at the issue another way, Ken Stone, reading Derrida and Levinas regarding "the question of the animal" and its potential for exploration in biblical studies, invites us to explore the "oppositional limits that configure [and complicate] the human and the animal."[43] The dogs of Exodus 11 are silent, and do not bark to alert the Egyptians of the escaping Israelite slaves. In contradistinction, the dogs of Revelation in my reading are not so compliant. In unveiling and deconstructing the oppositional limits between animal and human, vice and virtue, the dogs outside bark neither in the service of empire nor of the "Israelites" inside the New Jerusalem. We have seen, and are seeing, the hypocrisy by which we are cast as outsiders so that others can convince themselves that they are insiders. In the transition from persecution to survival to flourishing, the dogs outside will bark for our own pleasure.[44]

## MISTAKEN (I)DE(NT)ITY

> I, John, am the one who heard and saw these things. And when I heard and saw them, I fell down to worship before the feet of the angel who showed them to me; but he said to me, "Do you not see that I am a fellow-slave with you and your comrades the prophets, and with those who keep the words of this book? Worship God"!
>
> REVELATION 22:8–9

The epilogue of Revelation is a summative statement of what has been communicated to the seven churches and the text's wider audience. It confirms Jesus as the Alpha and Omega, the first and the last, the beginning and the end; and the one who is surely coming soon to reward the faithful (22:12). No one is to add to or take away from the prophecy detailed within his book, lest they risk the plagues described in it. All who hear and are thirsty are bid by the Spirit and the bride to partake and participate in the vision. Indeed, "the Spirit and the bride say 'come', and let everyone who hears say, 'come.' And let everyone who is thirsty come (22:17)."

John attests that his vision is true. However, after describing the arrival of the rider on the white horse, the final battle(s), the bride, and the New Jerusalem in meticulous detail, he falls on the ground to worship at the feet of the angel who showed these things to him (22:8). This angel happens to be one of the seven angels having one of the seven bowls of the seven last plagues (17:1). The first-person narrator of the Apocalypse worships the wrong deity, making it necessary for his fellow slave (*syndoulos*) to redirect his worship to God (22:9). This detail is explained away by some biblical scholars as typical of the Judeo-Christian apocalyptic genre and is ignored by believers for whom Revelation is authoritative.[45] John worships the wrong deity (each time the angel accompanying John in the vision) not once but twice (19:10; 22:8).

These facts from the text lead me to conclude that the dejection, demonization, and damnation of queer folks are caused by believers worshipping the wrong deities: heteronormativity, totalizing concepts of proper masculinity or femininity, liberation that frees only certain members of the community, and respectability politics, among others—practices that make them idolaters and those who love and practice deceit (22:15). Whereas the "dogs outside" are compared to homosexuals doomed to hell, and are the cause (according to popular televangelists) of hurricanes, tsunamis, and other natural disasters, we should not miss the fact that the angel of the seven bowls and seven plagues is *inside* the New Jerusalem with John. The seven plagues are *inside* heaven, Reverend Robertson![46]

From my Africana queer standpoint, even as I imagine my own version of the last days, I notice that John himself was outside—exiled on the island of Patmos (1:9)—yet he wrote himself into the victorious space of the narrative. There is nothing, besides perhaps the threat of adding to John's prophecy (22:18–20), preventing any of us outside from writing our own visions of the future, including an ultimate, fabulously happy end that includes a deity that knows who we are. Why worry about enduring and conquering the apocalyptic *here and now*, if the *then and there* is always already outside in *"God's garbage can,"* the lake of fire and sulfur? (Rv 20:10, 15).[47] We can disidentify with these messages, querying and naming what "gods" our detractors are worshipping, and suggest that they tend to the issues inside their own constructions of New Jerusalem instead of forecasting the futures of Others.

John, "the one who heard and saw these things" (22:8), is clearly not the only one capable of being in the spirit on the Lord's Day with something to say to the churches about persecution, and the kingdom, and patient endurance, and exile (1:10). Other apocalypses attributed to Paul, James, and Peter (among others), were circulating contemporaneously with John's apocalypse by the second century CE.[48] Among Africana queer folks there are lots of *revelations* to share, on the one hand, regarding what it means to be called a *faggot* from a pulpit, or molested by a deacon, called demonic by religious organizations, and written out of national histories. On the other hand, we have dreamed of "flinging our arms wide in some place in the sun," and are already articulating our longings for alternative racially queer futures.[49] Can I get a witness?[50]

## *LAMBNESIA*: THE SILENCE OF THE LAMB

> But the throne of God and the Lamb will be in it, and his slaves will worship him.
>
> REVELATION 22:3

The heavenly throne room (Rv 5–6) is a contentious site of origin for the intersection of LGBT, Asian, Rastafarian, African American, and Africana queer appropriations of Revelation. The queer theologian Patrick Cheng links the symbol of the rainbow (Rv 4:3; 10:1; cf. Gn 9:9–17; Ez 1:28) with queer, Asian, and African queer theologies.[51] Margaret Aymer in an article remarking on Rastafarian alter-empire praxis in the Little Five Points section of east Atlanta notes how foundations of Jamaican Rastafarianism are constructed with religiocultural appropriations of Revelation's "Lion of the tribe of Judah" (Rv 5:5), the fall of "Babylon" (Rv 18, associated with the demise of colonialism), and "New Jerusalem" (Rv 21–22).[52] Brian Blount in the context of the Black Church uses the imagery of the Lamb standing as if slaughtered (5:6) to argue for "an active ministry of resistance that would witness to the singular lordship of Jesus Christ."[53]

For marginalized believers, the throne room is a volatile contact zone for multiple and combative articulations of theological meaning. John is called to the presence of the throne and the one seated upon it surrounded by a rainbow (4:1–3; as in LGBTQ and Asian appropriations). The Lion of the Tribe of Judah has conquered so that he can open the scroll and its seven seals (5:5; as in Jamaican Rastafarian appropriations). The Lamb standing as if slaughtered opens the seals, revealing the souls under the altar who are given white robes as reward for their testimony of the word of God (6:1–11; as in African American appropriations). In his commentary on Revelation, Brian Blount writes, "The dazzling robes mark the souls as defiant witnesses who actively engaged in testimony to the lordship of Christ."[54] These are they who are among the blessed ones who wash their robes.

For SGL people however, the blessings on the ones who wash their robes (Rv 22:14) are tantamount to destroying the evidence of the violence against Africana queer folks. Black queer folks are among the souls under the altar who had been murdered asking Jesus (in the form of a Lamb standing as if slaughtered) "How long will it be before you judge and avenge our blood on the inhabitants of the earth?" (6:9–11). In contemporary times, (white) robes are given to SGL believers so that while they wait for spiritual vindication, dignity, and justice, they can sing in their respective church choirs. Brian Blount argues that "according to John, God's victorious way is the slaughtered way; it not only *de*scribes the path God's Son took, it *pre*scribes the path God's people will take on their way to the new heaven and new earth their combative effort will help God create."[55] However it is difficult to accept the homophobia-arousing evil that has been *a*scribed to Africana queer folks. From our multiple standpoints we are still asking how long transgender women like Islan Nettles and innumerable unnamed others will be beaten to death in the daylight of their own neighborhoods?[56] How long will it be okay for reggae dancehall artists to write songs encouraging the murder of queer folks (e.g., Buju Banton's "Boom bye bye in a Batty bwoi head)?"[57] How long will it be that lesbians from various African countries like Ugandan-born Aidah Asabaare are forced to apply for asylum in Europe and Canada for fear of being raped and killed?[58] How long will African Americans sing their national hymn "Lift Ev'ry Voice and Sing" while ignoring the fact that the *blood of the slaughtered* they *treaded their path through* was oftentimes that of their own SGL, queer, and transgender children, family members, and kin? True to Christian and neocolonial chrononormativity, we will have to "rest a little longer until the number of those yet to be killed is complete" (Rv 6:11), and "tell God all of our struggles when we get home."[59] Until then, "let the unjust one still be unjust, and the filthy one still make things filthy, and let the righteous one still be righteous, and the one who is holy still be holy" (22:11)—while we wait.

According to J. Halberstam, Black (gay and SGL) lives do not even warrant the attention of white gay and lesbian activists because the victims are neither Matthew Shepard nor Brandon Teena.[60] In July 2014, a person of transgender experience was brutally assaulted in the very Atlanta neighborhood (Little Five Points) described by Margaret Aymer above. Rather than calling police, onlookers recorded the attack on their cell phones, posting their videos to the internet.[61] Pleas for justice from the souls under the altar were made to the lamb that was standing as if slaughtered—surely a Jesus who "knows all about our struggles"[62]—among the ancient seven churches in Asia Minor and onward through time to our present day. The slaughtered lamb eventually transforms into the conquering warrior on the white horse (19:11–16), and reverts to the lamb once more in the climactic vision of the New Jerusalem (21:22–23; 22:1, 3). However, the transformation of the lamb into the avenging warrior apparently causes the lamb to develop *lambnesia* in the New Jerusalem.

Thus, in the apocalypse of John, queer folks are confronted with a God who is not necessarily on the side of all the oppressed, and a lion of Judah that condones murder in John's apocalypse and in Jamaican (Rastafarian) culture—*a Jesus who does not save*.[63] We cannot wash the blood evidence off our robes. We owe it to the ones who were lost in the tribulation as a result of violence, external imperial politics, or internal respectability politics to remember their names. Disidentification and erotohistoriography require us to speak the names of Sylvia Rivera and Marsha P. Johnson, when talking about Stonewall, and to look for the liberation yet to come for racial-ethnic transgender persons. We must remember that "Brother Outsider" Bayard Rustin organized the March on Washington, making it possible for the world to hear Martin Luther King's apocalypse-vision in 1963. We must talk about the work of J-FLAG in Jamaica, Uganda's David Kato, and others who sought to conquer on behalf of Africana queer folks. We can disabuse ourselves of the myths that queer intersections with Africana culture begin in the 1960s and originate in the United States.[64] These acts of remembering are part of the Sankofa project of world re-visions for Africana queer folks.

## WE WILL MAKE OUR OWN FUTURE TEXTS: AFRICANA QUEER CODICES

> I warn everyone who hears the words of the prophecy of this book: if anyone adds to them, God will add to that person the plagues described in this book; if anyone takes away from the words of the book of this prophecy, God will take away that person's share in the tree of life and in the holy city, which are described in this book. The one who testifies to these things says, "Surely I am coming soon." Amen. Come, Lord Jesus! The grace of the Lord Jesus be with all the saints. Amen.
>
> REVELATION 22:18–21

For many Africana queer folks, Revelation as a Christian canonical text endures as a religiocultural object through which homophobic, heteronormative, misogynist believers (and nonbelievers) justify their prejudice against queer folks "from every nation, from all tribes and peoples and languages" (Rv 7:9). It is one of the many ways that the Bible is deployed to justify hatred in the name of the "surely coming soon" Jesus (22:20). To question, critique, or ignore it is to be damned and left outside of community ("Outside are the dogs . . ." [22:15]). Revelation's placement as the last book of the biblical canon acts to seal the authority of the other sixty-five texts chosen to represent the Christian God's teachings for believers. This power position strengthens other texts deployed as weapons against queer people. This religiosocial condition creates a crisis for those deemed ineligible to share in the tree of life and in the holy city (22:19). It is a crisis both of religious fundamentalism and of internalized homophobia. One way to mitigate this crisis is to co-opt and confront the Bible as one text that is part of a larger queer canon.

Jacqueline Hidalgo notes that Cherríe Moraga's "Chicano Codex" includes Revelation as part of "*our* book of Revelation," along with script written on the walls of the barrio, and the L.A. riots.[65] In response to Hidalgo, Lynn Huber suggests that "the project of queer biblical hermeneutics involves assembling, revealing, claiming a 'Codex Queer.'"[66] According to Huber, Codex Queer "is not simply about recalling the past or envisioning a future, but it is about drawing together in the present those who have an oblique relationship to the Bible, strengthening and comforting them as they resist its social sway."[67] I suggest that cultivating a Codex Queer allows us to disidentify with histories of scholarship that limit and exclude the possibility for meaning making in scriptural or other texts. Lived queer experiences of the past and present can be brought into dialogue with texts and interpreting communities. We do not have to add to or subtract from the Apocalypse of John. Following Ishmael Reed and Vincent Wimbush, "We will [continue to] write our own future texts,"[68] texts, performances, documentaries, and retellings of historical narratives that explore worlds beyond the here and now. Brian Blount reminds us that "when the voices of cultures 'from below' [or outside] take themselves seriously enough to propel themselves into the exegetical, hermeneutical, and interpretive debate, the imperium claimed and held by dominant cultures is broken."[69]

From my Black SGL standpoint, employing erotic subjectivity with the concept of Sankofa, *our* Africana queer book of Revelation recognizes forebears including those listed above (i.e., Rivera, Johnson, Rustin, Lorde, Cullen, Hughes, Baldwin, and others, as well as the unnamed and unknown "souls under the altar") alongside heavenly and earthly co-laborers in the project of practicing honor, liberation, and transformation.[70] It reclaims precolonial African ancestors who lived in sexual and gendered fluidity. It imagines Africana queers yet to be born who are *fierce*, resourceful, and confidently aware of their intrinsic value, into a world that celebrates their difference.

As a starting point for enumeration, I posit that Africana Codex Queer includes the historical contributions of Black queer folks throughout African diasporas: in the construction of Black church aesthetics since Emancipation; the impact of their artistic and political contributions to the Harlem Renaissance; Baldwin's participation (alongside Senghor, Césaire, and others) in the first Congress of Black Writers and Artists in Paris (1956) to articulate the launch of the Negritude movement; the wisdom of radical women of color from anthologies such as *This Bridge Called My Back* and *Homegirls*; the publication of anthologies and writings by Black Gay Men such as *In the Life*, *Sweet Tea: Gay Men of the South*, as well as queer anthologies from the diasporas including *Queer Latinidad: Identity Practices, Discursive Spaces*; *Our Caribbean: A Gathering of Gay and Lesbian Writing from the Antilles*, and the *Queer African Reader*; along with blogs, essays, and social media postings by the queer organizers of the #blacklivesmatter movement.[71] As Vincent L. Wimbush states, "For Black and subaltern critical consciousness there is no meaning in any Western-translated narrative, script, text, and tradition unless such is first ripped, broken, and then 'entranced,' blackened, made usable for weaving meaning."[72]

By engaging Africana codices queer, I can pleasurably counternarrate historical and cultural erasures (cf. erotohistoriography) while having improper relations with biblical texts in the practice of queer scripturalization.[73] In doing so, I can privilege African ancestral lineages over Foucauldian genealogies to explore and unveil systems of power and knowledge on behalf of my community of accountability. "The eroticism of affective historiography allow[s] us to think that history is not only what hurts but what arouses, kindles, whets, or itches. . . . We might [even] say that history is what pleasures."[74] Rather than focusing on Revelation's Christ as conqueror-amnesia victim, I can choose to think of the African Christological trope of Christ as Ancestor.[75] Recognizing the Christ in the book of Revelation as ancestor, I claim the angels that corrected John (19:9–10; 22:9) as part of our Africana queer lineage.[76] I can now pleasurably and improperly co-opt the heavenly beings as "angels watchin' over me"[77] on behalf of Africana queer folks outside.

Furthermore, since Countee Cullen is my gay ancestor from the Harlem Renaissance, I can employ his sexual status in order to be *improper* with James Cone's argument in *The Cross and the Lynching Tree* for the theological implications of this move. Cone foregrounds Cullen's poem "Christ Recrucified" as a discursive pillar (cf. Rv 3:12: "If you conquer, I will make you a pillar in the temple of my God . . .") in his claim that "in the United States, the image of the crucified Christ was the figure of an innocent Black victim, dangling from a lynching tree."[78] Cone helps us to see that Michael Brown lying on a Ferguson street for four hours is a lynching. We help Cone (and others) see that the mob who murdered the Black transgender woman Islan Nettles, dragging her dead body to a Harlem police station, was a lynching. Seeing things John's way (with a nod to David deSilva),[79] Nettles is considered one of the abject, along with us on the outside. The angels prevent interpreters from worshipping the deity of conquering hegemonic homophobia. Counterbalancing John's error, the angels direct us to worship God: the God of oppressed queer folks, the Jesus as Ancestor who saves—and they direct us to the community of our fellow servants in the struggle for honor, justice, liberation, and transformation.

## AFRICANA QUEER PROLOGUE

> See, I am making all things new.
>
> REVELATION 21:5

John's apocalyptic epilogue can become an Africana queer prologue to imagine a *then and there* that will transform our *here and now*. The potential of the futures we imagine are relative to our willingness to develop erotic subjectivity, our ability to become Sankofa people managed against our sociogeographical constraints. This must become a praxis deployed by queer folks that is visible, translatable, and teachable. Freeman argues that "unbinding time and/from history means recognizing how erotic relations and the bodily acts that sustain them gum up the works of the normative structures we call family and nation, gender, race, class, and sexual identity, by changing tempos, by remixing memory and desire, by recapturing excess."[80] I have attempted in this essay to demonstrate some of these examples by suggesting that endings (like the epilogue of Revelation) can inspire beginnings. I have interrupted some historical narratives that locate Africana queerness in a post-Stonewall era, and claimed transformation for those whose kinship groups disqualify from liberation. I have located my story in the book of other stories that until now were sealed, and call for Africana queer stories yet to be told. We do not need to wait until the apocalypse to imagine futures outside of the prison house of the here and now. We can begin today.

John in his apocalypse made the error of cementing what utopia will be. As soon as utopia is articulated, it ceases to be utopia. However, since all of our sociogeographical locations are different, we can begin activating multiple versions of the future from our multiple standpoints. The Africana queer futurity formula I propose is another way of working toward Muñoz's concept of queerness that is on the horizon born of "hope spawned out of a critical investment in utopia."[81] It is the promise of hope for those who were never meant to survive. As we reconstitute ourselves to build communities of support and accountability, we must learn the lesson not to create "dogs outside" to our newly found social inside(s).

When necessary, we need to employ our oppositional gaze toward Revelation and those who use it to persecute us while not turning into oppositional gays toward another subaltern group. This was the sin of our Africana communities: to claim independence from colonial oppressors, by the providence of a God who is on the side of the oppressed, that sanctions abjection, violence, and murder of their own queer people. As we cruise Africana queer utopias, we can reclaim who we are in all of our difference—as Sankofa people with a past worth reclaiming—as erotic subjects capable of changing our conditions and our world. Ultimately, we will call ourselves home to a new heaven and a new earth having reconciled with families of origin and simultaneously cultivating families of choice. That is my queer hope.

Perhaps that is also the hope of the final invitations of Revelation's epilogue. Revelation is not known as a text of reconciliation. You obey and endure, or you disobey and perish. However, a disidentification in Africana queer context might imagine the invitation of the Spirit and bride that all who hear and all who are thirsty should come to take the water of life as a gift (22:17), as the potential to repair damaged relations with ourselves and our communities. Might this be how we co-create the making of all things new? After the cosmic battle, and the destruction of the beast, and the outside, what is the significance of the summons of verse 17 to "come"? Only the futures outside can tell.

While we wait, we will learn from Ntozake Shange and her colored girls to find the God inside ourselves and *love her* fiercely.[82] Instead of singing songs by the rivers of our respective Babylons in the strange land outside, we should dance. And since "hard times require furious dancing,"[83] we will take our shirts off in the Paradise Garages of our imaginations, chanting to Gloria Gaynor's "I Will Survive"—we will vibe to house music all night long.[84] As Jafari Allen writes,

> The Black gay club may in fact be the only place a trans person, gay man, or lesbian—shut out from other spaces of divine communion—may witness or participate in a vision of beloved community. This vision is not a substitute for church any more than it is a substitute for organizing. In fact, it represents a more ecumenical, democratic, honest, and expansive ethic of humanity than religion or formal politics. Classic house club refrains implore the dancer to "free your body," "move your body," "give it up," and "let yourself go" which may be interpreted as sexual innuendo, and is also understood in the space of the dance club as an exhortation to a deeper psychic and spiritual freeing that only takes place through the pleasures of the body.[85]

We are the beloved community we've been waiting for. Surely, our change is coming soon! The grace of the (Audre) Lord(e) be with all saints. Amen (Rv 22:21).

## NOTES

1. Translations from the Greek text are my own.
2. Same/similar gender loving, or SGL, in this context is associated with the work of the Black activist Cleo Manago in the 1990s. It is a culturally affirming identity that decenters the concept of a white, male, middle-class, Western world subject as the starting point for everyday queer experience. This definition is multiply articulated by contemporary SGL scholars and activists who add to, contest, and elaborate on it—including more fluid subjectivities that seem to be erased in it. See http://www.bmxnational.org/what-is-bmx/ (accessed August 31, 2015). I locate myself as a Black SGL man of Africana queer experience in solidarity with LGBTQ people in Africa and throughout the African diasporas.
3. Audre Lorde, "A Litany for Survival," in *The Black Unicorn: Poems by Audre Lorde* (New York: W.W. Norton, 1978), 31–32.
4. José Esteban Muñoz, *Cruising Utopia: The Then and There of Queer Futurity* (New York: New York University Press, 2010), 1.
5. José Esteban Muñoz, *Disidentifications: Queers of Color and the Performance of Politics* (Minneapolis: University of Minnesota Press, 1999), 1.
6. Ibid., 5.
7. Ibid., 11–12.

8. This surety is an example of Elizabeth Freeman's concept of *chrononormativity*, "a technique by which institutional forces come to seem like somatic facts." Elizabeth Freeman, *Time Binds: Queer Temporalities, Queer Histories* (Durham, N.C.: Duke University Press, 2010), 3.
9. The slashes that separate the categories are indicative of the separate yet porous boundaries of each construction, especially as Africana queer folk cross them.
10. For examples of queer of color critique, in addition to the above-mentioned works by José Esteban Muñoz, see Roderick A. Ferguson, *Aberrations in Black: Toward a Queer of Color Critique* (Minneapolis: University of Minnesota Press, 2003), Dwight McBride, *Why I Hate Abercrombie & Fitch: Essays on Race and Sexuality* (New York: New York University Press, 2005), and essays in "Black/Queer/Diaspora," ed. Jafari S. Allen, special issue, *GLQ: A Journal of Lesbian and Gay Studies* 18, nos. 2–3 (2012).
11. Jafari S. Allen "Black/Queer/Diaspora at the Current Conjuncture," *GLQ: A Journal of Lesbian and Gay Studies* 18, nos. 2–3 (2012): 213.
12. I pluralize *diasporas* to note movements to and from the African continent, as well as to and from the multiple geographical locations where people of African descent reside, emigrate from/to, and traverse (e.g. the Jamaican diaspora).
13. My purposeful use of the possessive "my" symbolizes my solidarity with and my practice of the ideal that my freedom is linked to the freedom of my LGBTQ sisters and brothers and all people of African descent.
14. Edouard Glissant, "History-Histories-Stories," in *Caribbean Discourse: Selected Essays*, trans. J. Michael Dash (1981; Charlottesville: University of Virginia Press, 1989), 61–95, 66.
15. Linda E. Thomas, "A Womanist Conjure on We Have Been Believers," in *We Have Been Believers: An African American Systematic Theology*, ed. James H. Evans Jr. (Minneapolis: Fortress Press, 2012), 185.
16. Cecil Conteen Gray, *Afrocentric Thought and Praxis: An Intellectual History* (Trenton, N.J.: Africa World Press, 2001), 28.
17. Thomas, "Womanist Conjure," 185.
18. Freeman, *Time Binds*, 109.
19. Ibid., 95–96.
20. Fredric Jameson, *The Political Unconscious: Narrative as a Socially Symbolic Act* (Ithaca, N.Y.: Cornell University Press, 2014), 102: "History is what hurts, it is what refuses desire and sets inexorable limits to individual as well as collective praxis, which its 'ruses' turn into grisly and ironic reversals of their overt intention." See also Freeman, *Time Binds*, 10.
21. Lyndon K. Gill, "Chatting Back an Epidemic: Caribbean Gay Men, HIV/AIDS and the Uses of Erotic Subjectivity," *GLQ: A Journal of Lesbian and Gay Studies* 18, nos. 2–3 (2012): 279.
22. Audre Lorde, "Uses of the Erotic: The Erotic as Power," in *Sister Outsider: Essays & Speeches by Audre Lorde* (Berkeley: Crossing Press, 2007), 53–59.
23. Gill, "Chatting Back," 279.
24. I define πόρνοι "as the ones who are sexually exploited" as opposed to "fornicators" (NRSV) or "sexually immoral" (NIV) to name the fact that in the first century,

this group includes male and female slaves and other subordinates who did not necessarily have agency over their bodies, and the fact that there can be no supply if there was no demand. As reception histories have been constructed through time, the moral and spiritual responsibility (blame) is placed on those who could be victims, as opposed to the perpetrators. In modern understanding, we assume that fornicators and the sexually immoral can choose to be so, which makes it easy to put this context onto the sexually marginalized (i.e., contemporary homosexuals). My definition disidentifies with this practice.

25. The book of Revelation repeatedly describes the action of heavenly figures proclaiming in "a loud voice" (Revelation 1:10; 5:2; 6:10; 7:2, 10; 8:13; 11:12, 15; 12:10, 14:7, 9, 15, 18; 16:1, 17; 19:1, 17; 21:3). Although I am writing in my own voice, it is amplified with energy from my ancestors who have gone to their eternal rewards before me (especially my queer ancestors) and with the energy of those yet to be born. See, for example, Elias Farajaje-Jonez, "Invocation of Remembrance, Healing, and Empowerment in a Time of AIDS," in *Equal Rites: Lesbian and Gay Worship, Ceremonies, and Celebrations*, ed. Kittredge Cherry and Zalmon Shermood (Louisville, Ky.: Westminster John Knox Press, 1995), 25–27.

26. Gaurav Desai, "Out in Africa," in *Post-Colonial, Queer: Theoretical Intersections*, ed. John C. Hawley (Albany: State University of New York Press, 2001), 148.

27. James Cone incorporates the thought of Countee Cullen, Langston Hughes, and James Baldwin in his book *The Cross and the Lynching Tree* without acknowledging that they were gay Black men. Cone's is an example of how gay and lesbian contributions are appropriated while ignoring or erasing sexual difference. See James H. Cone, *The Cross and the Lynching Tree* (Maryknoll, N.Y.: Orbis Books, 2011), esp. 93–119. Cf. A. B. Christa Schwartz, *Gay Voices of the Harlem Renaissance* (Bloomington: Indiana University Press, 2003), 48–87; William J. Spurlin, "Culture, Rhetoric, and Queer Identity: James Baldwin and the Identity Politics of Race and Sexuality," in *James Baldwin Now*, ed. Dwight A. McBride (New York: New York University Press, 1999), 103–21. On the subject of Africana citizenship, see M. Jacqui Alexander, "Not Just (Any) Body Can Be a Citizen: The Politics of Law, Sexuality and Postcoloniality in Trinidad and Tobago and the Bahamas," *Feminist Review* 48 (1994): 5–23.

28. Desai, "Out in Africa," 157.

29. See Arnaldo Cruz-Malavé and Martin F. Manalansan IV, "Introduction: Dissident Sexualities/Alternative Globalizations," in *Queer Globalizations: Citizenship and the Afterlife of Colonialism*, ed. Cruz-Malavé and Manalansan (New York: New York University Press, 2002), 1–12.

30. In the subhead I have substituted the houses of the Black and Latino/a ballroom community made (in)famous in Jenny Livingston's documentary *Paris Is Burning* for the seven churches of Asia Minor to which Revelation was addressed. See Jennie Livingston, *Paris Is Burning*, DVD (Miramax Films, 1990); Edgar Rivera Colón, "Getting Life in Two Worlds: Power and Prevention in the New York City House Ball Community," PhD diss., Rutgers University, 2009; Marlon M. Bailey, *Butch Queens Up in Pumps: Gender, Performance, and Ballroom Culture in Detroit* (Detroit: University of Michigan Press, 2013).

31. Traditional African American spiritual ("I Want to Be Ready").

32. See, e.g., Ex 11:7; 22:31; 1 Kgs 6:4; 14:11; 21:19, 23–24; 22:38; 2 Kgs 9:10, 36; Jb 30:1; Pss 22:16; 68:23; Is 56:10–11; Jer 15:3; Mt 7:6; Lk 16:21; Phil 3:2.

33. See especially Mark D. Nanos, "Paul's Reversal of Jews Calling Gentiles 'Dog' (Philippians 3:2): 1600 Years of an Ideological Tale Wagging an Exegetical Dog?" *Biblical Interpretation* 17, no 4 (2009): 448–82. I am grateful to Joseph A. Marchal for bringing Nanos's article to my attention.

34. Ancient Greek examples of many characteristics of ancient dogs are listed in Henry George Liddell et al., *A Greek-English Lexicon*, 9th ed.(Oxford and New York: Clarendon Press and Oxford University Press, 1996), s.v. "κύων." Also see the various references to dogs in Ingvild Saelid Gilhus, *Animals, Gods and Humans: Changing Attitudes to Animals in Greek, Roman and Early Christian Thought* (New York: Routledge, 2006).

35. Among them are J. Massyngberde Ford, *Revelation* (New Haven, Conn.: Yale University Press, 1975), 345; Bruce M. Metzger, *Breaking the Code* (Nashville, Tenn.: Abingdon Press, 1993), 106; Robert L. Thomas, *Revelation 8–22* (Chicago: Moody, 1995), 507; Robert H. Mounce, *The Book of Revelation* (Grand Rapids, Mich.: Eerdmans, 1998), 408; and David E. Aune, *Revelation 17–22* (Nashville, Tenn.: Thomas Nelson, 1998), 1222–23. I am grateful to Stephen D. Moore for bringing these sources to my attention.

36. Metzger, *Breaking the Code*, 106.

37. Aune, *Revelation 17–22*, 1222.

38. In the New Testament, see, e.g., Mt 15:19; Mk 7:21–22; Rom 1:29–31; 13:13; 1 Cor 5:10–11; 6:9–10; 2 Cor 6:9–10; 12:20–21; Gal 5:19–21; Eph 4:31; 5:3–5; Col 3:5, 8; 1 Tm 1:9–10; 2 Tm 3:2–5; Ti 3:3; Jas 3:15; 1 Pt 2:1; 4:3, 15; Rv 9:21; 21:8; 22:15.

39. See Max Fisher, "Mugabe Says of Obama's Gay Rights Push, 'We ask, was he born out of homosexuality?'" *Washington Post*, July 25, 2013 http://www.washingtonpost.com/blogs/worldviews/wp/2013/07/25/mugabe-says-of-obamas-gay-rights-push-we-ask-was-he-born-out-of-homosexuality/ (accessed September 9, 2013).

40. Stewart Maclean "'To hell with you': Robert Mugabe in rambling anti-homosexual rant at David Cameron's call for global gay rights," *Daily Mail*, February 26, 2012 http://www.dailymail.co.uk/news/article-2106720/Robert-Mugabe-rambling-anti-homosexual-rant-David-Camerons-global-gay-rights.html (accessed September 13, 2014).

41. Jeff Chu, "My Day at Westboro Baptist: 'Yes, Jesus Hates You,'" Sunday, March 24, 2013 http://www.salon.com/2013/03/24/my_day_at_westboro_baptist_yes_jesus_hates_you/ (accessed September 12, 2015); James Michael Nichols, "ATLAH, Anti-Gay Harlem Church to Be Protested by LGBT Activists," March 26, 2014 http://www.huffingtonpost.com/2014/03/26/anti-gay-harlem-church-protest_n_5035773.html (accessed September 12, 2015).

42. See Judith Halberstam, *The Queer Art of Failure* (Durham, N.C.: Duke University Press, 2011), 1–8; bell hooks, "The Politics of Radical Black Subjectivity," in *Yearning: Race, Gender, and Cultural Politics* (Boston: South End Press, 1990), 15–22.

43. Ken Stone, "The Dogs of Exodus and the Question of the Animal," in *Divinanimal-*

*ity: Animal Theory, Creaturely Theology,"* ed. Stephen D. Moore (New York: Fordham University Press, 2014), 36–52, 43.

44. See Halberstam's concept of the "unexpected pleasures" of failure: Halberstam, *Queer Art of Failure*, 2–4.
45. Brian K. Blount quoting Aune writes, "The motif of the angel who refuses worship from a seer in the context of an angelic revelation (as in Rv 19:10 and 22:9) is a *literary motif* with many parallels in apocalyptic literature, though the motif is not restricted to the apocalyptic." *Revelation: A Commentary* (Louisville, Ky.: Westminster John Knox Press, 2009) 347–48; see also Aune, *Revelation 17–22*, 1036.
46. E.g., *Advocate*, "It's All Our Fault! 10 Disasters the Gays Supposedly Caused," October 21, 2012, http://www.advocate.com/politics/2012/10/31/10-disasters-gays-were-blamed-causing (accessed September 12, 2015).
47. See Stephen D. Moore, *God's Gym: Divine Male Bodies of the Bible* (New York: Routledge, 1996); and *God's Beauty Parlor and Other Queer Spaces in and around the Bible* (Stanford, Calif.: Stanford University Press, 2001).
48. See Marvin W. Myer and Elaine H. Pagels, *The Nag Hammadi Scriptures: The International Edition* (New York: Harper Collins, 2007), 313–20, 321–42, 487–98.
49. See Langston Hughes, "Dream Variations," *The Collected Works of Langston Hughes: The Poems, 1921–1940*, vol. 1 (Columbia: University of Missouri Press, 2001), 33; as well as Juana María Rodríguez, *Sexual Futures, Queer Gestures, and Other Latina Longings* (New York: New York University Press, 2014).
50. This question signifies on the notice that there is no evidence of gay, lesbian, bisexual, transgender, or queer people in Brian Blount's African American church or community. See Brian K. Blount, *Can I Get a Witness? Reading Revelation through African American Culture* (Louisville, Ky.: Westminster John Knox Press, 2005). Also, Lee Edelman notes that fantasies of the future include the eradication of the abjectness that is named by queerness: "Every political vision *as a vision of futurity* must weigh on any delineation of a queer oppositional politics. For the only queerness that queer sexualities could ever hope to signify would spring from their determined opposition to this underlying structure of the political" (Lee Edelman, *No Future: Queer Theory and the Death Drive* [Durham, N.C.: Duke University Press, 2004], 13).
51. On African theologies, Cheng writes, "The rainbow is a symbol of gender fluidity in the Yóruba and Santería traditions. The rainbow deity is called Oshumaré and sie [*sic*] is an androgynous serpent figure with both female and male elements." Patrick S. Cheng, "The Rainbow Connection: Bridging Asian American and Queer Theologies," *Theology & Sexuality* 17, no. 3 (2001): 238.
52. Quoting Ennis Barrington Edmonds, Aymer writes:

    The use of the term *Babylon* constitutes a symbolic delegitimation of those values and institutions that historically have exercised control over the masses of the African diaspora . . . the most immediate referent is the gut-wrenching experience of suffering, hardship, and estrangement faced by the underside of Jamaican society. It is not only the pain of economic hardship, *but a sense of not belonging, of cultural alienation. It is a feeling of uprootedness and of being "out of whack" with one's environment.* (Margaret Aymer, "Empire, Alter-Empire, and the Twenty-First Century," *Union Seminary Quarterly Review* 59, nos. 3–4 [2005]: 144; Ennis Barrington Edmonds, *Rastafari: From Outcasts to Culture Bearers* [New York: Oxford University Press, 2003], 44)

53. Blount, *Can I Get a Witness?* 88.
54. Blount, *Revelation*, 135. Blount makes the connection between the souls (in 6:9–11) with those from the great tribulation (7:13–14) and "our comrades" (12:10–12).
55. Blount, *Can I Get a Witness?* 70.
56. In addition to transphobic violence, Nettles was a victim of chrononormativity in that she walked through her neighborhood in the daytime, not the night when transgender women are stereotypically assumed to be "productive." Her failure to pass, as a credible "woman," and to traverse the distance between her attackers and her destination in the contact zone of the queer and Black communities epitomized by Harlem, warrants erotohistoriography to ensure her death will not be forgotten. See Christian Fuscanno, "Islan Nettles' Murder and the Shameful (Non-) Response of LGBs," *HuffPost Gay Voices*, November 20, 2013 (updated January 25, 2014) http://www.huffingtonpost.com/christian-fuscarino/islan-nettles-murder-and-the-shameful-non-response-of-lgbs_b_4310858.html (accessed July 5, 2015).
57. See Donna P. Hope, "'Dons' and 'Shottas': Performing Violent Masculinity in Dancehall Culture," *Social and Economic Studies* 52 nos. 1 & 2 (2006): 115–31; idem, *Inna di Dancehall: Popular Culture and the Politics of Identity in Jamaica* (Kingston, Jamaica: University of the West Indies Press, 2006), 79–85.
58. See Fred McConnell, "Home Office to Review Gay Ugandan Woman's Deportation Order," *Guardian*, May 23, 2014, http://www.theguardian.com/uk-news/2014/may/23/home-office-review-ugandan-lesbians-deportation-order (accessed July 5, 2015).
59. See African American spirituals and hymns, including "I'm Gonna Tell God All of My Struggles," "Glory, Hallelujah (When I Lay My Burdens Down)," "Have a Little Talk with Jesus," and "I Must Tell Jesus."
60. Judith Halberstam, *In a Queer Time and Place: Transgender Bodies, Subcultural Lives* (New York: New York University Press, 2005), 30.
61. Patrick Saunders, "Trans Woman Attacked in Little Five Points," *GA Voice*, July 3, 2014. hegavoice.com/trans-woman-brutally-attacked-little-five-points/ (accessed July 13, 2015).
62. Johnson Oatman, "No, Not One!" (Christian hymn), http://www.hymnary.org/text/theres_not_a_friend_like_the_lowly_jesus. (accessed August 30, 2014).
63. In his preface to the 1997 edition of *God of the Oppressed*, James Cone wrote, "Building on my previous work in *Black Theology and Black Power* (1969) and *A Black Theology of Liberation* (1970), I sought to deepen my conviction that the God of biblical faith and Black religion is best known as the Liberator of the oppressed from bondage." James Cone, *God of the Oppressed*, 2nd ed. (Maryknoll, N.Y.: Orbis Books, 1997). Also, Lee Edelman names how queerness will always be ascribed to some groups of people even if it is thrown off others. See Edelman, *No Future*, 24–31. Thanks to Kent Brintnall for pointing out these connections.

64. See, for example, Stephen O. Murray and Will Roscoe, *Boy-Wives and Female Husbands: Studies in African Homosexualities* (New York: Palgrave, 1998), and Nadia Ellis, *Territories of the Soul: Queered Belonging in the Black Diaspora* (Durham, N.C.: Duke University Press, 2015).
65. See the following chapter, by Jacqueline M. Hidalgo.
66. Lynn R. Huber, "Apocalyptic Orientation: A Response to Jacqueline Hidalgo's 'Scriptures as (Dis)Orientation Devices'" (response given at the Fourteenth Transdisciplinary Theological Colloquium, Drew Theological School, September 27, 2015).
67. Ibid.
68. Ishmael Reed, *Mumbo Jumbo* (New York: Scribner, 1972); and Vincent L. Wimbush, "We Will Make Our Own Future Text: An Alternate Orientation to Interpretation," in *True to Our Native Land: An African American New Testament Commentary*, ed. Brian K. Blount (Minneapolis: Fortress Press, 2007), 43–53.
69. Blount, *Can I Get a Witness?*, 24.
70. On sacred textures in biblical texts, see Vernon K. Robbins, *Exploring the Texture of Texts: A Guide to Socio-Rhetorical Interpretation* (New York: Bloomsbury, 1996), 120–131.
71. James Baldwin, "Princes and Powers," in *Nobody Knows My Name* (New York: Dial Press, 1961); Cherríe Moraga and Gloria Anzaldúa, eds., *This Bridge Called My Back: Writings by Radical Women of Color* (New York: Kitchen Table/Women of Color Press, 1983); Barbara Smith, ed., *Home Girls: A Black Feminist Anthology* ((New York: Kitchen Table/Women of Color Press, 1983); Joseph Beam, ed., *In the Life: A Black Gay Anthology* (Boston: Alyson Publications, 1986); E. Patrick Johnson, ed., *Sweet Tea: Black Gay Men of the South* (Chapel Hill: University of North Carolina Press, 2008); Rodríguez, *Queer Latinidad*; Thomas Glave, ed., *Our Caribbean: A Gathering of Lesbian and Gay Writing from the Antilles* (Durham, N.C.: Duke University Press, 2008); Sokari Ekine and Hakima Abbas, eds., *Queer African Reader* (Dakar, Sen.: Pambazuka Press, 2013); and Alicia Garza, "A Herstory of the Black Lives Matter Movement," *Feminist Wire*, October 7, 2014, http://www.thefeministwire.com/2014/10/blacklivesmatter-2/ (accessed July 24, 2015). This list is by no means complete, but it offers examples of resources from an Africana Codex Queer.
72. Wimbush, "We Will Make Our Own Future Text," 51.
73. See Joseph A. Marchal, "Queer Approaches: Improper Relations with Pauline Letters," in *Studying Paul's Letters: Contemporary Perspectives*, ed. Joseph A. Marchal (Minneapolis: Fortress Press, 2012), 209–27.
74. Freeman, *Time Binds*, 117.
75. See Clifton R. Clarke, *African Christology: Jesus in Post-Missionary African Christianity* (Eugene, Ore.: Pickwick, 2011), 35–41. Clarke notes that Jesus-as-Ancestor Christology has two trajectories—one intercultural and one associated with a liberationist approach. "This latter approach is linked to North American Black Theology and is also influenced by Latin American theology of liberation" (35).
76. See womanist readings of the character of Hagar for implications in the contemporary lives of African American women, including Renita J. Weems, "A Mistress, a

Maid, and No Mercy (Hagar and Sarah)," in *Just a Sister Away: A Womanist Vision of Women's Relationships in the Bible* (Philadelphia: Innisfree Press, 1988), 1–22; Delores Williams, "Hagar in African American Biblical Interpretation," in *Hagar, Sarah, and Their Children: Jewish, Christian, and Muslim Perspectives*, ed. Phyllis Trible and Letty M. Russell (Louisville, Ky.: Westminster John Knox Press, 2006), 171–84.

77. "All Night, All Day (Angels Watchin' Over Me My Lord)," African American spiritual. These angels can be contemporary guides that can include Audre Lorde, James Baldwin, or the deceased gay uncle many of us had, among others.
78. Cone, *The Cross and the Lynching Tree*, 93.
79. Cf. David deSilva, *Seeing Things John's Way: The Rhetoric of the Book of Revelation* (Louisville, Ky.: Westminster John Knox Press, 2009).
80. Freeman, *Time Binds*, 173.
81. Muñoz, *Cruising Utopia*, 12.
82. Ntozake Shange, "A Laying on of Hands," in *For Colored Girls Who Have Considered Suicide / When the Rainbow Is Enuf* (New York: Scribner Poetry, 1997), 87.
83. Alice Walker, *Hard Times Require Furious Dancing: New Poems* (Novato, Calif.: New World Library, 2010).
84. The Paradise Garage was a popular dance club in New York City from the disco era until its closing in 1987. The Garage (as it was known) was one of the only night spots where people of all genders and sexualities (gay, straight, and fluid) partied together, with music as their unifying force.
85. Jafari S. Allen, "'For the Children' Dancing the Beloved Community," *Souls: A Critical Journal of Black Politics, Culture, and Society*, 11, no. 3 (2009): 311–26.

# "*Our* Book of Revelation . . . Prescribes Our Fate and Releases Us from It": Scriptural Disorientations in Cherríe Moraga's *The Last Generation*

JACQUELINE M. HIDALGO

Invoking a range of religious intonations, Cherríe Moraga frames her essay collection, *The Last Generation: Prose and Poetry* (1993), as "a prayer" even though she "no longer remember[s] how to pray."[1] She writes in a moment of temporal convergence as she reflects upon the five hundred years since Christopher Columbus arrived in the Americas.[2] She reminds readers of the "catastrophic consequence" of this advent, a catastrophe that still ripples through the early 1990s. The essays in the collection, all written between 1990 and 1993, respond to varying local and international crises: "the Gulf War, the collapse of the Soviet Union, Indigenous peoples' international campaigns for sovereignty, the hundreds of thousands of deaths of gay people, women, and people of color from AIDS and breast cancer, the Los Angeles Rebellion, and the blatant refusal by the United States to commit to environmental protection."[3] Tying her present act of writing to the sorrows of the *tlamatinime* (Nahua sages) who watched their sacred codices burn to ash under the gaze of Spanish missionaries in 1524, she fears the dying of "Chicanos, mestizos, and Native Americans"; the imminent loss of their memories, knowledge, and futures demarcate the title of her collection. She concludes the collection with an essay, "Codex Xerí: El Momento Histórico," which both reflects on Mesoamerican codices and presents itself as a "Chicano codex," as a religious offering and "a closing prayer for the last generation."[4]

As a Latina student of scriptures, particularly Christian scriptures, I have long found myself drawn to Moraga's concluding essay, "Codex Xerí," because that essay plays with notions of glyphs, scriptures, revelations, and other worlds that might be glimpsed when we examine "scripturalization,"[5] the social processes of making and engaging scriptures, although Moraga ignores the term *scripture* in her essay. In another context, I argue that Moraga's codex provides an example of the ways that scriptures, broadly understood to incorporate texts and practices that carry a certain sacred and centering tenor, can act as what Sara Ahmed terms *homing devices*, those objects by and through which unhomed persons can find, make, and remake homes.[6] In this essay, I want to press particularly at a conversation between Moraga's "codex" and Ahmed's work on "orientations" in order to show how such homing devices and homing processes are fundamentally ambivalent, disturbing and uncomfortable as much as they are comforting. Historically, scriptures have been used to justify the unhoming of colonized subjects, and practices of textual fetishization have often served to police the boundaries of normative cis-gender heteropatriarchy. A lesbian Chicana feminist such as Moraga can embrace scriptures only from an oblique angle, one that draws attention to and challenges us to rethink normative relations between peoples and their sacred texts. Scriptures that get employed as homing devices are also scriptures employed as disorientation devices, where scriptural disorientations can offer both tragic and transformative potentialities.

## REACTIVATING CHICANX CODICES

Moraga initially drafted her "Codex Xerí" as a response to an art exhibition, *The Chicano[7] Codices: Encountering Art of the Americas*, which the art historian Marcos Sánchez-Tranquilino curated at San Francisco's Mexican Museum in 1992. Moraga's specific essay reflects on lost Mesoamerican codices as well as the quite diverse codices created for the exhibition; thus she joined multiple artists who worked to "reactivate" their own codex practices that drew on Mesoamerican traditions in combination with other sources they view as revelatory, including sources from their daily lives.[8] Wanting to provide "a new vision of American culture," the museum asked artists to relate themselves to "the codex, or picture book, developed by North American cultures centuries before the arrival of Europeans. The pre-Conquest codex is an especially appropriate source of inspiration and interpretation, as it articulates social and historical information through visual artistic means."[9] Although Europeans also had *codices*, a term for the technological revolution of bound pages that we most associate with *books*, Mesoamerican codices rely on different technological styles, visual grammar, and reading practices.

Over the course of her career, Moraga cultivated an approach to her writing as a reactivation of codex practices. She titled one of her most recent collections *A Xicana Codex of Changing Consciousness, 2000–2010*.[10] Whereas European codices, especially after Gutenberg and increased literacy, came to be regarded as loci for solitary and quiet reading, Mesoamerican codex rituals rely on interpreters and performance. Moraga specifies Mesoamerican codices as not just texts but also ritual practices around texts when she conflates ancient Mesoamerican *tlacuilo* (scribes) with the *tlamatinime* (sages) in the crafting of modern Chicanx codices.[11] By taking up the codex as a practice of oral performance in search of storytelling revelation, in need of embodied and moment-to-moment interpretation, Moraga imagines codices as devices with ritualized and mutable meanings. Codices only mean through the people who read them ritually, with the people who "giv[e the codices] voice, body, propósito."[12] Moraga's stories are read in embodied ways, and thus meanings shift depending on the bodies who take up, inhabit, and transform the texts she has written. In "Codex Xerí," Moraga switches back and forth between a singular and plural, "Chicano codex" and codices. Meanings are always in the moment and in the people who read and access texts; they are never singular. Although many contemporary scholars would characterize all writing in this way, these scholars are reading against the dominant assumptions of European and Euro-American traditions. Moraga, instead, tries to locate a performance-based reading practice as prior to and beyond European traditions.

Each work of art in the 1992 exhibition reactivated the codex by drawing on ancient Aztec and other Mexican visual and cultural religious traditions as well as other sources and media, such as "family histories, personal memories, folk practices, and language."[13] Within this context, and among the many other Chicanxs who play with codices and glyphs, Moraga imagines a specifically *Chicano Codex*.[14] Moraga's codex is a meditation on and a reinvention of writing by taking up and reimagining a format of Mesoamerican "text," by pushing both European and Aztec scriptures into a hybrid dialogue and understanding well beyond the contexts for which Mesoamerican codices may have first been intended.

Although Moraga's essay first appeared with the exhibition, she incorporated the essay as the conclusion to *The Last Generation*. Perhaps writing the essay so as to evoke the nonlinear practice of the folding screens found in Aztec codices, Moraga's essay does not follow a neat linear structure, and thus I find it difficult to offer a simple content summary. She traces a serpentine trajectory through a plurality of topics, pressing at the pains and possibilities of the 1990s as a particular moment of temporal resonance. After describing then-current crises such as urban violence, poverty, environmental disaster, and AIDS in broad strokes, she then conjures a different past, a beginning named with "God, Ometeotl." Yet from this sacred beginning she rushes through five hundred years of settler colonial and heteropatriarchal violence, both Spanish and U.S., and she demands restitution. She then tasks "Chicano scribes" with "deciphering" unwritten histories found in images of daily life. Granting scribes a role of prophetic witness, she discusses the Aztec prophecy of the end of the Fifth Sun cycle, invoking it as a promise that all empires fall, and that the United States too must pass; indeed all of the current crises will pass, albeit painfully, as a new day dawns on the horizon.

## CODEX DISORIENTATIONS AND SCRIPTURES AS ORIENTATION DEVICES

The nonlinear movement and employment of contradictory images can trigger a disorienting feeling while reading "Codex Xerí." In order to redescribe Moraga's work here, I borrow terms such as *disorientation devices* and *angles of approach* from Sara Ahmed's *Queer Phenomenology* (2006). Ahmed's work on orientations and objects can help recontextualize Moraga's "Codex Xerí" and a few other Chicanx literary texts within the study of religion. I am necessarily pressing both Ahmed and Moraga beyond their own terms of engagement, but I also hope that Ahmed's focus on orientations may be a fruitful conversation partner for Latinx religious studies. I choose Ahmed's work because she describes orientations and disorientations as social directioning of bodies in space and time, directioning that makes and remakes bodies and the paths that they follow. Certain objects can become loci of orientation and the objects toward which and through which we are oriented. In her attentions to the varying ways that orientations shape bodies as sexual, gendered, and raced, Ahmed considers how those orientational shapings make bodies tend toward certain paths, putting certain objects and not others, certain people and not others, within reach.[15]

Ahmed's work provides a textured reading of the ways that bodies get shaped and reshaped in daily life through "tending toward" certain objects and not others. Certain objects become socially constructed, with physical processes and ramifications, and these objects then become receptive to certain bodies who approach the objects from appropriate angles. These objects also then direct and redirect the bodies that come to them so that other objects move to the foreground while placing others in the background.[16] By drawing our attention to "devices," to objects that get used for orientations and disorientations, Ahmed depicts objects as both material artifacts and ideas that have social power and get used for social directing. Although Ahmed does not discuss the Christian bible[17] specifically as an orientation device, she describes what a "bible" as an object can do. Ahmed designates the novel *The Well of Loneliness* as "the lesbian bible." Ahmed's identification of this novel illustrates something about what a bible is and can mean as a social object, "as [an object] that acquires its sociality by being passed around, by *changing hands*."[18] A bible gets exchanged through and connects bodies. The Christian bible is also a material object that gets passed around, and any bible's status as a "bible" may have to do with its work as a communally perceived "orientation device," as a starting point or a locus for redirection, an object that we turn to in order to follow certain paths with other people.

Understanding the Christian bible as an orientation device both aligns with and redirects religious studies scholarship on scriptures as phenomena, if, following Wilfred Cantwell Smith we think about scriptures as connoting a relationship that people have with texts. Through their relationships with these texts, people also negotiate, shape, and contest relationships with each other; scriptures then become domains of power shaping.[19] One might understand scriptures as signaling an affective relationship, as Smith claims that "the quality of being scripture is not an attribute of texts. It is a characteristic of the attitude of persons—groups of persons—to what outsiders perceive as texts. It denotes a relation between a people and a text."[20] It is not the content per se that matters but the shared object and practices of relating to that shared object.

Seeing a bible as an orientation device also explains how and why the import of the Christian bible, and other scriptures, rarely have to do with the specific content of scriptures but rather what people imagine the texts must direct us toward. As Ahmed argues about nationalism and shared texts, "The very act of reading means that citizens are directing their attention toward a shared object, even if they have a different view upon that object, or even if that object brings different worlds into view. So we might face the same direction. We could even say our faces 'face' the same way, creating a collective force."[21] The shared objects have a certain socially binding power because people turn toward them together. As socially powerful objects, scriptures function as binding sites for human communities. Scriptures are just special examples of how broader texts can work in binding groups.[22] The Christian bible then exists as an affective object because of a shared social construction of its role: "All objects of emotion are fantasies of what objects can give us."[23] Distinct ritualized relationships to scriptures—relationships whereby people interpret, perform, and iconize special texts—can yield sociopolitical ramifications, especially in domains of authority, inspiration, and structural legitimation.[24] Scriptures then become loci of power, and the practices of engagement around scriptures foster hierarchies, constructing those whose bodies arrive "naturally" at scriptures and those whose bodies are marginalized and must approach scriptures obliquely. Such socialities of scriptural power, or scripturalization, may also be redescribed in terms of orientations; scriptures become orientation devices that direct people to follow certain social paths and not others.

## SCRIPTURES AS DISORIENTATION DEVICES

Moraga's "Codex Xerí" meditates on scriptures, though she names them as "codices" instead, thereby redescribing the history of scriptures in the Americas and imagining alternative "texts" that could be scriptural for Chicanxs. To some extent, Moraga offers up her Chicano codex as an alternative scripture, one that provides a homing orientation: "The Chicano codex is the map back to the original face. Its scribes are the modern-day tlamatinime. . . . We hold up the obsidian mirror, tell them, 'Look, gente, so that you might know yourselves, find your true face and heart, and see.'"[25] The codex, as a mirror object passed around, an object whose meaning is in interactions between people, then offers a path, a presumed line that falls from turning toward a Chicano codex. The Chicano codex is also a locus of revelation, whereby a people's sight is transformed and the world can be differently understood. An obsidian mirror does not provide a simple, correlative reflection. Despite a seeming emphasis on "originality," Moraga also accentuates the plurality of the scribes and faces that can be seen in an "obsidian mirror," thus undercutting any simple drive toward a unity of codices or people interacting with them.

To imagine the Chicanx codex as an obsidian mirror that offers an imperfect reflection also speaks to scriptures as orientation devices, but what happens to those who encounter scriptures in ways that deviate from the predetermined script? Especially in the case of U.S. history, what about the religious, racial, gender, and sexual others who, because of their relationships of power and construction within a broader sociality, of necessity encounter the Christian bible not for its orientations but for the ways that it disorients? Human socialities tend to produce certain alignments, and people will then feel out of place and time when they do not match up with the lines, especially the "straight" lines that have been generated.[26] Thus avoiding the term *scriptures*, Moraga employs the terms *codex* and *codices* as a response to racialized and heteropatriarchal histories of conquest; in so doing, she underscores how European scriptures have manufactured disorientation and unhoming for colonized populations.[27]

"Codex Xerí" incorporates the historical moments of May 1992 after the Los Angeles uprising following the "not guilty" verdicts issued for three of the four officers charged in the beating of Rodney King.[28] She takes up that one moment as a refraction of the legacies of competing scriptures and practices of scripturalization in the Americas. Both Spanish and U.S. settler colonialism wielded the Christian bible, albeit in different ways, in the subjugation of Chicanx populations. This subjugation was economic, religious, racial, gendered, and sexual, and Moraga phrases the interconnection between religion and conquest in terms of militarism, theft, and rape: "Our rapist wears the face of death. In a suit of armor, he rides us—cross in one hand, sword in the other. And this is how they've always taken us with their gods of war and their men of god."[29] She depicts a history of brutal and sexually violent conquest as justified and legitimated by a Christian religion that was also used as an orientation object along a path of greed.[30]

In her emphasis on the codex, Moraga foregrounds the scriptural logics of hemispheric American conquest as bound with other dominating practices.[31] European conquest of the Americas often relied on a patriarchal and heterosexual gender binary construct, and indigenous systems that refused the binaries of heteropatriarchy were most often targeted for transformation so as to enable settler colonial domination.[32] Heteropatriarchy then not only becomes bound to settler colonial domination but then gets invoked in the very imagination of "races" as depending on certain strands of heteronormative reproductive futurity, tracked backward in time. Race becomes a product of heteronormative descent and reproduction.[33] Partially to counter this attempted eradication of native gender and sexual systems, Moraga traces the survival of *jotería* and "two-spirit" peoples among queer Chicanxs, invoking them as one of the many glyphs found in Chicanx daily life and drawn into her Chicanx codex.[34]

Moraga connects heteropatriarchal conquests of people and land to the conquest of sacred writings, and in this regard, she uses her essay to underscore how scriptures have functioned as disorientation and unhoming devices for the colonized peoples of the Americas. Moraga emphasizes codices, rather than scriptures, in her essay not only because of the exhibition for which she writes but because of the European antagonism to native traditions of "writing" that did not mesh with alphabetic scripts.[35] This destruction of Mesoamerican writings has entailed a theft of language leaving too many Chicanx subjects disoriented, lost at sea, and thus she describes Chicanxs as "Decapitated, our speech scrolled tongues float in a wordless sea. *How did we grow so speechless?*"[36] In order to disorient our assumptions about writing, Moraga's "Codex Xerí" renames the Latin alphabet as "Roman hieroglyphs" so as to undercut the ways that the Latin alphabet became "script" while the Spanish construed Mesoamerican writings as idolatrous pictures, as icons and hieroglyphs, and not script.[37]

A Chicanx codex then remembers tragic histories of unhoming and disorientation that have been elided in other texts. She casts the Chicanx codex as a record of disorientation and a mandate for transformation: "The Chicano codex is a demand for retribution—retribution for land and lives lost. Our records show the sum of Chicano existence engraved on tombstones: World War I, World War II, Korea, Vietnam, Iraq. Our records show a five-century-long list of tributes paid to illegal landlords."[38] She casts the lives lost of disoriented bodies as objects of tribute, but she also connects such tribute to larger histories of displacement within the land, the ways that Chicanxs have been made distant from lands they viewed as their own.

While the Chicanx codex supplies a record of disorientation, Moraga constructs the Chicanx codex as a disorientation device in relationship to dominant cultural narratives and norms. Its serpentine structure is not only unsettling for the reader trained in Euro-North American literary modes, but the varying "glyphs" that she narrates within the Chicanx codex directly challenge and contradict other scripturalized narratives in dominant U.S. mythology; specifically, she takes on Manifest Destiny by promising that another destiny awaits the New World, something other than the promise of everlasting U.S. civilization. Referencing the Nahua expression for writing, *in tlilli, in tlapalli* (the black, the red),[39] she scripturalizes her contemporary moment of crisis under the Los Angeles rebellion as a glyph in the promise of destined transformation that undoes Manifest Destiny's claim on the southwestern United States: "Amid the fires of the Los Angeles Rebellion, on the eve of a fading Quinto Sol and a rising new época, I paint in scribe colors—the black of this ink, the red of those fires—my own Chicano codex. I offer it as a closing prayer for the last generation."[40] Moraga names the Aztec myth of the "Fifth Sun," which, especially within Chicanx interpretations of Nahua thought, refers to the view that there have been four prior cycles of creation and destruction before the current universe (the fifth sun). Some day the fifth sun will cease and the gods will destroy this present creation and begin anew, a sort of apocalyptic expectation within Chicanx cultural production that has often acted as a prophetic promise that the current unjust order will be overturned as Chicanxs return to their "homeland," Aztlán/the southwestern United States. Having been a student of Revelation, I cannot help but recoil at the resonant images contained in the promise of destruction that will be visited on a dominating empire so that its colonized people will have justice.

Even as her use of the Aztec myth of the fifth sun resonates with biblical Revelation, Moraga casts Mesoamerican texts and prophecies as disorientation devices that conflict with the colonizers' bibles: "Half a millennium after the arrival of Columbus, the Mesoamerican prophecies are being fulfilled. The enslaved have taken to the streets, burning down the conqueror's golden cities."[41] In further describing Los Angeles as one of these burning cities, Moraga allusively conflates Revelation's Babylon and new Jerusalem in her description, drawing from Revelation 17–22. Moraga's cities of gold sound like the new Jerusalem (Rv 21:21 describes the city's golden streets), a city which belongs to "those who conquer" (21:7) even while the city is full of God's enslaved worshippers (22:3). She further describes Los Angeles as a "temple," and some readings of the new Jerusalem suggest that the city is itself a temple, and thus it has no temple inside.[42] Moraga's temple, however, now "is falling into flames."[43] Though the conquerors' cities sound like the new Jerusalem, Moraga prophesies their destruction, in part because they are cities of exploitative trade, economic abuse, and human enslavement, and the crimes of these cities sound like the wares of Babylon (18:11–13).[44] The new Jerusalem is not a simple ideal utopia, but instead another source of human misery amid practices of conquest; Moraga does not draw any utopian aspiration from biblical imagery, and she only draws on the Christian bible allusively, never quoting it directly. Thus her codex promises disorientation to readers who presume the sole supremacy of the Christian bible and certain ways of reading it. She both trades on the power of John's Apocalypse and displaces its power as being on equal terrain with other scriptures when she claims, "The Chicano codex is *our* book of revelation."[45]

## SCRIPTURAL DISORIENTATIONS AS HOMING PROCESSES

In playing with the Apocalypse and other sources of disorienting revelation as she does, Moraga calls for a relationship to scriptures that is far more pluralistic in objects, slippery in spatial grasp, and fleeting in temporality; she models a counterapocalyptic[46] angle of approach whereby she embraces apocalypse, prophecy, and revelation, as a way of desiring an altered futurity and a recuperation of subjugated historical memory and knowledge. She comes to construe revelation differently as a process of mixed and ambiguous disorientation. Because of the uprising in and burning of Los Angeles, Moraga also imagines the possibilities of revolution: "The Chicano scribe remembers, not out of nostalgia but out of hope. She remembers in order to envision. She looks backward in order to look forward to a world founded not on greed, but on respect for the sovereignty of nature. And in this, she suffers."[47] Thus, such a counterapocalypse is not to embrace a straight and linear futurity, a futurity whose hope rests on "the presence that reconciles meaning with being in a fantasy of completion."[48] Instead, Moraga's futurity refuses such reconciliation or completion, rather hoping to sunder prior practices of meaning, remake new and lost memories, and imagine more hybrid scripturalizations.[49] Still, she emphasizes that all such practices entail suffering, including and especially on the part of the scribe.

To some extent, a consonance might be found between Moraga's sense of "revelation" and Ahmed's, because neither imagines that total truth can be grasped. Moraga's codex reveals a history of disorientation and also creates disorientation, but even if she hopes for a transformation on the horizon, she does not grant that transformation in the space of her text. For Ahmed, revolutionary sight, rather than completely envisioning a better world beyond a veil, actually reveals the veils that mask certain areas of our sight: "The veil is not unveiled to reveal the truth; the veil is revealed, which is a revelation that must be partial and flawed."[50] Some contemporary biblical scholars have tried to interpret the Christian book of Revelation along these lines as well. Instead of construing Revelation as the spatial, temporal, and economic compass of Columbus's and settler colonial mapping, a compass that proves disorienting and unreachable for Moraga, Harry O. Maier, for instance, contextualizes Revelation as a disorientation device for revealing the veil of social structures as they mask unjust power dynamics: "It is to read the Apocalypse as a revelation, not of what is to come but of present structures of domination and tyranny—as a revelation of empire and one's place within it."[51] Instead of the ways that Revelation has been read in the "exegesis of empire," one might approach the Apocalypse as a revelation of how imperial power circulates, even of how one participates in imperial power structures. Moraga's essay likewise describes imperial power structures, and the Chicanxs that live within burning golden cities, but she also provides an incomplete picture. She disorients readers into seeing the veils of imperial dominating practices, including practices of scripturalization, but she can never fully promise a world beyond such domination.

Minoritized communities also maintain their own internal structures of domination that Moraga seeks to expose.[52] In other essays, Moraga writes of how it took her years to come to the Chicanx movement because the seventies movement "was only deformed by the machismo and homophobia of that era."[53] She had to travel years "to bring all the parts of me—Chicana, lesbiana, half-breed, and poeta—to the revolution [. . . and she] found a sense of place among la Chicanada. It is not always a safe place," but it is her place.[54] In such a discussion she redescribes homing as a project of ongoing disorientation, where to find and make home is not necessarily to set things right, to come into perfect alignment, to feel "safe." Because such disorientation is part of being Chicana, a Chicanx sage must read obliquely and amid disorientations: "to interpret the signs of the time, read the writing on barrio walls, decode the hieroglyphs of street violence, unravel the skewed message of brown-on-brown crime and sister-rape. The Chicano codex is *our* book of revelation. It is the philosopher's stone, serpentine and regenerative. It prescribes our fate and releases us from it."[55] Here, writings of sacred power are often also violent acts between peoples, not idealized utopic visions; these glyphs represent messages that are "skewed" and that require a "serpentine" reading strategy.[56] Nevertheless, Moraga holds on to the possibilities of the biblical Apocalypse as a book of Revelation among others that can be accessed for disorienting effects, where such disorientations, for all their tragic histories, also make alive other possibilities for the world, also open up other lines toward and from scriptures, other relationships to texts. Such codices both bind Chicanxs and release them, and in this way Moraga models a recognition of scriptures as always ambivalent homing devices, where disorientation both entails colonial violence and new lines of sight, often at the same time.

In reimagining scriptures as codices, Moraga also moves beyond the written word: "The Chicano codex es una peregrinación to an América unwritten."[57] In using "peregrinación," Moraga conjures a sense of religious pilgrimage, again emphasizing "scripture" in the case of the Chicano codex as an orientation object along a path, but it also becomes the path itself. Moraga, in imagining the codex as somehow an unwritten pilgrimage, requires a letting go of complete mastery of meaning because some powerful glyphs will always remain outside any writing system.[58] The power of writing is restrictive and restricted because scriptures as written texts have hidden and elided lives for whom she seeks to make space.[59]

To move past a valuing of only the written word, Moraga constructs and imagines multiple forms of scriptures as mixing, mingling, coming together, and sliding past each other, in order to speak better to her own "hybridity of home," which, as Ahmed argues, "is premised . . . on the comings and goings of different bodies as they remake homes in what at first might feel like rather strange worlds."[60] For example, Moraga's scriptures incorporate more than written codices or scripts on barrio walls; they also incorporate a fleeting gathering of queer Chicanxs coming together in a memorial: "*In the circle of this oración we form a contemporary urban Chicano glyph. A small group of jotería, 'two-spirited' people, standing in the shadow de Los Pechos de La India (San Francisco). Two lush green mounds of female protection. A radio tower piercing her breast. . . . We sprinkle his ashes in the comadre's yard. . . . Y todavía we remember ceremony.*"[61] Here a gathering of queer Chicanxs in prayer and memorial transforms the ways that San Francisco can be encountered, and this one moment becomes a glyph of revelatory import within a larger Chicanx codex.

## SCRIPTURAL DISORIENTATIONS AND THE STUDY OF LATINX RELIGIONS

Moraga's emphasis on the glyphs that come out of a plurality of Chicanx daily lived experiences and Ahmed's approach to orientations can together bridge certain facets of queer theory and the study of Latinx religions because of a directed focus on the social objects and directions of daily life. Historically, Latinx religious studies scholarship has emphasized *lo cotidiano* (daily life) as a locus of not only Latinx theological reflection but also as the appropriate focus for much study of Latinx political and religious subjectivity.[62] Moraga presents her notion of a "Chicano codex" as "a portrait of our daily lives" but one that emphasizes the motion of low-riding or picking nopales or other fleeting activities; scriptures, no longer restricted only to the written word, thus become such daily activities.[63] Similarly, the theologian Carmen Nanko-Fernández constructs pluralistic Latinx identities beyond the hyphen; she describes how transformed identities necessarily are in a digital age, when "boundaries are porous" and we must read ourselves as "situatedness in motion."[64] The dynamic approach Ahmed takes to orientations can be brought to bear on the strategies and complexities of such situated motion.[65]

For Moraga, though, turning to codices that reflect such situatedness in motion requires a belonging in anticipatory disorientation, of squinting at the horizon, of finding such disorientation revealing, but of never fully glimpsing the world beyond the horizon, of never quite reorienting oneself out of disorientation. In this regard, the closing frame of "Codex Xerí" might be cast within the queer utopian horizonal squinting that José Esteban Muñoz describes: "It is an invitation to look to horizons of being. Indeed to access queer visuality we may need to squint, to strain our vision and force it to see otherwise, beyond the limited vista of the here and now."[66] Moraga traffics in the ambiguity of an apocalyptic utopia, both promising crisis and imagining that crisis prefaces revolutionary transformation:

> It is 1992, and we are witnessing a new breed of revolucionario, their speech scrolls are slave tongues unraveling. Feathers in full plumage, they burn down the Alamo, Macy's San Francisco, the savings and loan, and every liquor store in South Central Los Angeles! . . .
> *And we, the Codex-Makers, remove the white mask*
> *We wait and watch the horizon*
> *Our Olmeca third eye*
> *begins to glisten*
> *in the slowly*
> *rising*
> *light.*[67]

With phrases such as "slave tongues" and a Fanonian "white mask," Moraga is pointing to a desired transformation away from a system that has controlled words, faces, and actions through enslavement. Yet her Codex-Makers can see beyond the world of U.S. scripturalization, glimpsing and expecting an alternative. Her essay ends with the Codex-Makers waiting in a liminal moment before the dawn breaks, ever in a fraught space of disorientation, one that remembers and promises violence, a glowing sun rising, even as the Codex-Makers critique such violence and long for a world otherwise made.

Even while imagining a utopian elsewhere founded on something other than greed, Moraga wrestles with her embeddedness in the ongoing structures of the present, recognizing herself as a mixed race and intersectionally named XicanaDyke.[68] This attention to the intersection of her ethnicity, race, gender, and sexuality also incorporates an attention to the messiness of belonging and identities, a messiness that resonates with the Cuban American historian and theologian Justo González's identification of the non-innocence of Latinx histories.[69] At the same time it presses us to incorporate a wider sense of intersectionality, of non-innocence in the study of Latinx religions and scriptures, one that attends to the wider reach of ambiguity when sexuality and gender are examined along with race, ethnicity, nationality, and religious identification and practice. It requires that any study of Christian and other scriptures also asks about how and why a XicanaDyke like Moraga needs to quest after her own nonbiblical texts while never fully forsaking a conversation with the biblical material. Moraga has different questions for and expectations of scriptures than what has been common in Latinx theological writings on the Christian bible.[70] Even while trying to provide another angle of approach to scriptures, Moraga tends to ground her discussions in messy, mixed, unsafe, and painful realities of the every day. She does not idealize the paths that lead to or fall from any scripture, bodily or written. Rather, she imagines all scriptural messages as fleeting; the Chicanx codex can never be affixed to firm solidity.

Moraga offers up her "Codex Xerí" as a prayer and a journey into and with disorientation, as a way of viewing the world off-kilter in "the hope of new directions."[71] She suggests that to view the world so is to reveal a veil of the white mask, which Codex-Makers must remove if they are to see an altered sun on the horizon.[72] A blending and mixture of codices, old and new, reinterpreted and remade still comes down to a project of revelation, of perceiving behind and beyond a certain kind of veil to glimpse the other possibilities that linger at the edge of sight.

## NOTES

1. Cherríe Moraga, "Introduction" to *The Last Generation: Prose and Poetry* (Boston: South End Press, 1993), 1.
2. Ibid.
3. Moraga, "Introduction," 3. Moraga's delineations of the crises that inspire her essay also share some in the historical moments (especially the impact of AIDS) that fostered discussions of queer temporality according to Jack Halberstam. J. Halberstam, *In a Queer Time and Place: Transgender Bodies, Subcultural Lives*, Sexual Cultures (New York: New York University Press, 2005), 2.
4. Cherríe L. Moraga, "Codex Xerí: El Momento Histórico," in *The Last Generation: Prose and Poetry* (Boston: South End Press, 1993), 184.
5. As the scriptural studies scholar Vincent L. Wimbush defines it, "Scripturalization should be conceived as a *semiosphere, within which a structure of reality is created that produces and legitimates and maintains media of knowing and discourse and the corresponding power relations*. Although this structure is not to be collapsed into texts, in the modern period of history—on this side of Gutenberg—it revolves mainly around issues having to do with texts." See Vincent L. Wimbush, *White Men's Magic: Scripturalization as Slavery* (New York: Oxford University Press, 2012), 46.

6. Sara Ahmed, *Queer Phenomenology: Orientations, Objects, Others* (Durham, N.C.: Duke University Press, 2006), 9. Also see chapter 6 of my book *Revelation in Aztlán: Scriptures, Utopias, and the Chicano Movement* (New York: Palgrave Macmillan, 2016).
7. In the last two decades, different individuals and communities have developed various strategies for interrupting the masculine normative, gendered binary of the Spanish language (such as Chicana / o or Chican@ instead of the more classic "Chicano"). Throughout this essay, I employ the "x" ending of "Chicanx" as one such strategy that moves past gender binaries while also evoking notions of crossing. I use the masculine "Chicano" when someone else deploys that term.
8. I draw the term *reactivate* from the work of Damián Baca in order to illustrate that many of these Chicanx artists are not retrieving ancient Mesoamerican practices, nor are they employing the practices that many indigenous communities presently use; rather, they are navigating their own hybrid traditions. Damián Baca, *Mestiz@ Scripts, Digital Migrations, and the Territories of Writing*, New Concepts in Latino American Cultures (New York: Palgrave Macmillan, 2008), 79.
9. Marie Acosta-Colón, "Acknowledgments," in *The Chicano Codices: Encountering Art of the Americas*, exh. cat. (San Francisco: Mexican Museum, 1992), 2; PDF available online: http://butisitart.wikispaces.com/file/view/Chicano+Codices+catalog.pdf.
10. Cherríe L. Moraga, *A Xicana Codex of Changing Consciousness: Writings 2000–2010* (Durham, N.C.: Duke University Press, 2011), in "Prólogo: A Living Codex," locations 40–51, Kindle edition.
11. Moraga, "Codex Xerí," 190. On *tlacuilo* v. *tlamatinime* and the reasons that Chicana artists might have to conflate these roles, see Laura E. Pérez, *Chicana Art: The Politics of Spiritual and Aesthetic Altarities* (Durham, N.C.: Duke University Press, 2007), 26.
12. Moraga, "Prólogo," location 45–47. As Kent Brintnall observed, there are striking resonances here in Moraga's approach and Laurel Schneider's discussions of Vizenor and the import of storytelling and survivance. See Schneider's essay in this volume.
13. Sánchez-Tranquilino, "Feathered Reflections on an Aztlantic Archaeology," *Chicano Codices*, 4.
14. For an examination of some of the ways that other Chicana artists have performed codices beyond the written word, see Micaela Díaz-Sánchez, "Body as Codex-ized Word/*Cuerpo Como Palabra (en-)Códice-ado*: Chicana/Indígena and Mexican Transnational Performative Indigeneities," in *Performing the U.S. Latina and Latino Borderlands*, ed. Arturo J. Aldama, Chela Sandoval, and Peter J. García (Bloomington: Indiana University Press, 2012), 31–50.
15. Ahmed, *Queer Phenomenology*, 14.
16. For instance, as Ahmed argues, "orientations of the body shape not just what objects are reachable, but also the 'angle' on which they are reached. Things look right when they approach us from the right angle." Ahmed, *Queer Phenomenology*, 67. Also see discussion of "orientation devices" in Sara Ahmed, "Orientations: To-

ward a Queer Phenomenology," *GLQ: A Journal of Lesbian and Gay Studies* 12, no. 4 (2006): 545–546.

17. In using "Christian bible," I refer most specifically to the canonically divergent bibles of Roman Catholicism and Protestantism, which get inflected differently in many ways as objects and devices, but for the sake of this essay, I will focus on the shared assumptions about them in the contemporary United States. Bibles in other eras and in other forms of Christianity both share and diverge from how the "Christian bible" currently functions in the U.S. context.
18. Ahmed, *Queer Phenomenology*, 104.
19. Wilfred Cantwell Smith, *What Is Scripture? A Comparative Approach* (Minneapolis: Fortress Press, 1993), ix. For an emphasis on scriptures as loci for human politics, see Vincent L. Wimbush, "Introduction: TEXTureS, Gestures, Power: Orientation to Radical Excavation," in *Theorizing Scriptures: New Critical Orientations to a Cultural Phenomenon*, ed. Wimbush (New Brunswick, N.J.: Rutgers University Press, 2008), 3.
20. See Smith, *What Is Scripture?* 18.
21. Ahmed, *Queer Phenomenology*, 119.
22. For instance, on the import of texts broadly, Benedict Anderson has described the import of print media in the rise of modern nationalisms. See Benedict Anderson, *Imagined Communities: Reflections on the Origin and Spread of Nationalism*, new ed. (New York: Verso Books, 2006). See, for instance, the discussion in chapter 3 of the power of the printing press and "the origins of national consciousness" (39–48).
23. Sara Ahmed, *The Promise of Happiness* (Durham, N.C.: Duke University Press, 2010), 189. Following in this vein, James W. Watts examines three social dimensions of scriptures that speak to the ways that people map and have certain orientations toward and expectations of scriptures. According to Watts, there are particular angles of approach that get taken in relationship to scriptures, whereby they get treated in distinct ways as ideas and material objects: the semantic, the performative, and the iconic. James W. Watts, "The Three Dimensions of Scriptures," *Postscripts* 2, nos. 2–3 (2006): 141–42.
24. Watts, "Three Dimensions," 148–49.
25. Moraga, "Codex Xerí," 187.
26. Ahmed, *Queer Phenomenology*, 11, 15–17. As Ahmed argues, when people deviate from those alignments, they can feel "'out of time' as well as 'out of place' with others" (12).
27. Moraga notably does not use the terms *scriptures* or *bible* in an essay that concerns itself with the terms *writing, codex, scroll,* and *scribe*. By favoring *codex* so as to evoke Mesoamerican traditions, she invokes a non-Euro-normative scripturalizing logic for these devices.
28. Because I first drafted this essay after protests erupted in Ferguson, Missouri, in August 2014, Moraga's essay can still feel hauntingly timely although more than two decades separate the 1992 Los Angeles uprising from my present. Moraga's essay presumes that "history will have advanced well beyond the time of this

writing," but her own approach to temporal fracture, in that same paragraph, likewise suggests a sense that the timing of her moment would stretch, because her essay did not memorialize "a beginning," but the historical "culmination" of what "took 500 years of conquest to create" ("Codex Xerí," 185). The varying legacies and manifestations of those 500 years remain with us today.

29. Moraga, "Codex Xerí," 187.

30. Ibid., 188.

31. Such an observation about the power of the Christian bible, especially the book of Revelation, as conquest orientation device, in the case of Columbus and other Spanish conquistadors, has also been prominent in the study of religion. See, for instance, Catherine Keller, *Apocalypse Now and Then: A Feminist Guide to the End of the World* (1996; Minneapolis: Fortress Press, 2005), esp. 153–63; Jean-Pierre Ruiz, *Readings from the Edges: The Bible and People on the Move*, Studies in Latino/a Catholicism (Maryknoll, N.Y.: Orbis Books, 2011), esp. chap. 9, "The Bible and the Exegesis of Empire: Reading Christopher Columbus's *El libro de las profecías*"; and David A. Sánchez, *From Patmos to the Barrio: Subverting Imperial Myths* (Minneapolis: Fortress Press, 2008), 47–82.

32. Andrea Smith, "Queer Theory and Native Studies: The Heteronormativity of Settler Colonialism," *GLQ: A Journal of Lesbian and Gay Studies* 16, nos. 1–2 (2010): 61.

33. See Ahmed's discussion of genealogy as "a straightening device" and myths of racial kinship and family resemblance (Ahmed, *Queer Phenomenology*, 122).

34. Moraga, "Codex Xerí," 189.

35. Ibid., 185. Forms of representing language existed among various populations indigenous to the Americas and sub-Saharan Africa. Yet their rituals around writing and their nonalphabetic scripts often diverged significantly from European orientations toward writing. Labeling these populations as "nonliterate," in the case of Mesoamerica, Spanish conquerors burned their writings as idolatrous, something Moraga discusses in her introduction to *The Last Generation*. See Walter D. Mignolo, "Signs and Their Transmission: The Question of the Book in the New World," in *Writing without Words: Alternative Literacies in Mesoamerica and the Andes*, ed. Elizabeth Hill Boone and Walter D. Mignolo (Durham, N.C.: Duke University Press, 1994), 220–70.

36. Moraga, "Codex Xerí," 184.

37. Ibid., 185.

38. Ibid., 187.

39. Or, as Baca would translate it, "the black ink, the red ink." See Baca, *Scripts*, 69.

40. Moraga, "Codex Xerí," 184.

41. Ibid., 185.

42. Consider how the new Jerusalem is connected to temple imagery in 3:12, and how the new Jerusalem's layout mimics idealized descriptions of the holy of holies. Celia Deutsch parallels the new Jerusalem with descriptions of the cubic shape of the Holy of Holies in 1 Kgs 6:20; 2 Chr 3:8–9; and Ez 41:21; 43:16; 45:1; 48:20. See Celia Deutsch, "Transformation of Symbols: The New Jerusalem in Rv 21:1–22:5," *Zeitschrift für die neutestamentliche Wissenschaft und die Kunde der älteren Kirche* 78, no. 1–2 (1987): 113.

43. Moraga, "Codex Xerí," 186 (see also 191). In Gil Cuadros's *City of God* (San Francisco: City Lights, 1994), he also employs revelatory imagery. Since Cuadros fell to the AIDS epidemic in the early 1990s and only ever published this one collection, his *City of God* has held a certain prominence in the study of queer Chicanx literature. Cuadros also depicts Los Angeles in much the same terms as Moraga here. The last essay in Cuadros's prose section, titled "Sight," also plays on notions of seeking revelation in reading "some ancient script," revelations that are a consequence of AIDS (93). He concludes that essay by invoking the veil of revelation and the connection between veils and endings: "But I have come to the end, thoughts of the world seem woven of thread, thinly disguised, a veil. I let the angels consume me, each one biting into my body, until nothing is left, nothing but a small glow and even that begins to perish" (99).
44. In an interpretive parallel to Moraga's here, Dagoberto Ramírez Fernández argues that economic cruelty causes and determines Babylon's downfall. Dagoberto Ramírez Fernández, "The Judgment of God on the Multinationals: Revelation 18," in *Subversive Scriptures: Revolutionary Readings of the Christian Bible in Latin America*, ed. Leif E. Vaage (Valley Forge, Pa.: Trinity Press International, 1997), 97.
45. Moraga, "Codex Xerí," 190.
46. For a discussion of the idea of "counterapocalypse," which "recognizes itself as a kind of apocalypse" that also "will try to interrupt the habit," see Keller, *Apocalypse*, 19.
47. Moraga, "Codex Xerí," 190.
48. Lee Edelman, *No Future: Queer Theory and the Death Drive* (Durham, N.C.: Duke University Press, 2004), 114.
49. As Rudy V. Busto observes about another of Moraga's essays, she also plays with Aztec myths in order to subvert some of their heteronormative and patriarchal history and deployment. She turns to them in hybridized ways that can be identified with the nahuatl concept of *nepantla* as a "middling" form of religiosity crafting itself between and amid different worlds. See Rudy V. Busto, "The Predicament of *Nepantla*: Chicano(a) Religions in the Twenty-First Century," in *New Horizons in Hispanic/Latino(a) Theology*, ed. Benjamín Valentín (Cleveland: Pilgrim Press, 2003), 238–49, esp. 243–49.
50. Ahmed, *Promise*, 166.
51. Harry O. Maier, *Apocalypse Recalled: The Book of Revelation after Christendom* (Minneapolis: Fortress Press, 2002), 37–38.
52. Another work of Chicanx literature that draws on Revelation in order to wrestle with internalized structures of domination is John Rechy's novel *Our Lady of Babylon* (New York: Arcade, 1996). In Rechy's novel, a woman (generally identified as "Lady" in the novel) is falsely accused of murdering her husband at her wedding, and, especially because of the involvement of the Roman Catholic hierarchy, she is labeled "a whore." In her escape into hiding, the Lady begins to have haunting dreams of various women from the Christian bible and other myths, especially women who have somehow been labeled as "traitorous whores," with Eve and Babylon as two prime biblical examples. In the case of Babylon, Rechy presents her

as a Roman streetwalker rather than a wealthy courtesan, and more than that, she is only a "whore" because John of Patmos continually constructs her as such (as a biblical scholarly parallel here, for instance, see the discussion in Jennifer A. Glancy and Stephen D. Moore, "How Typical a Roman Prostitute Is Revelation's 'Great Whore'?" *Journal of Biblical Literature* 130, no. 3 [2011]: 551–69, esp. 555). As Babylon, in much biblical reading, becomes an ambivalent, "genderqueer, statusqueer" figure in Revelation that readers both desire and revile, Rechy flips that script around, making John of Patmos into the ambivalent, queer object of desire and revulsion as seen through Babylon's eyes. For discussion of the ambivalence of desiring and reviling Babylon, see Erin Runions, *The Babylon Complex: Theopolitical Fantasies of War, Sex, and Sovereignty* (New York: Fordham University Press, 2014), esp. 238.

53. Moraga, "Queer Aztlán: The Re-formation of Chicano Tribe," in *Last Generation*, 156.
54. Ibid., 146–47. The import of constructing places of belonging more as shared disorientation than "safe space" also occurs in Gil Cuadros's short story "Unprotected," in *City of God*, 59–70. I came to this sense of the import of mixed rather than "safe spaces" through Julie Avril Minich's analysis of Cuadros in her conference paper, "Whose Aztlán? HIV/AIDS and Gil Cuadros's Decolonial Imaginary," which she retitled as "Aztlán Unprotected: Reading Gil Cuadros in the Aftermath of an Epidemic," in *An International Latina/o Studies Conference: Imagining the Past, Present, and Future* (Chicago, July 17, 2014).
55. Moraga, "Codex Xerí," 190.
56. Such a play with a serpentine reading state is also reminiscent of Gloria Anzaldúa's discussions of the Coatlicue state, a state of ongoing struggle and revelation with many different and at times conflicting angles of vision, a state wherein may be found "my thousand sleepless serpent eyes blinking in the night, forever open." Gloria Anzaldúa, *Borderlands/La Frontera: The New Mestiza* (San Francisco: Spinsters/Aunt Lute, 1987), 27–51, with quotations from 48 and 51.
57. Moraga, "Codex Xerí," 187.
58. Ibid.; and Pérez, *Chicana Art*, 6.
59. Moraga emphasizes the "unwritten" partially because much Chicanx history has been denied a place in writing. For instance, Richard T. Rodríguez explains how gay Chicanos' experiences often get eradicated from the written versions of life in the United States: "Chicano gay male articulations of experience, identity, and desire that forge a Chicano gay male consciousness do exist—and have existed—yet they take form mostly in nontextualized, noncanonical arenas." See *Next of Kin: The Family in Chicano/a Cultural Politics* (Durham, N.C.: Duke University Press, 2009), chap. 4: "Carnal Knowledge," 145/257, Nook edition. José Esteban Muñoz emphasized the import of gesture and ephemera in constructing "a queer past." See José Esteban Muñoz, *Cruising Utopia: The Then and There of Queer Futurity* (New York: New York University Press, 2009), 65.
60. Ahmed, *Queer Phenomenology*, 150.
61. Moraga, "Codex Xerí," 189. See also Ahmed, *Queer Phenomenology*, 106.

62. Although a number of Latinx theologians, ethicists, and scholars of religion make this point, perhaps the work of Ada-María Isasi-Díaz is the most cited. In her estimation, the focus on daily life requires an attention to complexity. Even while daily struggles are the bases of understanding moral, political, and theological agency of Latinas, such daily struggles should not be overly romanticized or idealized. See, for instance, her discussion in Ada-María Isasi-Díaz, *Mujerista Theology: A Theology for the Twenty-First Century* (1996; Maryknoll, N.Y.: Orbis Books, 2001), 69.
63. Moraga, "Codex Xerí," 188–89. The fuller quotation depicts daily life as filled with mixed and contradictory histories and trajectories whose meaning cannot be precisely pinned down: "The Chicano codex is a portrait of our daily lives. Images of spam next to a stack of store-bought tortillas in the family panadería. We are a codex of lotería and boxing matches. We pick nopales, graduate from college, are elected County Supervisor. We low-ride in East Los, bumper to bumper in minitrucks. We light candles at La Placita. *For whom do we pray?*"
64. Carmen Nanko-Fernández, *Theologizing en Espanglish: Context, Community, and Ministry*, Studies in Latino/a Catholicism (Maryknoll, N.Y.: Orbis Books, 2010), 35.
65. As the literary theorist Mary Pat Brady argues about Moraga's construction of the mythical Aztec homeland of Aztlán, Moraga's approach to codices looks to craft "a structure of feeling that would allow Chicana/os to formulate rebeldía, to resist the deprivations of the present. But for Moraga, reformulating Aztlán involves allowing room for contradictions, desire, and play; it also means formulating a concept of community and belonging (i.e., tribe) that does not maintain the structures of dominance (racism, misogyny, homophobia) encouraged by patriarchy and capitalism." Mary Pat Brady, *Extinct Lands, Temporal Geographies: Chicana Literature and the Urgency of Space* (Durham, N.C.: Duke University Press, 2002), 150.
66. Muñoz, *Cruising Utopia*, 22.
67. Moraga, "Codex Xerí," 192.
68. For instance, in Moraga's essay in *The Last Generation* titled "The Breakdown of the Bicultural Mind," she grapples with the complexities of desire and her own mixed-race descent as the daughter of a Mexican-Sonoran woman who also had ancestors who were San Gabriel mission Indian and an Anglo-U.S. father. Even after she revises the Freudian script of familial desire as desire for her mother, she also reconsiders other women of color she has desired and queries the extent to which such desire comes out of the warring selves of whiteness that struggle within her as an inheritance. As Yvonne Yarbro-Bejarano suggests, "Even as Moraga tries to evacuate her white privilege, there is a sense in which the whiteness in herself that seeks the Indian woman echoes the very system she critiques, a system in which whiteness desires and needs the dark Other to re-create and renew itself." See Yvonne Yarbro-Bejarano, *The Wounded Heart: Writing on Cherríe Moraga*, Chicana Matters (Austin: University of Texas Press, 2011), 110. See also her essay "A XicanaDyke Codex of Changing Consciousness," first written in 2000 and republished in *A Xicana Codex of Changing Consciousness: Writings, 2000–2010* (Durham N.C.: Duke University Press, 2011). Although that essay describes how she used to identify as a

"Chicana lesbian" so as to underscore the primacy of her lesbian identity, she now finds herself distant from a white-dominant gay and lesbian feminist movement.

69. Justo L. González, *Mañana: Christian Theology from a Hispanic Perspective* (Nashville, Tenn.: Abingdon Press, 1990), 39–40.

70. Fernando F. Segovia has provided a helpful tracing of some of the dominant trends among male Latino biblical scholars and biblically minded theologians that points out the import of "reader-response" approaches to Christian scriptures, while observing that for most scholars a certain authority is often granted to these texts, with Efrain Agosto and Jean-Pierre Ruiz representing the most significant departures. They both represent an approach that questions notions of scripture and revelation while privileging the import of the reader and the historical legacies that brought the Christian bible into the hands of Latinx readers. Fernando F. Segovia, "Introduction: Approaching Latino/a Biblical Criticism: A Trajectory of Visions and Missions," *Latino/a Biblical Hermeneutics: Problematics, Objectives, Strategies*, ed. Francisco Lozada Jr. and Fernando F. Segovia, Semeia Studies 68 (Atlanta: SBL Press, 2014), 1–39.

71. Ahmed, *Queer Phenomenology*, 158. As Moraga suggests, writing is about "hope." See "Codex Xerí," 190.

72. Moraga, "Codex Xerí," 192.

# ❧ Queer Persistence: On Death, History, and Longing for Endings

MAIA KOTROSITS

"The one thing we thought we knew for sure about infection with HIV—that it is invariably fatal—has become, in recent years, ever more uncertain," writes Tim Dean in 2008, in an essay called "Bareback Time."[1] Noting the changing timeline for HIV (at least for some populations) in the wake of new and very welcome medical treatments, Dean explores the anxiety experienced by some gay men as a result of the uncertainties around HIV positivity: "A sexual life story whose conclusion gay men dreaded but quickly came to know by heart has morphed, without sufficient warning, into a drama whose ending remains so unpredictable that some of us are left unsure about how to locate ourselves in it."[2] They experience, he suggests, an alarming sense of asynchrony. "Those who remember the early years of the plague, with its traumatizing images of healthy young people withering and dying, inhabit two temporalities at once: that of HIV as a surefire death sentence and that of HIV as a chronic manageable disease."[3] In the face of this asynchrony, Dean suggests that in the refusal to protect oneself from the risk of HIV, barebacking subculture constitutes (among other things) an experiment with temporal relations that, on one level, seems to resolve the question of the future.[4] But he also suggests that voluntary seroconversion is a kind of erotic haunting: "The point is to serve as a host for not only a virus but also another time, one that viscerally connects a body in the present to a period—and, indeed, a set of socio-sexual relations—in the historical elsewhere."[5] He claims that this hosting of another time is not necessarily or only nostalgia; because the past is perpetually unfinished, this self-conscious exposure to and hosting of another time constitutive of bareback culture "blows the future wide open."

I am less interested in the radical possibility of blowing the future wide open (at least for the moment) than I am in the suspense that seems less bearable than the prospect of certain death. "That awful waiting is gone," Dean quotes one man as saying on finding out he tested positive. Dean comments,

"The desire to seroconvert, to become HIV-positive—which appears unfathomable to most people outside the subculture—may be the clearest example of an attempt to resolve the anxiety-inducing doubleness of occupying two different time zones at once. To choose seropositivity—or to participate in practices that make seroconversion likely if not inevitable—entails a commitment to the irreversible."[6]

It is true that desiring HIV positivity may seem unfathomable outside barebacking subculture, but a sense of just wanting to *know*—a desire to end the terror of temporal suspense—is far from unrelatable.[7] Dean himself suggests another example, "Marriage, like barebacking, promises the seductive illusion that one can be sure about which temporality he or she inhabits; it offers an answer to questions that may barely have been formulated. Marriage, like barebacking, seems to make the future less uncertain."[8] If death is frightening, more frightening still is thinking that our future is unforeseeable.

I would like to pick up on this anxiety of temporal suspense and the difficulty of living without a foreseeable future—that is, the difficulty of living with inconclusiveness. Not exactly knowing how our lives might turn out in the end is, of course, a condition of being alive in the first place. But the pressure of suspense seems to take on a particular intensity around the perimeters of loss, trauma, sickness, and violence—in the duress of our extreme vulnerability, when we are decentered from our lives, or our lives are thrown "off course." This longing for an ending does not necessarily always or only appear as a longing to die, of course, but the fact that it regularly arises that way is significant. What could be more absolute an ending than death? Neither only metaphorical nor completely identical with suicide ideation, a desire for it all to be finally over—for something/one else to come and end not just our pain, but our waiting—is, I want to suggest, a surprisingly theological impulse. Put us out of our misery, oh Lord. And yet it is also surprisingly sanguine about the possibility for closure. Death means relief, conclusion, a legible narrative arc. The narrative impulse of longing for death is even underscored in Dean's own language: "A *sexual life story* whose conclusion gay men dreaded but quickly came to know by heart has morphed, without sufficient warning, into a *drama* whose ending remains so unpredictable that some of us are left unsure about how to locate ourselves in it."

In a similar tale of asynchrony and longing for endings, Mark 13 tells the story of waiting for the end of everything: "Tell us when this will be, and what will be the sign when all of this is drawing to its close?" (13:4) Peter, James, John, and Andrew ask Jesus, after he predicts the destruction of the temple in Jerusalem. Jesus answers with a long description of chaos, violence, and natural disaster. Families will be torn apart, nations will war, there will be earthquakes and famine—all of which will culminate in the disintegration and darkness of the cosmos.

The original question of "when," however, is not answered directly. "Not yet," he says. Then he adds that no one knows, only the Father (13:32). Be on your watch, though, he warns them. You do not want to be caught unaware. This entire chapter, often called Mark's "little apocalypse," is wracked with questions of time: not just when will all this disaster happen, but how long will it last? Oh, not too long, Jesus says. God will be merciful to his chosen people so he will limit the days of suffering, and he will gather his people together from the ends of the world.

However, this passage was written in a different present than the one presumed by its characters, as scholarship has long noted: The Gospel of Mark was written in the aftershocks of the Jewish-Roman war and the very chaos that Jesus is made to predict (*ex eventu* prophecy, as it is typically termed). The present or the near past is made to seem inevitable, predictable, an obvious development, at least to some knowing souls.

There would seem to be an obvious teleology inherent in this literary mechanism—the world has long been leading up to this climactic moment. Indeed this phenomenon often coincides with what has been termed "apocalyptic" literature—literature that envisions, broadly speaking, cataclysmic resolution to the world's woes. The true state of the world and the ends to which it will return are revealed.[9]

In fact, for a vision of the end of the world, the whole passage ends up coming off as oddly reassuring. Not only will there be restoration at this end—Israel will be gathered together from the ends of the earth—but it will come at exactly the right time (whatever that time turns out to be). "Learn the lesson taught by the fig tree," Jesus waxes. "As soon as its branches are full of sap and it is bursting into leaf, you know that summer is near" (13:28).

This apparently teleological bent does not quite win the day in Mark 13, however. The question of "how long" until they all die and Jesus' vague and vexing reply suggest both a sense of doomed inevitability and a terrifying lack of resolution in the extended moment in which Mark is composed, a lack for which a definitive course of history would seem to compensate. Jesus knows what, and how, but as far as "when" goes, he only really knows that the time will be right. "Learn the lesson of the fig tree." Yet earlier in the story Jesus cursed and withered a fig tree, that exemplar of propitious timing, for not giving fruit even though (as the story says) "it was not the season for figs" (11:12–14). Was the suspense of waiting too much to bear?

Mark 13 archives a survivor's frustration, the frustration of not only having seen too much pain, but having to go on afterward. Notably, much of Mark is written in what is called the "historical present"—a past event narrated in the present tense.[10] The practically emphatic use of the historical present in Mark paired with the temporal suspense of Mark 13 not only illustrates a fluidity between past and present or the queerness of time. It also represents a juncture in which the apparent queerness of time meets the demands of story. It is problem of *history*, in fact. To write history—to by necessity relegate some things to the past—is to long for something to be over, to impose an ending on it, even as we attest to its continuing pressure on us.

As a narrative, Mark garbles beginnings, middles, and ends. It is worth noticing that this vision of the end in the Gospel of Mark erupts in the middle of the story. After the end of the world, the story goes on, upending expectations of resolution at all, let alone "at the right time." In fact, the rest of the Gospel of Mark echoes Mark 13 in both its building toward dramatic resolution and its withholding of one. Jesus dies in a climactic fashion, but not only is this the penultimate chapter of the book (the story pressing on beyond that ending), but what is supposed to be the moment of his recognition is ironized,[11] and the final chapter hardly ties up loose ends: Jesus is not "resurrected" per se; he is "raised," the text says ambiguously, and he is notoriously absent.[12] The women who have gone to the tomb "do not tell anyone" and run away scared, leaving readers with at the very least a lot of questions, if not an overriding sense of dissatisfaction.[13] Jesus outruns death only to be poised between resurrection and forgetting. He can neither be grieved nor celebrated.

The Gospel of Mark includes several such moments of frustrated memorializing. When Jesus is anointed in Bethany (cf. 14:3–9), it is by a woman whose act is criticized by the disciples for its wastefulness, but hailed by Jesus for its prescience in preparing his body for burial. "Wherever the good news is proclaimed in the whole world," he says in a dramatic gesture, "what she has done will be told in remembrance of her" (14:9). Not only is the woman's act temporally queer (as a kind of anticipatory grieving), but Jesus' words subtly undercut what would be a more expected insistence at the moment, to commemorate Jesus. That is to say that Mark undercuts the very thing, according to the noble death tradition, that makes a martyr's death meaningful—the memory of the martyr carried on by those who follow after him.[14] Mark gives that weighted remembrance to a woman without a name—the painful irony of which has been thoroughly documented.[15] The woman knows Jesus will die, but "Mark" (regularly an omniscient narrator) does not know her name. Around the perimeters of grief, the question of who knows what can be unnervingly tricky, and the subjects of our memorials are often hard to pin down.

• • •

What happens when a story keeps going long after it should have ended? What might our longing for absolute endings, that historical impulse, tell us about time? Eve Sedgwick's book *Tendencies* closes with a frustrated act of memorializing compatible with Mark. Although the book is dedicated to the memory of Michael Lynch, Sedgwick's friend who died from AIDS in 1991, when she wrote the final essay—an essay about Lynch—she "thought it was going to be an obituary."[16] She is of course glad that it is not, but she repeats only a page later a similar sentiment: "When I decided to write 'White Glasses' four months ago, I thought my friend Michael Lynch was dying."[17] However this time she adds that at that time she also thought she was healthy. Since beginning the essay, she had learned that she had breast cancer. Sedgwick writes,

> Unreflectingly, I formed my identity as the prospective writer of this piece around the obituary presumption that my own frame for speaking, the margin of my survival and exemption, was the clearest thing in the world. In fact it was totally opaque: Michael didn't die; I wasn't healthy: within the space of a couple of weeks, we were dealing with the breathtaking revival of Michael's energy, alertness, appetite—also with my unexpected diagnosis with a breast cancer already metastasized to several lymph nodes. So I got everything wrong. (Sedgwick, *Tendencies*, 255)

Jane Gallop, in her own close reading of this essay, gives prominence to this disjoint—the coincidence of Sedgwick's "unexpected diagnosis" and Lynch's "breathtaking revival"—noting the difficult irony. Gallop carefully observes the many temporal markers in *Tendencies*, ones that do not always cohere chronologically, but instead produce a "twisting temporality" of which irony is a significant part.[18] Connecting the twisted temporality of "White Glasses" to Sedgwick's foreword in *Tendencies*, which states almost incidentally that queer is "a continuing moment," Gallop concludes:

> The unsettling temporality of "White Glasses" is, in a way, the temporality of the entire volume. Not only is it positioned as *Tendencies'* final essay, but something of its uncanniness can be seen in the dedication which opens the book. The text of the dedication reads: "In memory of Michael Lynch, / and with love to him." Like "White Glasses," the dedication has a double address—and a twisted temporality. The first line locates Lynch in the past, in memory; the second line sends love "to him," thus placing him in the indefinite future of reading. In the dedication, like in the uncanny obituary of May 9, 1991, Lynch is still alive and already dead. The dedication thus locates the volume itself in that peculiar moment, which becomes, as the Foreword puts it, "a continuing moment . . . recurrent, eddying, *troublant*."[19]

It is true that Sedgwick's essay and the entire volume of *Tendencies* are jammed with language both tracking and contorting time. But it interests me that this is also specifically an essay and a volume full of death and grief. It contains not one memorial piece, but two. Not only does the volume begin with a memorial dedication to Michael and end with Sedgwick's frustrated memorial to him, but speaking directly to the heaviness of grief and death on her work in general, Sedgwick begins her introduction to *Tendencies* with the heading "A Motive" followed by the sentence, "I think everyone who does gay and lesbian studies is haunted by the suicides of adolescents."[20]

Haunting and grief: If one might presume that these experiences happen "after" a death, Sedgwick suggests otherwise. Sedgwick cites the statistics of queer teen suicides, thus haunted not only by their occurrence but by their ongoing regularity—the intensive risk and real possibility of suicide among queer teens. She is haunted by what *could have* happened to her friends: "I look at my adult friends and colleagues doing lesbian and gay work, and I feel that the survival of each one is a miracle."[21] In "White Glasses," too, Sedgwick's frustrated memorial is not one in which she is deprived of the grieving that she needs to do, exactly: "I thought [this essay] was a good way to deal prospectively and perhaps lucidly with a process of shock and mourning about Michael's loss that had, indeed, already become turbidly disruptive in my life to a degree I found I couldn't share more directly with Michael."[22] Reminiscent of the woman anointing Jesus at Bethany, Sedgwick performs her own anticipatory memorial. She is *already* grieving, *already* disrupted by the loss of Michael, and she is only deprived of dealing "perhaps lucidly" with her grief, already in process. Instead of dealing lucidly, she finds herself maddeningly caught in the "opacity" of her own sickness as well as her friend's, and the tension of her illness and his "breathtaking revival": in other words, the parallel, if ironic, suspense of their unfinished stories.

Sedgwick is clearly beset with the specter of untimely deaths. But if queer is a "continuing moment," its continuity is (at least by Sedgwick's account) one that transverses death in important ways without wholly undoing it. It is a moment of grief that extends before loss. It is a moment of haunted survival: life that goes on after it should have ended; goes on haunted by terrible possibilities that never occurred, almost did, or still might; goes on despite itself and in the face of other losses; or simply just *goes on*. Sedgwick's queer continuing moment suggests a queer persistence of life that seems to frustrate her even while it is also sometimes "breathtaking" or a "miracle." Importantly, because although Sedgwick's "continuing moment" (what I want to call "queer persistence") is associated with miracle, surprise, vexation, and grief, it is not the same as narrative continuity. It is not about progression or forward movement or otherwise making one's way to an end because although Sedgwick's haunted survival drives her longing for endings, the queer continuing moment thwarts possibilities for lucidity and closure. (Mark, too, has its miracles and surprises alongside its vexations and grief: Think of the persistence of seeds against the odds and despite an incompetent sower in 4:1–9, the feasts for thousands that erupt suddenly in chapters 6 and 8, or the surprise of the transfiguration—the momentarily luminous body, no less precarious than it was before.)

Sedgwick's twisted temporality, a temporality embedded in her grief and rubbing up uncomfortably against her longing for endings, suggests that time is only queer against the narrative/normative demands of history. That is also to say that Sedgwick reminds me of what it feels like to do history: writing an obituary for that which, much to your surprise, is not yet dead; seeking lucidity while buried in the opacity of the middle. History is the work of dealing with "remains." It consoles in the face of life's exasperating and simply disappointing inconclusiveness.

In the wake of Freud and Lacan, we are more inclined to theorize death with regard to lack, and thus we are probably missing the ways we implicitly associate death with completion. But death is, in terms of endings, far from absolute, with its effectively endless and totally uneven ramifications. Even aside from death's ongoing impacts, death's narrative and theological function as the absolute end toward which we all tend (or are driven, as it were) interferes with some of the presumed radicality it has taken on as a concept following Freud.[23] The polarity of life and death and the associations of life with narrative, progression, continuity, and future, and death with annihilation and narrative impossibility, fly in the face of what we know about the ways that death and life are necessarily co-implicated (biologically, ecologically, politically, affectively). In an ecological landscape of agentic assemblages, to die is only to reinfuse and reassemble, to enter into new agentic assemblages.[24] In a landscape built on biopolitical and necropolitical regimes, one population's death is another population's future.[25] The dead animate (literally, give life to) the present in the form of haunting.[26] Death is only annihilation and futurelessness from the perspective of a single human subject. As Dean writes: "I'm persuaded by [Adam] Phillips's claim that barebacking involves a distinctly impersonal relation to not only the past but also the future ('Barebacking is a picture of what it might be for human beings in relation with each other not to personalize the future')."[27]

Proximities to and traumatized preoccupations with death have long been catalysts for queer theory. By now they have also become a knot of theoretical interest in and of itself within the field, most obviously in the swell of projects specifically theorizing grief, loss, precarity, trauma, and spectrality. Sedgwick's *Tendencies* particularly reminds us that affect and temporality, however general they would appear as themes, have some deep roots in this sense of hauntedness: queer theory's relationship not just to death but to the very specific and anguishing deaths of queer individuals and populations.

Contending with violence is a crucial dimension of not just queer theory, but also the Gospel of Mark.[28] Christian theology has so often historicized its triumphalism in the Jesus who is vindicated on the cross through the earliest gospel, the anxious and uncertain subtext of the empty tomb exchanged for a lightness unbearable in its own way. The Gospel of Mark, as a book written in the waves of grief after having seen not only dreams of Judean political sovereignty fall, but simply after having suffered the loss of too many lives, is not a charter for meaning and justice in the face of death. It is rather—not unlike barebacking or Sedgwick's reparative practices[29]—a reckoning with survival and a barbed flirtation with connection and possibility when meaning and justice collapse.

Having to go on is a privilege, and often a terrible one. I am reminded of how Ann Cvetkovich begins the introduction to her book *An Archive of Feelings: Trauma, Sexuality and Lesbian Public Cultures* with an anecdote about first hearing Le Tigre perform "Keep on Livin." She loves the song in part for how it musically represents the difficulty of surviving trauma:

> because it captures the way surviving can be as simple and elusive as being able to "taste that sweet sweet cake." I hear the insistent refrain of "you gotta keep on (keep on livin'!)" as part curse and part celebration; [Kathleen] Hanna's cry of "you gotta keep on" sounds like an impossible demand for survival, but when the chorus answers "keep on, keep on livin,'" it sounds like the cheer that can help sustain you.[30]

Cvetkovich, Sedgwick, and Dean highlight some very uneasy frictions in the project of survival that make the valorization and romanticization of either life or death feel like not just a strange bifurcation of intensely related phenomena, but almost beside the point.

Surfacing these particular "moments" in queer theory may seem quite heavy. But I want to suggest that we give some of this heaviness in queer theory its due, even if that heaviness may dampen the more sublime or rapturous experiences some of us have traditionally had with queer theory. That is not to make queer theory less compelling or necessary, of course. Indeed as the history and narrative arc of queer theory gets written, the palpable heaviness and friction of these moments within queer theory might provide us with a break from the dizzying and somewhat repetitive question "What is queerness?" or from the endless locating/diagnosing of what is "truly queer." It might be not only importantly relativizing, but a kind of ethical obligation as well, to give honor to some of the tensive, knotted experiences that typically get overwritten in overenthusiastic renderings of queer radicality.[31]

In addition, it may be likewise important to surface some of the theological impulses in queer writing, ones that are deeper and perhaps disavowed because of the serious historical antagonisms between (especially) Christianity and various forms of queerness. The Gospel of Mark is, then, an interesting foil for such a project since, as I have suggested here, the Gospel of Mark has a number of antitheological moments, ones that are also antiteleological, if we read it in the absence of later Christian presumptions about its meaning. As a text, the Gospel of Mark claims and undoes so many theological desires and longings. Its refusal to offer either promise or resolution at the end is profound and complicated, and thus Mark archives some difficult experiences, but ones that (I would emphasize) are not ultimately different or more important than Dean's or Sedgwick's.

Dean, Sedgwick, and the Gospel of Mark together suggest that although history may be written by the winners, it is also written by the survivors who have lost a lot, the ones making sense not of the past but of their presence, and their difficult place in the endurance of things—justifying, marveling, mourning, decrying. How we long to kill the suspense, long for a god of mercy to place us again in the story of our lives, giving us the ending we all think we deserve.

## NOTES

1. Tim Dean, "Bareback Time," in *Queer Times, Queer Becomings*, ed. E. L. McCallum and Mikko Tuhkanen (Albany: State University of New York Press, 2011), 75.
2. Ibid., 78.
3. Ibid.
4. Ibid., 76.
5. Ibid., 93.
6. Dean continues: "It may be startling to realize that the sense of relief following a positive HIV test result was common, if far from universal, *before* protease inhibitors existed, during a time when such a diagnosis was more readily apprehensible as a death sentence. Widespread relief at knowing one's irrevocable status—the relief of finally having seroconverted and thus knowing for certain the trajectory on which one is embarked—have been documented by clinical and sociological studies." Dean, "Bareback Time," 82.
7. A similar impatience is expressed in the question "How soon is now?" which is the title and inspiration for Carolyn Dinshaw's book on queer temporality. She borrows the phrase from the title and lyrics of a song by the Smiths, which expresses a lovelorn loneliness and frustration with *still* not yet having met someone. Dinshaw writes, "The sound of desire in 'How Soon Is Now?' is restless, but through this impatience even bigger questions press forth: is there any other way to understand time, or a *life*-time, beyond this vacant sequence of isolated, and isolating,

present moments? Is there another way to value waiting, other than as exasperating and without promise?" *How Soon Is Now? Medieval Texts, Amateur Readers, and the Queerness of Time* (Durham, N.C.: Duke University Press, 2012), 3. Although Dinshaw wants to envision another, less "desolate" way of experiencing "now," she (along with the Smiths' song) attests to an experience of the present as unbearably suspenseful.

8. Dean, "Bareback Time," 83.
9. Although I myself am not too interested in (or convinced by) categories such as "apocalyptic literature" or apocalypticism, preferring to simply entertain all kinds of visions of the end as psychosocial (and perfectly mundane) expressions of particular experiences and desires, there has been some really wonderful work on texts that typically fall under the heading of "apocalyptic," work that offers some nicely phenomenological descriptions of the texts themselves and the connective tissue between them. See for instance Tina Pippin, *Apocalyptic Bodies: The Biblical End of the World in Text and Image* (New York: Routledge, 1999), John J. Collins, *The Apocalyptic Imagination: An Introduction to the Jewish Matrix of Christianity* (New York: Crossroads, 1984), and Catherine Keller, *Apocalypse Now and Then: A Feminist Guide to the End of the World* (Minneapolis: Augsburg Fortress Press, 1996).
10. The Gospel of Mark uses the historical present 151 times, which means the tense strongly inflects the gospel. Just for comparison: The longer gospels of Matthew and Luke use it only twenty times and one time, respectively. See Ben Witherington III, *The Gospel of Mark: A Socio-Rhetorical Commentary* (Grand Rapids, Mich.: Eerdmans, 2001).
11. The moment in which Jesus dies has typically been read as a moment of recognition of his divinity or significance. The centurion's words at the moment of Jesus' death are often translated, "Truly, this was God's son!" This hardly suits Mark's larger sense of irony, however, and it does not make much sense given that Jesus has just cried out that he has been abandoned by God. I have argued elsewhere that the centurion's words should be read as consonant with the darkness and humiliation overriding the rest of the scene, something more like, "This one. God's son. Really?" The lack of punctuation in Greek allows for this reading. Maia Kotrosits and Hal Taussig, *Re-reading the Gospel of Mark Amidst Loss and Trauma* (New York: Palgrave Macmillan, 2013), 11. See also Dennis R. McDonald, *The Homeric Epics and the Gospel of Mark* (New Haven, Conn.: Yale University Press, 2000), 142–44.
12. Likewise striking for its sense of temporal suspense is one of Mark's major and more characteristic literary devices: *intercalation*, in which one story begins only to be interrupted by another brief story before the first one can reach its conclusion. The "beginning" of the good news, and the beginning of Mark's story of Jesus, is the middle of Jesus' life. This is obviously troublesome for the other canonical gospels, which try in their own respective ways to get as far back to the beginning of Jesus' story as possible. Even in its textual afterlife, Mark seems to be perpetually caught in the middle: Although the earliest written gospel, it lives its canonical eternity between Matthew and Luke. On intercalations in Mark, see G. Van Oyen,

"Intercalation and Irony in the Gospel of Mark," in *The Four Gospels*, ed. F. van Segbroek et al. (Leuven: Peeters, 1992), 2:949–74.

13. Testifying to this sense of dissatisfaction is a tradition of textual additions that just cannot leave that ending alone. Added to the inconclusive ending is the "shorter" ending in which Mary, Mary, and Salome dutifully tell Peter what they had seen, and the "longer" ending in which Jesus appears to Mary Magdalene and some of his disciples, commissions his disciples, and gets "taken up."

14. Mark's relationship to the Greco-Roman noble death tradition is recounted in Burton Mack, *A Myth of Innocence: Mark and Christian Origins* (Philadelphia: Fortress Press, 1988), 247–311; as well as Stephen J. Patterson, *Beyond the Passion: Rethinking the Death and Life of Jesus* (Minneapolis: Fortress Press, 2004), 39–67. Both Mack and Patterson build on the work of George W. E. Nickelsburg, "Genre and Function of the Markan Passion Narrative," *Harvard Theological Review* 73, no. 1–2 (1980): 153–84.

15. Most famously, Elisabeth Schüssler Fiorenza's *In Memory of Her: A Feminist Theological Reconstruction of Christian Origins* (New York: Crossroads, 1984), takes this unnamed woman for its inspiration. It should be noted that most women are not named in Mark, with the exception of Jesus' mother and the women at the empty tomb (Mary, Mary, and Salome).

16. Eve Kosofsky Sedgwick, *Tendencies* (Durham, N.C.: Duke University Press, 1993), 254.

17. Ibid., 255.

18. Jane Gallop, "Sedgwick's Twisted Temporalities, 'or even just reading and writing,'" in *Queer Times, Queer Becomings*, ed. E. L. McCallum and Mikko Tuhkanen (Albany: State University of New York Press, 2011), 64.

19. Gallop, "Sedgwick's Twisted Temporalities," 70.

20. Sedgwick, *Tendencies*, 1.

21. Ibid.

22. Ibid., 256.

23. The associations between sex and death, for instance, most notably and influentially in the work of Leo Bersani, rely on death's radicality to theorize the self-shattering potentialities of sex. See Leo Bersani, "Is the Rectum a Grave?" *October* 43 (Winter 1987): 197–222.

24. This is Jane Bennett's thesis in *Vibrant Matter: A Political Ecology of Things* (Durham, N.C.: Duke University Press, 2010).

25. Jasbir Puar argues that the upward mobility and limited inclusion of some LGBTIQ folks, on the basis of their alignment with certain normative-national goals, is deeply connected to the disenfranchisement, queering, and death of other populations. *Terrorist Assemblages: Homonationalism in Queer Times* (Durham, N.C.: Duke University Press, 2007).

26. This is implicit in both Dinshaw's "crowded" present and Carla Freccero's proposal of an ethics centered on both an "openness to being haunted" and recognizing the past's ongoing felt effects in and through us. Dinshaw, *How Soon Is Now?* Carla Freccero, *Queer/Early/Modern* (Durham, N.C.: Duke University Press, 2006).

27. Dean, "Bareback Time," 93.
28. Readings of Mark since the late '90s have been darker and less triumphalist, in general, than the bulk of Christian tradition, which has read the gospel as a story confirming Jesus' clear identity as messiah, the salvation of the world from sin and death. This is especially true of work emerging from postcolonial and empire critical considerations, but also true of scholars such as George Aichele, *The Phantom Messiah: Postmodern Fantasy and the Gospel of Mark* (New York: T & T Clark, 2006), and McDonald, *The Homeric Epics and the Gospel of Mark* (New Haven, Conn.: Yale University Press, 2000), who have picked up on more somber themes and complex moments in the Gospel of Mark. Before these books Mary Ann Tolbert's *Sowing the Gospel: Mark's Work in Literary-Historical Perspective* (Minneapolis: Fortress Press, 1996); and Werner Kelber's *Mark's Story of Jesus* (Philadelphia: Fortress Press, 1979) made an even earlier case for a less triumphalist reading of Mark.
29. In *Touching, Feeling: Affect, Pedagogy, Performativity* (Durham, N.C.: Duke University Press, 2003), Eve Kosofsky Sedgwick delineates (and, really, longs for) modes of queer reading that are not so bent on the "paranoid impulse" that is so characteristic of theory since the 1990s, particularly theory following Foucault. She borrows from the terminology of the psychoanalyst Melanie Klein, who contrasted the depressive versus reparative position, the latter being associated with "additive and accretive" impulses, and which is not necessarily some happy picture of existence. Giving camp as one example of reparative practices in an otherwise traumatized landscape, Sedgwick writes of the reparative impulse that "its fear, a realistic one, is that the culture surrounding it is inadequate or inimical to its nurture; it wants to assemble and confer plenitude on an object that will then have resources to offer to an inchoate self. . . . What we can best learn from such practices are, perhaps, the many ways selves and communities succeed in extracting sustenance from the objects of a culture—even of a culture whose avowed desire has often been not to sustain them" (*Touching Feeling*, 149–51). On Sedgwick's paranoid and reparative impulses and the Gospel of Mark, see Kotrosits and Taussig, *Re-reading the Gospel of Mark*, chap. 9.
30. Ann Cvetkovich, *An Archive of Feelings: Trauma, Sexuality, and Lesbian Public Cultures* (Durham, N.C.: Duke University Press, 2003).
31. Radicality may not be a political virtue, perhaps, as much as it is a positioning born of steep experience, anyway.

# Who Weeps for the Sodomite?

KENT L. BRINTNALL

*Flee for your life; do not look back or stop anywhere in the Plain; flee to the hills, or else you will be consumed.*
—GENESIS 19:17B

With the possible exception of Lot and his daughters, it seems virtually no one in the history of the West has obeyed the injunction not to look back on the fiery devastation rained down on the Cities of the Plain. Although gendered injustice most certainly appears to have played a role in the punishment meted out to Lot's wife, when one begins to rack up the shame, terror, anger, and hate experienced by those who have tried to discern—or think they understand—what happened in Sodom and Gomorrah, and to whom, and why, it may be that no one who has looked back has been left unscathed.[1] This compulsion to survey the wreckage carefully is more than understandable. As Mark Jordan notes in *The Invention of Sodomy in Christian Theology*, Sodom and Gomorrah are "a trope for divine wrath. . . . What happened at Sodom is not an exotic, foreign vice that cannot be mentioned. It is, on the contrary, a most articulate reminder of the consequences of rebelling against God."[2] The smoldering rubble cautions all who survived the initial blast to be wary lest sodomitic vice—whatever *that* might be—once again catch heaven's attention. After all, God may have experienced a change of heart after the flood waters receded (Gn 8:21–22), but there is no comparable record of divine compunction as the smoke cleared.

Jordan also reminds readers that although "Sodomite," in the strictest sense, "is . . . the proper name for the inhabitant of a historical city," it has been "extended metaphorically to others, who are counted covert or honorary citizens."[3] Given the disaster that befalls Sodom's inhabitants, religious authorities and political pundits across the ages have anxiously tried to ferret out Sodomites living in diaspora. And although it took several centuries before prying eyes caught a glimpse of sexual perverts among the charred remains, once such bodies came into view, it would be almost two millennia before anything else could be seen.[4] Given this calamitous history of identifying Sodom's actual and honorary citizens, sexual perverts have tried valiantly to adjust the gaze of those who fix their eyes on this desolation. Rather than adding another installment to the overlong series of efforts to name—finally, definitely, assuredly—the sin of Sodom, I want to think instead about what efforts to unname homosexuality as Sodom's sin can teach us. How might these important, valuable, life-saving efforts to see the devastation of Sodom and Gomorrah with fresh eyes help us think about the ways efforts to witness and remember catastrophe sometimes go awry? Although neither witnessing nor memory receive attention in his work, I am guided by Lee Edelman's *No Future* in this endeavor.[5] Best known for its vitriolic denunciations of the Child, reproductive futurism, and perhaps even the future itself, Edelman's work is fundamentally an attempt to identify, expose, and respond to the antagonism at the heart of the self and the social.[6] He understands the "ethical value" of queerness as revealing this irresolvable antagonism and its unacknowledged consequences. Pro-LGBT interpretations of the Sodom and Gomorrah story illustrate the dynamics Edelman traces in *No Future*: They seek to displace queerness onto other bodies without recognizing the violence of that gesture. I argue that attending to Lot's wife helps us see more clearly not only the dynamics of the biblical text but also the dynamics that inform the actions of the text's interpreters. If we liken the calamity of the antagonism Edelman analyzes to the catastrophe that Genesis 19 narrates, we may gain new insight into what is "gained" by refusing to look away—by trying to distance ourselves—from the destruction of Sodom.[7]

• • •

Since the Sodom and Gomorrah story is most likely familiar to readers of this essay and since my primary exegetical concerns relate not to the text itself, but rather to pro-LGBT readings of it, I forgo a recounting of the story here.[8] Even a word-for-word reproduction of the relevant text would do little to explain how and why Genesis 19 became "the most well-known, [and] certainly the most influential" anti-gay passage in the Bible.[9] Interpretations usually turn on the meaning assigned to the men of Sodom's demand that Lot bring out the visitors he has invited into the city and welcomed into his home, so that they "may know them" (Gn 19:5). Given that the Hebrew word translated "know" (*yada*) often has sexual connotations, and given that Lot offers the mob his daughters, "who have not known a man" (Gn 19:8), many readers have concluded that the crowd's demand is sexual.[10] The men's demand to have sex with the visitors coupled with their refusal of Lot's daughters as substitutes has prompted many readers to impute homosexual desire to the Sodomites.

Others note that the purported homosexual character of the sex is incidental; these readers insist that it is the violence of the mob's demand that is most significant. Insofar as sex is present in the story, it is an instrument the Sodomites intend to use to degrade and humiliate the visitors—and Lot.

Focusing on the Sodomites' hostility toward outsiders, many pro-LGBT readers have insisted the story should not be read as a tale about sexual morality at all, but rather as a denunciation of the degradation of the foreigner, the subordination of the other, the humiliation of the outsider.[11] The Catholic theologian John J. McNeill was among the first to connect the violence the story denounces to the homophobia the church so often practices. "For thousands of years in the Christian West homosexuals have been the victim of inhospitable treatment. Condemned by the Church, they have been the victim of persecution, torture, and even death. In the name of a mistaken understanding of the crime of Sodom and Gomorrah, the true crime of Sodom and Gomorrah has been and continues to be repeated every day."[12] Expressing a similar sentiment, but using more highly charged rhetoric, the historian Connell O'Donovan pronounced, "Let Sodom be the symbol of what heterosexism and homophobia do to us, like the Holocaust has become for Jewish people."[13] The biblical scholar Michael Carden argues that the history of homophobic interpretations makes it especially important to always think the inhospitality of the Sodomites alongside their willingness to rape foreigners: This story narrates not some general violence, but a specifically heterosexist and homophobic violence that depends on conceptions of sexual penetrability as a humiliating and degrading mark of subordination.[14]

Some authors quite confidently name homophobes as the "real" sodomites,[15] whereas others note the irony that homophobic readings have perpetuated the inhospitality critiqued in the story.[16] In *No Future*, Edelman identifies irony as a trope that reveals the inevitable excess of language, illuminating the impossibility of narrative closure and the difficulty of making definitive statements.[17] The willingness of pro-LGBT supporters both to interpret decisively this story's meaning and to characterize its interpretive history as "ironic" should strike us, at the very least, as odd. Recognition of ironic misreadings of the story should trouble the certainty with which pro-LGBT readers announce its meaning.

Although readings of Genesis 19 that emphasize inhospitality and violence may offer the best interpretations of the text, pro-LGBT readers frequently enact the very dynamic of othering that the story purportedly denounces, even when—perhaps especially when—relying on such readings to denounce homophobia.[18] As Carden observes, with its "thrill of divine retribution," Genesis 19 "appeals to the moralist inside us."[19] Or, as Nancy Wilson, former moderator of the Universal Fellowship of Metropolitan Community Churches, has observed, by focusing on inhospitality, gay and lesbian theologians have the chance to turn the tables on those who have been inhospitable to them.[20] The genocidal rage at the heart of this story is not—huge sigh of relief—directed at *us*, Sodomites marked by sexual perversion; it is instead—stifled giggle of delight—directed at *them*, Sodomites marked by sexual anxiety. It is *still*, however, a story with genocidal rage at its heart: a "lethal Hate Crime text."[21] As the theologian John Linscheid asks, "Do queer theologians, who note the rapacity or inhospitality of the city's inhabitants, unwittingly pitch camp with right-wing theologians who preach Sodom as the homosexual archetype? In both arguments we seek refuge by emphasizing our differences from those who were destroyed."[22] And neither argument, it seems important to add, grapples with the story's justification of the decimation of entire communities based on the wicked deeds of some of their members.[23]

Lest it seem that I am focusing on a formal equivalence where there is a clear substantive distinction—after all, rape, homophobic violence, exploitation of the poor, subordination of the immigrant all seem like genuine wickedness that deserve harsh judgment in a way that same-sex desire does not—let me present some specific examples of how this othering appears textually in pro-LGBT treatments of the Sodom and Gomorrah story. In *Stranger at the Gate*, Mel White relates his first encounter with the term "sodomite." The word was hurled at him in junior high when he confessed a desire to dance with another boy.[24] When he was directed to Genesis 19, he found "the story was as frightening as it was unclear."[25] It was particularly puzzling to White that anyone would think the story had anything to do with his confessed desire because a story about rape "certainly didn't apply to me."[26] Although this distinction between homoerotic desire per se and the act of rape is unassailable, White goes further: "If the story of Sodom is really about wicked, greedy, self-centered people who refused hospitality to strangers and even threatened to abuse them or to rape them as a sign of contempt, what did the story have to do with people like me?"[27] Although the amplified version of the question still distinguishes White and people like him from rapists—simply because they experience homoerotic desire—it also suggests they are not wicked, greedy, self-centered, inhospitable, or abusive. Although I would certainly want to challenge any idea that there is a *necessary* connection between homoerotic desire and such traits, I would also want to challenge any notion that homoerotic desire somehow immunizes a person from such dispositions. In his essay "Is the Rectum a Grave?" Leo Bersani offers a biting critique of the conflation of gay identity with progressive politics:

> Many gay men could, in the late 60s and early 70s, begin to feel comfortable about having "unusual" or radical ideas about what's OK in sex with-

> out modifying one bit their proud middle-class consciousness or even their racism. Men whose behavior at night at the San Francisco Cauldron or the New York Mineshaft could win five-star approval from the (mostly straight) theoreticians of polysexuality had no problem being gay slumlords during the day and, in San Francisco for example, evicting from the Western Addition black families unable to pay the rents necessary to gentrify that neighborhood.[28]

These comments should be kept in mind when reading Connell O'Donovan's "Reclaiming Sodom." O'Donovan suggests that gay men own Sodom, having paid for it with their blood. He proclaims: "Let's take back Sodom. Let's rebuild there. They always give us wastelands and we always turn them into music and gardens, full of our passion, desires, beauties." Positioning gay men as the victims of homophobic and heterosexist violence, O'Donovan conveniently forgets that we have perfected these skills of beautification—also known as gentrification—on the backs of other people.[29] The history of misogyny, racism, classism, biphobia, transphobia, and erotophobia—as well as domestic violence and sexual assault—within LGBT communities should serve as sufficient reminder that stories that seek to encourage kindness toward the stranger using the threat of God's wrath might need to be told loud and often to "people like us." And although it has been said ofttimes before, it always bears repeating: Even the moniker "LGBT" elides histories of violence and abuse. Gay men have hardly always treated lesbians (or other women) with respect; lesbians and gay men have frequently maligned and humiliated bisexuals, and far too many examples from historical and contemporary political contests show the frequency and ease with which lesbians and gay men will sever their ties with trans* folk to further their own perceived interests.

• • •

In *Our Tribe*, Nancy Wilson asserts that "gay and lesbian culture—or *sensibility*, if you will—include[s] the spiritual gift of hospitality."[30] By acknowledging that "not . . . all gay and lesbian people are angels," she signals an awareness that gay and lesbian cultures and sensibilities are all too often typified by distinct kinds of *in*hospitality as well.[31] When explaining how her congregation enacted this spirit of hospitality—by ministering to people with AIDS and people in prison—Wilson describes services offered solely to gay men. Some congregants may very well have perceived those to whom they ministered as "other," but these ministries, as presented by Wilson, are demographically narrow in scope.[32] The hospitality in question demonstrates the limitation, as noted by Tim Dean, of a Christian ethic of loving one's neighbor as one's self, which all too often gets translated into loving only those neighbors who resemble one's self.[33]

But Wilson's introduction of the Sodom and Gomorrah story is even more telling.[34] Following her observation that interpretations of Genesis 19 as a denunciation of same-sex desire rest on a superficial familiarity with the biblical text, Wilson describes an encounter with one of the homeless men who lived on the street in front of the church she pastored in Los Angeles. "A young, handsome man named John" approached her because "he'd seen two women leaving the church walking arm in arm or holding hands. He said that this bothered him, them walking down the street like that because wasn't it *against the Bible?*"[35] Immediately after reporting his question, Wilson situates John. "Now, mind you, this man was a crack addict and a panhandler who spends half his life in and out of county jail. He lies, steals, and is throwing his life away because he is sick with addiction. But he was morally shocked and offended by two lesbians he had seen touching each other in public." Wilson—not John—has moral authority. "I gave John a very short version of 'Homosexuality and the Bible.' I also told him I was a lesbian, and his eyes widened." John's confession follows Wilson's disclosure: "He looked over his shoulder to see if any of his buddies were watching. . . . [He] let me know that he had had homosexual experiences." John "was clearly conflicted," and while "sure God [would] forgive him everything else," he was equally convinced that God would not forgive this. Despite John's confession, which identifies him, at least in part, with the community on which Wilson's ministry focuses, and despite his obvious pain, Wilson "shifted the conversation" from John's concerns to what she thinks is important: telling him to practice safe sex and letting him know that free condoms were available in the church. "With that I got in my car and left [John] to sort it out for himself." Wilson reports that this "incredible conversation" stayed with her for days. Her ruminations were not about John's turmoil, or the accuracy of her assumptions about him, or whether she had responded with the appropriate level of pastoral care, but rather how "*amazing*" it was that "a poor, young black male crack user who long ceased caring about his own life, who has long since given up hope for anything but another day of survival and using, can *still* be shocked and frightened by observing two women breaking the alleged sexual norms of his day—and frightened by his own secret desires and sexual feelings" because of the cultural pervasiveness of a mistaken reading of a biblical text. If this is the charism of lesbian and gay hospitality in action, one might legitimately wonder what distinguishes it from the inhospitality that typifies homophobia.[36]

We can find similar—if subtler—tropes in work much more fully conscious of Sodom and Gomorrah's complex terrain. In his contribution to Ken Stone's *Queer Commentary and the Hebrew Bible*, Michael Carden engages midrashic materials relating to Sodom and Gomorrah. He calls to mind a young girl named Pelotit, executed by the people of Sodom for giving a poor man food. It is her cry from the executioner's scaffold that reaches Yahweh's ears and triggers an investigation of Sodom's wickedness.[37] Along with Pelotit, Carden wants to remember Lot's wife, given the name Edith in some midrashic sources. Carden highlights accounts that suggest Edith looked back on Sodom because she felt compassion for those being burned alive. Her turn was "an act of martyrdom, in protest against the genocidal dimension of the divine vengeance."[38] Fully aware of the story's "genocidal dimension," Carden writes his own midrash, "imagin[ing] an underground sorority of tribades . . . in the cities of the plain . . . in ongoing conflict with their fathers . . . , [and] a fraternity of fairies standing beside their dyke sisters" with Pelotit as their guardian angel.[39] She carries a sword, but it is only a prop. She does not kill; she only saves. In the face of God's wrath, Pelotit "rescue[s] every Sodomite who was remotely queer."[40] Although it is certainly satisfying to imagine this intervention that saves the queer remnant from the conflagration, why this limitation? Why does Carden not imagine Pelotit saving *everyone*? If even Carden—who acknowledges the problem of mass destruction at the heart of the story, who recognizes that interpretations of the tale can too easily be simple inversions rather than radical transformations, who worries about the allure of the story's homicidal rage—cannot reimagine the story more expansively, what does that tell us?

In light of Genesis 19's history, we should not be surprised at the treatments it has been given by pro-LGBT readers. Philo of Alexandria, the first-century Jewish philosopher credited by most sources as the first to name same-sex desire as the sin of Sodom, used his characterization as part of a larger critique of Hellenistic culture.[41] Carden identifies several Christian apocalypses that use Sodom and Gomorrah in anti-Jewish polemics, and highlights a passage from the *Acts of Paul* which contains both allusions to the sexual sins of Sodom and anti-Jewish polemic.[42] In *The Invention of Sodomy*, Jordan notes that some accounts of Pelagius's martyrdom rely on sexual meanings of the Sodom and Gomorrah tale to fund anti-Muslim critique.[43] Even without relying on contemporary examples, which are legion, we have ample evidence that the Sodom and Gomorrah story is like a machine for producing us-them narratives.[44] And, of course, this is how the canonical gospels record Jesus' understanding of the story. When sending out emissaries to proclaim the gospel, Jesus reassures them that if a town does not welcome them, "It will be more tolerable for the land of Sodom and Gomorrah on the day of judgment than for that town" (Mt 10:15; see also Lk 10:12). With this pronouncement, Jesus builds on the horrific judgment of Sodom and Gomorrah in the past and predicts they will be judged in the future. They *have been* decimated; they *will be* decimated. With this pronouncement, Jesus compounds the genocidal wrath of the original tale. Not only does he participate in the narrative's insider-outsider logic, promising that the outside will be destroyed, but he promises a hyperbolic harshness: The outsider will be destroyed in perpetuity.[45] Many pro-LGBT interpreters of Genesis 19 refer to Jesus' statements to bolster their case that the sin of Sodom should be identified as inhospitality, without also noting that Jesus' statements evince an insider-outsider logic that includes a promise that the outsider will be treated harshly, giving lie to the notion, along with many other "hard" sayings and apocalyptic fantasies, that any strong version of radical inclusion is the organizing principle of Jesus' ministry.

• • •

But it is ultimately Lee Edelman's articulation of the meaning and function of queerness that provides the most telling and trenchant perspective on the dynamics of pro-LGBT treatments of Genesis 19. In the opening pages of *No Future*, Edelman writes, "*Queerness* . . . figures . . . the place of the social order's death drive. . . . More radically, though, . . . queerness attains its ethical value precisely insofar as it accedes to that place, accepting its figural status as resistance to the viability of the social while insisting on the inextricability of such resistance from every social structure."[46] Queerness marks the site of that which must be demeaned, denied, excluded, foreclosed, negated, vilified, denounced, or resisted so that the social can cohere. Every social order requires a queer, and efforts to move the queer into the heart of the social order do not eliminate queerness; they displace it. "The *structural position* of queerness, after all, and the need to fill it remain."[47] Contrary to what several critics claim, Edelman is not arguing that queerness *is* the death drive, or that queers should try to *become* or *occupy the place* of the death drive. Rather, he is calling attention to processes of figuring—of conceptualizing, of representing—the social order's viability, and suggesting that we may realize something important about the constitution of the social if we accept, rather than resist, the notion of queerness as *ineradicably, irredeemably* oppositional. Rather than trying to show how regnant norms and ideals can be transformed, expanded, reinterpreted, or resignified to include particular instances and expressions of queerness, the figure of queerness Edelman champions may reveal that sociality itself is a form of, because formed by, violence.[48] Edelman helps us see that efforts to determine the legitimate, "worthy" targets of genocidal rage are still very much invested in genocidal rage. The desire to be spared violence is not necessarily a nonviolent desire.

By putting pressure on a representation that marks it as inimical to communal flourishing, by acceding to its figuration as eruptive jouissance—to an excessive, ecstatic, overwhelming, alluring, but not altogether pleasant pleasure—queerness exposes "the fantasies necessary to sustain the social order."[49]

Like the unrelenting pulsion of the drive that exceeds domestication in desire, a queerness that forgoes attempts at reconciliation with dominant mores exposes "the inescapability . . . of . . . access to jouissance."[50] The desire to quell the disruptive excess of queerness—whatever form or figuration it assumes—is fueled by the very energy that this desire seeks to quell. Jouissance, and its violent pulsions, Edelman helps us understand, will always out. Those marked as threats to the viability of the social—because of race, gender, nationality, political ideology, religious affiliation, sexuality, disability—may very well be able to make progress in showing how they can help support and sustain the social order, how their attributes, dispositions, virtues, habits, and desires are only mistakenly perceived as dangerous and disruptive, that their "otherness" depends on faulty perception. But, Edelman insists, the *structural position* of queerness will always remain even if those who are called on to figure this position changes.[51] Depending on one's political commitments, the queer may be the one who is perceived as other or the one who perceives otherness: Either can be the target of vicious repudiation as a threat to the ongoing viability of the social. In some narrative framings, the queer is the sodomite-as-pervert; in others, the queer is the sodomite-as-inhospitable-rapist.

When discussing how Scrooge in Dickens's *Christmas Carol* occupies the structural position of queerness, how he is a prototypical *sinthomo*sexual,[52] Edelman observes, "If, as the terroristic adage of our culture's long children's hour proposes, 'it takes a village to raise a child,' then, we might add, it takes, albeit perversely, a villain too."[53] By identifying a villain, by identifying the *sinthomo*sexual who embodies a disruptive jouissance that threatens the village's ongoing survival in some fashion, the community accesses the pulsive force and unsettling pleasure of the drive's negativity by reviling, excluding, and containing queerness—all under the cover of protecting the fate of the social order. The compassionate gesture to welcome Scrooge into the community of those who celebrate Christmas requires that Scrooge sacrifice precisely those traits that make him Scrooge. Similarly, the compassionate gesture of welcome to those struggling with same-sex desire into the community of those who celebrate the family comes at the cost of a "healing" that keeps such desires at bay. "That compassion can look like callousness . . . suggests that compassion and callousness differ only by *decree*."[54]

> We, the *sinthomo*sexuals who figure the death drive of the social, must accept that we will be vilified as the agents of that threat. But "they," the defenders of futurity, buzzed by negating our negativity, are themselves, however unknowingly, its secret agents too, reacting, in the name of the future, in the name of humanity, in the name of life, to the threat of the death drive we figure with the violent rush of a jouissance, which only

returns them, ironically, to the death drive in spite of themselves. Futurism makes *sinthom*osexuals, not humans, of us all.[55]

Lot's wife functions like Edelman's *sinthom*osexual:[56] a figure that reveals and exposes, a figure that helps others recognize the violent fantasy constituting the social,[57] not, of course, because she figures the pulsive force of jouissance—her transformation into a pillar of salt makes her an epitome of stillness and calcification, just the form of identity that the *sinthom*osexual seeks to undo. But by turning to look on the catastrophe occurring behind her, she necessarily directs our gaze to that cataclysm. In her rejection of the angels' directive, in her reluctance to move forward, she forces us to confront something we know but long to forget. Because the biblical text is silent about her motives, various sources have supplied them: She looks back out of grief for the dying, due to abject terror, because of sadistic glee, from curiosity. Lot's wife turns toward the cataclysm like Benjamin's angel of history, but she remains steadfast, refusing to be moved by the storm of "progress," resisting the desire to stitch together the fragments of catastrophic loss.[58]

Whatever her motive—whether it contrasts with the disaster's violence or is consistent with it—Lot's wife's look directs us to look: "Behold. This is happening. This happened. This may very well happen again."[59] But a look is just a look: It does not interpret, explain, intervene, prevent. A look registers and records; Lot's wife bears witness. By bearing witness without seeking to understand, Lot's wife does not draw a boundary around the catastrophe thereby limiting it to a specific moment, population, or code of justice. She compels us instead to remember the cataclysm itself, in all its horror, rather than moving immediately to justification's domestication. Lot's wife's look connects her—either through compassion or cruelty—to the calamity befalling the Cities on the Plain. And through her look we risk being (re)connected to the Sodomites. She is indelibly marked by the calamity, but she bears this mark because she decides—for whatever reason—to remain intimately involved in the eruptive apocalypse ravaging her former townspeople, friend and foe alike.[60] Like the *sinthom*osexual, and quite unlike the pro-LGBT interpreters of this story, Lot's wife reveals—by bearing witness to, by memorializing, in perpetuity—the catastrophic violence that forges communities.[61]

In addition to observations about how towns inhospitable to those proclaiming the gospel will fare on the day of judgment, the gospel of Luke ascribes another reference to Sodom and Gomorrah to Jesus' teaching. When telling his disciples about the coming of the Son of Man, Jesus likens it to the "days of Lot" (Lk 17:28). Jesus emphasizes the speed and unexpectedness with which this coming will occur and notes that people must be ready to abandon their belongings and not turn back. "Remember Lot's wife," he tells them, and then immediately adds, "Those who try to make their life secure will lose it, but those who lose their life will keep it" (Lk 17:32–33). Just as his wife looked back, Lot "lingered" after learning about Sodom's imminent destruction (Gn 19:16). And although he fled without looking back, he pled with the angels to let him retreat to a place other than the one they originally indicated so that he could save his life (Gn 19:20).

After what fashion, then, does Jesus want his disciples to remember Lot's wife? Is she the moral failure who turns back or the moral exemplar who willingly loses her life to reveal, like Jesus, what the coming of God looks like? Or does the question itself—insofar as it wants to sort the world into moral failures and moral exemplars, into those who deserve the wrath of God and those who do not—repeat the dynamic I have examined here?

As Edelman notes in his dialogue with Lauren Berlant, "Queerness . . . is . . . an ongoing effort of divestiture, a practice of undoing."[62] As Carden notes in his queer midrashic ruminations, Lot's wife's self-erasure "sets up the situation" for Lot's daughters to ply him with wine and have sex with him thus "initiat[ing] the line of the Messiah. The Messiah comes from Sodom, and Edith's looking back is a messianic moment."[63] And as Jesus is remembered to insist, messianic moments, like Lot's wife's looking back or his own execution, will always be typified by great suffering and violence (cf. Mk 8:29–36). Pro-LGBT interpreters of the Sodom and Gomorrah story, like Lot, seek to save their lives by fleeing the conflagration and shifting the figural burden of sodomy elsewhere. Lot's wife, like Edelman's *sinthom*osexual, casts her lot with the Sodomites in order to bear witness to the catastrophic violence that overwhelms them.[64] Pro-LGBT interpreters of the story operate as if it is sufficient to show that they are not the targets of divine wrath; Lot's wife takes on the impossible, queer task of opposing the divine will by succumbing—and thereby bearing witness—to its devastatingly arbitrary excess.

## NOTES

1. For an argument that the Hebrew text does not support a reading that Lot's wife turned into a pillar of salt, but rather that she looked as the plain itself turned into salt, see Yehuda Sama, "The Salt Saga: Lot's Wife or Sodom Itself," *Nachalah* 1 (1999): 75–84. As part of his argument, Sama explains that Lot also disobeyed the angels' directives and received no punishment; therefore, we should be reluctant to read a different fate for Lot's wife (77).
2. Mark D. Jordan, *The Invention of Sodomy in Christian Theology* (Chicago: University of Chicago Press, 1997), 32.
3. Ibid., 6.
4. Most authorities credit the first-century Jewish philosopher Philo with naming same-sex desire as the sin of Sodom. Derrick Sherwin Bailey's *Homosexuality and*

*the Western Christian Tradition* (London: Longmans, Green, 1955) is cited as one of the first modern sources to challenge this interpretation and (re)assert that the sin of Sodom is, in fact, inhospitality. For histories of the interpretation of the Sodom and Gomorrah story, see Michael Carden, *Sodomy: A History of a Christian Biblical Myth* (London: Equinox, 2004); Bryan Fone, *Homophobia: A History* (New York: Picador, 2000), 75–110; and Jordan, *Invention of Sodomy*, 29–44.

5. Lee Edelman, *No Future: Queer Theory and the Death Drive* (Durham, N.C.: Duke University Press, 2004).
6. For a discussion of the antagonistic constitution of the self, see Lee Edelman, "Unbecoming: Pornography and the Queer Event," in *Post/Porn/Politics: Queer-Feminist Perspective on the Politics of Porn Performance and Sex-Work as Culture Production*, ed. Tim Stüttgen (Berlin: b_books, 2010), 194–211.
7. Edelman, *No Future*, 3. For the use of the language of calamity to describe this antagonism, see Lee Edelman, "Ever After: History, Negativity, and the Social," in *After Sex? On Writing since Queer Theory*, ed. Janet Halley and Andrew Parker (Durham, N.C.: Duke University Press, 2011), 110–18.
8. Readers unfamiliar with the tale can find it in Genesis 18–19.
9. John Boswell, *Christianity, Social Tolerance, and Homosexuality: Gay People in Western Europe from the Beginning of the Christian Era to the Fourteenth Century* (Chicago: University of Chicago Press, 1980), 92. On the anti-gay history of the text, see also Bailey, *Homosexuality and the Western Christian Tradition*, 1; Carden, *Sodomy*, 5; Brian Doyle, "The Sin of Sodom: *yada, yada, yada*—A Reading of the Mamre-Sodom Narrative in Genesis 18–19," *Theology & Sexuality* 9 (1998): 86; George R. Edwards, *Gay/Lesbian Liberation: A Biblical Perspective* (New York: Pilgrim Press, 1984), 24; Fone, *Homophobia*, 81; Victor Paul Fumish, "The Bible and Homosexuality: Reading the Texts in Context," in *Homosexuality in the Church: Both Sides of the Debate*, ed. Jeffrey S. Siker (Louisville, Ky.: Westminster John Knox Press, 1994), 19; Robert Goss, *Queering Christ: Beyond Jesus Acted Up* (Cleveland: Pilgrim Press, 2002), 193; John J. McNeill, *The Church and the Homosexual*, rev. ed. (Boston: Beacon Press, 1988), 42; and Jay Michaelson, *God vs. Gay? The Religious Case for Equality* (Boston: Beacon Press, 2011), 67. Despite this history, one marker of a certain kind of progress is that when I teach this story in various contexts, it takes some work to convince even my students with conservative theological views that it has been read to condemn homosexuality.
10. For interpretive approaches that challenge a sexual reading of the story, see Bailey, *Homosexuality*, 3; Boswell, *Christianity*, 93–94; Doyle, "Sin of Sodom"; and Martti Nissinen, *Homoeroticism in the Biblical World: A Historical Perspective*, trans. Kirsi Stjerna (Minneapolis: Fortress Press, 2004), 45–49.
11. Boswell, *Christianity*, 93; Fone, *Homophobia*, 81; Goss, *Queering Christ*, 193; Michaelson, *God vs. Gay?* 68; Michael S. Piazza, *Gay by God: How to Be Lesbian or Gay and Christian* (Dallas: Sources of Hope, 2008), 38; Matthew Vines, *God and the Gay Christian: The Biblical Case in Support of Same-Sex Relationships* (New York: Convergent Books, 2014), 64; and Nancy Wilson, *Our Tribe: Queer Folks, God, Jesus, and the Bible* (San Francisco: Harper Collins, 1995), 167. This reading takes its cue from Ezekiel 16:49–50:

"This was the guilt of your sister Sodom: she and her daughters had pride, excess of food, and prosperous ease, but did not aid the poor and needy. They were haughty, and did abominable things before me; therefore I removed them when I saw it."

12. McNeill, *Church and the Homosexual*, 50. See also Fone, *Homophobia*, 81–82; and Mel White, *Stranger at the Gate: To Be Gay and Christian in America* (New York: Simon and Schuster, 1994), 39.
13. Connell O'Donovan, "Reclaiming Sodom," in *Reclaiming Sodom*, ed. Jonathan Goldberg (New York: Routledge, 1994), 248.
14. Carden, *Sodomy*, 13, 29; see also Holly Joan Toensing, "Women of Sodom and Gomorrah: Collateral Damage in the War against Homosexuality," *Journal of Feminist Studies in Religion* 21, no. 2 (2005): 61–74. For similar understandings of this relationship between inhospitality and rape in the story, see Edwards, *Gay/Lesbian Liberation*, 25–26; Tom Horner, *Jonathan Loved David: Homosexuality in Biblical Times* (Philadelphia: Westminster Press, 1978), 48–51; Arthur Frederick Ide, *The City of Sodom and Homosexuality in Western Religious Thought to 630 CE* (Dallas: Monument Press, 1985), 19; and Vines, *God and the Gay Christian*, 65. For an argument that revaluing penetrability and powerlessness is a mode of contesting homophobia, heterosexism, and misogyny, see Leo Bersani, "Is the Rectum a Grave?" in *Is the Rectum a Grave? and Other Essays* (Chicago: University of Chicago Press, 2010), 24–30.
15. Daniel A. Helminiak, *What the Bible Really Says about Homosexuality* (Tajique, N.M.: Alamo Square Press, 2000), 49–50; and Piazza, *Gay by God*, 39.
16. Carden, *Sodomy*, 196; Helminiak, *What the Bible Really Says*, 49–50.
17. Edelman, *No Future*, 23–24, 91–93.
18. Of the pro-LGBT engagements with Genesis 19 that I considered, only Letha Scanzoni and Virginia Ramey Mollenkott suggested that the passage could have any relevance for LGBT persons. "The only real application to homosexuals would have to be a general one: homosexuals, like everybody else, should show hospitality to strangers, should deal justly with the poor and vulnerable, and should not force their sexual attentions upon those unwilling to receive them." See *Is the Homosexual My Neighbor? Another Christian View* (San Francisco: Harper and Row, 1978), 59.
19. Carden, *Sodomy*, 15.
20. Wilson, *Our Tribe*, 167.
21. Stephen Sprinkle, "A God at the Margins? Marcella Althaus-Reid and the Marginality of LGBT People," *Journal of Religious Leadership* 8, no. 2 (2009): 68.
22. John Linscheid. "Surviving Fire: A Queer Look at Sodom," www.gayoldsouls.com/JL/Sodomtxt.html (accessed July 25, 2014). In *No Future*, Lee Edelman notes that cultural critics on the right and the left, while articulating different rhetorics regarding queerness, enact similar structural logics. See Edelman, *No Future*, 27–28. Consistent with both Edelman and the reading of Lot's wife I offer below, Linscheid suggests that a queer engagement with the story involves bearing its violence and refusing the temptation to shift either the violence—or responsibility for the violence—elsewhere.
23. For an argument that the text functions to show that, although God punishes wickedness, God also factors in individual guilt and innocence, see J. A. Loader, *A*

*Tale of Two Cities: Sodom and Gomorrah in the Old Testament, Early Jewish and Early Christian Traditions* (Kampen, The Netherlands: J. H. Kok, 1990), 41–47. Loader relies, in part, on the punishment of Lot's wife as evidence for this conclusion.

24. White, *Stranger at the Gate*, 36–37.
25. Ibid., 37.
26. Ibid.
27. Ibid., 39.
28. Bersani, "Is the Rectum a Grave?" 11.
29. O'Donovan, "Reclaiming Sodom," 240.
30. Wilson, *Our Tribe*, 167.
31. Ibid., 212.
32. The prison ministry's hospitality is circumscribed even further by a footnote Wilson adds to her discussion of how the prison refused to allow for a worship service for gay inmates: "I was fascinated and, I must admit, somewhat horrified to read in an issue of the *Christian Century* that a U.S. federal judge had ordered a federal prison to allow a self-proclaimed Satanist to perform Satanic rituals in prison. In our country, Satanists will get their religious civil liberties *before* homosexuals, apparently." Ibid., 292n15.
33. Tim Dean, *Unlimited Intimacy: Reflections on the Subculture of Barebacking* (Chicago: University of Chicago Press, 2009), 212.
34. The narrative I discuss in this paragraph can be found in Wilson, *Our Tribe*, 165–67. Eighteen years later, having had time to reflect not only on the events recounted in this narrative but her mode of recounting them, Wilson reproduced the passage verbatim in *Outing the Bible: Queer Folks, God, Jesus, and the Christian Scriptures* (Indianapolis: LifeJourney Press, 2013), 68–69.
35. Although Wilson characterizes the relations between her congregation and the people living on the street in front of the church as friendly, respectful, and even "symbiotic," the fact that one of these men would be surprised to find that the congregation ministered to lesbian and gay couples offers a significant challenge to her perception of the intimacy of this relation between congregation and community.
36. For a secular account of gay hospitality that is similarly unaware of its own inhospitality, compare Dean, *Unlimited Intimacy*, 189–90, with Kent L. Brintnall, "Erotic Ruination: Embracing the 'Savage Spirituality' of Barebacking," in *Negative Ecstasies: Georges Bataille and the Study of Religion*, ed. Jeremy Biles and Kent L. Brintnall (New York: Fordham University Press, 2015), 64–65.
37. Michael Carden, "Remembering Pelotit: A Queer Midrash on Calling Down Fire," in *Queer Commentary and the Hebrew Bible*, ed. Ken Stone (Cleveland: Pilgrim Press, 2001), 155–58. In some versions, Pelotit is Lot's daughter. Recalling that Lot's position at the gate possibly signifies his role as a judge, could we also imagine Lot sentencing his own daughter to death? Does Lot's condemnation of Pelotit remind us of the way that far too many parents react to their queer children?
38. Ibid., 165.
39. Ibid., 157. In *Sodomy*, Carden frequently notes the story's genocidal violence and even quotes Linscheid's "Surviving Fire." But in his quest to "detoxify" this story

for contemporary LGBT people, he never grapples with what it means to position one's self outside this genocidal violence. For attempts to understand Lot's wife by placing her in conversation with similar characters from Asian sacred texts, see Samuel Cheon, "Filling the Gap in the Story of Lot's Wife (Genesis 19:1–29)," *Asia Journal of Theology* 15, no. 1 (2001): 4–23; Mai-Anh Le Tran, "Lot's Wife, Ruth, and Tô Thị: Gender and Racial Representation in a Theological Feast of Stories," in *Ways of Being, Ways of Reading: Asian American Biblical Interpretation*, ed. Mary F. Foskett and Jeffrey Kah-Jin Kuan (St. Louis: Chalice Press, 2006), 123–36.

40. Carden, "Remembering Pelotit," 161.
41. See Bailey, *Homosexuality and the Western Christian Tradition*, 21–23, 27; Carden, *Sodomy*, 61; Edwards, *Gay/Lesbian Liberation*, 33; Fone, *Homophobia*, 87, 91; Loader, *Tale of Two Cities*, 86; Michaelson, *Gay vs. God?*, 71; and Robert L. Treese, "Homosexuality: A Contemporary View of the Biblical Perspective," in *Loving Women/Loving Men: Gay Liberation and the Church*, ed. Sally Gearhart and William R. Johnson (San Francisco: Glide Publications, 1974), 31–32.
42. Carden, *Sodomy*, 117–18.
43. Jordan, *Invention of Sodomy*, 10–11, 27.
44. Oddly, the one possible counterexample might be Peter Damian's *Book of Gomorrah*, which Jordan credits with creating the theological category of sodomy in the eleventh century. Damian's primary worry, it seems, is not about the sodomite "out there," but the sodomite in the church, the sodomite who is posing as a priest. In addition, Damian addresses the sodomite directly, trying to persuade him to acknowledge the enormity of his depravity. Of course, Damian is quite clear that he—and other members of his audience—are not citizens of the wicked city, so there is still a strong us–them dynamic in his diatribe's address. See Peter Damian, *Book of Gomorrah*, in *Peter Damian: Letters 31–60*, trans. Owen J. Blum (Washington, D.C.: Catholic University of America Press, 1990), 3–53; and Jordan, *Invention of Sodomy*, 45–66.
45. I thank Stephen Moore for helping me elaborate this point.
46. Edelman, *No Future*, 3.
47. Ibid., 27. See also ibid., 114–15.
48. In "Is the Rectum a Grave?" Bersani also attends to the figuration of queerness, grounding his argument in "an arduous representational discipline" that depends on homophobic constructions of gay male sex to "explode th[e] ideological body" responsible for homophobic, AIDSphobic, and male supremacist violence. See Bersani, "Is the Rectum a Grave?" 15.
49. Edelman, *No Future*, 7, 101; Edelman, "Ever After," 112, 114.
50. Edelman, *No Future*, 5.
51. Ibid., 27, 107–8, 114.
52. This is Edelman's neologism, "grafting, at an awkward join, the sounds of French and English, to the benefit of neither," that he uses interchangeably with queerness. Ibid., 33. It seeks to highlight how queerness figures the link between the *sinthome* (symptom), sexuality, and homosexuality in an incoherent, unspeakable mesh of pathology, unknowability, and specificity. See ibid., 33–39. *Sinthom*osexuality

develops Edelman's earlier exploration of the ways that homosexuality figures the unknowability and incoherence of sexuality generally. See Lee Edelman, *Homographesis: Essays in Gay Literary and Cultural Theory* (New York: Routledge, 1994), xiii–23.

53. Edelman, *No Future*, 45.
54. Ibid., 90.
55. Ibid., 153.
56. Given what I say here about Lot's wife and how she may support a reading of the Sodom and Gomorrah story quite different from those offered by pro-LGBT interpreters, it is noteworthy that so many of such interpreters, especially those writing for more popular audiences, leave her out of their recounting of the story.
57. See ibid., 6–7, 17, 30, 152.
58. Walter Benjamin, "Theses on the Philosophy of History," in *Illuminations*, ed. Hannah Arendt; trans. Harry Zohn (New York: Schocken Books, 1968), 253–64.
59. Given the importance of looking in Genesis 18–19 and in John's Apocalypse, one could potentially read the whore in Revelation 18–19 as a *sinthomo*sexual who bears witness to the violent constitution of community, figured as the justifiable wrath of God.
60. This characterization of Lot's wife owes a debt to Heather Love's *Feeling Backward: Loss and the Politics of Queer History* (Cambridge, Mass.: Harvard University Press, 2007), 127–28, 146–63, Amy Hollywood's "ethics of catastrophe" from *Sensible Ecstasy: Mysticism, Sexual Difference, and the Demands of History* (Chicago: University of Chicago Press, 2002), 60–110, and my engagement with the work of Georges Bataille in *Ecce Homo: The Male-Body-in-Pain as Redemptive Figure* (Chicago: University of Chicago, 2011), 20–24, 185–88.
61. Writing in the second century, Irenaeus understands Lot's wife as a "type of the church." She is a pillar of salt, and the church is the salt of the earth. Both endure, even though subjected to suffering; both witness to something beyond themselves. See Carden, *Sodomy*, 122.
62. Lauren Berlant and Lee Edelman, *Sex, or the Unbearable* (Durham, N.C.: Duke University Press, 2014), 19.
63. Carden, "Remembering Pelotit," 165. For another reading of Lot's wife's turn as an act "of love and defiance" that resists genocide, see Sprinkle, "God at the Margins," 70–74.
64. Of course, the other option is the one pursued by Abraham—try to convince God not to destroy Sodom and Gomorrah (Gn 18:23–32). This strategy, as the story treated here evinces, was unsuccessful.

# "They Had No Rest from This Torment": Encountering the *Apocalypse of Peter*

BROCK PERRY

"At one point, Rev. Lovejoy described Hell in so much detail that Mrs. Addison, a dignified lady with yellow feathers in her yellow hat, burst into tears and ran right out of the church. A bunch of people, including me, followed her with their eyes, guessing why she thought she was going to Hell."[1] So recalls Gary Gray, the black protagonist of James Hannaham's novel *God Says No*, of his visit to the A.M.E. Zion Church of Charleston, South Carolina—his home church—during Thanksgiving break of his freshman year of college. Gary, a devout Christian since he was a child, was home for the first time since moving to Kissimmee to attend Central Florida Christian College, where he had gotten off to a bit of a rough start.

Returning to his dorm room one day earlier in the semester, he found that Russ, his racist roommate, had divided their room into two halves with a strip of tape. Amid other of Gary's belongings that Russ had shoved to his side of the room, Gary noticed the statue of Jesus that he prayed to nightly was lying broken on the floor. In a fit of rage at Russ for having broken his beloved icon, Gary shoved him and started a fistfight. The boys' skirmish incurred disciplinary action from the school's Elders, who threatened to call their parents if they did not resolve the issue between themselves. And so over the following weeks, Gary and Russ managed to get along much better, and Gary even thought that maybe Russ wasn't so bad after all.

Back in Charleston, walking home from the aforementioned fire-and-brimstone sermon, Gary narrates: "I couldn't stop praying for forgiveness and worrying about seared flesh bubbling. I imagined the skin on my forearm melting like pizza topping. I've got to tell Russ about Rev. Lovejoy, I said to myself. He'd love Rev. Lovejoy. Russ loves a tough sermon like Rev. Lovejoy's. I love that guy."[2] As he arrives at the front gate of his house, he is suddenly paralyzed, powerless to open the latch, his mind blank. "I love Russ. I'm in love with Russ, I thought, laughing to myself and shaking my head. I knew that wasn't possible. Russ hated me more than he loved Jesus, and plus he was a boy! A laugh rumbled up in my stomach, but then I got that seasick feeling you get when something's so weird and bad and wrong that it's got to be true."[3]

It is unlikely that Gary Gray is the only person to have experienced such a visceral connection between descriptions of hell as a reality and the unbearable ache that grows in your stomach when you realize your desires might land you there. Regardless of one's personal religious convictions there is no shortage of popular and public messages informing LGBTQ folk that they are quite literally going to hell, coming from places as varied as pulpits, public school principal's offices, and witness stands in federal court.[4] "Hell Houses," parodies of haunted houses that guide visitors on a tour of hell that includes performances depicting sinners and their punishments, continue to be held by some Christian organizations around Halloween each year, drawing in an estimated 1.6 million visitors in 2006.[5] These events (kits for which can be purchased online, complete with scripts and effects tracks) typically revolve around scenes regarding homosexuality.[6] One kit, for example, includes a scene in which demons harass a young lesbian to the point that she commits suicide; another shows a gay man surrounded by demons and dying of AIDS after marrying a man. Certainly, one need not look hard or far for public displays of hostility toward queer folk that draw on historically Christian ideas about salvation and damnation. From the spectacular hatred displayed by the Westboro Baptist Church's iconic signs (God Hates Fags! You're Going to Hell!), to the insidious (if likely more harmful) theologically justified homophobia and transphobia preached in pulpits throughout the United States, many LGBTQ people find themselves subject to a hellish violence in the name of Christianity.

## ON THE EDGE OF HISTORY

> We've reached a moment in history where it's very difficult, if not impossible, to go back.
>
> —ERIC MARCUS

To open an essay with reference to the association of LGBTQ people and hell feels a bit anachronistic, when LGBTQ people in the United States appear to be at the edge of a massive shift in history, away from such associations.[7] A quick glance at the "Our Victories" page on the Human Rights Campaign's website would seem to indicate LGBTQ people have experienced unprecedented progress in the past several years.[8] The United States military eliminated their "Don't Ask, Don't Tell" policy in 2011 after Congress passed the Don't Ask Don't Tell Repeal Act of 2010. Two years later, the Supreme Court's decision in *United States v. Windsor* extended the federal definition of marriage to include same-sex marriages, a decision that led Fred Sainz, the

Human Rights Campaign's vice president for communications and marketing, to call 2013 the "gayest year in gay history."[9] And two years after that decision (2015), the Supreme Court decided in *Obergefell v. Hodges* that same-sex marriage is a fundamental right guaranteed by the United States Constitution. These judicial decisions, often hailed as "historic," certainly mark a change in the status of the rights of LGBTQ people in a country where same-sex sexual activity was still illegal in fourteen states as of 2003. These federal rights, in addition to increased visibility of LGBT people in popular media, publicly out politicians, athletes, and celebrities, LGBT inclusion in many mainline Protestant denominations and other communities of faith—all seem to serve as indications of our arrival into a very different future from a not very distant past.

There is another side to this edge of time, however, in which time is moving forward more slowly for others whose venerated place in the course of history is less certain. Despite the advances touted by mainstream activists, LGBTQ youth, for example, are at increased risk of violence, homelessness, and suicide than their straight peers.[10] Indeed, on March 28, 2013, which fell not only during Holy Week of the Christian liturgical calendar, but also only one day after the United States Supreme Court heard arguments regarding gay marriage that would lead to its decision in *United States v. Windsor*, the Ali Forney Center—the largest organization providing housing and other resources to homeless queer youth in the United Sates—posted a press release on its website calling for "Christians to wake up to the terrible fact that far too many LGBT youth are being abused and rejected in Christian homes." The press release continues, "Again and again we hear young people tell us tales of torment and abuse in their homes. Told that they are disgusting, that they are sinners, that they are abominations. Made to hate themselves. Made to wish that they were dead."[11] In addition to being at an increased risk of violence, suicide, and homelessness, transgender and gender nonconforming people, especially those who are people of color, face disproportionate poverty, police violence, and discrimination in employment, housing, and health care.[12] The disparity between these stories of progress and disenfranchisement belies any simple and universal claim of advancement.

What is clear is that whether Christian, secular, or something in-between, not all LGBTQ people find themselves in the same irreversible moment of historical progress. If the present time is one in which a better history is being made for some, what is to be said for those still living, presently, in the bad history that so many others are getting past? My interest here is in exploring how this apparent disorientation of progress into the future might be better understood through encounters with the past. If Christian beliefs and their historical precedents have been influential in the marginalization of LGBTQ people, those precedents, far from being merely historical, may reveal something about the ways they occupy us in the present. Progressive and liberal Christian responses to claims that gay people are going to hell have tended to take the shape of reading Christian history in light of the experience of LGBTQ people in order to show how the two are not opposed to one another. These approaches to history assume that LGBTQ people have every bit as much a right to heaven as their normative counterparts. The historical encounter staged in this essay, however, is with the apocryphal *Apocalypse of Peter*, a text that does not lend itself so easily to a reading that would support Christian affirmation of LGBTQ people. Rather, the queer figures in this popular second-century CE text appear being tortured in the flames of hell—forever. The apocalyptic is a genre in the history of Christianity that combines the telling of time and history with ideas of salvation and damnation. It is a form of writing in which the representation of an "End," a closure, serves as the foundation for hope and community in an imperfect present, as well as a social and political rubric for what threatens such hope and community as it seeks that end. Encountering these tortured queer figures in the *Apocalypse of Peter* may dis/close (*apo/kalyptein*: uncover, disclose, reveal) the paradoxically un/ending temporal and ethical complications and entanglements of our own—and every—present moment.

## QUEER ENCOUNTERS

Since the 1990s, considerations of gender and sexuality, often under the rubric of queer theory or queer studies, have increasingly made their way into the academic study of religion. With reference to biblical texts in particular, Joseph Marchal has outlined three predominant approaches to "queering"—or queer reading—that, while not necessarily mutually exclusive, operate according to different methodological and normative assumptions. Marchal's first approach, the historical-critical, focuses on the sociolinguistic context of a text's production in order to emphasize the differences between past and present understandings of erotic relationships.[13] The second approach, in contrast, takes an "explicitly gay-affirmative" orientation that foregrounds themes and persons in texts with which queer folk might be drawn to positively identify and to take as indicators of their right to be included in Christian communities.[14] Whereas the first approach depends on a proper understanding of what the texts *did not* mean then and so *do not* mean today, the second depends on a proper (if unorthodox) understanding of what the texts *did* mean then and so *do* mean today.

These two approaches lend themselves to a binary logic of rejection (in the first case) and reclamation (in the second) on the basis of the validity of particular interpretations of what are taken to be transhistorically stable meanings. Although reclamation and rejection often have an expedient strategic value for the project of securing the inclusion of LGBT people in institutions that have marginalized or excluded them, they are limited as approaches to texts and history insofar as they do not draw attention to their own normalizing functions and epistemological limitations. Methods of reclamation take for granted what queerness, sexuality, gender *are*—both past and present—insofar as they encourage readers to identify unproblematically with historical figures as an approach to securing a place for queers in Christian history and in communities for which that history is meaningful. In an inverse movement, outright rejection often fails to fully consider the ramifications of the past in the present, the ways that disregarding injurious texts allow us to turn away from their continued—if veiled—influence in both religious and cultural contexts today.

Alternatively, Marchal's third, and more "queerly resistant" interpretive approach begins not from a fidelity to proper historical understandings or from the abstracted perspective of an identity position, but rather from a contestation and interrogation of normativity, including the normalizing functions of historical and literary interpretation. The third approach involves "a shift in focus from the text or from the history as 'source' to a development of the process of interpretation as itself a critical 'resource' for engaging the persistent rhetorical function of biblical argumentation."[15] This approach suspends identitarian and disciplinary boundaries and invites what he calls "'inappropriate relations' with queer studies from outside of religious studies."[16] Although Marchal formulates his categories of queer approaches in relation to biblical texts in particular, they are helpful for thinking about queer approaches to Christian apocryphal and historical texts in general.[17]

It is in the spirit of Marchal's third approach to queer reading that I want to consider the experience of the encounter with the past itself in order to explore the implications of queer theories of negativity for approaches to Christian history and the Bible. Approaching history as an encounter in the present with the past falls in line with what Elizabeth Freeman calls "erotohistoriography." In Freeman's words, "Erotohistoriography is distinct from the desire for a fully present past, a restoration of bygone times. [It] does not write the lost object into the present so much as encounter it already in the present, by treating the present itself as a hybrid. And it uses the body as a tool to effect, figure, or perform that encounter."[18] Thus in erotohistoriography, temporal and historical consciousness does not depend on a proper objective or empirical understanding of things from the past as facts (already a significant departure from the historical inquiry that characterizes much of Christian historical and biblical studies), but rather on the bodily sensations and dispositions experienced by the reader in the present as a form of understanding themselves. Freed from the belief in "history," pleasurably in relation to the past in the present, and ultimately temporally disoriented, the erotohistoriographer experiences reconfigurations of desire and intensifications of pleasure that usefully reveal different possibilities for the future, according to Freeman. The emphasis on tactility in particular in erotohistoriography evokes the "queer touch" of medievalist Carolyn Dinshaw's approach to queer historiography. For Dinshaw, queer historiography is "sensible" and "tactile," a "history of things touching."[19] Insofar as queer touch connects the present to the past, it is also contingent and partial, "a history of displacements (of signs, of things, of people), of signifiers knocked loose and whose signifiers knock others loose, in turn."[20] For both Freeman and Dinshaw queer historiography is an embodied, affective relation to the past, with real (if contingent) implications in the present.

It will be helpful to consider the historiographical work of Freeman and Dinshaw alongside a sustained study of the concept of the encounter itself—Lauren Berlant and Lee Edelman's *Sex, or the Unbearable*. This text stages an encounter between the two authors as a dialogue, performing in text the promises and problematics that mark any encounter. In the co-written preface, they write that encounters, as scenes of relationality, are structured by negativity. "Negativity," they write, "refers to the psychic and social incoherences and divisions, conscious and unconscious alike, that trouble any totality or fixity of identity. It denotes, that is, the relentless voice that unsettles the fantasy of sovereignty."[21] As what undoes us and is beyond our control, marking the limit of our capacity to truly know our selves and those with whom we are in relation, negativity is often experienced as overwhelming, or "unbearable." It is what causes Gary Gray to laugh, and then to get "that seasick feeling you get when something's so weird and bad and wrong that it's got to be true." However, it is not reducible to what is merely negative in experience. Certainly, negativity often comes into experience as something traumatic or painful, as in the racism that Gary's roommate Russ expresses when he separates their dorm room with a strip of tape, which leads Gary to believe Russ hates him "more than he loves Jesus." However, negativity is not limited to what is painful and can just as often be experienced in relation to what feels funny or pleasurable, as it is when Gary realizes he is in love with Russ. Negativity does not point singly to pain or pleasure, but what can be overwhelming, troubling, or unbearable about both.

If our relations to our selves and to others are what enable us to become subjects, they are also the source of the disruption of that very subjectivity in that they always exceed our capacity to know them. "To encounter ourselves as nonsovereign," Berlant and Edelman continue, "is to encounter relationality itself, in the psychic, social, and political senses of the term."[22] Given that relationality is that in which experiences of negativity occur, it is scenes of relationality—encounters—on which the authors focus in order to interrogate negativity's consequences. The negativity inherent in relationality, however, makes a definition of the encounter a difficult task, marked as it is from the start with an aspect of incomprehensibility. The encounter is never purely and simply direct, but rather requires a "a scenic component, a fantasmatic staging" that "puts into play reaction, accommodation, transference, exchange, and the articulation of narratives."[23] These various maneuvers that the negativity at the heart of relationality necessitate in the encounter are what enable change—or not. As that which undoes and troubles the self in the form of a limit to knowledge, negativity is an epistemological limit in the ontology of relationality, experienced in encounter. How we conceptualize the encounter, the way we do or do not think (if we can) about its constitutive negativity, influences our understanding of relationality and everything it encompasses, including our erotic and haptic relations to the past.

Marchal invites us to consider the "process of interpretation" of biblical texts as a critical resource for thinking through the normalizing effects of the meaning-making procedures of historical inquiry, bringing the past into the present. In doing so, we can think of the process itself as an encounter, in the present, with the past—not by a disembodied subject—but one with all the trappings of eros and affect that characterize Freeman's erotohistoriography. Freeman shows us that, by shifting our orientation to the past and foregrounding the embodied experience of pleasure in the encounter in historiography, the past itself becomes a place of future possibility. Thinking of historiography as an encounter with the past, however, requires attention to the encounter's inherent negativity, which has the capacity to bring both pleasure and pain into sometimes unbearable proximity to each other in a way that leaves us scrambling when we try to make the sensible comprehensible and politically useful. As Berlant and Edelman make clear, the inherent negativity of encounter always frustrates our capacity to understand both negativity and the encounter itself. Queer encounters with the past, then, are also necessarily marked by a negativity that would call into question any attempt to have fully grasped their meaning. Insofar as we encounter the past, it is always a partial connection: touching, but contingent.

## THE ORIGINAL HELL HOUSE

The encounter with the past staged here is with the *Apocalypse of Peter*, an early second-century text and the earliest Christian apocalypse to describe hell in addition to paradise.[24] In the revelation to Peter, the future events of the last days and the final judgment are revealed, wherein God banishes the sinners to a fiery hell where they will be punished eternally—a future many queer folk, much like Gary Gray, have imagined quite viscerally for themselves, seared flesh and all. The text is a literal "tour of hell"—the term Martha Himmelfarb has given it and other apocalypses like it—wherein Jesus dramatically describes to Peter scenes depicting the fate of sinners and their various torments and tortures before heading to paradise, where the gates are opened for the righteous, after which "the heaven shut, that had been open."[25] The righteous and the damned, separated eternally.

While earlier apocalyptic texts were also concerned with revealed visions of heaven and history, the fate of the persecuted and righteous dead, the last judgment, and the end of the world, the *Apocalypse of Peter* marks a certain shift in apocalyptic literature in its focus on hell and the fate of sinners in eternity.[26] Catherine Keller writes that earlier apocalypses, composed as they were in contexts of persecution, provided hope for an end to the day-to-day rhythm of finitude and suffering. In this mode the apocalypse *"kills time,"* she writes, "before it kills us."[27] Less concerned with morality than temporality, the hope of the earliest Christians was in an end to the imperfect time of their experience and the creation of a new and better one. That apocalyptic resolution to their suffering did not come in the time they expected, but the binary between the present and the future it instituted remained, taking on moral dimensions. The temporal splitting of time between a suffering present and a better future enabled further a moral splitting between the evil of the past and present ages and the perfection of the future to come. The collective end less imminent, the early church became increasingly concerned with individual ends and the ordering of its community.[28]

In that context the *Apocalypse of Peter* and other such tours of hell served not only as a popular mode of speculation about the fate of the dead and the end of time, but also as an outlet for moralizing instruction.[29] The sins described in the *Apocalypse of Peter*, many of which are of a sexual nature, incur punishments that typically mirror the sins themselves by incorporating some part of the body used to commit the offense, with the severity increasing proportionately to the magnitude of the sin.[30] Because the sins described are typically those that would not necessarily be apparent to the community (e.g., speech and sex), they would not have been easily regulated. Thus, the documents served as a way for the communities that produced them to publicly state what should not be done in private.[31] Further, Greg Carey has argued that given the importance of group identity for withstanding the persecution the early church faced, "deviance from a group's norms threaten[ed] its identity."[32] Thus, "fear—fear that outsiders might harm the religious community, fear that insiders might succumb to the pressure and abandon the faithful, and fear that behaviors among the faithful might undermine group solidarity," governed the normalization of social and erotic behaviors.[33] The prophetic hope of the apocalyptic tradition, transformed into a moralized disjuncture between ages, allowed the early church to project its fears on those figures in the present that would threaten its entrance into the future to come.

## HELL OF A TIME

In Jesus' revelation to Peter he describes scenes of the torture performed on blasphemers, murderers, liars, adulterers, women who commit abortion, persecutors of Christians, usurers, and idolaters, along with the following:

> And other men and women being cast down from a great precipice fell to the bottom and again were driven by those who were set over them to go up upon the rock and thence were cast down again to the bottom and thus they had no rest from this torment. And these were the ones who defiled their bodies, behaving as women: and the women who were with them were those who lay with one another as a man with a woman.[34]

Whereas the men in this passage are in hell for their gender deviance, the women are punished for having sex with one another "as a man with a woman."[35] Another manuscript of the text indicates more direct sexual contact between the men: "These are they who have cut their flesh as apostles of a man: and the women with them . . . and these are the men who defiled themselves together as women."[36] Apparently failing to conduct themselves according to the proper sexual and gender norms in both accounts, the *Apocalypse of Peter*'s "queers" are driven to ceaselessly climb and fall from the edge of a cliff as punishment. They are figures whose gender and sexual deviancy causes them to be excluded from the early Christian community as it sought to secure a better future for itself.

Insofar as that is true, there is perhaps a touch to be felt between these "queer" characters and those marked queer in our own social order, especially in light of the concepts of negativity and queerness developed by Lee Edelman in his book *No Future* and in his contributions to *Sex, or the Unbearable*. According to Edelman, negativity is, by its very nature as negativity, completely inassimilable to conscious thought or any meaning whatsoever. It is the real force exerted by what cannot be thought on thinking itself.[37] As such, theorizations of negativity and its consequences cannot, ultimately, approach negativity per se. Any attempt to harness negativity for some political purpose, to transform it into something useful or meaningful, into any kind of knowledge whatsoever, is necessarily a fantasy, a departure from the constitutive negativity of reality.[38] Negativity structures, but is not explainable or recuperable by, the social. It is simultaneously formational and deformational; that is, it induces the formation of the social as the maintenance of relationality's coherence in the face of that which would undo it.

In the social order, Edelman argues, politics works in contradistinction to negativity in order "to *affirm* a structure, to *authenticate* social order, which it then intends to transmit to the future."[39] This commitment to the continuation of the social order, as that which structures the very idea of the political, is what Edelman refers to as "reproductive futurism." Reproductive futurism is "an ideological limit on political discourse as such, preserving in the process the absolute privilege of heteronormativity by rendering unthinkable, by casting outside the political domain, the possibility of a queer resistance to this organizing principle of communal relations"[40] Reproductive futurism demands that the negativity of the present be figured as a particular threat within the social to the social and to its life to come.

What undoes the social is, however, just as much a part of the social as that which forms it, bringing the social and the social subject into constant encounter with what it cannot bear. Our sense of ourselves and others, the languages we use to communicate, the norms and laws that govern us, and our political aspirations all emerge as attempts, in the realms of meaning and knowledge, to make relatable that which is unrelatable in relationality itself. Edelman draws on Lacanian psychoanalysis to develop his concept of negativity, arguing that negativity is the force of the incomprehensible register of the Real—the death drive—that insistently disrupts the fantasy that negativity can be overcome.[41] Within the social's political machinations, the burden of negativity's persistence, the social's death drive, comes to be represented by the queer as that which the social must abject as it attempts to ensure its continuity and coherence, its reproduction into the future. The negativity of the encounter, unapproachable in its own right, is interpreted as the queer.

Queerness is resistant to the "organizing principle of the social order," and occupies "the space outside the framework within which politics as we know it appears and so outside the conflict of visions that share as their presupposition that the body politic must survive."[42] By this definition, "the queer comes to figure the bar to every realization of futurity, the resistance, internal to the social, to every social structure or form."[43] Acceding to its figuration as that which is inassimilable to the social's narratives of historical continuity and their continued reproduction into the future, queerness reflects to the social its own constitutive negativity. Queerness, rather than affirming reproductive futurism's violent denials of its own negativity, is the constant, unending insistence of the reality of that negativity.

Following Edelman's description of queerness as what comes to be represented as the social order's death drive, we may perhaps begin to see the ceaselessness of the climb and fall that the *Apocalypse of Peter*'s gender deviants suffer at the prodding of their tormentors in a different light. As figures that represent death rather starkly within an extreme vision of the future—i.e., eternity—they are the queer others over against which early Christians secure their entry into paradise. Given that repetition of a traumatic experience was Freud's first insight into the death drive,[44] and that the *Apocalypse of Peter*'s queers are forced to repetitively climb and fall in perpetuity, they evoke the death drive itself. While the author of the apocalypse and the community it represents attempt to secure their future, those that represent a threat to that future—the damned queers—are figured as the constant driving force of a negativity that is not only no use to the future, but undermines the future as such. As figures of the death drive, they are made to stand (fall?) in for what the early Christians saw as the inconceivable evil of their time, obstructing their entrance into the pristine and peaceful age to come. In the *Apocalypse of Peter*'s vision of the future, heaven is no place for queers.

## CHRISTIAN HISTORY AS QUEER INJURY

Why read such a disturbing text at all? Why go out of the way to drag these tortured queers from history? If negativity is not reducible to the merely negative, what is negative—trauma, injury, loss—does warrant its own consideration in light of the way Christian beliefs, often justified on the basis of historical authority, have been wielded against queers. Foregrounding the negativity of queer historiography may at first seem counterproductive to the undeniably important and necessary project of addressing Christianity's contributions to homophobia, transphobia, and heterosexism. Readings that settle out along the lines of reclamation or rejection seem to have clearer political value in that direction, where political value lies in the possibility that the marginalized might be given rights and included in the normative institutions that have historically excluded them. That political value, however, does not necessitate any challenge to the theological and social norms that enable—and even require—exclusion in the first place. Thus the invocation of political value as an ethical standard in approaches to injurious texts has the capacity to elide the efficacy of their continued power to injure.

It is helpful to consider these observations in light of Heather Love's claim that

> for groups constituted by historical injury, the challenge is to engage with the past without being destroyed by it. Sometimes it seems it would be better to move on—to let . . . the dead bury the dead. But it is the damaging aspects of the past that tend to stay with us, and the desire to forget may itself be a symptom of haunting. The dead can bury the dead all day long and still not be done.[45]

If this is true, if the dead continue to haunt us even after we have performed all the appropriate rites of queer interpretation such that we must repeat them again and again, then the stubborn reality of loss and the repetition of interpretation it provokes warrant further attention. This is a potentially unpopular move, however. In refusing to march queer historiography forward into an ever-brighter future to the chant of "it gets better," one risks being left behind.

While dwelling in a past marked by loss and injury may be unpopular at a time when the future of LGBTQ rights is upon us, it is precisely because not all queers have the same access to that future that it is necessary. Jasbir Puar has helpfully described the ways narratives of LGBT political progress depend on upward mobility and bodily capacity that is most available to "a particular class of white gay men."[46] A parallel may exist, then, between those queer discourses and figures of the past deemed unfit for a political platform based on progress and those queers of the present deemed too backward for the future. The apocalyptic splitting of the evil past from the redeemed future takes shape in the present politics of LGBTQ liberation. If, as Love suggests, "texts or figures that refuse to be redeemed disrupt not only the progress narrative of queer history but also our sense of queer identity in the present,"[47] then those who find the critical value of queerness in its ability to *disrupt* processes of identification, which are necessarily processes of exclusion, will want to think within the tension these figures evoke.

## UN/ENDING

What then could the *Apocalypse of Peter*'s cliff-jumping gender deviants mean for queer reading today? Do they mean anything at all? Are they lost to us forever in their eternal suffering? Is it the queer historiographer's job to reach back in time and redeem them? Or is there queerer pleasure that comes with leaving them in hell, and lingering with them there to imagine how they feel when they fall, curious about whether there is some thrill to it? To speculate about whether it might not only be the painful fall of a queer kid pushed to the ground, but also like the pleasurable rush of coming—that is, whether falling off is like getting off? Or to wonder about just what kind of relationship tormentor and tormented share here, whether it might not just be the fist of a pushy bully, but also the touch of a very different kind of fist that sends the damned over the edge? These questions have preoccupied my own encounters with the *Apocalypse of Peter* and its tortured, queer sinners. In those encounters, to which I have been drawn again and again, any clear distinction between their pleasure and their pain has continuously escaped me, along with any resolution about what either might mean. Whatever pleasure I have felt in my own interpretive speculations about the possibility of secret pleasures between tormenter and tormented has been constantly accompanied by a keen awareness of the visceral power of images of hell in many people's lives—its capacity to bring a touch of pleasure into unsettling proximity with the pain of "seared flesh bubbling" and skin "melting like pizza topping," as Gary Gray describes it. Imagining pleasure where it is apparently proscribed is not unfamiliar and even seductive to many queer folk, to be certain, and Freeman's erotohistoriography foregrounds the affective experience of the historiographer in encounters with the past in order to highlight the capacity for pleasure (and not just pain) to disorient and reconfigure temporal and relational modes of being in the world at present. Pleasure and pain are not, however, mutually exclusive, and encounters characterized by even the most intense pleasures can be experienced as terrifying or threatening, as likely to provoke retreat into the security of the same as a rush into the new and different. Encounters with the past—even difficult ones—are often crossed over with both pleasure and pain in a way that exceeds our capacity to understand them once and for all, or to put them to good use.

Love argues that it is difficult to discuss the relation between the positive and negative feelings of readers in critical contexts, because in those contexts "ambivalence tends to resolve itself into critique and gestures toward political utility." Explaining further, she writes, "The premium on strategic response in queer studies has meant that the painful and traumatic dimensions of these texts (and of the experience of reading them) have been minimized or disavowed."[48] Queer historians have typically either attempted to create positive historical narratives in which they could locate themselves or reinterpreted the losses of queer history in terms that give them positive political power. Love is concerned that these approaches to the history, while understandable and not without their importance, have left queer politics unable to come to terms with the ways that damaging (and damning) aspects of the past continue to exert their influence in the present. Instead of rescuing the *Apocalypse of Peter*'s queers with a historiographical parachute that would save them in the name of their untold pleasures, perhaps it is better to see the constancy of their climb and fall—their representation as early Christianity's death drive—as a demonstration of the queer impossibility of resolving the tension and ambiguity that characterize every encounter, past or present. Their meaning, as it were, is to represent what ceaselessly thwarts the desire to make meaning, the same desire that draws us again and again into the encounter with the past in the first place. It is the story of an End with un/ending consequences. None of us, it seems, has any rest from this torment.

No doubt, a queer historiographical approach to Christian history that locates—and leaves—queers in hell hardly provides an obvious platform from which to argue for inclusive ecclesial policy or LGBTQ rights. But as Laurel Schneider writes, hell may very well be heaven's queer closet, and queer closets have a tendency to explode, "exposing the lies upon which [the rest of the house] is built."[49] What the *Apocalypse of Peter* discloses may not be something about its queer figures after all, but rather about the community that found it so compelling as a vision of the future. Still waiting on that future today, many Christians throughout history have hardly ceased repeating the damnations it demands. In so doing, they betray the impossibility of getting beyond the negativity those damnations attempt to contain. Edelman writes that queers,

> who figure the death drive of the social, must accept that we will be vilified as the agents of that threat. But "they," the defenders of futurity, buzzed by negating our negativity, are themselves, however unknowingly, its secret agents, too, reacting, in the name of the future, in the name of humanity, in the name of life, to the threat of the death drive we figure with the violent rush of a jouissance, which only returns them, ironically, to the death drive in spite of themselves.[50]

The pleasures of the damned in the *Apocalypse of Peter*'s tour of hell are no secret in the end: The pleasures they share between themselves are what land them in hell in the first place. If there is a secret pleasure to be uncovered in the text, it is the disavowed pleasure of a community that sought to eliminate its queers in the name of the future, its negations of negativity that enabled them to imagine a perfect future—a future without negativity, without difference, and, ultimately, without relationality itself.

By following Edelman's lead and leaving the *Apocalypse of Peter*'s queers in their hellish configuration, and by leaving ourselves open in the present to their presence in the historical archive, there is a chance we allow for a different kind of queer historiography, one that Carla Freccero has described as "queer spectrality." This approach, which neither forgets the dead nor properly mourns them, "involves an openness to the possibility of being haunted, even inhabited, by ghosts."[51] Queer figures of the past are allowed to remain other, to perform visitations, to get under our skin. From the perspective of queer spectrality, encounters with the *Apocalypse of Peter* are less about what we can *do* with them and more about what they do to *us*. Frecerro acknowledges that this method, which Freeman dubs a "bottomy historiography,"[52] may seem passive to the point of encouraging quietism or nihilism, but argues that its passivity may also be its strength. Drawing on Leo Bersani's development of jouissance as the self-shattering that occurs when getting fucked, she claims:

> Passivity—which is also a form of patience and passion—is not quite the same thing as quietism. Rather, it is a suspension, a waiting, an attending to the world's arrivals (through, in part, its returns), not as a guarantee or

security for action in the present, but as the very force from the past that moves us into the future.[53]

In encountering the queer figures inhabiting the *Apocalypse of Peter*'s hell, we open ourselves to being haunted by the unsettling indeterminacy and insistence of their negativity. Bersani writes of his own archive of such negative figures that "*they act on us*, freeing mental spaces for possibilities that, without this traumatic expansion of consciousness, we would have been unable to imagine."[54] The *Apocalypse of Peter*'s queers might disclose something as they touch us after all: not about a heavenly future, or the kind of political program that would eventually get all of us there. Instead, they are haunting evidence of the violence with which a community's vision of the future, even the most perfect one imaginable, can be enacted on those who are made to represent the cause of its unending deferral.

## NOTES

1. James Hannaham, *God Says No* (New York: McSweeny's, 2009), 9.
2. Ibid., 11.
3. Ibid., 12.
4. See, for example, Kate Abbey-Lambertz, "Gay People Are Going to Hell, Says Expert Witness in Michigan Gay Marriage Trial," *Huffington Post*, March 3, 2014, http://www.huffingtonpost.com/2014/03/07/michigan-gay-marriage-trial-gay-people-go-to-hell_n_4914470.html?utm_hp_ref=gay-voices; Matt Stopera, "Tennessee Principal Tells Gay Students They're Going to Hell," *BuzzFeed*, March 1, 2012, http://www.buzzfeed.com/mjs538/tennessee-principal-tells-gay-students-theyre-goi#.xt42oQz7x.
5. Sarah Kennedy and Jason Cianciotto, "Homophobia at 'Hell House': Literally Demonizing Lesbian, Gay, Bisexual and Transgender Youth," The National Gay and Lesbian Task Force, October 2006, http://www.thetaskforce.org/static_html/downloads/reports/reports/Homophobia_Hell_House.pdf.
6. "Hell House Outreach How-To Kit," New Destiny Christian Center, http://www.godestiny.org/#!hell-house-how-to-kit-order-page/c1c30.
7. See Alan Greenblatt, "How 2013 Became the Greatest Year in Gay Rights History," *NPR*, December 3, 2013, http://www.npr.org/sections/itsallpolitics/2013/12/03/248217871/how-2013-became-the-greatest-year-in-gay-rights-history. The epigraph for this section, which is a quotation from Eric Marcus, is found in this article.
8. "Our Victories," Human Rights Campaign, http://www.hrc.org/the-hrc-story/our-victories.
9. Greenblatt, "Greatest Year."
10. "LGBT Youth," Lesbian, Gay, Bisexual, and Transgender Health, Centers for Disease Control and Prevention, last updated November 12, 2014, http://www.cdc.gov/lgbthealth/youth.htm; "LGBTQ Youth Homelessness in Focus," United States

Interagency Council on Homelessness, http://usich.gov/issue/lgbt_youth/lgbtq_youth_homelessness_in_focus/. Eve Kosofsky Sedgwick's 1993 essay "Queer and Now" opens with a reflection on queer youth suicides, and she cites their haunting reality as a major motivation for many doing "gay and lesbian" studies. She writes, "To us, the hard statistics come easily," before then listing statistics that are depressingly similar to those still listed on the present-day CDC website, and which are as easy to quote today as they were then. Eve Kosofsky Sedgwick, *Tendencies* (Durham, N.C.: Duke University Press, 1993), 2.

11. Carl Siciliano, "A Long Way from Home: Christianity and the Parental Rejection of LGBT Youth," Ali Forney Center, http://www.aliforneycenter.org/index.cfm?fuseaction=cms.page&id=1123.
12. Jaime M. Grant, Lisa A. Mottet, Justin Tanis, Jack Harrison, Jody L. Herman, and Mara Keisling, "Injustice at Every Turn: A Report of the National Transgender Discrimination Survey," National Center for Transgender Equality and National Gay and Lesbian Task Force, 2011, http://www.thetaskforce.org/static_html/downloads/reports/reports/ntds_full.pdf.
13. Joseph A. Marchal, "Queer Approaches: Improper Relations with Paul's Letters," in *Studying Paul's Letters: Contemporary Perspectives and Methods*, ed. Joseph A. Marchal (Minneapolis: Fortress Press, 2012), 216.
14. Ibid., 217.
15. Ibid., 218.
16. Ibid.
17. Which is not to elide the particularity of the traditional authority of the Bible as it is used in contemporary debates about sexuality and gender, a particularity to which Marchal attends carefully in his essay.
18. Elizabeth Freeman, *Time Binds: Queer Temporalities, Queer Histories* (Durham, N.C.: Duke University Press, 2010), 95.
19. Carolyn Dinshaw, *Getting Medieval: Sexualities and Communities, Pre- and Postmodern* (Durham, N.C.: Duke University Press, 1999), 39.
20. Ibid. Dinshaw emphasizes the Latin root of contingent, "tangere," meaning "to touch."
21. Lauren Berlant and Lee Edelman, *Sex, or the Unbearable* (Durham, N.C.: Duke University Press, 2014), viii.
22. Ibid.
23. Ibid.
24. Martha Himmelfarb, *Apocalypse: A Brief History* (Malden, Mass.: Wiley-Blackwell, 2010), 98.
25. James K. Elliott, *The Apocryphal New Testament: A Collection of Apocryphal Christian Literature in an English Translation Based on M. R. James* (Oxford: Oxford University Press, 1993), 612.
26. Himmelfarb, *Apocalypse*, 1.
27. Catherine Keller, *Apocalypse Now and Then: A Feminist Guide to the End of the World* (Boston: Beacon Press, 1996), 85.
28. Ibid., 92–94.

29. Martha Himmelfarb, *Tours of Hell: An Apocalyptic Form in Jewish and Christian Literature* (Philadelphia: University of Pennsylvania Press, 1983), 1.
30. Ibid., 69; and Himmelfarb, *Apocalypse*, 99.
31. Himmelfarb, *Tours of Hell*, 73.
32. Greg Carey, *Ultimate Things: Introduction to Jewish and Christian Apocalyptic Literature* (St. Louis: Chalice Press, 2005), 221.
33. Ibid.
34. Elliott, *Apocryphal New Testament*, 606. The *Apocalypse of Peter* is recorded in two main manuscripts, a shorter Greek manuscript (quoted here) and an Ethiopic manuscript.
35. Bernadette J. Brooten, *Love between Women: Early Christian Responses to Female Homoeroticism* (Chicago: University of Chicago Press, 1996), 306.
36. Elliott, *Apocryphal New Testament*, 607. Elliott maintains that the Ethiopic manuscript from which this quote is taken is likely closer to the original text than the Greek manuscript. Brooten notes that other translators have translated the Ethiopic variously as "the men who, like (with) women, defile one another," and "men who defiled themselves with one another in the fashion of women." On these translations, see Brooten, *Love between Women*, 306n5.
37. Berlant and Edelman, *Sex*, 10.
38. Ibid., 98.
39. Lee Edelman, *No Future: Queer Theory and the Death Drive* (Durham, N.C.: Duke University Press, 2004), 2.
40. Ibid.
41. Ibid., 9–10.
42. Ibid., 30.
43. Ibid., 4.
44. See Sigmund Freud, "Beyond the Pleasure Principle," in *The Freud Reader*, ed. Peter Gay (New York: Norton, 1989), 611–12.
45. Heather Love, *Feeling Backward: Loss and the Politics of Queer History* (Cambridge, Mass.: Harvard University Press, 2007), 1.
46. Jasbir K. Puar, "The Cost of Getting Better: Suicide, Sensation, Switchpoints," *GLQ: A Journal of Lesbian and Gay Studies* 18, no. 1 (2011): 151.
47. Love, *Feeling Backward*, 8.
48. Ibid., 3–4.
49. Laurel Schneider, *Beyond Monotheism: A Theology of Multiplicity* (New York: Routledge, 2007), 102.
50. Edelman, *No Future*, 153.
51. Carla Freccero, *Queer/Early/Modern* (Durham, N.C.: Duke University Press, 2006), 80.
52. Freeman, *Time Binds*, 109.
53. Freccero, *Queer/Early/Modern*, 104.
54. Leo Bersani, *Thoughts and Things* (Chicago: University of Chicago Press, 2015), 93.

# Excess and the Enactment of Queer Time: Futurity, Failure, and Formation in Feminist Theologies

BRANDY DANIELS

The Anglican theologian Sarah Coakley is a particularly notable, if provocative, figure in feminist theology, a discourse often at odds with traditional systematic theology—either in perception or by its own avowal. A central endeavor in Coakley's scholarship has been to rethink this complicated, often fraught, relationship between feminism and systematics via a turn to contemplative prayer.[1] In her acclaimed collection of essays titled *Powers and Submissions*, for instance, Coakley challenges feminist theologians to rethink their skepticism toward submission and proposes a Christian feminism grounded on a "fundamental and practiced dependency *on God*," arguing this dependency as a "fulcrum from which our (often necessary) dependencies on others may be assessed with critical discernment, and the assumed binary gender associations of such dependencies called into question."[2] Coakley further pursues this endeavor in the first volume of her systematic theology, *God, Sexuality, and the Self: An Essay "On the Trinity,"* foregrounding the interconnections between prayer, systematics, and gender / sexuality / feminism as central to her theological system and, as the subtitle intimates, situating these themes under and alongside the doctrine of God.[3]

The key locus where prayer, systematics, and sex meet for Coakley is desire. In the prelude of *God, Sexuality, and the Self*, Coakley explains that "the questions of right contemplation of God, right speech about God, and right ordering of desire all hang together," and within this entanglement, desire is primal, "more fundamental than sex."[4] As in *Powers and Submissions*, Coakley persuasively argues that (right) theological discourse must be preceded and accompanied by vulnerability and surrender to the divine—necessary affects and acts that eschew idolatry (which, Coakley then points out, is a sense of mastery that often manifests in and through masculinist and racist ideologies)—and engendered by the "particular graced bodily practices" of prayer and contemplation.[5] In this first volume of her systematics, Coakley not only presents key tenets of her doctrine of God—a historical retrieval of a patristic Trinitarian formulation recast through the lens of desire in a way that addresses sexuality and gender—but also presents a theological methodology grounded by this particular theological-ontological-epistemological framework and its attendant assumptions. The methodology she presents, which she dubs *théologie totale*, "bind[s] questions of theological method, contemplative practice, and desire into a new tether," via "a specifically trinitarian understanding of God," and in doing so, offers fresh insight for feminism that secular gender theory is unable to provide.[6]

Whereas the doctrinal and metaphysical assertions of Coakley's theology as well as her theo-ethical embrace of submission have been the subject of much criticism and debate (as well as praise) particularly from feminist perspectives, less critical attention has been given to her methodology.[7] This essay, then, critically examines Coakley's *théologie totale*—the effects it seeks and claims to accomplish, and the theo-onto-epistemological assumptions that undergird it. Coakley outlines nine distinctive hallmarks of this approach, but this essay will focus primarily (though not solely) on contemplation—the pinnacle of her methodology.[8] Coakley's *théologie totale* seeks to engender a middle way, a theology *in via*, an "unsystematic systematics," that "inculcates mental patterns of 'un-mastery,' . . . opens up a radical attention to the other, and instigates an acute awareness of the messy entanglement of sexual desires and desire for God."[9] Turning to recent scholarship in queer theory on temporality, this essay suggests that the teleological thrust and attendant theo-onto-epistemological assumptions undergirding *théologie totale* (and how contemplation functions within it) betray and thwart precisely what the approach seeks to engender. In assuming and proffering a narratively cohering and linear account of subjectivity that takes as given a clear telos of desire, I argue that *théologie totale* ultimately reifies the mastery Coakley is seeking to eschew and forecloses openness to the other—that it adheres to what José Esteban Muñoz calls "straight time's choke hold."[10]

Though Coakley seeks to craft a methodology that affirms and stems from the "messy entanglement of sexual desires and desire for God," I argue that *théologie totale* and the presuppositions underlying it function to untangle, to straighten, to tidy up.[11] On subjecting Coakley's methodology (and concomitant account of formation) to a queer temporal critique, the latter half of this chapter suggests that a theological imagination and method that align with the aims of *théologie totale* approach "the future" not by asking "how do we secure or obtain it?" but rather "who are the 'we' that make up and enact it?" Placing the work of José Esteban Muñoz and Wendy Farley—of queer theory and feminist theology, respectively—in conversation, I conclude by gesturing toward what such a feminist theological method and account of contemplation might look like—offering some hallmarks of a feminist theological method in a queer time and space.

## COAKLEY ON THE (DESIRING) SUBJECT AND (TELOS OF) STRAIGHT TIME

To grasp how Coakley operates with an account of subjectivity and desire that has a particular (straight) teleology, it is important to closely examine Coakley's project in *God, Sexuality, and the Self*, where she not only explicates the methodology that will guide her systematics but also presents her Trinitarian doctrine of God. Coakley's account of the doctrine of the Trinity is the key theo-onto-epistemological assumption undergirding *théologie totale*; it is also simultaneously influenced by this methodology, which thus highlights the epistemological foregrounding of and in her claims that "the problem of the Trinity cannot be solved without addressing the very questions that seem least to do with it," questions of "sexual justice . . . of the meaning and stability of gender . . . of the final theological significance of sexual desire."[12] The foregrounding claim that guides Coakley's method, then, is that of a "contemporary trinitarian *ontology of desire*—a vision of God's trinitarian nature as both the source and goal of human desires, as God intends them."[13] In this vision and account, where "God the 'Father,' in and through the Spirit, both stirs up and progressively chastens and purges the frailer and often misdirected desires of humans and so forges them, by stages of sometimes painful growth, into the likeness of his Son," Coakley explains that "ethics and metaphysics may be found to converge" and "divine desire can be seen as the ultimate progenitor of human desire, and the very means of its transformation."[14] This trinitarian doctrine marks both the ontological foundation of desire as well as its ideal telos.

Contemplation is the tool through which our desires are (re-)formed toward and taken up into the divine—"privileging contemplation" and "desire as the constellating category of *théologie totale*" are hallmarks one and nine, respectively, of *théologie totale*; these themes serve as the bookends of her methodology.[15] This transformation of our desires by and toward the divine is that which eschews and resists idolatry and a false sense of human mastery. Contemplating God as "the source and sustainer of all being" means understanding "the dizzying mystery encountered in the act of contemplation as precisely the 'blanking' of the human ambition to knowledge, control, and mastery."[16] But is there an inherent contradiction, a (theo-)logical flaw, in so systematically seeking such unmastery and, moreover, proposing such a clear path toward achieving it? This essay, as I have already intimated, suggests that there is—that such a path assumes a narratively cohering, linear subject-formation toward an ideal end that ends up foreclosing an openness to the other, and that the positing of such a path is reflective of mastery.

*Mastery and the Origins and Formation of Subjectivity/Desire*

Many of the scholarly debates in queer temporality center on questions of futurity, making it a preoccupying theme in the literature—a theme that this chapter also focuses on in its critique of Coakley's methodology.[17] A theme that marks these debates and couches them together under the broader frame of the antisocial thesis (and, even more broadly, queer theory) is a shared recognition and critique of how the construction of subjectivity has been ontologized and naturalized.[18] The historicization of (sexual) subjectivity stems from both Freud and Foucault, forefathers of queer theory, and queer theorists since then have relied and built on both of these thinkers to highlight ways essences or origins assumed as given (sexuality, gender identity, etc.) obscure the role power plays in their very constitution—Foucault calls this "the regime of power-knowledge-pleasure that sustains the discourse on human sexuality."[19] This regime that constructs identity and claims it as natural, Foucault explains, works to "impose a law of truth" that creates a pattern of recognition that makes us "subject to someone else by control and dependence," a pattern that is governed by assumed norms and ideals that then limit and oppress.[20] As the Foucauldian scholar Lynne Huffer puts it, "Modern sexual subjectivity comes at the cost of what Foucault, following Deleuze, calls *assujettissement*: a subject-producing subjection that simultaneously creates and subjugates sexual subjects within an increasingly differentiated grid of deviance and normalization."[21] In explaining *assujettissement* within the context of her broader argument, Huffer notes how scholars doing work in queer temporality and antisociality are distinctive in this regard.[22] While queer theorists working on temporality have been at odds about how individuals or communities should, or if they even can, resist this normalization and its constraining and oppressive effects, they hold in common a recognition of how power operates temporally, constructing identities that are then assumed as originary, and that thus have ideal forms; the antisocial account, unlike more intersectional-based strands of queer theory, critiques and challenges "investments in subjectivity." Huffer quotes, and aligns with Edelman, noting that "queer negativity *opposes the subject* of humanistic teaching."[23] And as subjects are formed, assumed, and idealized, and thus must be opposed, so too are accounts of time and space themselves.

Coakley operates with an account of identity that is formed through our desires and the various influences that can shape and direct them—and that thus can be transformed, via contemplation: as she puts it, "a vision of selfhood reconstituted participatorily in the triune God"—which leads her to suggest that hers is a "form of theology that can appropriately be undertaken in a postmodern age."[24] If Foucault and the queer theorists who followed him are at all indicative of postmodernism, however, then Coakley's account of selfhood is found wanting, as she posits an ontology and ends of desire and identity that postmodernism would eschew. Moreover, and more significantly, queer theory identifies this assumed ontology of desire that Coakley operates with as a "regime of power-knowledge-pleasure"—as indicative of and participating in "human ambition to knowledge, control, and mastery."[25] This is evidenced not only through Coakley's account of subject formation but also through her identification of a clear originary, and teleological, value (of divine desire) to which the subject should conform.

The critique of originary values is another insight Huffer offers through her reflections on Foucault's genealogical method. Huffer begins her book *Are the Lips a Grave?* by offering an important corrective to the genealogical method as it is now commonly evoked, explaining that it is now popularly used, "*contra Foucault* to denote the tracing of influence or lines of filiation."[26] Huffer points out that this is not what Foucault was doing, that he distinguishes genealogy "from the continuities that characterize history writing: genealogy eschews the search for origins and reconfigures the past as disparate, discontinuous, and radically contingent."[27] Genealogy is not about tracing a theme or pattern as it functions throughout history; rather, it is about discovering and revealing the inconsistencies and gaps. The genealogist does not seek to identify a clear origin and path; rather, it is the precise opposite—in critquing "the value of values, the genealogist exposes the creation of values as a problem of origin."[28] In identifying this search for coherence as a false production of (an assumed, given) origin, Huffer—following Nietzsche and Foucault (and, later, the feminist theorist Luce Irigaray)—demonstrates how the assumption of and search for origins is a function of and desire for mastery. This mastery relies on and reinforces "the rational-moral premises of Western thought" and in doing so "both produces origin as the source of truth and masks the violence of that production."[29]

Huffer's Foucauldian return to genealogy highlights a key problem with Coakley's project, in that it firmly claims a clear origin of desire despite its concomitant claims to eschew mastery. Coakley assumes a stability of the subject and the origin of the subject's desires without questioning or even attending to the way one's being, desires, and relationships are formed and delimited by (theo-)onto-epistemological regimes of knowledge-power-pleasure. In that assumption, she (re-)performs an "uninterrogated epistemic authority of moralizing critical subjects" that not only "masks the violence of that production" and limits possibilities for flourishing but also contradicts the unmastery and destabilization of identity through contemplation that she is claiming to seek.[30] The originary and teleological value Coakley gives to desire of and for the divine at times overtly presses against her claims of unmastery, which is revealed through Coakley's reflections on rationality.

For Coakley, it is the third person of the Trinity, the Spirit, that enables our participation in the divine—"constantly and 'reflexively' at work in believers in the circle of response to the Father's call."[31] In incorporating us, the Spirit is also responsible for this transforming unmastery: In having to "yield to the Spirit's 'sighs too deep for words,' it follows that prayer at its deepest is God's, not ours, and takes the pray-er beyond any normal human language or rationality of control."[32] Turning to Patristic resources for a Spirit-led Trinitarian theology based in prayer, in chapter 6, "Batter My Heart," Coakley juxtaposes Gregory of Nyssa with Augustine, looking at how their respective accounts "might mutually illuminate one another."[33] Although Coakley acknowledges how Augustine's account of desire, which argues that the "rightful *harmony* between the rational activities of the mind," is in stark contrast to "Gregory's spiritual emphasis on the indispensability of loss of mental control," she argues that Augustine's account is nuanced and eschews mastery in that it is "only *God* who can finally supply the (graced) control that human, ascetic effort constantly fails to achieve."[34] With divine desire as the originary value, God then becomes the agent through which rational knowledge and order can occur—mastery is now not so much upended as it is displaced onto and through the divine. This expansion, rather then eschewal, of rationality that Coakley calls for also reflects the telos of desire in Coakley's account and the linear account it relies on.

### *The Telos of Desire and the Linearity of Straight Time*

Coakley's *théologie totale* assumes and contends a specific telos of the desiring subject that, grounded in this originary tale, performs the same anti-Foucauldian genealogical move and (thus) has the same effects; here, especially, the insights of queer temporality reveal the limits and contradictions of her frame. Coakley calls for, and thus (re-)produces, an ideal modern (sexual) subjectivity—a subjectivity that, for her, is where our desires are rightly ordered, forged "into the likeness of [God the Father's] Son."[35] Whereas Coakley suggests this telos opens up "a radical attention to the 'other,'" Huffer, for instance, points out that for Foucault, it is participating in a pernicious "dialectical logic" that produces the subject "within a grid that differentiates subjects in relation to others," differentiating us in a "grid of deviance and normalization."[36] The teleology of desire that Coakley posits, in binding subjects to a particular vision of the good, actually closes us off from the other, including even the otherness within ourselves as it subjectivates us—as it constructs us as subjects.[37]

Lee Edelman is the most vociferous among a wide range of queer theorists in eschewing a clear telos of desire and the good, arguing that to claim such a good is to participate in a logic of "reproductive futurism," whereas queerness marks the outside of such a frame, "the place of the social order's death drive."[38] Even the very frame of temporality is problematic for Edelman. In a roundtable titled "Theorizing Queer Temporalities," Edelman notes how beginning their "conversation with a series of questions presupposing a 'turn toward time' already establishes as our central concern not the movement *toward* time but *of* it," and argues that this "very framing repeats the structuring of social reality that establishes heteronormativity as the guardian of temporal (re)production."[39] Getting the final word in the roundtable, Edelman wonders if "we need to consider that you *don't* get 'from here to somewhere else,'" and proposes queerness as a "a nonteleological negativity that refuses the leavening of piety and with it the dollop of sweetness afforded by messianic hope."[40]

Whereas Edelman's eschewal of an account of futurity in toto has been a key site of debate among queer theorists of temporality, even those who reject his totalizing commitment to negativity share his critique of the linearity of time, of its "narrative accountings" that, in positing an ideal end, also rely on and (re-)create "social scripts that usher even the most queer among us through major markers of individual development and into normativity."[41] Queerness and queer time challenge and resist this linear path that normalizes and idealizes, and thus excludes. It does not suffice for the path to be expanded and transformed. Coakley's use of Freud in her call for an expansion of rationality is particularly salient here. While she ultimately argues that "Freud must be . . . turned on his head" and that *"desire is more fundamental than 'sex,'"* not the other way around, Coakley highlights—and lauds—how Freud became "more attuned to the Platonic view of desire" and "argued that sublimation is entirely necessary for civilization to endure."[42] Coakley calls for "spiritual practices of attention that mysteriously challenge and *expand* the range of rationality, and simultaneously darken and break one's hold on previous certainties."[43] For Coakley, eros/desire is linear rationality transformed toward this ideal end of divine desire—erotic excess is reined in and transformed.

What Coakley lauds in Freud is precisely what Lynne Huffer reads as eros's problematic recoding as a function of biopower, "eros-as-bios," which "captures the psyche in a patriarchal system," a system that "incites and imprisons us as sexual beings."[44] What is telling in this juxtaposition is not the validity (or lack thereof) of Huffer's and Coakley's interpretations of Freud, but their differing diagnoses of the function and place of eros within that reading.[45] Whereas Coakley reads erotic transformation of desire as a narrative, linear, formative process, grounded in a rational-moral frame, Huffer reads eros

> as a disappearance: a profile dissolving at the edge of the horizon, a shadow cast as it falls. Eros becomes the name for that which is lost in the moral rationalization of modern sexuality as the site of our intelligibility. In a moment that leaves eros behind as the unintelligible form of a fading unreason, it can only reemerge, in the historical present, as an atemporal rupture—as the lightning-quick flash of a "mad" mode of knowing—within the scientific specification of the sexual *dispositif's* ever-proliferating list of perversions.[46]

Eros does not merely transform and reorient the subject, it (ethically) dissolves the subject, shattering the subject through and by the encounter of alterity, what Huffer explains as "a heterotopian *ethopoiesis*, an ethical remaking of the erotic relation."[47] Similarly, Edelman's queer temporal critique, which is grounded in psychoanalytic theory, also counters this linear Coakleyian logic, as "queerness marks the excess of something always unassimilable that troubles the relentlessly totalizing impulse informing normativity."[48]

Whereas Edelman and Huffer highlight how linearity and narrative coherence subjectivize and limit, Coakley's account overtly demands the practice of contemplation as the clear path one must travel, in such a way that forecloses a recognition of otherness rather than an ability to attend to it. Coakley argues that "if one is resolutely *not* engaged in the practices of prayer, contemplation, and worship, there are certain sorts of philosophical insights that are unlikely, if not impossible to occur to one."[49] Coakley places firm boundaries around a clear path toward such unmastery—the boundaries and clarity of which queer temporality reads as oppressive and limiting. Do the insights and critiques of queer temporality then countermand contemplation and theological formation in toto?

## ASTONISHED CONTEMPLATION: TOWARD A QUEER TIME AND SPACE (OR, WHO IS THE WE?)

In the preceding section, I hoped to demonstrate how, in her failure to note, interrogate, or even recognize, straight time, Coakley undermines her own aim of openness to the other and reproduces the problem of mastery she seeks to overcome. In this latter half of the chapter, then, I gesture toward the possibility of an account of formation in a queer time and space. Although Edelman argues that queer temporal critiques demand a rejection of futurity—and thus, one might surmise, of formation altogether—that queerness marks the "place of the social order's death drive," and therefore we are to embrace "'epistemological self-destruction' for all," even he gestures, ever so slightly, toward an alternative: that such "queerness proposes, in place of the good, something . . . 'better,' though it promises, in more than one sense of the phrase, absolutely nothing."[50] What might such an account look like?

Whereas Edelman argues that queerness figures as the negative of the social order, and futurity must be rejected, for Muñoz, it is not the future per se that is the problem but rather the ways in which straight time constricts the future by demanding conformity to a norm. In *Cruising Utopia: The Then and There of Queer Futurity*, Muñoz calls for a queer time that is not bound to this linear, coherent, teleological narrative of straight time, a "future in the present" that is not so much to be grasped and attained (as this too would fall under a logic of straight time) but enacted and glimpsed.[51] Even though Muñoz's vision is utopic, it does not operate with the same kind of prescriptive linear telos of success as Coakley's *théologie totale* does. Queerness, Muñoz argues, if it "is to have any value whatsoever . . . must be viewed as being visible only in the horizon," and it is not reached via a graspable future, but experienced in the glimpses of the perpetual horizon, within the quotidian examples of "utopian bonds, affiliations, designs, and gestures that exist within the present moment."[52] Rather than a linear trajectory toward an ideal end through particular contemplative practices, queer temporality resists the linear by envisioning a future in the present and resists a linearly prescriptive path by using as raw material for enacting that future not perfected practices but the detritus, through excesses and everydayness. In doing so, queer time liberatively engenders inclusion over the exclusionary enactment of particular ideals.

Muñoz begins *Cruising Utopia* with an examination of a 1971 revolutionary queer manifesto that he argues is "especially radical and poignant [in its demands] when compared to the anemic political agenda that dominates contemporary LGBTQ politics in North America today."[53] The "we" that these activists refer to in their manifesto, Muñoz explains, "does not speak to a merely identitarian logic but instead to a logic of futurity." This "'we,'" he continues, "speaks to a 'we' that is not yet conscious, the future society that is being invoked and addressed at the same moment."[54] Muñoz thus begins his argument about queer time by focusing on the community that enacts the potential future, rather than in seeking clear answers as to how it might be secured. The account of queer time that Muñoz offers in *Cruising Utopia* offers a useful alternative framework, and his methodological and formational assumptions that I have already outlined—the future in the present, queerness as horizon, potentiality through excess—speak to the kind of liberative praxis that Coakley's theology calls for but doesn't engender. Muñoz's text offers a panoply of aesthetic and performative examples—practices—that evidence and engender this queer utopic vision, where "queerness' ecstatic and horizontal temporality" takes us out of straight time and in doing so offers "a path and a movement to a greater openness to the world."[55]

The examples Muñoz offers provide a vision of formation that is markedly different from the teleological linearity that guides Coakley's *théologie totale*, as they assume a temporality that subverts and upends clear binaries between past-present and present-future, gesturing instead toward muddled and circular accounts of formation and method—which open up possibilities for freedom, what Muñoz explains as "freedom as unboundedness."[56] "I do not wish to render a picture of utopia that is prescriptive," Muñoz asserts, explaining that he instead wants "to connote an ideality—a desire for a thing, or a way, that is not here but is nonetheless desirable, something worth striving for."[57] In speaking of a future present that envisions and engenders potentialities of utopias that are to be found as traces, glimmers, and kernels in performances, aesthetics, and the ways in which we organize our lives, Muñoz offers examples rather than prescriptions, and even his examples are mere gestures toward and traces of "certain mode[s] of nonbeing that [are] eminent, thing[s] that [are] present but not actually existing in the present tense."[58]

Moreover, like Coakley, Muñoz also proposes a methodology—what he calls "hope's methodology"—that he employs in his own understanding of the practicing of queer time: that of "astonished contemplation," which admittedly juxtaposes nicely with Coakley's emphasis on contemplation.[59] A sense of astonishment, the invitation of surprise and mystery into our spiritual, social, and moral formation enables us to think beyond the coherent, narrative, linear account of subjectivity, and the place of practices as securing that path that marks straight time, and thus helps us see and imagine anew.

The feminist theologian Wendy Farley's account of contemplation speaks to this sense of astonishment. In *Gathering Those Driven Away: A Theology of Incarnation*, she offers an account of formation that is rooted in belonging, ultimately rooted in the incarnation of Christ and the ecclesiastical implications of the incarnation of the God-man. In explaining the influences that underlie the text, Farley explains that "the wound that moves in this particular piece of writing is the fight over sexual minorities in the Christian churches. . . . The situation of queer Christians," she continues, "reveals this wound in so much of Christianity: it cannot perceive in its own members the beauty of Christ's body."[60] Grounding her reflection in this reality demands for Farley an eschewal of a clear teleology of success, a rejection of a particular account of the good. As Farley, after recounting various womanist and mujerista theologians' analyses that "the good" really translates as "whiteness," puts it:

> Womanist writers call out this lie and insist that obedience and docility are not marks of faith. They separate us from our true selves and therefore from the divine image in us. For women, for subjects of violence, for gay and lesbian and transgendered people, it is necessary to counter the supposed virtues professed by the church if we are to rediscover our faith. We are in the disorienting situation of being embedded in a religious community that trains us to despise the very things that our Beloved created us to be.[61]

Whereas Coakley's account speaks solely to the benefits of contemplation and articulates it as engendering an openness to the other, she fails to speak to the ways in which some communities are societally demarcated as "other" in such a way that could potentially be exacerbated by personal and communal religious practices. Farley conversely notes how personal and communal practices are not always positive for those who do not materially embody the ideal form of the straight white male.

Moreover, as I have discussed in the section above, in positing formation as a linear path toward an ideal form—even a path and form that functions to expand and subvert our previous certainties—Coakley not only fails to attend to how normalization and idealization can affect the psychic and material conditions of minorities, but she also participates in the constitutions of norms that can operate as "preemptive and violent circumscription[s] of reality," establishing the "ontological field in which bodies may be given legitimate expression."[62] Coakley puts boundaries on the possibilities of identity formation while failing to attend to how those boundaries, and the subsequent subjectivities these boundaries produce, are often negatively affected by the vision of formation she outlines.

Farley's recognition of the limiting, exclusionary, and oppressive experiences faced by minority groups leads her to also recognize, and reject, a singular, clearly bounded linear account of formation and history; she explains that "the reflections in this volume work on the hypothesis that the institutional churches and their canonical theologians do not represent the only lineage of apostolic witness from whom we know something about the mystery of the incarnation."[63] A clearly bounded, narrative linear account of history and formational processes is not only problematic because of where it leads, Farley points out, but because of who it leaves out in its account of the past and thus in its vision of the future. Farley seeks an account and calls for an ethic that align with queer time and space because she believes that this reflects the incarnation itself. "Mother Christ no doubt vilifies the institutional church," she asserts, "but she also wanders outside the church, no more constrained by it than by the body that Rome crucified."[64] Christ, for Farley, is found outside of the clearly conscribed path, glimpsed wandering around a variety of noninstitutional locales. Moreover, our path toward participating in and being transformed by the divine does not travel a clear, defined path. "The process of sanctification," for Farley, is one in which we participate in practices where we discover the "kingdom in which we wander: immigrants and refugees just learning how to live in a land of freedom."[65]

In the final chapter of her book, Farley "meditates on examples of practices through which we can learn to embody our own incarnation."[66] While, like Coakley, Farley recognizes and embraces contemplation—as it "augments this [conceptual acceptance of the namelessness of Divinity] with a practice that moved awareness beyond conceptual apprehension"—Farley does not focus solely, or even primarily, on it.[67] Just as Muñoz seeks glimpses of queer time through the quotidian, where a "surplus" can emerge that points us to a potentiality of "something that is not quite here," Farley recognizes the significance of the excess through the everyday.[68] "One practice might be going to church," she notes, "but practice is also all of the things we do in the course of everyday life." Through everyday acts such as cooking, playing with children, eating and drinking, making love, Farley explains, "our blind eyes have opened to one another's beauty" and we "see Christ in ordinary pleasures."[69] Whereas Coakley argues that "a particular set of bodily and spiritual practices (both individual and liturgical) are the *precondition* for trinitarian thinking of a deep sort," and that, once this is granted, "one is already admitting that the task of theology—on this view—cannot simply be 'conformed to the world,'" Farley suggests that it is through such worldly acts that we see and find Christ.[70]

• • •

This chapter has sought to detail how Coakley's *théologie totale*, in operating with a linear, narrative-driven, teleological account of desire and formation that one attains/achieves via contemplation is stuck within what Muñoz calls "straight time's choke hold," which thereby impedes and limits the potentialities for theological and personal transformation for which Coakley calls; I have turned to Farley and Muñoz to further elucidate the limits of Coakley's approach as well as to gesture toward an account of method and formation that avoids these constraints through a nonlinear, queer account of time that might enable us to envision and enact new and liberative "future presents" to work toward and participate in Christ's redemptive work in the world.

Following Muñoz's emphasis on the potentialities in the aesthetic and performative, I conclude this chapter with two brief poetic examples that speak to formation in a queer time and place, one by the womanist ethicist Emilie Townes, and the other by the queer spoken-word artist Andrea Gibson. Although Coakley not only accepts but also possibly calls for hierarchy of order—writing that "where hierarchy simply means order, then, it is not at all clear that feminism should oppose it"—Gibson's poem "Pole Dancing to Gospel Hymns," speaks to the glimpses and excesses Muñoz notes.[71] As Gibson puts it:

> She pole-dances to gospel hymns. Came out to her family in the middle of Thanksgiving grace. I knew she was trouble two years before our first date. But my heart was a Labrador Retriever, with its head hung out the window of a car, tongue flapping in the wind on a highway going 95 whenever she walked by. So I mastered the art of crochet, and I crocheted her a winter scarf, and one night at the bar I gave it to her with a note that said something like, I hope this keeps your neck warm. If it doesn't, give me a call. The key to finding love, is fucking up the pattern on purpose, is skipping a stitch, is leaving a tiny, tiny hole to let the cold in and hoping she mends it with your lips.[72]

Gibson's poetic reflection on "finding love," on desire and relationality, suggests, like Muñoz's reflection on utopic potentialities and Huffer's account of eros as atemporal rupture, that it is found in that which is out of sync with time and space—not just in spite of the excesses and failures, but precisely in and through them.

Finally, whereas Coakley's methodology seeks a clear formational process through a specific practice, Townes, in a poetic reflection that resonates with Farley's work, concludes *Womanist Ethics and the Cultural Production of Evil*, with a reflection on the everyday. "Ultimately, somewhere deep inside each of us we know that perhaps the simplest, yet the most difficult, answer to the challenge of what we will do with the fullness and incompleteness of who we are as we stare down the interior life of the cultural production of evil is *live your faith deeply*," Townes explains, noting that doing so "is not a quest for perfection, but for what we call in Christian ethics the everydayness of moral acts. It is what we do every day that shapes us and where both the fantastic hegemonic imagination and the challenge and hope to dismantle it are found."[73]

Like Coakley, Townes emphasizes embodied practices as theologically and formationally significant, but like Farley, Townes locates such "graced" practices in ordinary, quotidian acts—the "everydayness" of events like "designing a class session or lecture or reading or writing or thinking," of "sharing a meal," of "facing heartache and disappointment [and experiencing] joy and laughter."[74] Rather than seeking a clear end and a clear path to travel to attain that end, an ethic in a queer time and place recognizes that everydayness is where we reside, and thus where new futures are imagined and communities and people are formed—the future present that Muñoz speaks of and calls for, a utopic vision that is inclusive, imaginative, and always on the horizon, and in that, is liberative and desirable. Townes's vision is undeniably one of inclusion and belonging. She recognizes people are formed through these daily practices, and formed in community, and that we thus "must live and be witness to a justice wrapped in a love that will not let us go, and a peace that is simply too ornery to give up on us."[75] Given how queer temporality calls into question the normalizing, exclusionary limits of linearity, and gestures instead toward potentiality and openness, the conclusion of her poetic reflection, an invitation to embrace the circuitous complexity of formation in and through everydayness is also apt here: "Won't you join me?"

## NOTES

1. In an interview with Rupert Shortt, Coakley explains that "time on my knees . . . provides one of the central themes for my entire project as a systematic theologian," and that the "loss of mastery" that prayer engenders "is not inimical to feminist empowerment, but—paradoxically—is its very condition" (Sarah Coakley, "New Paths in Systematic Theology," in *God's Advocates: Christian Thinkers in Conversation*, ed. Rupert Shortt [Grand Rapids, Mich.: Wm. B. Eerdmans, 2005], 71). And in an introduction to a symposium on Coakley's work, Gösta Hallonsten notes that "the characteristic features of the theological work of Sarah Coakley" are "clearly feminism and gender theology" as well as "the emphasis on prayer, especially contemplative prayer, and also on practice as a locus for doing theology" (Gösta Hallonsten, "Sarah Coakley—A Symposium," *Svensk Teologisk Kvartalskrift* 85, no. 1 [2009]: 49, 50). Finally, it is important to note that though this is a central theme in Coakley's work, her oeuvre is extensive in both its depth and breadth. Coakley has written on a variety of topics ranging from the liberal christology of Ernst Troelstch to disputes within patristic Trinitarian formulations to evolution and the rationality of religious belief, to name just a few.
2. Sarah Coakley, *Powers and Submissions: Spirituality, Philosophy and Gender* (Malden, Mass.: Wiley-Blackwell, 2002), xx (emphasis mine). As Mark Oppenheimer puts it in a review of the text for the *Christian Century*, "In the thicket of verbiage are two main clearings, general themes that reappear. The first is that feminist theory is a powerful tool not always well used. The second is that prayer needs to be a central category of theology" (Mark Oppenheimer, "Sarah Coakley Reconstructs Feminism," *Christian Century*, June 28, 2003, 27).
3. Sarah Coakley, *God, Sexuality, and the Self: An Essay "On the Trinity"* (New York: Cambridge University Press, 2013).
4. Ibid., 1, 10.
5. Ibid., 19.
6. Ibid., 34.
7. For critiques of Coakley, see Anna Mercedes, *Power For: Feminism and Christ's Self-Giving* (New York: Bloomsbury T&T Clark, 2011); Beth Felker Jones, "The Spirit Helps Us in Our Weakness: A Review of *God, Sexuality, and the Self*," *Other Journal*,

accessed April 7, 2015, http://theotherjournal.com/2014/06/09/the-spirit-helps-us-in-our-weakness-a-review-of-god-sexuality-and-the-self/; Jodi L. A. Belcher, "Subversion through Subjection: A Feminist Reconsideration of Kenosis in Christology and Christian Discipleship" (Master's thesis, Vanderbilt University, 2008); and Jonna Bornemark, "Kenosis as Mirroring," *Svensk Teologisk Kvartalskrift* 85, no. 1 (2009): 75–80. Coakley's methodology has been subject to less critical attention, likely because of the book's recent publication.

8. "Privileging contemplation," is the first of the nine distinctive methodological hallmarks of *théologie totale* that Coakley outlines in list form (Coakley, *God, Sexuality, and the Self,* 87). For the full list, see 87–97.
9. Ibid., 43.
10. José Esteban Muñoz, *Cruising Utopia: The Then and There of Queer Futurity* (New York: New York University Press, 2009), 182.
11. Coakley, *God, Sexuality, and the Self,* 43. See also Coakley, *Powers and Submissions,* 52, 54.
12. Coakley, *God, Sexuality, and the Self,* 2. At the end of the same introductory chapter, Coakley writes that "theology involves not merely the metaphysical task of adumbrating a vision of God, the world, and humanity, but simultaneously the *epistemological* task of cleansing, reordering, and redirecting the apparatuses of one's own thinking, desiring, and seeing" (20).
13. Ibid., 5.
14. Ibid. Coakley's account is grounded in early patristic Trinitarian formulations, a "critical retrieval of this spiritual nexus," where "the right ordering of desire was not, of course, alien to some of the greatest early Christian thinkers of the late antique era," that, rather "the perception of 'perfect relation in God' (the Trinity) was fundamentally attuned, and correlated, to their concomitant views about men and women, gender roles, and the nature of 'erotic' desire" (5, 2). Coakley offers an archaeology of how this approach faded from modern theology and proposes her method as a way to retrieve it.
15. Ibid., 105.
16. Ibid., 44.
17. See, for instance, Carolyn Dinshaw et al., "Theorizing Queer Temporalities: A Roundtable Discussion," *GLQ: A Journal of Lesbian and Gay Studies* 13, no. 2 (2007): 177–95; Robert L. Caserio et al., "The Antisocial Thesis in Queer Theory," *PMLA* 121, no. 3 (2006): 819–28.
18. See Caserio et al., "The Antisocial Thesis in Queer Theory."
19. Michel Foucault, *The History of Sexuality*, vol. 1: *An Introduction*, trans. Robert Hurley (New York: Vintage Books, 1978), 11.
20. Michel Foucault, "The Subject and Power," *Critical Inquiry* 8, no. 4 (1982): 781.
21. Lynne Huffer, *Are the Lips a Grave?: A Queer Feminist on the Ethics of Sex* (New York: Columbia University Press, 2013), 31.
22. Huffer explains that it is "a commitment to the queer undoing of modern subjectivity that distinguishes the antisocial thesis from other strands of queer theory" (ibid., 33).

23. Ibid. 17. See also n. 47: "I want to reiterate what Edelman points out in response to his critics," Huffer writes, "that the differences between the intersectional and antisocial strands of queer theory revolve more around differing investments in subjectivity than they do around success or failure in diagnosing an unjust present order."
24. Coakley, *God, Sexuality, and the Self*, 26, 27.
25. Ibid., 44; Foucault, *History of Sexuality*, vol. 1, 11.
26. Huffer, *Are the Lips a Grave?* 2.
27. Ibid.
28. Ibid., 3.
29. Ibid., 4.
30. Ibid., 17.
31. Coakley, *God, Sexuality, and the Self*, 111.
32. Ibid., 114. Coakley bases this account of Spirit-led prayer and its effects on Romans 8.
33. Coakley, *God, Sexuality, and the Self*, 276.
34. Ibid., 279.
35. Ibid.,, 6.
36. Ibid., 83; Huffer, *Are the Lips a Grave?* 47, 31.
37. "Subjectivation" refers to the Foucauldian notion of the ways in which the self is constructed as a subject, and constrained or subjugated in that construction by power—a process that is both passive and active. It is the term scholars have used as a translation for the French term *assujettissement*. See, for instance, James W. Bernauer, *Michel Foucault's Force of Flight: Toward an Ethics for Thought* (Atlantic Highlands, N.J.: Humanities Press, 1990), 123; Mark G. E. Kelly, *The Political Philosophy of Michel Foucault* (New York: Routledge, 2009), 88.
38. Lee Edelman, *No Future: Queer Theory and the Death Drive* (Durham, N.C.: Duke University Press, 2004), 3.
39. Dinshaw et al., "Theorizing Queer Temporalities," 180–81.
40. Ibid., 195.
41. Ibid., 182.
42. Coakley, *God, Sexuality, and the Self*, 9, 7.
43. Ibid., 33.
44. Huffer, *Are the Lips a Grave?* 31.
45. Not all scholars writing on temporality and antisociality would agree with Huffer's, and thus Coakley's, reading of Freud (and subsequent critique of psychoanalysis). Edelman, for instance, turns *to* psychoanalytic theory (though he relies on Lacan, not Freud) as a frame for his critique of linearity and teleology. See also Leo Bersani, *Is the Rectum a Grave? and Other Essays* (Chicago: University of Chicago Press, 2009); Kent L. Brintnall, *Ecce Homo: The Male-Body-in-Pain as Redemptive Figure* (Chicago: University of Chicago Press, 2012).
46. Huffer, *Are the Lips a Grave?* 12.
47. Ibid., 43.
48. Dinshaw et al., "Theorizing Queer Temporalities," 189.

49. Coakley, *God, Sexuality, and the Self,* 16.
50. Edelman, *No Future*, 3, 5; Dinshaw et al., "Theorizing Queer Temporalities," 195.
51. Muñoz, *Cruising Utopia*, 49.
52. Ibid., 11, 22–23.
53. Ibid., 19, 20.
54. Ibid., 20.
55. Ibid., 25.
56. Ibid., 32.
57. Ibid., 121.
58. Ibid., 9.
59. Ibid., 5. Muñoz himself takes the term from Bloch. See Ernst Bloch, *The Utopian Function of Art and Literature: Selected Essays*, trans. Jack Zipes and Frank Mecklenburg (Cambridge, Mass.: MIT Press, 1989), 18–70.
60. Wendy Farley, *Gathering Those Driven Away: A Theology of Incarnation* (Louisville, Ky.: Westminster John Knox Press, 2011), 2.
61. Ibid., 10.
62. Judith Butler, *Gender Trouble: Feminism and the Subversion of Identity* (New York: Routledge, 2006), xxiii. Although Coakley argues that through contemplation, the Divine transforms gender expression, rendering gender more "labile," she nevertheless claims an ontological two-ness of gender (Coakley, *God, Sexuality, and the Self,* 35, 55–58, 87, 115, 252). For instance, in discussing the "secular riddle of gender," Coakley argues that it can only be solved when "its connection to the doctrine of a Trinitarian God" is understood and embraced (54). This claim and the argument that follows make a number of epistemological assumptions that are concerning, the most obvious one being that there *is* a sort of ontological twoness of gender, even if it is fallen and subject to a "transfiguring interruption" (58). Coakley goes on to claim that the Trinity and our participation in the triune life of God "does not obliterate the twoness of gender" but rather transforms and redeems it (59).
63. Farley, *Gathering Those Driven Away*, 10.
64. Ibid.
65. Ibid., 206.
66. Ibid.
67. Ibid., 12.
68. Muñoz, *Cruising Utopia*, 6.
69. Farley, *Gathering Those Driven Away*, 223.
70. Coakley, *God, Sexuality, and the Self,* 16.
71. Ibid., 319.
72. Andrea Gibson, "Pole Dancer," in *Pole Dancing to Gospel Hymns* (Nashville, Tenn.: Write Bloody Publishing, 2008), 7.
73. Emilie M. Townes, *Womanist Ethics and the Cultural Production of Evil* (New York: Palgrave Macmillan, 2006), 164.
74. Ibid., 164–65.
75. Ibid., 165.

# The Madness of Holy Saturday: Bipolar Temporality and the Queerdom of Heaven on Earth

KAREN BRAY

Is there an end to capitalism? As in, "Does capitalism have an end time, an apocalyptic thrust—the apex of which we might be nearing?" *And* as in, "Does capitalism have an end goal, a telos toward which it strives?" Further, what does it mean to live in the *time* of twenty-first-century neoliberalism? As in what are the "signs" (mores, theologies, affects) of our time? *And* as in under what constructs of temporality do we labor? Questions of ends, times, and End Times have been at the forefront of contemporary political theologies. For instance, in *The Theology of Money*, Philip Goodchild warns of the eschatological judgment of money. Money defines value and, through its promissory nature (as in the promise "One day I'll have enough money," or, in other words, "One day I will finally be enough"), money holds us in suspense of achieving value. The sovereignty of money fortifies an eschatological hope akin to what Lauren Berlant has diagnosed as cruel optimism: "A relation of cruel optimism exists when something you desire is actually an obstacle to your flourishing."[1] In other words, as Goodchild has noted, under neoliberalism spending time is subordinated to saving it.[2] If, as the saying goes, "time is money," then we have to use our "time wisely," by saving as much of it as possible. In other words our hours need to be spent productively or, better, profitably. We bring our laptops on the bus so that travel time is also work time. We don't saunter errands; we run them. No one ever says, "You wouldn't believe what a great unitasker she is!" Conversely, spending time—time to play, to make love, to lie in the grass and just be—places us in debt. To spend time unproductively, neoliberalism tells us, is to have "wasted our time." Hence, even as we are held in suspense of the moneyed eschaton we must be ever more efficient producers of promised wealth. By promising its fulfillment in a nearly unattainable state of future wealth, the eschatological judgment of money holds our flourishing at bay.

The effects of such cruelly optimistic demands must be of critical importance to theologies that take seriously the question of how we might ethically spend time instead of obsessively saving it. Although I affirm Goodchild's diagnosis of the moneyed eschaton, there is still more to ask of political theologians and the counters they offer to the hold on us this eschatological promise has. For instance, few have adequately addressed how post-Fordist temporalities feel. And as such how we might learn to embody a different sense of time. For this we may need queer theory. Hence, throughout this essay I hope to trace the following framing contentions. First, I argue that theologians must confront the spread of neoliberalism in all facets of life. This is in part owing to what I, and others, have diagnosed as neoliberalism's theological character, which includes the above-mentioned eschatological dimensions. Second, I propose that the field of radical political theology, while it addresses neoliberalism, still contains problematic universal claims and anemic concepts that seem to elide the effects neoliberalism has on our bodies, psyches, and collectivities. Third, I surmise that these overdeterminations and lacunae can be brought to light in an examination of the different approaches to temporality undertaken by radical orthodox and radical democratic theologians. Fourth, I suggest that although at times mirroring some of the same contentious issues found in democratic/orthodox debates, queer approaches to temporality offer invaluable resources for a political theology that takes seriously the affectual consequences of neoliberalism. In particular, I suggest that those whose temporal and affectual orientations impede productivity and efficiency have something crucial to teach us about the dire effects neoliberalism has on us all. Finally, through an engagement with queer theories of temporality and affect as well as theologies of Holy Saturday, I propose the concept of bipolar time as a queer temporal reorientation, one that resists the eschatological demands of neoliberalism. It is my hope that bipolar time might reorient us toward different modes of feeling and living. These modes offer neither resurrection out of the pain of neoliberalism such that we might come to be its productive agents once more (happy customers, efficient laborers), nor nihilistic acceptance of the pains endured in the quotidian crucifixions perpetrated in service of neoliberalism's cruelly optimistic promise. Bipolar temporality in its disordering of time disrupts this crucifixion/resurrection binary. Ultimately, this essay explores what embracing our senses of disorder might have to do with challenging the econo-political and theological orders of the day.

## RADICAL THEOLOGIES OF OUR TIME

To the moneyed eschaton radical political theologians have sought counters.[3] Radical orthodoxy (RO) proposes a return to the Christian Kingdom. Others, whom we might call radical democratic theologians, propose the eventiveness of the multitude—an in-breaking of democratic potential. For both orthodox and democratic theologians the temporality of the "event" is key to the making of theological value judgments. According to RO's standard-bearer John Milbank, "The Church is the most fundamental of events, interpreting all other events."[4] The seemingly uniform church becomes the standard by which all other historical events must be judged. The judgment of the church rejects a temporality that does not move forward because of a certain end-goal, one nurtured by the often eruptive, fractured, and discontinuous movement of the immanent world. For Milbank this sense of "directionless" time cannot be accepted by a truly Christian ontology, one necessarily predicated on the one true Good. For RO more broadly, teleological ordering modeled by the event of the church implies a temporal pull toward a historical given.[5] Milbank's understanding of the all-interpreting event of the church is a statement against both an open-ended future and a slippery past.

Conversely, radical democratic theologians such as Clayton Crockett and Jeffrey Robbins embrace a discontinuous temporality. For these thinkers, the event is precisely that which cannot be interpreted by uniform, imperial structures that demand obedience. Robbins argues:

> The political potency that is key to radical democracy's resistance to all forms of hegemony comes not by a way of transcendent authority—by an appeal to some power outside ourselves—but by way of an exodus emanating from within: "In Postmodernity," [Negri] writes, "the eminent form of rebellion is the exodus from obedience, that is to say, from participation in measure, i.e., as the opening to the immeasurable."[6]

Participation in the immeasurable moves us away from a providential time measured by proper eschatological ends and certain Christological beginnings.

Crockett finds a similar move in Gilles Deleuze's study of cinema. Crockett finds political weight in Deleuzian thought when in *Cinema 2: The Time Image*, Deleuze asks what happens when we realize that a progressive history is no longer a viable way to view time in the world.[7] He finds temporal openings in new forms of political cinema in which "the cinematographic image becomes a direct presentation of time, according to non-commensurable relations and irrational cuts. . . . This time-image puts thought into contact with an unthought, the unsummonable, the inexplicable, the undecidable, the incommensurable."[8] This image of time in which one can no longer trace a universal procession from old to new asks what and who have been left out of history. For Deleuze, the temporal inconsistencies brought to the fore by political cinema remind us that a people have been missing.[9] In suggesting that a people have been missing, Deleuze is pointing to the ways in which stories of the marginalized are often both left out of official histories and excluded from mainstream cultural production. Hence, for Crockett, via Deleuze, the possibility of the event is the opening in time for the radicalization of democracy. Such a radicalization would take, Crockett proposes, an impossible future that is not a clear temporal extension of the present, but rather exists in the shadow of an "unforeseen event."[10] And yet might these democratic ideas of event and exodus lend themselves to abstraction, eclipsing the historical realities of subjects living within the flux of time and eclipsing the functions of power that determine who is made more vulnerable by the providential ordering of time?

Although RO theologians often sidestep such questions of power, it is in the slide into abstraction that Milbank and his fellows find the need for the regulation of values through the judgment of the orthodox church. Liberal theologies, they argue, too easily lend themselves to the free play of desire viewed as characteristic of capitalism. According to RO theologian William Cavanaugh, true freedom comes in the freedom to choose obedience to Christ over the market.[11] The critique of an untethered desire in his *Being Consumed: Economics and Christian Desire* is emblematic of the issue of desire found in RO writings. Cavanaugh argues that, unlike the neoliberal assertion that freedom is freedom from interference by others, true freedom comes in the freedom to choose one's proper desires. But is there really no end to capitalist desire? In other words, is there no goal toward which a faith in the market is oriented? Is capitalistic freedom a freedom without the regulations of imperial demands? Let us return to the opening questions of this essay. What is the time of neoliberal capitalism? Or rather what is the arc of time? What does it mean to be held in suspense of the moneyed eschaton? Is it not similar to being held in suspense of the Christian one? In other words, can we really avoid the resonance between the temporal structure nurtured by an orthodox, and so particularist, interpretation of value found in RO writings and the temporal structure proposed by the promissory nature of money?

The commonalities of effects of such temporal orientations—those structured around providence—between that of the Christian Kingdom and that of the market are many. We can see some in William Connolly's concept of the evangelical-capitalistic-resonance-machine. The ECRM is bound together by shared fundamentalist faiths: The belief in an omnipotent God resonates with that of an omnipotent market. In addition to its exclusionary nature, the return to orthodoxy sought by RO theology feeds an untenable situation: "Both religious and economic fundamentalists dream an impossible dream of a world of simplicity in which complete redemption is possible, overseen by a rational and dependable God."[12] Neoliberalism relies on keeping the majority of the population dreaming while systematically making that dream more impossible. Radical orthodox theologians rely on the universal particular that excludes those who do not hold Christianity as the arbiter of value (or who do not fit into their idea of what a Christian is) from reaching their salvific dream. Without this exclusionary nature Milbank's claim to seriousness, which he finds in the particularity of Christian virtue over and against a generalization of virtue, crumbles.[13]

Perhaps we are in need of a crumbling seriousness, in need of a different dream, one resistant to such a closed and determinate telos. As Robbins might say, we need a time of exodus from such cruelly optimistic systems. Still, queer theory's embrace of the entanglement between affect and temporality may help us better recognize how this exodus is radically felt by those in processes of fleeing. Although radical democratic theologians resist the programmatic nature of time proposed by Milbank, few have sensitively engaged the strictures of captivity and those of resistance found not in the event but rather in the refusal of the productivity of a time-in-action undertaken by queer theorists. Left in the shadow of the moneyed eschaton and the wake of the uniform church, theologians seeking a middle way between a utopian future and a nostalgic past can look to queer temporalities that nurture the potency found in the equivocacy between capture and flight.

## QUEER TIME: NO DAY BUT TODAY?

> There can be no future for queers, as they are to bear the bad tidings that there can be no future at all: that the future, as Annie's hymn to the hope of "Tomorrow" understands, is "always / A day / Away."
>
> —LEE EDELMAN, *No Future: Queer Theory and the Death Drive*

> Queerness is also a performative because it is not simply a being but a doing for and toward a future. Queerness is essentially about the rejection of a here and now and an insistence on potentiality or concrete possibility for another world.
>
> —JOSÉ ESTEBAN MUÑOZ, *Cruising Utopia*

Over the last few decades queer theory has taken a critical turn toward the "antisocial" thesis. According to Robert L. Caserio, this thesis, first developed in Leo Bersani's 1995 work *Homos*, proposes that, "If there is anything 'politically indispensable' in homosexuality, it is its 'politically unacceptable' opposition to community."[14] Antisociality refuses demands for productivity and civic assimilation made by heteronormative society. The work of Lee Edelman perhaps best represents the temporality proposed by the antisocial thesis. For Edelman, politics rests on a reproductive futurism, in which the hopes of a better life are dependent on the figure of the Child, for whom we are told we must fight. Queerness, he writes in his 2004 polemic *No Future: Queer Theory and the Death Drive*, is what "names the side of those not 'fighting for the children,' the side outside the consensus by which all politics confirms the absolute value of reproductive futurism."[15] Edelman's refutation of the promise of the future opens up new temporal possibilities, ones resistant to the eschatological judgment of money.

This critique of futurism can also be used to challenge an orthodox focus on the all-interpreting-event of the church under which a promised future holds us similarly in suspense. Yet we might find problematic resonances between Edelman's universal particular in which queer experience becomes essentialized in the death drive and the universal particular in assigning the Christian God (as interpreted by the orthodox church) as the value of all values. Edelman announces:

> Fuck the social order and the Child in whose name we're collectively terrorized; fuck Annie; fuck the waif from *Les Mis*, fuck the poor, innocent kid on the Net; fuck Laws both with capital *Ls* and with small; fuck the whole network of Symbolic relations and the future that serves as its prop.[16]

Here, affirming a collective "we" terrorized by the figure of the Child, Edelman risks turning the negative into the affirmative. For instance, Lynne Huffer argues that:

> Precisely because queer performativity cannot let go of the "psyche" or "soul" which constitutes the rationalist modern subject, the moral violence of the swamp remains—even, and especially, in morality's dialectical negation as a resistance to sociality or a queer death drive. Indeed, from a Nietzschean perspective, the death drive of the queer antisocial thesis epitomizes the self-hating violence of the moral "I": "wild, free, prowling man turned backward against man himself." In dialectical terms, negation alone does not undo the "I." As Beauvoir puts it pithily with regard to surrealism: "every assassination of painting is still a painting." Every assassination of morality is still a morality.[17]

Fucking the figure of the Child (assassinating it) on whom all politics is based still creates a politics in which it is the figure of the queer pessimist for whom we now must fight. If negation does not eliminate the "I," then the question becomes, "On whose effacement is the 'I' of the queer pessimist built?" In other words, who lurks in the shadows of the symbolic created by the alignment of the queer with the death drive? This is not a novel question and was, in a manner, provocatively answered by José Esteban Muñoz in his entry in the oft-referenced 2006 issue of *PMLA: Publications of the Modern Languages Association of America*:

> I have been of the opinion that antirelational approaches to queer theory were wishful thinking, investments in deferring various dreams of difference. It has been clear to many of us, for quite a while now, that the antirelational in queer studies was the gay white man's last stand.[18]

This effacement of difference is perhaps nowhere clearer, or commented on, than in the fact that black children were never promised a future in the first place. To fuck the figure of the Child is actually to fuck the figure of the white Child, but this distinction goes undertheorized by Edelman. And this is the problem; by remaining in the universe of figures, Edelman loses track of the particularities of experience that might helpfully multiply queer approaches to feeling, temporality, and subjectivity. A similar elision takes place under Milbankian fundamentalism in which the figure of the church supersedes the particular historical experiences of those bodies that enflesh any ecclesial one.

Edelman does make clear that his target is not an actual child:

> In its coercive universalization, however, the image of the Child, not to be confused with the lived experience of any historical children, serves to regulate political discourse—to prescribe what will *count* as political discourse—by compelling such discourse to accede in advance to the reality of a collective future whose figurative status we are never permitted to acknowledge or address.[19]

And yet what makes the figure of the queer aligned with the death drive any less coercive or universal? As long as Edelman seems to be compelling us to accede to an antisocial collective present, can the figure of the queer pessimist escape the prescription of what will *count* as political discourse? Additionally, as Tim Dean has pointed out, in Edelman's use of the figure of the Child, Edelman misses certain psychoanalytic features of children, and this "enables [Edelman] to overlook all those ways in which, far from the antitheses of queerness, children may be regarded as the original queers."[20] Although I do not wish to follow Dean into the psychoanalysis of children—a path that might lead us to once again make singularities into figures—Dean helps me unravel the myopic strains in Edelman's vision. For instance, in terms of capitalist time, children and queer folk might embody a similar nonproductive function. Children are not old enough to labor in the marketplace (at least legally in the United States, although this is far from the case in much of the world), or to biologically reproduce. They take up the resources for which others have toiled; they are a burden and a waste.

Although I find Edelman's rejection of an overdetermined future compelling, and a useful counter to the imperial teleology found in RO writings, *No Future* does not escape its problematic universalizing. Both Milbank's insistence on seriousness or particularity and Edelman's elision of difference miss the ways in which unexpected actors and collectivities (the gay Christian, the black child, the mad prophet) destabilize both ultimate transcendence and ultimate annihilation.

Although democratic theology might escape this troublesome exclusivity, the temporality of the event proposed by RD thinkers could be an apt target for Edelman's critique of futurity. Indeed, if we were to replace the word "queerness" in this section's epigraph from Muñoz (whose work on queer futurity is often placed as a prime example of queer opposition to the antisocial turn) with "event" such that it became: "The event is essentially about the rejection of a here and now and an insistence on potentiality or concrete possibility for another world," we would be at the heart of radical democratic temporality. In embracing queer collectivity—an embrace that resists the elision of difference and so escapes some of the universal-particularist tendencies of Edelman—Muñoz's utopian performatives provide alternative visions of how one might spend time over saving it. Refusing pure negation, Muñoz proposed the concrete performance of hope from within queer communities. This concreteness of hope provides a key difference in the futurism found in his work and that risked by radical democratic theologians' deployments of amorphous concepts of immeasurability and exodus. According to Muñoz, "In our everyday life abstract utopias are akin to banal optimism. . . . Concrete utopias are the realm of educated hope."[21] A concrete utopia must be performed in the present, and so is felt concretely by those embodying such performances. For instance, although I find it hard to touch on how exactly an exodus from obedience and an opening to the immeasurable looks and feels, I can get physically lost and loosed from my chains on the dance floors where Muñoz wishes to take ecstasy with me. I can vibrate with the screams of Vaginal Crème Davis in the punk bar as she helps undo any sense of stable separation between my pleasure and my pain.[22] As discussed further below, with the affect theorist Ann Cvetkovich I can caress the crocheted sides of artist Alison Mitchell's "Hungry Purse," and slip into a sense of being together with others gathered in the art piece and with the material threads that encompass us.[23] And with Elizabeth Freeman I can tremble with expectation—time finally slowing down to the point where it is pleasurably unproductive—as I wait to be dominated in the S/M club.[24] From within these material enactments, ones in which one is both still here in the present and feeling one's way through a dream of a different becoming, binaries between future and past, crucifixion and resurrection, and pleasure and pain begin to fissure under the weight of the uncontainability of time and affect. Further, the concrete utopias found in the work of Muñoz, because they are enacted by collectives of people in the present, are textured with histories and bodies that confront and are confronted with moments of inscriptional violence. Hence, these utopias contain the undeniable potency of feeling that comes from being out-of-joint with the temporal demands of capitalism.

However, both utopian and the time of a Deleuzian-inflected event may still contain a problematic temporal deference to the future. In other words, can an exodus from totalizing narratives, even when conducted through utopian performances in the present, aptly contain a persisting past? Looking to the time of Holy Saturday as proposed by Shelly Rambo in *Spirit and Trauma: A Theology of Remaining* might better touch this persistence. Exploring a Saturday temporality returns us to queer theory through a new theological lens, which looks not only to what might come next, but more particularly to what remains in the wake of traumatized pasts and uncertain futures. This strain of queer theory, represented here in the works of Elizabeth Freeman and Heather Love, clears paths for bipolar temporality.

## HOLY PRESENCE OF PAST AND FUTURE

According to Shelly Rambo, "In the aftermath of trauma, death and life no longer stand in opposition. Instead death haunts life."[25] Rambo looks to what remains in the time between crucifixion and resurrection, the experience of witnessing to what remains of life, which is an encounter with what is not recognizable. This encounter involves the interplay of the senses in an attempt to find one's way.[26] Following Rambo we can ask: What if the temporality of the post-Fordist moment is one of Holy Saturday—a day lived in the wake of crucifixion and the shadow of an uncertain resurrection? The wake of a failed American dream and the shadow of fractured revolutions? Indeed, might we be living in a moment reflective of a life haunted by death? And if so how does this Holy Saturday feel? Even as we are beckoned forward, held cruelly captive to the promise that Sunday is coming, we feel ourselves pushed back, pulled asunder.

In constructing a Holy Saturday pneumatology, Rambo looks to the writings of Hans Urs von Balthasar, deeply influenced by his partner Adrienne von Speyr's mystical experiences with Jesus' descent into hell. Agreeing with Rambo, I suggest that although Balthasar and Speyr construct a Holy Saturday that still relies too heavily on Sunday's redemption (a suggestion resonant with Edelman's critique of a political reliance on the promise of the future), there is great potential for the rethinking of temporality found in their work.

For instance, Balthasar argued that the time of Holy Saturday describes an indecipherable time that resists a sense of mere waiting for the event of resurrection.[27] The time of Holy Saturday is a time-out-of-joint, or reading with Deleuze, a crack in history that might open us to the people whom official histories have left out of the narrative. We might find similar Deleuzian resonances between political cinema's revelation that the people have been missing[28] and what Rambo describes as "the middle-day [as] the site of witness to the truths that are in danger of being covered over and buried."[29] As explored further below, this refusal to be covered over is similarly demanded by a turn to bipolar time; bipolar time asks us to feel what is to be that which neoliberalism has worked so hard to suppress.

Holy Saturday as described in Speyr's mystical experiences marks not a faith in redemption, but rather one of endurance. This is a persistence found in the space not of God's victory, but rather God's abandonment.[30] The sense of what it is to live in the wake of crucifixion and the face of uncertain resurrection saturates Holy Saturday. The temporality of what Rambo names as a middle spirit marks a crucial equivocacy between being locked in the narrative of the past and being held captive to the often cruelly optimistic belief in a fully unchained new life. It resists both an overemphasis on an active exodus from the dead God and an unwavering faith in the new life promised by Milbank and market fundamentalisms. Holy Saturday time, as theorized by Rambo, favors instead a focus on the materiality of a present in which the binary between death and life no longer holds.

The materiality of a life lived in this time is often unproductive. Balthasar, recounting the experiences of Speyr, narrates the temporality of Holy Saturday thus:

> It is a beginning without parallel, as if Life were arising from Death, as if weariness (already such weariness as no amount of sleep could ever dispel) and the uttermost decay of power were melting at creation's outer edge, were beginning to flow, because flowing is perhaps a sign and a likeness of weariness which can no longer contain itself, because everything that is strong and solid must in the end dissolve into water. But hadn't it—in the beginning—also been born from water? And is this wellspring in the chaos, this trickling weariness, not the beginning of a new creation?[31]

This is a present-future less resonant with the eruptive event of the multitude or that of the resurrection than with the quotidian process of feeling one's way through the weariness of a life penetrated by the past. It is a finding of flow from within the stuckness of those worn down so much that not even sleep is redemptive. It is a time not of stable beginnings and ends but of watery wellsprings (manic life flows), and a trickling weariness (depressive attention to mortality). As Rambo notes, "This residue of love [that found between Father and Son even in utter abandonment] is not powerful but weary and impotent."[32] It is in this sense of Holy Saturday in which temporality shifts such that we no longer see utter despair in such impotence, but rather what remains of love. This sense of time is a particularly apt theological referent for queer temporalities, for these theories, like Holy Saturday, can throw our senses of success, production, and redemption into crisis.[33]

## QUEER SATURDAYS

Feelings of witnessing to our traumatized past, of waiting, and attempting another way resonate with the reading of queer time found in Heather Love's *Feeling Backward*. Love frames the temporal problem in queer studies as such:

> Insofar as the losses of the past motivate us and give meaning to our current experience, we are bound to memorialize them ("We will never forget"). But we are equally bound to overcome the past, to escape its legacy ("We will never go back"). For groups constituted by historical injury, the challenge is to engage with the past without being destroyed by it.[34]

The tension between never forgetting and never returning frames Heather Love's question of how best queer life in the present might deal with its past and its future. She notes that while utopian desires have been primary in the project of queer studies, the future vision on which they build has too often impeded the act of facing the past from which that vision is trying to escape. Here we might remember the problematic sense of a time of exodus, and the worry that it has not yet fully addressed that from which it flees. Although radical democratic theologians seem too eager to flee toward the impossible, Love reminds us that neither the present nor the future is ever fully free of the past. This is in part owing to the affectual legacy that the past holds on the future. Often faced with the choice of either moving on to happier times or clinging to the past, even as they are beckoned forward, queers, Love argues, can't help but feel "backward."

Feelings not only persist, they also have critical work to do; these "backward feelings," are "all about action: about how and why it is blocked, and about how to locate motives for political action when none is visible."[35] Further, "backward" feelings arise through the experience of being marked as "backward." Whether one is "backward" because one is queer, disabled, indigenous, black, woman, impoverished, or mad, the feeling of being so arises through plays of power that have allowed certain bodies to flow easily into societal space and others to be impeded. In this way, "backward" feelings can interrogate the irruptive flow of time proposed by radical democratic theologians and the providential time, which has historically served as an imperial rationale for marking certain people divergent, proposed by radical orthodoxy. Hence, one need not overcome these feelings as much as learn from them, feel them in order to feel a different kind of future, what Love calls a backward future, one "apart from the reproductive imperative, optimism, and the promise of redemption."[36] Rather than a project invested in voiding the future, we might say that Love seeks to unvoid the past by refusing to avoid it, and so to feel our way toward more viable lives beyond reproductive futurism. Hence, a backward future might be another name for the time of Holy Saturday. Holy Saturday theologies can view the day between crucifixion and resurrection not merely as a time of reflection on our way to happier futures, but rather as *the* place and *the* time from which we can find alternate ways of living and structures of feeling that better enflesh a democratic temporality.

Where might we practice these backward feelings in such a way that we are opened to new forms of temporal existence? Perhaps it will be in enacting rituals of temporal disorientation. For instance, might we view sadomasochistic practices as queer ritual enactments of time? In *Time Binds* Elizabeth Freeman "treat[s] S/M as a deployment of bodily sensations through which the individual subject's normative timing is disaggregated and denaturalized."[37] Through an analysis of Isaac Julien's film *The Attendant*, Freeman further argues that this disorganization is collective and that "sadomasochistic sex performs a dialectic of a rapid-temporal 'modernity' and a slower 'premodernity,' the latter indexed by any number of historical periods and, crucially, by forms of labor and affiliation that do not accede to capitalist imperatives."[38] The very sensory practice of S/M resists giving in to the coming of the moneyed or Christian eschaton. Further, to denaturalize bodily time such that demands for efficiency are thrown into disorder by our most intimate plays of desire is to feel a backward future. Quoting Carla Freccero, Freeman locates in S/M a "passivity—which is also a form of patience and passion—[that] is not quite the same thing as quietism. Rather it is a suspension, a waiting, an attending to the world's arrivals (through, in part, its returns)."[39] This is the attendant's attendance, but this might also be the witness of Holy Saturday, of the love that remains instead of redeeming.

The need to witness is also described by Clayton Crockett. In *Deleuze beyond Badiou*, Crockett asks, "So what is to be done? Do we militantly wait for another event, and hope that it happens before we die or become extinct? Or do we create an event of thinking?" He continues, "As Paola Marrati suggests, Deleuze believes that concepts like History, God, and Self are too big to function for any effective political action, and that, in fact, politics based on action runs into serious problems because the movements become programmed in advance and then reduced to clichés, or else captured by state and capitalist apparatuses."[40] Here we recall the programmatic nature of Milbank's event of the church, which has been used to justify the neocolonialism of global capitalism and earlier forms of "civilizing" colonial projects. In Freeman's reading of S/M, we find not only an event of thinking but also of feeling, a felt event that resists a programmatic politics of action without falling into apathy.

I find great potential in Freeman's reading of S/M; yet I am left wondering if there is another approach to time that can address the temporal and affectual precarity nurtured by neoliberalism, without re-performing the master/slave dialectic. I do not wish to deny the political potential in the ritual time of S/M, but rather to ask if we can find a temporal structure that disorganizes the self and the political not through flipping a script as much as refusing it. I propose that we might find it by looking to temporal shifts within so-called mental "illness," most particularly bipolar disorder.

## DISORDERED TIME

What would it mean to view the "disorder" we name bipolar as a site from which to question the value of order? Following Ann Cvetkovich's work on depression, I argue that we can deindividualize and depathologize bipolarity and affirm that good politics need not only come from good feelings.[41] Hence, I propose bipolar time as a protest and potency from within the eschatological shadows of capitalism.

Following the crip theorist Robert McRuer, it would be possible to name the indictment to save time as a heteronormative insistence on able-bodiedness.[42] Bipolar time argues further that this indictment is also an insistence on able-mindedness. Viewing bipolarity as a crip sensibility disrupts its pathologization in order to reveal, while acknowledging its pain, its pleasurable potential.[43] Embracing the crip reformulation of disability as not that which should be fixed, but rather as a site from which we might learn to resist society's demands for productivity and efficiency, I argue that bipolarity can question the thrust of normativization inherent in neoliberal temporality and sociality. Further, bipolar disorder opens up questions of redemption or cure similar to those brought to the fore by crip theory. Hence, bipolar time returns us to Holy Saturday time, taken now not from the point of view of divine abandonment, which in Balthasar's reading will be redeemed, but rather from a stance that says resurrection may be not only unattainable but also unnecessary. Bipolar time is a kind of queering of Holy Saturday theologies as it serves not only in Balthasar's words as a "radically disorienting space of death and hell," but also as a radical reorientation of the meanings of life and heaven.

Like the time of S/M, which according to Freeman can serve as "a dialectic between the will to speed up and annihilate and the will to slow down and dilate,"[44] bipolar time illuminates the ties and tensions between the soul-deadening effects of capitalism and the mad feeling that things might be otherwise. Further, bipolar temporality marks the inseparability of time and feeling. Counter to Rambo's assertion that the middle spirit of Holy Saturday "[attests] to a form of divine presence that is difficult to see, to feel, and to touch,"[45] bipolar time, a time saturated by unnerving feelings, marks how we might better learn to touch and feel God in mania, depression, and their interpenetration. Hence, bipolar temporality refuses the cruel optimism and happy efficiency of neoliberalism and affirms a different sense, one enacted through microtactics of the self: collapsing into bed, embracing one's feelings of overwhelming exhaustion, or living into one's porosity to the world, collectivizing connections and so insisting that we need not be alone in facing that which has got us so tired. Bipolar time does not seek to construct, reveal, or capture subjects of depression and mania. Rather, bipolar time attempts to clear space for different styles of life, those dependent on the paying of greater attention to where moodiness takes us. Bipolar time asks us to attend to what our moods reveal about the world and to what feelings will us to do. Hence, although the rupturing of a certain time and self is key for a bipolar sensibility, bipolar time might not cohere to queer pessimism as much as to queer attentiveness. To queerly attend to one's moods is to find both manic joy and deadening depression ethically interesting. To find moods ethically interesting is not to sublate one into the other, but rather to follow moods where they will and to practice a multiplicity of moody responses, for, in practicing both the fall into the bed and the flight into the world, bipolar time seeks not a final end to its penetrative flows of despair and desire (a Sunday for its Friday), but rather questions the very nature of resurrection.

Bipolar time is a dream of a temporally reordered world, in which worth is divorced from work, value from efficiency, and the raison d'être from redemption. In many ways it is reflective of the temporal eventiveness (a time structured by an in-breaking of the new) proposed by democratic theologians and resistant to the providential time advocated by the radical orthodoxy. Yet because bipolar time is a nonlinear penetrative time in which with every speedup there is also a slowdown, it can interrogate excessive foci on rapidity, newness, and action implied by radical democratic theologians' concept of the event. Within a time of bipolarity mania is always haunted by depression and depression by mania. Hence, to live into such a time would also be to resist a sense of irruptive change out of a kind of captivity into any sense of an ultimate freedom-to-come. In this way bipolar temporality questions both a radical democratic narrative of exodus and a radical orthodox narrative of salvation.

Further, to radical theologies, both democratic and orthodox, bipolar time adds the acknowledgment that each moment of past, present, and future is deeply felt and so carries affectual resonances that matter for how we imagine and presently live out our political, theological, and social lives.

Further bipolar time shakes any sense of clear agency. One does not choose to be chained to depression or to take off in flights of manic exodus. Yet there is a partial agency of response. This partial agency of response cannot be simply individual. There are microresponses that individuals might attempt in pleasure and in pain. One might choose to cry in public or private. One might choose to call in sick or go to work. One might choose to live or to die. However, I want to propose that it is not in how each person individually feels (or separately responds to such feelings) as it is in how each person comes to be more sensitively oriented toward another where the greatest agential and ethical hope might lie. In other words the agency of response is present even if that agency is simply to better attend to how both the world and we feel. Everyone can respond more sensitively. Persons can look to what remains of love in a mania haunted by depression and a depression haunted by mania. They can respond to the anxiety produced by demands for efficiency and productivity by feeling these alternate emotional states in such a way that refuses to subordinate spending time to saving it. Indeed, the depressive side of bipolar temporality is a reminder that inaction is also a way of faithfully remaining. It attends to how the love that remains in the wake of the collectivizing trauma of neoliberalism is often weary and impotent. Therefore, the inaction implied in microtactics like the fall into the bed confronts demands for action implied in the politics of event, exodus, and utopia. And yet we can still find a sense of performativity in one's attempts to feel oneself through bipolar time, reorienting macro senses of value.

This reorientation might be philosophically traced in the thought of mad thinkers and thinkers of madness. For instance, in *The Rebellious No: Variations on a Secular Theology of Language*, Noëlle Vahanian, drawing on discussions of madness in the works of Foucault, Nietzsche, and Derrida, writes:

> What is called reason is a form of blindness, a suspension of thought which produces sanity—the ability to desist from willing, a "being caught up and carried along." She's hyper-aware of the saliva in her mouth or the ticking of her heart; hyper self-conscious to the point of self-alienation, unable to let be and let go; he's a model citizen, an average consumer, a good soldier, a man of the crowd, a cog in a wheel.[46]

The hyperawareness that madness nurtures is the kind of resistance to order found within a life lived in bipolar time. Characteristic of both phases of depression and mania is an "oversensitive" orientation toward the world. Whether it comes in the form of a manic reading and feeling of the world or the depression that comes when the world feels like too much to bear, living in a bipolar time means being the person who cannot let be and let go. It is to be unable to become the model citizen and average consumer. Through the madness of living into a bipolar temporality one can resist becoming a cog in the wheel.

Additionally, although some might understand depression as the very shutting down of the will, Vahanian, quoting Louis A. Sass, counters: "What prevents [the insane] from returning to a more normal existence is no simple failure of will but, in a sense, an inability to desist from willing—an inability to let themselves be caught up in and carried along by the ongoing flow of practical activity in which normal existence is grounded."[47] To refuse to be carried along by the temporal pull of practical activity, when practical activity has become monetized and often cruelly optimistic, is at the heart of performing bipolar temporality. Hence, bipolar time is resistant to the flows of productivism and captivity demanded by the eschatological judgment of money.

Further, the madness of the mad, like the backwardness of the queer, brings to the fore power relations that have shaped the history of the model citizen known as "rational man." Reading with Foucault's *History of Madness*, Lynne Huffer notes that "madness is the 'ransom' paid by the 'other' for the historical rise of the rational moral subject."[48] Further, as Huffer artfully argues, the ransomed mad cannot be disentangled from the ransomed queer:

> At stake in Foucault's tracing of these figures in their historical appearance and disappearance are ethical questions about subjectivity and alterity within a modern rationalist moral order. Faced with an objectifying language of reason for the telling of history, *History of Madness* refigures those sexual subjects transformed by science into objects of intelligibility—as homosexuals, onanists, perverts, and so on—by allowing them to hover as "fantastical" ghosts. They haunt our present but we can't quite grasp them.[49]

The sensibilities of those who are mad not only serve to diagnose how the post-Fordist moment feels, they also pose ethical questions about the historical sacrifice of certain people—queers, perverts, the impoverished, the differently abled, the differently minded—for the construction of Modern *Man*. Like the hauntings of trauma felt within Holy Saturday, the mad of the past haunt our present asking not for resurrection but rather for a reorientation of feeling and attending, or what Huffer names, "an archival listening: the creation of a pathway for a different hearing."[50]

Bipolar time as a crip time is not necessarily a queering of the symbolic order, but rather the breakdown of this order. As Vahanian has offered in her response to my concept of bipolar time:

> [It] offers a different resistance, one beyond a psychic disordering of drives failing "normal" accession to the symbolic where such so-called failed accession would be a resistance, a subject-less resistance to this symbolic. Why? Because bipolar time is not a production of linear time. It is not a response to capitalistic time, and in that sense it does not develop as a resistance to it. But yet, it resists.[51]

Bipolar time does not develop in direct reaction to neoliberalism; neoliberalism cannot be traced as its origin or as its ultimate target, as though if once neoliberalism were destroyed, we would no longer need processes of feeling and responding differently to whatever norms arose in its place. It is not a linear or particularly revolutionary state of being. Bipolar resistance comes not from the programmatic politics worried over by Deleuze and found in Milbank, but rather wells up from the ways in which we are always already "disordered."

Bipolar time, as representative of disordered time, is not interested in being "saved." It will not be saved by an ordering cure, nor does it need to save time over spending it. Indeed, bipolarity makes saving in either sense nearly impossible. It is this impossibility that returns me to the appropriateness of Rambo's reading of trauma as a time of Holy Saturday. Bipolarity asks us how one should better remain, and so live, when unsure whether one really wants a resurrection that may not be coming. Crucial to bipolar time's sense of disorder is that those with alternate mental orientations to the world often can't live temporally in the constant demand for efficiency. The dis-ordered may experience times of rapid creativity and production, but also times in which the slowdown of depression means saving time is no longer an option. Hence, bipolar time can throw one's sense of self into a spiral of worth. This spiral might force one to divorce oneself from what we produce. This is not an easy feat in light of a societal ethos that, as McRuer and Mollow remind us, affirms Joseph Conrad's assertion, "A man is a worker. If he is not then he is nothing."[52] Not easy, but crucial, as growing wealth disparities are throwing more people out of work and into their beds or worse.

So what might happen if this ever increasingly collective "disorder" is viewed not as something that needs to be overcome but rather as a site from which one might question the demand to be productive and efficient? And if in doing so one concedes that time should be spent saving it, just how might one enact such a need?

## BIPOLAR PRACTICES, CONCRETE HEAVENS

Although bipolar time helps us resist even a democratic overemphasis on the future, I suggest if we are to practice spending time over saving it we may still need utopian dreaming, a dreaming performed within the smallest quotidian moments as well as in the utopias described by Muñoz. Concrete utopias are a doing for and toward the future. The doing rather than the telos is of utmost importance. For instance, Muñoz viewed the queer punk scene as a collective space in which identity and acceptability—even that of acceptable queer identity—was challenged and in which this challenge was communal. Ann Cvetkovich describes a similar utopian moment when she writes of the collective singing of cover songs performed by Feel Tank participants.[53] During a gathering in Toronto the line "My loneliness is killing me" from Britney Spears's "Baby One More Time," embodied the loneliness felt by Cvetkovich, while also, because it was sung collectively, helping her feel a little less lonely.[54] This is the performance of a utopia in which the love that remains in loneliness, although not curing loneliness, feels like concrete hope.

This insistence on the concreteness of utopia, in its performability, aids in contextualizing political theology, and reins in the risk of crucial concepts of event, potentiality, and the multitude remaining too amorphous and disembodied. Further, it is in the concreteness of queer utopias where we might find resonance with and so (ironically) a resistance to RO's conception of the salvific church. According to James K. A. Smith, "[For RO] the church does not have a cultural critique; it is a cultural critique. Its politics is an ecclesiology."[55] If we were to replace "church" here with "queerness," such that queerness doesn't have but is a cultural critique, we would be onto a Muñozian (and an Edelmanian) ecclesiology. Like Milbank's church, the queer utopias found in the work of Muñoz can function as interpreting events and cultural critiques. Yet it seems unlikely that most RO theologians would accept queerness as a "proper" part of creation and revelation. Further, the demand that this is not all there is enacted in queer utopian performance does not dictate what "this other is" has to be. Conversely, RO's "other than this" relies on a particular and unwavering telos. Unlike the kind of transcendence in immanence found in queer utopian dreaming, one which opens a myriad of immanent possibilities, RO's transcendence in immanence actually shuts down the potency of the immanent.

In his concluding chapter, "Take Ecstasy with Me," Muñoz writes, "Knowing ecstasy is having a sense of timeliness's motion, comprehending a temporal unity, which includes the past (having-been), the future (the not-yet), and the present (the making-present)."[56] Drawing on the etymological meaning of ekstasis as to stand or be outside of oneself, Muñoz conceives ecstasy as a moment in which one is brought not only beyond oneself spatially but also temporally. This movement resonates with Edelman's refusal of reproductive futurism. Although Edelman insists that this move must be made as though the present were all there is, Muñoz insists it must be made precisely because the present is *not* all there is. Yet they may both be invitations to, as Muñoz puts it, "desire differently, to desire more, to desire better."[57] This call to desire differently, more, and better is also a call made by radical theologians of both camps. However, in their assertion that this desiring must direct itself toward the church and nowhere else, orthodox theologians miss the very heart of desire. Hence, Muñoz's invitation to take ecstasy with him might be the open communion rejected by radical orthodoxy, but demanded when we take seriously the inexhaustibility of divine desire.

Therefore, it is this type of eschaton, a concrete Queerdom of Heaven, one performed in the punk bar and through the collective singing of cover songs, but also in quotidian moments of the weary love that remains—those often not about novel becoming, but rather unbecoming—where I hope to spend some bipolar time. Perhaps I will spend it in the hours of teaching that remind me that the event of thinking matters; perhaps I will spend it in the moment of sharing both a weariness from and a mad hope for the world, a moment that reminds me that the event of collective feeling matters; or perhaps I will spend it in the hours of not getting out of bed, which remind me that impotency is also a way of witnessing to how this world feels. Perhaps, taking a note from Cvetkovich, I will spend it at the karaoke bar singing St. Dolly's great lament against saving time: "9 to 5, what a way to make a livin,' barely gettin' by, it's all takin' and no givin', they just use your mind and you never get the credit, it's enough to *drive you crazy* if you let it." There, spending time surrounded by the collective out-of-tuneness of my fellow patrons, this disordered space might become a reminder of our attunement, or perhaps better our attend-ment to one another, an attendance that reminds us that we need not let the rich man's game take our time and use our mind, but too that we need not be on pitch in order to sing out. We need not be fleeing toward certain redemption—an all-curing salve in the church or the market—to avoid becoming a slave to the cubicle, the commodity, or consumption. For this life of faith, one in which none of us need find our pitch in order to know our (im)potency, is the embodiment of the Queerdom of Heaven on Earth as it concretely refuses the eschatological judgment of money.

## NOTES

1. Lauren Berlant, *Cruel Optimism* (Durham, N.C.: Duke University Press, 2011), kindle location 24.
2. Philip Goodchild, *Theology of Money* (Durham, N.C.: Duke University Press, 2009), 188.
3. I define radical political theology as a field of theology that takes postmodernism and postsecularism as a starting point for the writing of theology. It is interested in questions normally considered political, such as sovereignty and economy. The field is greatly indebted to Carl Schmitt's famous assertion that "all modern concepts of the state are secularized theological concepts" (Schmitt 1922). Radical political theology for the purposes of this essay encompasses two strands of contemporary political theology. The first, often called "radical theology," for the purposes of clarity I refer to as "radical democratic theology," or RD, the second, "radical orthodox theology," or RO. Radical theology / radical democratic theology is a contemporary field of theology that draws on constructive theology, process theology, secular theology, and death-of-God theologies and is deeply influenced by continental thought (particularly the writings of Gilles Deleuze and Félix Guattari, Alain Badiou, Slavoj Žižek, and Michael Hardt and Antonio Negri). It offers a theology written from within an immanent frame, and it is dependent on the potency of people over and against a transcendent God. Radical orthodox theologians, although similarly writing from within and in response to postsecularism and engaging in issues of sovereignty and economy, argue for a return to the transcendent sovereign God as a counter to what many see as the loss of value in a liberalism run amok.
4. John Milbank, *Theology and Social Theory: Beyond Secular Reason* (Oxford: Blackwell, 1990), 388.
5. For further examples of such temporal structure in radical orthodox writings, see William T. Cavanaugh's *Being Consumed: Economics and Christian Desire* (Grand Rapids, Mich.: Wm B. Eerdmans, 2008); D. Stephen Long's *Divine Economy: Theology and the Market* (New York: Routledge, 2000), and Catherine Pickstock's *After Writing: On the Liturgical Consummation of Philosophy* (Oxford: Wiley Blackwell, 1997).
6. Jeffrey W. Robbins, *Radical Democracy and Political Theology* (New York: Columbia University Press, 2011), 191. Robbins is here quoting Antonio Negri, *Time for Revolution* (New York: Continuum, 2003), 260.
7. Clayton Crockett, *Deleuze beyond Badiou: Ontology, Multiplicity, and Event* (New York: Columbia University Press, 2013), 99.
8. Gilles Deleuze, *Cinema 2: The Time Image*, 6th ed. (Minneapolis: University of Minnesota Press, 2001), 214.
9. Ibid., 215–18.
10. Crockett, *Deleuze beyond Badiou*, 192.
11. Cavanaugh, *Being Consumed*, 10–11.
12. William E. Connolly, *Capitalism and Christianity, American Style* (Durham, N.C.: Duke University Press, 2008), 13.
13. Milbank, *Theology and Social Theory*, 331.

14. Robert L. Caserio, "The Antisocial Thesis in Queer Theory," *PMLA: Publications of the Modern Language Association of America* 121, no. 3 (2006): 819. The PMLA roundtable's opening provocation is drawn in part from Leo Bersani, *Homos* (Cambridge, Mass.: Harvard University Press, 1996).
15. Lee Edelman, *No Future: Queer Theory and the Death Drive* (Durham, N.C.: Duke University Press, 2004), 2.
16. Ibid., 28.
17. Lynne Huffer, *Mad for Foucault: Rethinking the Foundations of Queer Theory* (New York: Columbia University Press, 2010), 115.
18. José Esteban Muñoz, "Thinking beyond Antirelationality and Antiutopianism in Queer Critique," *PMLA: Publications of the Modern Language Association of America* 121, no. 3 (2006): 825.
19. Edelman, *No Future*, 10.
20. Tim Dean, "An Impossible Embrace: Queerness, Futurity, and the Death Drive," in *A Time for the Humanities: Futurity and the Limits of Autonomy*, ed. James L. Bono, Tim Dean, and Ewa Plonowska Ziarek (New York: Fordham University Press, 2008), 128.
21. José Esteban Muñoz, *Cruising Utopia: The Then and There of Queer Futurity* (New York: New York University Press, 2009), 3.
22. See José Esteban Muñoz, *Disidentifications: Queers of Color and the Performance of Politics* (Minneapolis: University of Minnesota Press, 1999).
23. See Ann Cvetkovich, *Depression: A Public Feeling* (Durham, N.C.: Duke University Press, 2012).
24. See Elizabeth Freeman, *Time Binds: Queer Temporalities, Queer Histories* (Durham, N.C.: Duke University Press, 2010).
25. Shelly Rambo, *Spirit and Trauma: A Theology of Remaining* (Louisville, Ky.: Westminster John Knox Press, 2010), 3.
26. Ibid., 162.
27. Ibid., 46.
28. For Gilles Deleuze the new basis on which modern political cinema was founded is the acknowledgment that a people have been missing. According to Deleuze, political cinema's rejection of linear time or a historical narrative that has served to absent the people is represented through juxtapositions of old and new that create absurdities and point toward the cracks in History. Deleuze, *Cinema 2*, 217–18.
29. Rambo, *Spirit and Trauma*, 48.
30. Ibid., 53.
31. Hans Urs von Balthasar, *Heart of the World*, trans. Erasmo Leiva (San Francisco: Ignatius, 1979), 152.
32. Rambo, *Spirit and Trauma*, 57.
33. Although I have chosen to focus on the writings of Heather Love and Elizabeth Freeman in order to illuminate the tie between certain theories of queer temporality, one could also look to the work of Jack Halberstam on queer failure in *The Queer Art of Failure* (Durham, N.C.: Duke University Press, 2011) or to crip critiques of productivity such as those found in the work of Robert McRuer.

34. Heather Love, *Feeling Backward: Loss and the Politics of Queer History* (Cambridge, Mass.: Harvard University Press, 2007), 1.
35. Ibid., 13.
36. Ibid., 147.
37. Freeman, *Time Binds*, 137.
38. Ibid., 137–38.
39. Ibid., 147. Of course, the play of pleasure and pain through ritual enactment is not unfamiliar to theologians and religious practitioners. There is a long history of Christian practice that involves bodily pleasure and pain in acts not only for worship but also for the enactment of a different kind of time.
40. Crockett, *Deleuze beyond Badiou*, 169.
41. Cvetkovich, *Depression*.
42. Crip theory is a form of disability studies that seeks not for accessibility and acceptance, but rather, similar to queer theory, looks—through the experience of the disabled—to destabilize heteronormative and ableist systems of accessibility and acceptability. In *Crip Theory: Cultural Signs of Queerness and Disability* McRuer explicates how compulsory heterosexuality is actually dependent on compulsory able-bodiedness in that compulsory heterosexuality is built around concepts of normate (what the mainstream marks as "normal") bodies and sexualities. Robert McRuer, *Crip Theory: Cultural Signs of Queerness and Disability* (New York: New York University Press, 2006).
43. In invoking bipolarity's pleasurable potential, I seek not to glorify depression or mania, but rather to uncover alternate desires for the world to produce in non-normate mental orientations. Additionally, following the work collected by editors Robert McRuer and Anna Mollow in *Sex and Disability* (Durham, N.C.: Duke University Press, 2012), to argue against the pathologization and desexualization of the crip (including the mentally crip).
44. Freeman, *Time Binds*, 153.
45. Rambo, *Spirit and Trauma*, 79.
46. Noëlle Vahanian, *The Rebellious No: Variations on a Secular Theology of Language* (New York: Fordham University Press, 2014), 70–71. The "she" referred to in the quotation is a general "mad" woman set up to be in contrast to the "he" who is the general model citizen.
47. Louis A. Sass, *Madness and Modernism: Insanity in the Light of Modern Art, Literature, and Thought* (Cambridge, Mass: Harvard University Press, 1994), 241.
48. Huffer, *Mad for Foucault*, 92.
49. Ibid., 56.
50. Ibid., 227.
51. Noelle Vahanian, email message to author, October 12, 2014.
52. Joseph Conrad, *Notes on Life and Letters* (1921), quoted in McRuer and Mollow, *Sex and Disability*, 25.
53. Feel Tank is the name of groups in Chicago, New York, and Toronto that have participated in the Public Feelings Project, which brings together activists, artists, and

academics, who do critical work in the study of theoretical, historical, and artistic materials engaged with political affects and the politics of affect.

54. Cvetkovich, *Depression: A Public Feeling*, kindle location 2401.

55. James K. A. Smith, *Introducing Radical Orthodoxy: Mapping a Post-secular Theology* (Grand Rapids, Mich.: Baker Academic, 2004), 80.

56. Muñoz, *Cruising Utopia*, kindle location 3366.

57. Ibid., kindle location 3433.

# The Entrepreneur and the Big Drag: Risky Affirmation in Capital's Time

LINN MARIE TONSTAD

The current socioeconomic order exerts immense pressure to convince us that significant change is impossible: We can practice amelioration—but not desired transformation—as we participate in the forced march toward willing acquiescence to the logic of economic rationality. Not a contradiction—this order is particularly insidious in its ability to orient our desires from the inside, as it were, so that our experiences of risk and futility turn into opportunities for self-realization, as we'll see.

Two different strategies naturalize the current order, increasing the power of both. One insists there is no alternative; any attempt to create one is utopian, unrealistic, and immature. As Harry Harootunian suggests, a new temporal order—"a boundless present"—has arrived, following the end of the Cold War and the beginning of the War on Terror. "The apparent difference today is the withdrawal of a foreseeable future as a perspective for figuring the aspirations of the present."[1] The other combines securitization and self-realization to push us through our fears and pull us through our desires. We are constantly reminded of our fragility and vulnerability so that we will make the choices that (might) keep us safe—education, insurance, savings, and so on. We are constantly reminded of the fragility and vulnerability of all that seems stable (a new incarnation of all that is solid melts into air?) so that we will fear time passing and leaving us the useless detritus of a history that once was. We are constantly reminded of the opportunities brought us by the current order: the chance to take a risk, to commit ourselves fully to a project of our own outside established institutional contexts, to snatch the opportunities presented by the difference between the future and the present under the threat of the risks presented by the difference between the future and the present. These simultaneous possibilities and threats shape what I call *entrepreneurial subjectivity* in this essay.

The odd, but unsurprising, result of these combined forces is the disappearance of the sense of a difference between the future and the present as an opportunity for willed transformation rather than simply an experience of vulnerability / possibility due to unforeseeable and incalculable risk. The dual strategies of naturalization embed us so fully in the current order that the present expands into a weirdly unchanging moment in which we constantly seek to catch up so that we can move freely into the glorious / dangerous future of our responsible, risky becoming. At any moment, we are always fully committed to something (we-know-not-what). This alignment constitutes an affirmation of finitude and contingency, the affirmation of the world as it is and as it presents itself to us. Such alignment (total commitment) is parodically world-affirming. Fluidity, in which there is no alternative but to adapt to whatever is required of us, ties us to the present moment. The future is at once already determined and radically open-ended: already determined in that we have no ability to change its course fundamentally; radically open-ended in that we have to conform ourselves utterly to whatever is demanded of us, and what will be demanded cannot be foreseen.

Living toward the apparently open-ended, fluid future requires total self-identification with the demands of that fluid future, total commitment to whatever unknowable threat-opportunity might arrive next. We know, we are told, that stable jobs, stable industries, and stable life paths will undergo disruption. We cannot expect the future to be like the past; we must always be prepared for radical disruption or, better yet, we ought to drive that disruption. The temporal outcome is the dual overdetermination of the present: At any moment, we must be ready for radical change, unpredictable in advance.

Each of us must adopt an entrepreneurial relation to an individual future. We undergo the "*financial subjectivation* of wage-earners"[2] that depends on assumptions of future productivity, self-transcendence, and fluidity. We lose any sense of a viable past—for the present is already different from the past, and the future will be more so yet, nor can we imagine how the future will differ from the present. We *know* that the future will be different from the present, that we ourselves, our relations to each other, and our relations to work will be different from what they now are, but we have no sense that the processes through which those differences will be established are processes that can be steered toward significant collective betterment. While there emerge ever more sophisticated critical discourses of settler colonialism, Afropessimism, queer theology, and animality—to name just a few important examples—the financial reordering of the world continues apace.

In this essay, I use the temporality of entrepreneurial subjectivity in the contemporary order of capital[3] to pose questions to some influential theological and queer-theoretical strategies for countering capitalism's rapacity and modernity's illusions of autonomous self-creation. Entrepreneurial subjectivity mobilizes risk and (both threat and certainty of) loss toward total commitment in the face of an unknown and unknowable future. It thus serves as a spectral double to the theoretical and theological hopes invested in what I term the ecstatic-ascetic subject of self-loss. The accompanying question for these debates, within and beyond theology, is that of finitude and its affirmation. Christianity, my primary archive, has often (and often rightly) been accused of a world-denying inability to affirm finitude. Christianity becomes ideology when it fails to reckon with the reality for all people (and for the world) of suffering, death, and loss—of futility. The same goes for any other discourse of transformation that pretends that better socialization, political structures, or economic relations might fully protect us against the risk and reality of suffering, death, failure, and loss. And yet. I share with many others the sense that although we all die, our lives might be better ordered than they are—that economic relations could be less cruel and exploitative, that horrendous suffering might be lessened (in part through less cruel and exploitative economic relations), and that there are futures that would be better than the present, and better than the futures the present presently promises. My worry is that some of the strategies we use to counter the depredations of the present intensify rather than ameliorate its strategies for self-perpetuation, and distract us from other possible resources for futural redirection and transformation. In a brief and suggestive closing section, I gesture toward some such resources.

## THE ECSTATIC-ASCETIC THEOLOGICAL SUBJECT

Many theologians (and theorists) have turned to the ecstatic-ascetic subject as a corrective to modernity's dreams of autonomy, self-presence, and self-determination and capitalism's creation of subjects of consumption who move ceaselessly from one unsatisfying object of desire to the next. Daniel Bell Jr. argues that the solution to the possessive nature of consumerist desire is a trinitarian transformation in which "desire is healed of its self-absorption . . . and turned outward as it is renewed as humble vulnerability."[4] Sinful human desire takes two distorted forms. First, humans want *"more than enough"*; second, desire becomes "self-referential . . . 'desire for desire.'"[5] Such desire must be chastened by a primary orientation to God that results in interhuman relations "that exceed any contract."[6] Beyond self-possession, possessive consumerism, and autonomous subjectivity, *Christian* desire creates risk-taking, endlessly self-giving subjects whose false delusions of self-having are shattered in the encounter with the vulnerable other.[7] Capitalism is transformed and overcome by Christian practices of desire. Bell calmly asserts that "God's provision . . . make[s] possible . . . a kind of asceticism. . . . Here we would do well to recall Christ's suffering obedience to which we are conformed. . . . God's abundance may take the form of martyrdom and resurrection."[8]

Dispossession, the ecstatic-ascetic (or kenotic) posture toward self and other, stands at the heart of Rowan Williams's theology. "The goal of the created order is to point the soul to self-transcendence."[9] Self-transcendence is costly, involving purification, other-directedness, self-sacrifice, and dispossession. The obedience on which self-transcendence is built "is no bland resignation. It is a change wrought by anguish, darkness and stripping. . . . Ascetical practice must involve a *concentration* of desire that can dispense with the ersatz and the comfortable."[10] Following Simone Weil, Williams argues, "The practice of selfless attention, self-forgetful attention, to any task is a proper preparation for contemplating God. To be absorbed in the sheer *otherness* of any created order or beauty is to open the door to God, because it involves that basic displacement of the dominating ego without which there can be no spiritual growth."[11] The ego, again, seeks mastery and establishment on its own foundations. The self-oriented ego must be overcome by a painful (re)orientation to the other.

The self must appropriate—affirm—the finitude of the world, its unmasterability. The *I* must give up the imagination that "the person [is] a self-subsisting terminus of desire."[12] Such sacrifice of self-identity conforms the person to God, since this is the very shape of God's existence:

> The single life of the Godhead is the going-out from self-identity into the other; that cannot be a closed mutuality (for then the other would be only the mirror of the same); the love of one for other must itself open on to a further otherness if it is not to return to the same; and only so is the divine life "as a whole" constituted as love (rather than mutual reinforcement of identity).[13]

Divine risk-taking makes up the atonement, which is a risky self-gift on the part of God that overcomes self-enclosure and self-protection. The illusion of autonomy and self-sufficiency causes us to "shore up our sense of independence" by "intensify[ing] our dependence on those external factors which assure us of worth and meaning."[14] There is a material aspect to this as well, not merely an intersubjective one: "The objects of the world, seen in the perspective of the eucharist, cannot be proper material for the defence of one ego . . . against another, cannot properly be tools of power, because they are signs of a creativity working by the renunciation of control."[15] Such self-sacrificial relations are built on the primary material of divine self-giving, a "divine dispossession" that is "more like renunciation than dominance."[16] Christian practice thus provides the corrective to "a discourse of rights and claims [that] becomes more and more strident."[17] Williams's essay "The Body's Grace," perhaps the most-cited essay in queer Christian theologies of a certain kind (especially influential for Eugene Rogers Jr. and Graham Ward), emphasizes similar themes: the importance of vulnerability and risk, the ecstatic shape desire takes in sex, and sex's capacity to destroy the illusion of autonomy. Since our society provides little to "reinforce a sense of common need or dependence, and a contingency and vulnerability we share as finite agents,"[18] Williams prescribes contingency, risk-taking, and vulnerability as therapies for subjects deluded about their own autonomy.

Sarah Coakley offers similar prescriptions. The subject must learn through pain, suffering, and purgation, her own vulnerability and fragility in order to encounter the other as other. Desire's purification takes place through an ecstatic/ascetic experience of encounter with God. Since I discuss Coakley at length elsewhere,[19] I will only briefly trace these themes. Coakley argues that contemporary discourse on desire, and the contemporary economic order, is riven by a "false . . . disjunction" between libertarianism and repression for which only asceticism provides a solution.[20] Ecstatic-ascetic desire, when bound in lifelong vows of fidelity, becomes a "martyrdom, . . . the commitment to some forms of loss, suffering and transformation in relation to the other."[21] Coakley's "ascetical theology" applauds the way sexuality involves a loss of control, a sacrifice of the illusion of self-sufficiency. In a world marred by "instantly commodified desire and massive infidelity," we need "erotic *saints*" to break down our illusions of mastery and teach us ecstatic-erotic fidelity.[22]

Graham Ward develops similar themes, although in a somewhat different direction. He worries that the (post)modern self is affected by a capitalist notion of desire as lack, in which the self moves endlessly from one object of desire to another, with no object of desire sufficient to hold the self or even to stanch desire for a moment.[23] The self seeks to own, to obtain the objects of its desiring. The answer to such desire is the coincidence of love and desire in Christianity, in which the difference of the other is respected; indeed, in which the self empties itself in order to be filled by the other. For Ward, "What is loved in love is difference. Such love . . . operates according [to] the economies of both kenotic and erotic desire."[24] That love always contains an element of suffering, for the self finds itself painfully vulnerable to the other, whose touch might destroy as well as heal.

The turn to the ecstatic, erotic, ascetic nonsubject as a counter to the autonomous subject of possessive individualism has become a theological strategy that allows Christian desire to be contrasted with non-Christian or secular desire and so prove the superiority of the former. It also suggests the relevance of Christianity to contemporary concerns with sexuality and economics. The prescription of ascesis, vulnerability, and risk-taking promises to counter Christian desires (real and imputed) for mastery while dissolving the fixed subjects of self-determination and self-possession that crop up in discourses of sex and money. The theological version of the ecstatic-ascetic subject finds its certainties of God and self dissolved into a God who is the ultimate ecstatic-ascetic subject of self-loss.

That subject of self-loss, in a nontheological version, is encapsulated most gorgeously in Leo Bersani's oft-quoted description of the rectum as "the grave in which the masculine ideal (an ideal shared—differently—by men *and* women) of proud subjectivity is buried. . . . Male homosexuality advertises the risk of the sexual itself as the risk of . . . *losing sight* of the self, and in so doing it proposes and dangerously represents *jouissance* as a mode of ascesis."[25] The divine subject of self-loss hangs on a cross on which the "masculine ideal of proud subjectivity is buried," for this is a self that sacrifices itself, that does not keep itself for itself but gives itself up, even unto death.[26] But Bersani is not my concern here; what interests me is the way the ecstatic-ascetic subject of self-loss emerges out of self-involving risk-taking in relation to an unknown and unknowable eventuation—dare I say, a future?

## THE ECSTATIC-ASCETIC ENTREPRENEUR

The ecstatic-ascetic subject of self-loss is found—or so I want to suggest—in another, rather unexpected form in the contemporary economic order: in the entrepreneur. The entrepreneur shares the following features with the ecstatic-ascetic subject: risk-taking, vulnerability, orientation to the other, irreversible commitment to an unpredictable future, self-transcendence, fluidity (and responsivity), and self-creation through ascetic practices. Entrepreneurialism is no longer limited to entrepreneurs. Entrepreneurialism has become a new form of governmentality and a fundamental form of subjectivity.[27] The "entrepreneur has become a general role model for the way social subjects should conduct themselves in order to maximize their own social security and employability." Even those normally considered middle managers are subjected to the "specter" of the entrepreneur as "a general dictum or ethos for the way in which a number of different social practices should be carried out."[28] The requirement of productivity enforced by the transformation of the worker into the entrepreneur demands that the subject "give himself unreservedly"[29] to his work life without holding anything back;[30] that is also his self-production. "The new techniques of 'personal enterprise' doubtless reach a peak of alienation in claiming to abolish any sense of alienation: following one's desire and obeying the Other who speaks softly within the self are one and the same thing. In this sense, modern management is a 'Lacanian' government: the desire of the subject is the desire of the Other."[31] Yet to give oneself to the desire of the other is not enough: Such commitment might capture only the old model of the "company man." We must also be risk-taking entrepreneurs who cannot be boxed in by traditional divisions of labor and responsibility.[32]

Ideals of creativity and artistry become instead entrepreneurial self-creation: "Everyone is an artist, so he or she should also work and live in a way that is accordingly flexible, spontaneous and mobile, or self-exploiting, without security and forced into mobility."[33] Indeed, the artist "has been turned into a general model for the overall project of neoliberal normalisation," for the artist's "specific skills . . . coincide with [the artist's] desire,"[34] and the latter condition is the ultimate identification with the desire of the other. The new economy's insistence on "lifelong learning" monetizes the presumptively fluid subject;[35] any remaining individual fixity is just another flaw unless it reaches the threshold of an illimitable economic resource. Entrepreneurialism extends its reach through every socioeconomic level. The lower-income entrepreneurial subject is expected to fit piecework into her daily life: the Uber driver who wants to pick up some "extra" money for her children's Christmas, the TaskRabbit who cleans houses for "spending" money, or the artist who supplements his income by delivering food for Caviar (a high-end take-out food delivery service). The "gig economy" is well summed up by Wolfgang Streeck as a way to "obscure the distinction between freely chosen and forced mobility, between self-employed and precarious work, between giving notice and being given the sack."[36] Although the ideal entrepreneur is often represented as a middle- to upper-middle-class subject, the fragmentation of labor means that precariously employed workers are forced into entrepreneurialism[37]—just without outsize rewards. The important similarities between the pressures of subject-formation at different socioeconomic levels need to be emphasized: It is not *generally* the case that "privileged" (white, male, heterosexual) subjects enjoy security while other subjects suffer precarity. Although "privileged" subjects have a wider array of protections available to them in times of crisis, and are much less likely to be subject to discriminatory injustice, they too experience these pressures.

At the highest socioeconomic levels, such subjects do as they are done to. Karen Ho's brilliant ethnography of Wall Street demonstrates the ways in which concrete cultural and structural norms of Wall Street—fluidity, total commitment, and risk-taking—expand throughout the economic order to determine the working conditions of those who operate without the particular safety net on which Wall Street's practices depend, namely the Street's outsize compensation packages. Ho examines the "particular investment banker habitus which allows [Wall Street bankers] to embrace an organizational model of 'employee liquidity' and to recommend these experiences for all workers."[38] The vulnerability and frangibility that Wall Street bankers experience in their own lives become their prescription for the lives of others, as do their long hours at work. Indeed, in addition to allowing an employee to work for his or her firm at all hours and places, the smartphone now allows a contractor to work for multiple companies whenever he or she "wants."

Entrepreneurialism far outstrips calcified models of self-interest as the motor of capital. Already in 1921, Frank H. Knight described the qualities of risk taken by the entrepreneur: "The only 'risk' which leads to a profit is a unique uncertainty resulting from an exercise of ultimate responsibility which in its very nature cannot be insured nor capitalized nor salaried."[39] Indeed, entrepreneurialism takes on an ethical dimension:

> Everybody who "just does" and avoids satisfaction with existing conditions fulfills the characteristics required to make oneself an entrepreneur. . . . Activation of oneself on behalf of the collective objectives of welfare and growth is best achieved when subjects conduct themselves in the manner of entrepreneurs.[40]

Tomas Marttila's language evokes not only the entrepreneur, but the activist and the Christian as well.[41] The distance between what *is* and what *might be* captures the way each of these three figures commits to existing conditions in order to change them, and to change the self as well—a change that takes place at risk of the self. These figures are neither world-denying nor straightforwardly built on the proud ideal of subjectivity; they avoid satisfaction with existing conditions and commit themselves to an unknown future.

The entrepreneur is the one who "just does": The entrepreneur passes to the act, takes risks, and makes use of whatever opportunities present themselves. The responsible self is no longer the responsible and reliable employee, rewarded by his employer with stability and a defined-benefit pension; the responsible self is now the one who is utterly responsible for himself. Crucially, the apparent openness of the future becomes the very means by which the present is determined. The subject must position himself to be flexible in the new, global marketplace; he needs to be ready at any moment to commit and take risks to enjoy the full advantage of unexpected opportunities that might open up. The subject must plan for an uncertain future, putting away money in health savings accounts and comparison shopping to take full advantage of high-deductible health insurance plans, adding "life happens" funds to life insurance and emergency funds, stashing away enough money to cover living expenses for six to twelve months in case of long-term unemployment, and so on.

Our shared (and real) vulnerability generates our fears; vulnerability's enforcement serves as the site of our desire's disciplining—precisely because we are constantly reminded of our vulnerability and frangibility. The knowledge that no form of protection is protection enough becomes the spur to potentially infinite efforts at self-protection. The potential for shattering becomes the site of autonomy's enforcement, just at the moment that certain critical discourses valorize fragmentation, self-emptying, and (self-)shattering as responses to modernity's dream of autonomy. The successful Silicon Valley entrepreneur's watchword and motto is "disruption," after all (and the disruptor may well become the disrupted); "today exposure puts everybody at the risk of irreparable loss."[42]

Thus, no reminder that all humans are subject to fragmentation, dissolution, limitation, and death can cut the knot that ties the desiring subject to the wheel of production and self-creation; indeed, the forms of self-shattering and self-dissolution that he may practice in "private" life ("the infinitely more seductive and intolerable image of a grown man, legs high in the air, unable to refuse the suicidal ecstasy of being a woman")[43] may be the outlets that he needs to conform ever more thoroughly and desirously to the demands placed on him in his work life.[44]

Margot Weiss analyzes just these patterns in her controversial *Techniques of Pleasure*.[45] Weiss remains relentlessly focused on the intertwining of BDSM mastery with concrete modes of consumption, as well as on the close relationship between the rise of BDSM as skilled practice and the development of a white technological economy in the Bay Area. In a recent essay, she emphasizes that "radical sexualities and communities serve as sites of semi-permitted *transgression*—not transformation."[46] Summarizing some of the arguments of *Techniques of Pleasure*, Weiss examines claims "not only that BDSM is queer (non- or anti-normative), but that it is *resistant to capitalism and the state*."[47] Contra Karmen MacKendrick, Jeremy Carrette, and Lewis Call, Weiss emphasizes that the admittedly transgressive practices of BDSM reveal rather "the *increased* intertwining of capitalism and sexuality," which invites the further question, "What do we make of the desire, on the part of scholars, to read BDSM in precisely the opposite way?"[48] What is interesting to me is not Weiss's emphasis on—put crudely—the amount of money BDSM practitioners spend on toys and technique or her demonstration that such practices do not exist outside the spaces of capital. I had not expected otherwise.

What I find interesting is the way Weiss reads the desire embedded in certain approaches to BDSM as "a more social desire for transformation" on the part of those of us who work in queer studies.[49] Rather than opposing critique and affiliation, or surface reading to paranoid reading, we might "see critique as a form of [our] desire."[50] Our readings of certain transgressive sexual positions and practices reflect—not perhaps only, but also—our own desires for some*where* to stand, a place and a practice from which resistance to the all-embracing claims of late capitalism may be practiced. We cannot rest content with the hope that the dissolution of the subject—the end of m/Man—will also be the end of capitalism. The dissolution of the subject may be one of the ways by which capitalism preserves itself; the practices enjoined on us—risk-taking, vulnerability, openness to failure, unexpected forms of affiliation—may not in themselves achieve the ends we seek by engaging in them. Instead, they may name or even intensify the pressures that keep the current economic order in place. If we want to hold onto our affective attachment to sexual transgression as a form of resistance, we need to think very hard about the mechanisms and social ontologies that would entail the dissolution (rather than enhancement) of one by the other.

The pair ecstasis-ascesis, serving in contemporary theological and some theoretical discourse as the promise of an anti- or unmodern "dispossessed" self, is not the arrival of the untimely future "man" of whom we dreamed and for whom we sought to labor as those who go under. The subject's surplus-enjoyment—"life itself, in all its aspects"—becomes just that which "establishes equivalence between the duty of performance and the duty of pleasure[,] . . . the imperative of 'ever more,'" for "subjects are enjoined to 'surpass themselves.'"[51] The result is what Pierre Dardot and Christian Laval term an "'ultra-subjectivation,' whose goal is not a final, stable condition of 'self-possession.'" It is "a form of *subjectivation as an excess of self over self*, or *boundless self-transcendence*."[52] The means of this self-transcendence? "Asceses of performance"[53] requiring self-knowledge and *phronesis*. The entrepreneur, the theological ecstatic-ascetic subject, and the theoretical subject of self-loss may have more in common than we thought. As a result, "the queer art of failure," which pretends to proffer the hope of "acceptance of the finite, the embrace of the absurd, the silly, and the hopelessly goofy,"[54] becomes instead the "key to success."[55] Since "the norm of entrepreneurial subjectivity is likely to be inhabited in the mode of failure,"[56] failure, like risk-taking, becomes internal to—rather than shattering—entrepreneurialism's patterns. Undoing the self may be a fancy way of establishing it, dispossession a way to draw attention away from the accumulation of possessions, acceptance of finitude and vulnerability a spur to ever greater disciplining of desire, willed or unwilled, or, worse, an intensified and ever more claustrophobic insistence that there is no alternative.

## QUEER TIMES: FINITUDE AND HOPE

Where, then, might we seek the time of change? Queer theory's turn to temporality in the last decade has taken a multiplicity of forms, but the debate over futurity between José Esteban Muñoz and Lee Edelman is perhaps the most prominent.[57] That debate focuses on Muñoz's Ernst Bloch–inflected description of the gestural performative invocation of an unrepresentable utopia, his answer to Edelman's (frequently misunderstood) refusal of a politics of futurism structured by the figure of the Child.[58] Edelman's challenge to utopian, future-oriented thinking involves a serious theological and theoretical question: How can one think—or learn to desire, or hope for—significant social change without denying finitude, fallibility, and loss?

One way of answering that question may be approached through another significant locus for thinking queer temporality: David Halperin's reconsideration (2007) of Michael Warner's discussion (1995) of "risky" sex practices in gay male communities, which Halperin uses to develop a rejoinder to psychological and psychoanalytic accounts of such practices (represented in Halperin's book primarily by Tim Dean).[59] In Warner's original essay, published just before the shift from what we might term "AIDS time" to "HIV time" among economically secure first-world gays—the shift from AIDS as an almost certain death sentence to HIV as a hostile or alien presence in the body that nonetheless can be controlled and restrained—he sought what might account for unsafe sex practices in an epidemic. Recognizing the role of risk in transgressive (or, importantly, any) sex, Warner's most interesting suggestion was that when seronegative men engage in "unsafe" sex practices, they are identifying with the "culture of articulacy about mortality and the expectations of 'normal life'" that seropositive gay men developed in the crisis. Seronegative men "are staking their interests with that culture and taking as their own its priorities, its mordant humor, its heightened tempo, its long view on the world."[60] Warner identifies a *temporality* and a *subjectivity* here. Unsafe sex raises the question, Warner suggests, "Under what conditions is life worth surviving for? . . . If surviving AIDS means surviving all your positive friends and lovers, is the *you* that survives someone that you can imagine?"[61] Unsafe sex thus mediates between identity, identification, and solidarity, as a place in which selfhood and kinship intertwine.

Tim Dean's notoriety derives primarily from his qualified affirmation of bugchasing in *Unlimited Intimacy*, in which he argues that seeking to seroconvert represents a working-out of the death drive, a form of affiliative kinship practice, and an affirmation of finitude.[62] In his essay "Bareback Time," he explores the transformed temporalities resulting from the difference the now-uncertain prognosis that an HIV-diagnosis entails. Dean argues that unsafe sex "entails a commitment to the irreversible" in a time when the multiple temporalities of modernity and their concomitant uncertainties make something that cannot be undone a response to the anxiety of unknowing.[63] In a rather different way than Warner, who wrote before the "accomplishment" of the shift from AIDS time to HIV time,[64] Dean says that "voluntary seroconversion" is a way to "viscerally connect . . . a body in the present to a period . . . in the historical elsewhere," a connection that has a "spiritual dimension."[65] These connections across different temporalities can correct the successive generational logics that not only mark heterosexuality, as Guy Hocquenghem suggests,[66] but also feminist and queer theories and communities. Such transtemporal connections also resist the historical present that is the time of capital.

David Halperin recognizes the way the "gay male subject of unsafe sex represents . . . a scandalous rebuke to neoliberal models of individual rationality." The subject becomes an object of "horrified fascination" in his inexplicable pursuit of pleasure in the face of risk and death.[67] Halperin seeks to depathologize such discussions by developing a notion of abjection as a quasi-political-ethical response to degradation.[68] Abjection is an identification with the socially despised and excluded, or an acceptance of being socially despised and excluded, in which a "spiritual release" from domination is realized "by derealizing its humiliating effects—by depriving domination of its ability to demean the subject."[69] If, then, abjection distills the continued social pathologization of gay male subjectivity, it neither reflects the death drive nor some inexplicable gay male pathology. Instead, abjection is a way to "transcend (at least in our imagination) the humiliating realities of social existence" through the "genius" that sex has "in its ability to transmute otherwise unpleasant experiences of social degradation into experiences of pleasure."[70]

The drug Truvada, which can prevent HIV transmission with something approaching 99 percent effectiveness, transforms the debate yet again, as exhibited by the July 14, 2014, *New York* magazine article titled "Sex without Fear." Among the many fascinating quotations included in the article, three stand out. Sean Strub said, "Rather than giving [HIV-negative people] the life skills teaching them how to be healthy about their sexuality . . . the idea [is unbelievable] that we are going to put tens of millions of gay men on PrEP and bankrupt the economy to spray people with Raid." In contrast, Walter Armstrong said,

> There's something really ugly about how some older gay men who've lived through AIDS say to younger guys, "After all we've been through, I can't believe you would take PrEP and risk your life for sex." When I consider all we've been through, I can't believe anyone wouldn't take it—or at least think about it.[71]

The article ends on a poignant note: Leo Herrera reflecting on the first time he had condom-less sex with his partner. "It feels like the future, like a new chapter. . . . I feel very proud because a lot of men have died for me to be able to do this."[72] Risking one's life for sex, in solidarity with or in opposition to earlier generations of gay men, shows how timely Warner, Dean, and Halperin's discussions remain.

These three accounts offer somewhat different approaches to time, risk, and subjectivity in an age of HIV-AIDS, an age that, in different ways for Warner,

Halperin, and Dean, stands as a metonym for finitude itself. For them, HIV-AIDS also corrects any delusion of the successful, self-transparent, calculating self that neoliberalism might have imbued us with. Yet we are now faced with something of an impasse: The neoliberal entrepreneur discussed in the earlier part of this essay might theoretically appear as such a calculating subject, but as we have seen, the pair ecstasis-ascesis, which in different ways names the "subject" as developed by Warner, Halperin, and Dean (ecstatic establishment of kinship; ascetic practices of affirmation of finitude), can equally well name the "lived" entrepreneurial subject. Commitment to irreversibility in the face of unknowable and uncontrollable risk, becoming someone unknown to oneself—these ineluctable features of human existence are heightened and intensified in importantly different and importantly similar ways in figuring the entrepreneur or risking one's life for sex.

The different temporalities of cross-generational and cross-social identification seen in the debates over PrEP suggest that the time of HIV-AIDS permits us to ask the question of a transformed utopian future that does not amount to the denial of finitude. Herrera and Armstrong identify with the desires of those who have come before, affirming what they were and wanted. The haunting past opens onto a present of "sex without fear," yet as Michael Warner points out, there is no sex without risk. Risk-management is the watchword of the corporation and the medical realm. Eric Cazdyn connects shifts in capital's time to the rise of the "new chronic, . . . a mode of time that cares little for terminality or acuteness, but more for an undying present that remains forever sick."[73] Management of chronic illness, within and beyond the medical, "effectively colonizes the future by naturalizing and eternalizing the brutal logic of the present,"[74] in a way that constitutes a particular temporal modality of contemporary capitalism.

In Cazdyn's view, the "new chronic" also entails the loss of revolution, for revolution requires the kind of radical change that the new chronic refuses. Cazdyn develops the notion of the "already dead" as someone who "has been killed but has yet to die."[75] Those who live as the killed who have yet to die operate within "a free zone in which the already dead can transgress the structural limits of the present situation."[76] Cazdyn seeks to reclaim the right to die, since it is "our right to dream—and live in—a radically different present than the one we now inhabit."[77] Death and the imagination stand or fall together, he suggests. Cazdyn suggests (in partial critique of Edelman as well as Judith Butler) that "the future cannot be abstracted out of capitalism. . . . Radical difference is impossible to represent, given the structuring limits of the present. . . . This historical trap . . . does not mean that a noncapitalist future is impossible, only that it is unimaginable from the current situation."[78] We might therefore retain elements of the readings of AIDS-time offered by

Warner, Halperin, and Dean—like the right to die and the centrality of cross-generational identification to queer social life—while thinking about other sites of dead-end temporality that exist in HIV-time, the time of the killed who have yet to die. "How," Cazdyn asks, "to challenge the new chronic by preserving the intensity, and even the utopian quality, of the terminal?"[79]

## PAST, PRESENT, FUTURE

The recovery of lost utopias is also the discovery of new utopias. As José Muñoz famously argues, performance can be a form of worldmaking that not only gives us a sense that there *is* an alternative—that something other than what is can be—but itself generates the oppositional counterpublic it seeks to mobilize.[80] These performances can connect us across the disjunctions of temporal transformations—from AIDS-time to HIV-time. The dreams of others, especially those dreams that the present teaches us to disdain, can estrange us from the naturalization of our current existence and can teach us where to seek an alternative.[81]

We might then seek out also the spectral spinsters of an earlier generation of lesbian-feminism, those who are / were / might be the "big drag" discussed by Elizabeth Freeman when she asks, "Where is the feminist, lesbian, or even queer 'now' in 1967, in 1997, or whenever you are reading this sentence?"[82] Kaitlin Noss describes the "sense of nostalgic loss" in relation to the lesbian feminism that she finds herself ambivalently desiring, a "risky desire" that might "braid together the radical roots of 'lesbian' as a robust political identity and the threads of intersectional critique that insist on effective antiracist, anticapitalist work."[83] We have recently seen a turn to something like lesbian (or perhaps lesbian feminist) time—"Deep Lez"—in order to "awaken the dissident and minor future once hoped for in the past," as Freeman summarizes, following Lucas Hilderbrand.[84] Discussing lesbian performances of gaiety as a way to resist discipline and commodification,[85] Sara Warner says, delightfully, that "a Fabian strategy comprised of dilatory dyke tactics may be our best hope for countering the forces of homoliberalism."[86] Looking backward, she suggests, may be the best way to "retard the progress of the current homosexual [and neoliberal] agenda and move instead gaily forward."[87] What would become possible if we learned not to disdain, but rather to desire, the dreams of those who came before us?

As David Halperin says, "Gay culture is a vestige from an earlier time. It is archaic, obsolete. Gay culture has no future."[88] In contrast to heteronormativity's reproductive sameness—or the reproductive sameness of the overdetermined time of capital—the culture all are inducted into no matter their sexual orientation, "gay culture doesn't just happen. It has to be made to happen. It requires material support, organization, and a queer public sphere."[89] Where can these institutional, social, and imaginative resources be found? Asked differently: How do we materialize impossible forms of life? The alignment of finitude, risk, contingency, temporal overdetermination and futural openness explored in the first part of this essay is a partial identification of quilting points of contemporary capital. Materialization toward change requires shifts in these relationships.

Kathi Weeks argues for the strange-making capacities of the utopian demand. Such a demand "prefigures . . . a different world in which the program or policy that the demand promotes would be considered as a matter of course both practical and reasonable." Significantly, she insists that "the political practice of demanding is of crucial importance."[90] The denaturalizing effects of a utopian demand draw attention to the possibility that the world might be otherwise than it is, but denaturalization alone is not enough. The demand is limited and specific; it is "both act and text, both an analytic perspective and a political provocation."[91] Weeks recognizes the challenge that utopia poses to the demand, and vice versa—the specificity of demand might stifle wide-ranging utopia—yet "the terms can be altered by their relationship."[92] The relationship reflects the doubling effect of the utopian demand: It "must be both strange and familiar, grounded in the present and gesturing toward the future."[93]

Sara Ahmed directly connects retro-temporality with the possibility of things being otherwise, learning about the past as a way to the "possibilities that have to be recognized as possibilities to become possible."[94] Halperin suggests that the distantiation he considers essential to gay culture is "characteristic of every artist, every stylist, every cook, and every theologian."[95] If we bring Halperin's attention to form together with Weeks's consideration of utopian forms, a possibility opens for challenging the way the openness, indeterminacy, and unknowability of the future enforces entrepreneurialism by drawing us through the threat of the difference between the present and the future.

Weeks considers the demand a narrower subset of the manifesto,[96] a form with deep roots in Marxist, black, white, and women of color feminist and queer political organizing. Classics of the genre include the Black Women's Manifesto, the Redstockings Manifesto, the Queer Nation Manifesto, and, of course, the Communist Manifesto,[97] suggesting the viability of the manifesto form for different but interrelated revolutionary projects. The manifesto, like the demand, refuses the threatening specter of the open future, the need fully to commit to whatever opportunity presents itself. Instead, the manifesto answers the individuating potential of the threatening, unknowable future with the collectivizing "we" of a determinate future. The manifesto "set[s] itself against the conventions of appropriate discussion and reasonable demands on which the reproduction of the status quo depends."[98] Manifestos "attempt to produce that which they seem to presume."[99] For Weeks, the collectivizing and determinate aspects of manifestos are risky because they predetermine the "we" and "risk closing rather than opening multiple and unexpected paths to the future."[100] For this reason, she prefers the demand, but for my purposes, the difference between them is not that significant; the manifesto may even be preferable to the demand *because* it forecloses some possible futures.

The manifesto makes demands that can constitute a "we." It has the capacity to redirect the dissatisfaction with existing conditions characteristic of the entrepreneur, but also of the activist, the queer (in the political sense), the feminist, and the Christian toward the willed transformation that entrepreneurialism refuses us. Recovering the manifesto form in order to challenge the dictates of total commitment also means recovering the dreams of the already dead: a queer past that may have resources for a different future. The lesbian feminist theologian and philosopher Mary Daly has become deeply unfashionable to most of my students—feminist and queer—in large part because of her absolutely indefensible transphobia, but also because as a lesbian feminist she must necessarily have been an essentialist, they believe, and their enemy is essentialism first and foremost. As I have argued implicitly throughout this essay, however, essentialism is increasingly a misguided target; not that we should be essentialists, but rather that the fluidity we offer as an alternative to essentialism is exactly the fluidity that capitalism expects of us, the fluid playfulness that it allows us so that we may find ourselves realized in these boundless forms of self-transcendence, so that our desire and our discipline will coincide.

One of Daly's diagnostic demands is for "Women-Touching women"[101]—relationships among women irreducible to the passing-on of patriarchal reproductive sameness. As Daly points out, "Woman-identified knowledge has been made to seem repugnant. Fixed by the pushers of pseudofeminism, women are 'purified' of even the desire to re-member."[102] Instead, Daly says, we need to "risk be-ing the Crazed Witch."[103] Without removing or overcoming the specificity of Daly's analysis, I want to play for a moment with the inversions characteristic of queer theological attempts to find same-sex and gender-fluid relations in Christian imagistic traditions. Queer theologians turn to the example of David and Jonathan whose loves surpasses that of women, or to traditions of gender fluidity in early Christian hagiographies, in which even women can become men—despite the extreme dearth of imagery of relations *among* or *between* women that are not mediated by a relation to a man. Daly's call for re-membering women and for Women-Touching women may orient us toward a nonexclusive "lesbian" temporality of recovering the dreams of the already dead in literal and symbolic ways. The dead and the already dead may come together here, where HIV-AIDS time meets a lesbian temporality of desiring toward a future that is no future. So let us take with us not only Daly but all the rest she left behind and "move gaily forward" past the limits of the possible.

The question of the affirmation of finitude has run throughout this essay. I have argued that the simultaneous affirmation of finitude, contingency, and fluidity can advance the totalizing capacity of the present order, in a parody of the Christian notion of the goodness of creation. Christian theology is often critiqued for its (purported) world-denying tendencies, but it also affirms that finitude is susceptible of transformation without becoming other than what it is.[104] We need to find that there is an alternative, that the current economic order has fractures and locations in which alternative economies may be built,[105] so that we learn to identify with a "we" that does not yet exist. The imaginative (and analytic) inhabitation of an alternative order offers the simultaneous promise of naming the present and learning where the quilting points are that might orient us toward an alternative future. As theologians and biblical scholars, we need to learn to speak our own desires for such transformation as a form of the critique that Weiss describes. The practices of legitimation in our various subdisciplines offer little reward—and often punishment—for the experiments in genre, form, and life that most benefit our abilities to tell such stories, though, and it may well be true that (at least some of) our subdisciplines and institutions teeter on the brink of disappearing—not that we are allowed to forget that for even a moment!

Perhaps our time is indeed short, whether measured by the time until tenure denial, until death, or until ecological catastrophe. In the interim, though, it seems to me that we must use the institutions we have to experiment with alternative temporal forms—in ways that have the power to seduce, to allure, to make desirable. Attempts at thickly theological approaches to the economy have often devolved into calling out the disordered desire represented by consumerism and the possessive desire to which the Christian response is thought to be the recovery of sacrifice. Neither move seems particularly germane to our contemporary economic situation, in which fragility, vulnerability, and sacrifice are already present throughout. Instead, I believe we need to marshal resources imaginative and institutional toward the visualization of forms of life that teach us—in direct but inverse parallel to contemporary economic naturalization—to make choices toward the actualization of a currently impossible future, accompanied by the living specter of that big drag.

## NOTES

1. Harry Harootunian, "Remembering the Historical Present," *Critical Inquiry* 33, no. 3 (2007): 472–73.

2. Pierre Dardot and Christian Laval, *The New Way of the World: On Neo-Liberal Society*, trans. Gregory Elliott (London: Verso, 2013), 280.
3. Entrepreneurial subjectivity is only one strategy of subject-formation among others—albeit one of the most pervasive—but it is a particularly instructive one for thinking queer temporality and queer theology.
4. Daniel M. Bell Jr., *The Economy of Desire: Christianity and Capitalism in a Postmodern World* (Grand Rapids, Mich.: Baker Academic, 2012), 154.
5. Ibid., 169.
6. Ibid., 171.
7. Ibid., 175, 185–86.
8. Ibid., 181.
9. Rowan Williams, *Christian Spirituality: A Theological History from the New Testament to Luther and St. John of the Cross* (Louisville, Ky.: John Knox Press, 1980), 164.
10. Ibid., 166.
11. Ibid., 176.
12. Rowan Williams, "Deflections of Desire: Negative Theology in Trinitarian Disclosure," in *Silence and the Word: Negative Theology and Incarnation*, ed. Oliver Davies and Denys Turner (Cambridge: Cambridge University Press, 2002), 131.
13. Ibid., 118.
14. Rowan Williams, *On Christian Theology* (Malden, Mass.: Blackwell, 2000), 70.
15. Ibid., 218.
16. Ibid., 216.
17. Ibid., 220 (emphasis removed).
18. Ibid., 221.
19. Linn Marie Tonstad, "Speaking 'Father' Rightly: Kenotic Reformation into Sonship in Sarah Coakley," in Linn Marie Tonstad, *God and Difference: The Trinity, Sexuality, and the Transformation of Finitude* (New York: Routledge, 2016), 98–132.
20. Sarah Coakley, "Beyond Libertarianism and Repression: The Quest for an Anglican Theological Ascetics," in *Other Voices, Other Worlds: The Global Church Speaks Out on Homosexuality*, ed. Terry Brown (New York: Church Publishing, 2006), 332.
21. Ibid., 338n7.
22. Sarah Coakley, "Ecclesiastical Sex Scandals: The Lack of a Contemporary Theology of Desire," in Sarah Coakley, *The New Asceticism: Sexuality, Gender and the Quest for God* (London: Bloomsbury Academic, 2015), 51.
23. See, for instance, Graham Ward, *Cities of God* (London: Routledge, 2000), 76.
24. Graham Ward, *Christ and Culture* (Malden, Mass.: Blackwell, 2005), 201. See Linn Marie Tonstad, "Suffering Difference: Graham Ward's Trinitarian Romance," in *God and Difference*, 58–97, for an extended discussion of Ward.
25. Leo Bersani, *Is the Rectum a Grave? and Other Essays* (Chicago: University of Chicago Press, 2010), 29–30.
26. See Kent L. Brintnall, *Ecce Homo: The Male-Body-in-Pain as Redemptive Figure* (Chicago: University of Chicago Press, 2011), especially chapter 1, for an examination of the way resurrection may undo the self-shattering potential of the male divine's death on the cross.

27. Tomas Marttila, *The Culture of Enterprise in Neoliberalism: Specters of Entrepreneurship* (New York: Routledge, 2013), 1. In "Debt Time Is Straight Time," *Political Theology* 17, no. 5 (2016), 434–448, I examine the subjectivity and temporality of debt as overdetermination of the present by the past and future. Debt-determined subjectivity is another primary form of subject-formation in the current order.
28. Marttila, *Culture of Enterprise*, 2.
29. Dardot and Laval, *New Way*, 263.
30. See also Frédéric Lordon, *Willing Slaves of Capital: Spinoza and Marx on Desire*, trans. Gabriel Ash (London: Verso, 2014).
31. Dardot and Laval, *New Way*, 260.
32. In "Playful Membership: Embracing an Unknown Future," *Management & Organizational History* 9, no. 2 (2014): 166–82, Niels Åkerstrøm Andersen and Justine Grønbæk Pors examine the way organizations use play as a way to encourage flexibility in their employees and to mediate between the fixity of decision making and the unknowability of the future. They emphasize the relationship between play and contingency: "In play, the future represents a horizon of contingent possibilities. And play brings this surplus of possibilities to the present, making the present undecided and contingent as well" (175). Play might allow organizations, otherwise (arguably) subject rather to the constraints of managerialism, to participate in the temporal indetermination of entrepreneurialism.
33. Gerald Raunig, *Factories of Knowledge, Industries of Creativity*, trans. Aileen Derieg (Los Angeles: Semiotext[e], 2013), 119. Although I do not explore this motif further here, it is crucial to note the differential mobilities and concomitant spatiotemporalities of bodies and money.
34. Lordon, *Willing Slaves of Capital*, 124. Interestingly, Lordon suggests that this "vanishing point" of capitalism could reactivate the old dream of capitalism's demise by its own self-transcendence in the face of total contradiction, since the implication of this vision of the worker is that "the very idea of employment as a relation of hierarchical subordination is fundamentally called in question." Nevertheless, Lordon admits that "employees will not all become artists, thus capable of escaping through the communist line of flight." Instead, the "complete possession of souls" demanded by capitalism is best understood as a "totalitarian" project (125–26).
35. "The imperative of life-long learning implies a twofold invocation of modulation: an invocation to mold and modularize not only education or work, to stratify, striate and count all relationships, the whole of life, and at the same time an invocation to be prepared to constantly change, adapt, vary." Raunig, *Factories of Knowledge*, 46. See also Dardot and Laval, *New Way*, 263.
36. Wolfgang Streeck, *Buying Time: The Delayed Crisis of Democratic Capitalism* (London: Verso, 2014), 31.
37. As Miranda Joseph points out, the especially vulnerable—in her study, women preparing for release from prison—may embrace "entrepreneurial subjectivity" because "it suggests that individuals have a great deal of agency" (*Debt to Society: Accounting for Life under Capitalism* [Minneapolis: University of Minnesota Press,

2014], 84). The especially vulnerable may replicate more general social logics in concentrated form.

38. Karen Ho, *Liquidated: An Ethnography of Wall Street* (Durham, N.C.: Duke University Press, 2009), 11.
39. Frank H. Knight, *Risk, Uncertainty and Profit* (1921; 1957; Mineola, N.Y.: Dover, 2006), 310–11.
40. Marttila, *Culture of Enterprise*, 6.
41. It may go without saying that I am treating these as ideal types. I focus on the Christian because I write as a theologian whose primary archives are Christian theology and the legacies of queer and feminist reflection, not in order to contrast the Christian with other possible figures.
42. Richard Dienst, *The Bonds of Debt* (London: Verso, 2011), 63.
43. Bersani, *Is the Rectum a Grave?* 18.
44. Lordon reads that relationship as "the production of a double imaginary, the imaginary of fulfilment, which makes the humble joys to which the dominated are assigned appear sufficient, and the imaginary of powerlessness, which convinces them to renounce any greater ones to which they might desire" (*Willing Slaves of Capital*, 109–10).
45. Margot Weiss, *Techniques of Pleasure: BDSM and the Circuits of Sexuality* (Durham, N.C.: Duke University Press, 2011).
46. Margot Weiss, "Queer Economic Justice: Desire, Critique and the Practice of Knowledge," in *Global Justice and Desire: Queering Economy*, ed. Nikita Dhawan, Antke Engel, Christoph H. E. Holzhey, and Volker Woltersdorff (New York: Routledge, 2015), 79.
47. Ibid., 83.
48. Ibid., 84. Weiss significantly oversimplifies the connections others draw between BDSM, transgression, and anticapitalist resistance.
49. Ibid., 79.
50. Ibid., 92.
51. Dardot and Laval, *New Way*, 283.
52. Ibid., 284.
53. Ibid., 268–69. They take the phrase from *Management et contuite de soi: Enquête sur les ascèses de la performance*, ed. Éric Pezet (Paris: Vuibert, 2007).
54. J. Jack Halberstam, *The Queer Art of Failure* (Durham, N.C.: Duke University Press, 2011), 187.
55. Megan McArdle, *The Up Side of Down: Why Failing Well Is the Key to Success* (New York: Viking, 2014).
56. Joseph, *Debt to Society*, 62.
57. José Esteban Muñoz's *Cruising Utopia: The Then and There of Queer Futurity* (New York: New York University Press, 2009) represents his answer to Edelman's *No Future: Queer Theory and the Death Drive* (Durham, N.C.: Duke University Press, 2004).
58. See Tonstad, *God and Difference*, 264–68, for a longer discussion of Edelman's project. I will not go into detail here about how he is generally misread; suffice it to say

that both the ethical aspects and the specific restrictions of his argument are often missed by critics.

59. David M. Halperin, *What Do Gay Men Want? An Essay on Sex, Risk, and Subjectivity* (Ann Arbor: University of Michigan Press, 2007). Halperin reprints the Warner essay in an appendix. Michael Warner's essay "Unsafe: Why Gay Men Are Having Risky Sex" first appeared in the *Village Voice* on January 31, 1995; I will cite the essay by page number in Halperin's book. Tim Dean will be represented here by his essay "Bareback Time," in *Queer Times, Queer Becomings*, ed. E. L. McCallum and Mikko Tuhkanen (Albany: State University of New York Press, 2011), 75–100.
60. Warner, "Unsafe," 166.
61. Ibid., 168.
62. Tim Dean, *Unlimited Intimacy: Reflections on the Subculture of Barebacking* (Chicago: University of Chicago Press, 2009).
63. Dean, "Bareback Time," 81.
64. "Accomplishment" here is intended to figure the only local contexts in which the transition from AIDS-time to HIV-time has been "achieved"; further, non-progressors and others trouble any simple discussion of HIV-diagnosis as either a death sentence or a manageable syndrome.
65. Dean, "Bareback Time," 93.
66. Guy Hocquenghem, *Homosexual Desire*, trans. Daniella Dangoor (Durham, N.C.: Duke University Press, 1993), 109.
67. Halperin, *What Do Gay Men Want?* 33.
68. See ibid., 107, for the ways in which abjection is and is not political.
69. Ibid., 79.
70. Ibid., 87.
71. Tim Murphy, "Sex without Fear," *New York Magazine*, July 14, 2014, 45.
72. Ibid., 47.
73. Eric Cazdyn, *The Already Dead: The New Time of Politics, Culture, and Illness* (Durham, N.C.: Duke University Press, 2012), 5.
74. Ibid., 6.
75. Ibid., 4.
76. Ibid., 194.
77. Ibid., 7.
78. Ibid., 141.
79. Ibid, 11.
80. José Esteban Muñoz, *Disidentifications: Queers of Color and the Performance of Politics* (Minneapolis: University of Minnesota Press, 1999), 195–96.
81. "This promissory union between communities lived and imagined can sound like a particularly historical kind of afterlife, in which the '*there*' of having been saved also houses the 'there' in which being saved commits the young saint to the adventure of the secular world." Christopher Nealon, *Foundlings: Lesbian and Gay Historical Emotion before Stonewall* (Durham, N.C.: Duke University Press, 2001), 182.
82. Elizabeth Freeman, *Time Binds: Queer Temporalities, Queer Histories* (Durham, N.C.: Duke University Press, 2010), 62, 76.

83. Kaitlin Noss, "Queering Utopia: Deep Lez and the Future of Hope," *WSQ: Women's Studies Quarterly* 40 (Fall/Winter 2012), 128.
84. Freeman, *Time Binds*, 85.
85. Sara Warner, *Acts of Gaiety: LGBT Performance and the Politics of Pleasure* (Ann Arbor: University of Michigan Press, 2012), 193.
86. Ibid., 26.
87. Ibid., 30.
88. David M. Halperin, *How to Be Gay* (Cambridge, Mass.: Belknap Press of Harvard University Press, 2012), 442.
89. Ibid., 453, 26.
90. Kathi Weeks, *The Problem with Work: Feminism, Marxism, Antiwork Politics, and Postwork Imaginaries* (Durham, N.C.: Duke University Press, 2011), 176.
91. Ibid., 219.
92. Ibid., 219–20.
93. Ibid., 221.
94. Sara Ahmed, *The Promise of Happiness* (Durham, N.C.: Duke University Press, 2010), 218.
95. Halperin, *How to Be Gay*, 454.
96. Weeks, *Problem with Work*, 218.
97. A digital copy of the Black Women's Manifesto, published by the Third World Women's Alliance, is available at http://library.duke.edu/digitalcollections/wlmpc_wlmms01009/. The Redstockings Manifesto can be found at http://redstockings.org/index.php/42-uncategorised/76-rs-manifesto. The text of the Queer Nation Manifesto is at http://www.historyisaweapon.com/defcon1/queernation.html. See https://www.marxists.org/archive/marx/works/1848/communist-manifesto/ for the Communist Manifesto.
98. Weeks, *Problem with Work*, 215.
99. Ibid., 217.
100. Ibid., 218.
101. Mary Daly, *Pure Lust: Elemental Feminist Philosophy* (Boston: Beacon Press, 1984), 247.
102. Ibid., 112.
103. Ibid., 113.
104. Kathryn Tanner makes much of this in the first three chapters of *Christ the Key* (Cambridge: Cambridge University Press, 2010).
105. As suggested, for instance, by J. K. Gibson-Graham, *The End of Capitalism (As We Knew It): A Feminist Critique of Political Economy* (Minneapolis: University of Minnesota Press, 2006).

# Queer Structures of Religious Feeling: What Time Is Now?

ANN PELLEGRINI

Freud's hostility toward religion and his, at best, condescension toward the religious are by now so well known as to have become part of the obviousness of the secular modern—and of classical psychoanalysis as secular discourse par excellence. For the Freud of *The Future of an Illusion* (1927), religion is akin to an obsessional neurosis of childhood; just as children may be hoped (and helped) to outgrow their neuroses, so too might humankind overcome the obsessional neurosis that is religion.[1] A few sentences later in the same text, Freud is even less sparing, and religion approaches the level of a psychosis: It "comprises a system of wishful illusions together with a disavowal of reality, such as we find in an isolated form nowhere else but in amentia, in a state of blissful hallucinatory confusion."[2] In the place of religion, Freud offers psychoanalysis and, with it, an education into the discomforting certainties of transience, mortality, and a primal helplessness.[3] Growing up does not rescue us from our helplessness, the multiple ways in which we are dependent and vulnerable and subject to experiences and events not of our choosing. And then, we're gonna die. But this *"education to reality,"*[4] Freud urges, might actually lead to a greater appreciation of living in the here and now.

But, what time is now?[5] Another way to pose this question: What is the time of psychic life?

My interest in these questions derives from my interest in the overlaps between psychoanalysis and queer theory—in a *Pink Freud*,[6] if you will—and in a related interest in deconstructing the religious/secular divide. Freud sought to position psychoanalysis on the side of science and secular rationality. There is something ironic in this, given Freud's interest in exposing the irrational forces that continually disrupt "His Majesty the Ego."[7] Does a science of the irrational undo its own will to know? The religious/secular divide has been structuring for much white Anglo-American queer theory and feminist studies, too, for both of which secularism has been epistemologically and morally central.[8] In this, and despite their anti-institutional positioning, queer and feminist studies well fit the dominant (i.e., Protestant secular) ethos of the North American academy, within which religion has been something of an embarrassment even for the academic study of religion.[9]

The, at best, conflicted feelings secular gender and sexuality studies have about religion may hold up a kind of mirror for the ambiguous place of both religion and sexuality in modernity. Both sex and religion are sites of excess in modernity, but they have been figured in very different ways. One, sexuality, is the mark of modernity and the modern—which is to say, the modern Western—subject. Sexuality is something to be examined, organized, brought under control, and/or examined, organized around, and liberated. The other, religion, is what a disenchanted modernity was supposed to have left behind, liberated itself from.[10] And yet religion has been remarkably persistent, and not just as some atavistic hangover or vestigial body part that has no ongoing function. Insofar as religion ("good" religion, anyway) is admitted space in the modern, it is often invited in—sometimes even by the secular state—as a way to discipline and organize otherwise unruly sexuality. The "bad" religion of "fundamentalism" is, by contrast, subject to scrutiny, surveillance, fear, condescension, psychologization, and control. Of course, one person's "good" religion is another's fundamentalism. Nonetheless, these different relations to time and good ordering—modern sex and sexual subjects "versus" antimodern religion and religious subjects, socially advanced societies "versus" primitive or still-developing nations—contribute to the public framing of religion and sexuality as opposed and antagonistic "identity positions." How might queer theories of temporality intervene in such an opposition? Not only that, how might an embodied psychoanalysis be part of that project of remapping the time/s of sexuality? One of the arguments I want to venture is that psychoanalysis puts forward, or can put forward, both a queer theory and a queer *practice* of temporality. By practice, I mean to draw focus away from arguments over the contents or dis-contents of psychoanalysis and toward the embodied encounter of time, and *in* time, that happens in the analytic relation.

Even before it became a body of theory identified with the proper name "Freud" (although he hardly exhausts psychoanalytic thinking or clinical practice), psychoanalysis was first and foremost an embodied and embodying practice that took place in a particular time and space between at least two subjects. It still is.

Although there are many reasons to criticize, with feminists, what Freud and psychoanalysis have to say about gender and sex, there is also much cause to point out, with Foucault, the ongoing ways in which psychoanalysis has historically participated in the incitement to speak of sex as our truth. Of course, even here, much depends on how we understand the psychoanalytic incitement to speech. If we think of the movement of speech in analysis as occurring between and across two spaces, then we might conceive this mediated and mediating talk not as a technology of self-revelation (of "the" truth) but of becoming. From this perspective, psychoanalysis as practice potentially offers itself as a means of becoming or trying out becomings over time and in it. These becomings could take a whole range of forms that contradict the ostensible social truths—and bounds—of self and each other. At its best, psychoanalysis is less about finding and speaking the "truth" of sex than in opening up the order of desire to other scenes, other possibilities, other ways of living the self. If psychoanalysis really is "what two people can say to each other if they agree not to have sex,"[11] then it may well constitute a practice of freedom, a novel relational and aesthetic mode in the Foucauldian sense.[12] Wouldn't that be deliciously ironic?

"For me intellectual work is related to what you could call aestheticism, meaning transforming yourself," Foucault says in the 1983 interview "The Minimalist Self," continuing, "This transformation of one's self by one's own knowledge is . . . something rather close to the aesthetic experience."[13] Alongside aesthetic experience, and perhaps as a version of it, psychoanalysis offers itself as a possible site for queer experimentation. Part of its experimental force derives from the ways psychoanalysis as practice changes, or can change, what time feels like. Psychoanalysis depends on time even as it suspends it. The clinical hour, repeated weekly, or even daily if the analysand is in classical psychoanalytic treatment, creates a set temporal and spatial frame precisely so that time as it is usually experienced can be relived, disrupted, retold. This disruption of time's everyday feeling may even have phenomenological overlaps with religious "time-outs," such as the Jewish Sabbath. This suggestion would have scandalized Freud, the self-proclaimed "Godless Jew," who forbade his wife from lighting the Shabbat candles.[14] Secularism, too, is not just a particular regime of knowledge / power / subjectivity, but a way of telling and living time.[15] Psychoanalysis can disrupt those tellings; it can also reinforce them. With one foot in the Sabbath and the other in the standardized clock time of factory, office, and train travel (a marvelous technology of the new in Freud's own time), psychoanalysis—Freud's proclamations notwithstanding—is neither wholly secular nor holy religious.

No doubt my suggestion that psychoanalysis offers a kind of queer time-out, a space for transformation and experimentation, will scandalize many readers of this essay. This suggestion also runs up against Foucault's own strong criticisms of psychoanalysis in *The History of Sexuality*, volume one,[16] and still more extensively, in *History of Madness*,[17] a 1961 text better known to English-language readers in abbreviated form and under the title *Madness and Civilization*.[18] In her fascinating and polemical re-turn to the full text of *Mad-*

*ness*, Lynne Huffer argues for the incompatibility between Freud and Foucault *and* between psychoanalysis and queer theory. I admire Huffer's study, its ambition, erudition, and important resurfacing of Foucault's early text. But it is not always clear in Huffer's reading if the incompatibilities concern psychoanalysis as theory or practice or both. Any which way, the psychoanalysis in question seems to me more Freudian than Freud himself. It also seems frozen in time, with Freud as originator of a technique of patriarchal mastery—the "doctor-patient couple"—that amplifies the authority of reason over madness by drawing itself (and secularizing?) the ancient power of priests and magicians.[19] To be sure, in its focus on the interior (of a subject, of a family cell) psychoanalysis has expanded the reach of power into the body—and so often in the name of liberation. Nonetheless, both Foucault's and Huffer's treatment of psychoanalysis seems to me partial if not outdated. In *Testo Junkie*, a text also highly critical of psychoanalysis, Paul B. Preciado updates Foucault—and Freud—by showing how pharmacological resolutions have taken power even further into the body and situated it at the level of the molecule.[20]

At a time when weekly talk therapy (let alone analysis multiple times a week) is a luxury few can afford, when insurance companies balk at subsidizing it for any extended period, and when pharmacology has largely displaced it, there is something almost quaint (and hopeful) about inveighing against the talking cure as ruse of power. But is it possible—to cite a term from a later set of investigations by Foucault, his 1977–78 lectures published under the title *Security, Territory, Population*—that psychoanalytic practice today functions, or could function, as a kind of *counter-conduct*? By "counter-conduct," Foucault means a form of resistance or "struggle against the processes instituted for conducting others," against, in other words, pastoral power.[21] "In its modern forms," Foucault argues, "the pastorate [the government of souls and their conduct] is deployed to a great extent through medical knowledge, institutions, and practices."[22] It is precisely by virtue of its investiture with the powers once associated with the Christian pastorate that medicine also becomes a site of contestation and struggle—"a whole series of revolts of conduct," as individuals and groups contest the terms on which they are being conducted, trained, and disciplined through medical knowledge.[23] His examples of "medical *dissent*" include the organized refusal to submit to vaccines and the development of alternative medicine.[24]

Adam Phillips has described psychoanalysis as one of the places in contemporary culture where we can reevaluate the history of our own obedience.[25] At its best, then, psychoanalysis might constitute counter-conduct against the forms of obedience in which we are trained to be/come and know ourselves as particular kinds of selves. Much of this potential derives from the "slow time" of psychoanalysis, the long patience of nothing happening, and the unsettling experience of talking and listening without having to know or ever being able to. This is psychoanalysis as will to un-know, un-do, and be un-done, practices of un-knowing and un-doing in which no one is or need be the master once and for all. It seems to me that so much of the project and the practice of lying on the couch is the invitation (discomforting, exciting, pleasurable, unnerving) to un-know the self you thought you had to be. In this regard, at least, I hear and experience so much in psychoanalytic practice that "rhymes" with Foucault's challenge to loosen the holds of time: "We are much more recent than we think."[26]

## CLOCK TIME

Religion and secularism are not universal categories, even as part of their promise (in different ways) is universalism. Janet Jakobsen and I examine the universal aspirations of the secular, and the exclusions and violences of this universalism, in our co-edited volume *Secularisms* (2008). One of our interests is to expose the network of temporal and moral associations—and binaries—that get put into play by the secularization thesis and by narratives that oppose the religious to the secular, assigning stasis, primitivism, regression to the former; movement, progress, futurity to the latter. The claim of the secularization narrative is that the secularism that develops from particular European and Christian origins is, in fact, universal and fully separate from Christianity. In fact, secularism and the progress narrative it proffers of the irrepressible forward march of freedom and reason remain tied to a particular religion, just as—to take an only apparently small example—the secular calendar remains tied to Christianity. In fact, the inspiration for our work in *Secularisms* was the remarkably unremarked upon fact that in the run-up to the new millennium there were worldwide fears of a "Y2K bug" and its potential to disrupt computer transactions and even crash financial markets. How did a particular religion's way of telling time—as the clock moved from 1999 to 2000 *anno domini*—become the secular calendar of global finance and world politics. Isn't secularism supposed to represent the overcoming of religion and its particularities? Nonetheless, other ways of telling time remain active.[27]

In his magisterial study of the *American Technological Sublime*,[28] the historian David E. Nye charts how great emotional experiences of "awe and wonder, often tinged with an element of terror," are mediated by encounters with "particular natural sites, architectural forms, and technological achievements." How did the new technologies of the early twentieth century reshape not just the experience of time and space, but also the experience of experience? The electrification of the urban American landscape in the late nineteenth century and into the twentieth certainly inspired wonder and awe. But electricity and the communications technologies it enabled also ushered in new forms of surveillance, social control, and, even, temporality.[29] A stark example of this is the establishment of standardized time and time zones across the United States in the 1880s, a development driven by profound transformations in technologies for traversing distance: the electric telegraph and the train. The telegraph and, later, the telephone both collapsed space, enabling instantaneous communication across large distances.[30] The discordance between local times became jarring. Railroads needed to coordinate—sync—the timetable of trains with the local times they traversed. Before the American Railway Association effectively imposed standard time and regularized time zones, in November 1883, there was a plurality of local times across the United States. In the mid-nineteenth century United States, there were thirty-eight different standard times in Wisconsin alone. By October 1884, 85 percent of U.S. towns with populations greater than 10,000 had switched to railway time.[31] This new practice of keeping time became federal law, when Congress passed the Standard Time Act, in 1919.

The standardization of time increased the efficiency of train travel and its safety, although train wrecks still occurred with disturbing frequency, attracting the horrified fascination of the American public. As Mark Aldrich has documented, by 1907, train accidents had become the leading cause of violent death in the United States.[32] Europe's railway record was not much better, and train derailments became a signature accident of their time.[33] Train accidents offered the spectacular shock of the new, horrifying to those who witnessed them firsthand but also fascinating to those who consumed stories of them in novels or newspapers—or medical studies. Indeed, in *Beyond the Pleasure Principle*, Freud names "railway disasters" as the leading example of the kind of "severe mechanical concussions . . . involving a risk to life" that can lead to "traumatic neurosis."[34]

Time's standardization also ratified and, in some sense, helped constitute the felt instantaneity of new communications technologies as they connected "there" to "here." Of course, the establishment of uniform time, along with an array of electrical devices to tell the correct time, also enabled the extension of surveillance deeper into the body, with implications far beyond the industrial factory. In Nye's cogent phrasing: "Once national time was in effect, being 'on time' became an absolute rather than a relative standard."[35] New technologies also gave rise to new "structures of feeling," to use Raymond Williams's famous term.[36] The telephone could magically connect us across space. But its prosthetic assistance was necessary only because—as Freud himself ventriloquized the mixed feelings of "progress" in *Civilization and Its Discontents*—"if there were no railway to make light of distances, my child would never have left home, and I should not need the telephone to hear his voice."[37] These new regularities—modern, technologized ways of being and moving and feeling through time and connecting across space—were overlaid on other ways of telling and experiencing time. What remained of these other ways of being in time? Can you be touched by two times at once and, if so, with what benefits and what losses? Arguably, the nineteenth- and early-twentieth-century explosion of interest, both popular and scientific, in the United States and Europe, in paranormal phenomena owes not a little to the electrical reorganization of temporality. So do the conceptualization and, I would suggest, the very experience of trauma as a fracture in secular time.

The regularization of time and its embodiment did not go uncontested. As the historian Carolyn Marvin argues, the new electrical media "precipitated new kinds of social encounters" that tested the bounds of previous ways of organizing social life, political power, and the meaning of the body. It is not simply that psychoanalysis straddled (at least) two ways of telling time; it also, I am arguing, stood at the threshold between reasserting hegemonic forms of control and unleashing new kinds of social encounters and possibilities.

There is a strong case to be made for the persistence of alternative temporalities even within the most secular scenes of the modern. Psychoanalysis offers a rich case in point, with its codes (linearity, developmental imperatives) and counter-codes. Past and present exist at the same "time." In a sense, the unconscious does not know how to tell time. Is the analytic process geared toward orienting the analysand to the right relation of time: the "chrononormativity" (Elizabeth Freeman's term)[38] of before and after, then to now, a completed past? Or/and might psychoanalysis be a way of acknowledging the haunting force of the past in the present, and making this co-presencing not just survivable but a force for flourishing in the present and toward an unknown future? It may be that psychoanalysis's capacity to help its practitioners (patient and analyst) live in and with the séance of the new requires suspending its own antipathy toward religion. In suggesting this, I am also gesturing towards psychoanalysis as a queer structure of religious feeling.

## PRACTICE, PRACTICE, PRACTICE

Arguably, psychoanalysis's spiritual dis-ease, its profound discomfort with religion, is owing not only to its secular Enlightenment lineage (dare I say: its quasi-religious faith in universal reason and universal mind), but also to a kind of mimetic rivalry—what, in the language of psychoanalysis we could also call a "narcissism of minor differences"[39]—with *other* spiritual techniques and traditions, such as private meditation, the Catholic confessional, and mesmerism. As the distinguished Indian psychoanalyst Sudhir Kakar puts it, both psychoanalysis and spirituality "essentially cultivate the same field—the self—and with not dissimilar methods that attempt to look inwards. Mutual irritation is bound to follow as the two keep on bumping against each other."[40]

Indeed, from its origins psychoanalysis was vying with competing Western and Christianizing spiritual disciplines for adherents committed to practices of self-care, self-discovery, and self-cultivation during a period of tremendous cultural and technological upheavals in the late nineteenth century and the early twentieth. The assertion of the term *self* here, as a kind of prefix, is one of the creative fictions of Western modernity. To put the "self" before "care," "discovery," and "cultivation" makes it seem as if there were a fixed self who comes temporally and substantially before these activities, perhaps even before all activity. To paraphrase Judith Butler paraphrasing Nietzsche: There is no doer before the deed.[41] Doing creates being and being*s*; acts forge and re-forge what commonly gets called "identity." There is no self prior to the relational webs—including language, embodiment, nonhuman and human-made environments—that produce and support the experience of human being as such. What's more, the kind of self I/you/we feel ourselves to be (empty or overflowing, autonomous or "dividual," to use Kakar's term) varies tremendously across time and culture, and may even change over the course of an individual lifetime. Perhaps even with the assistance of psychoanalytic practice. And/or perhaps with the assistance of other religious or spiritual practices.

Freud himself had a complicated relationship to (other?) spiritual practices. He scandalized Ernest Jones and others among his followers by his belief in telepathy. Freud published a number of essays in which he seeks to distinguish psychoanalysis from the wrong kind of dream interpretations (premonitory dreams, for example). But he was personally fascinated by telepathy, saw some connections between telepathy and the unconscious communications that took place between analyst and analysand, and engaged in experiments—probably attempts at thought-transference—with Anna Freud and Sándor Ferenczi. Pushed by Jones to disavow telepathy because of the way it was being used to smear psychoanalysis and its practitioners as occultists and quacks, Freud responded, in a March 1926 letter: "If someone should reproach you with my Fall into Sin, you are free to reply that my adherence to telepathy is my private affair, like my Jewishness, my passion for smoking and other things, and the theme of telepathy—inessential for psychoanalysis."[42]

Practice does not make perfect. But it does make up many things—including persons and lifeworlds. Practice is the warp and woof of spiritual-religious life. Nevertheless, there is a tendency in the United States (and in other national contexts shaped by Reformed Protestantism) to make "belief" or "faith" the leading edge of religion, thereby locating (projecting?) religious identity into the interior, private realm of soul, mind, or conscience. This belief-centered and privatized view of religion dominates political and legal discussions of religion (and religious freedom) in the United States with grave effects for many religious outliers, where religious outliers also includes those who are not religious at all. Jakobsen wryly observes that in the United States, religious freedom means getting to act Protestant—even when you're not.[43] This is a great line, with a very serious point. The history of U.S. jurisprudence shows what happens when a particular religion is the model for what all religions are supposed to look, act, and feel like. In 1995, the conservative legal scholar Frederick Mark Gedicks[44] could accurately write, "No Jewish, Muslim, or Native American plaintiff has ever prevailed on a free exercise claim before the Supreme Court. Fundamentalist Christians and sects outside so-called mainline Protestantism have had only mixed success in seeking exemptions." Twenty years later, exactly one non-Christian plaintiff—a Muslim American prisoner in Arkansas—has prevailed on a free exercise claim,[45] possibly two depending on how Santeria is understood and categorized (a question that may reinstate the problem).[46]

## JEWISH QUESTION

Sudhir Kakar suggests another point of friction between psychoanalysis and religion: namely, the former's need to establish itself as a proper science, with the secular respectability that came with it. This was certainly a keen concern of Freud's: to establish the scientific bona fides of psychoanalysis in line with Enlightenment rationality. Religion was too coated with the stink of particularity, emotion, unreason, the body. Psychoanalysis already dwelt too much in the precincts of unreason (the unconscious) and the vicissitudes of embodiment. How much more it thus needed the secular legitimation of science. Science offered the cover of objectivity, universality, reason. But, for Freud and his immediate heirs, the desire for science was also powered by a wish to distance psychoanalysis from Jewishness as religious, racial, and sexual difference—hence the otherwise curious linkage in Freud's letter to Jones between telepathy, his Jewish identity, and his passion for smoking and other pleasures. All these were to be declared off limits, Freud's "private affair." Where his Jewishness was concerned, this was certainly an example of Freud's own wishful thinking.[47] Though Freud and his immediate family made it to London not long after the annexation of Austria, four of his sisters died in the camps.

The origin moments of psychoanalysis date to a historical period when the medical and natural sciences were deeply concerned with biological theories of race. In the historical context of psychoanalysis, race means "Jewishness." Nor is this only because of the historical fact that the founders and leading practitioners of psychoanalysis were Jewish.[48] Freud's proclaimed atheism did not cancel out his Jewishness—something he never sought to deny in any case. Nor did it erase what he himself called his "emotional" identifications with Judaism. But the larger point is that Freud could not have escaped his Jewishness even if he tried. Within the "thought-collective" of late nineteenth-century

Austro-German medical science, "race" called up the opposition "Jew/Aryan."[49] In the increasingly secular, urban landscape of nineteenth-century Europe, categories of religious difference, Christian/Jew, were transformed into categories of "racial" science, Aryan/Jew.[50]

As has been documented elsewhere by such scholars as Sander Gilman, Jay Geller, and Daniel Boyarin, one of the ways to detect the supposed racial difference of "the Jew" (where "the Jew" almost always meant the *male* Jew) was via bodily signs of sexual and gender deviance. There are many examples of this crisscrossing of racial, gender, and sexual stereotypes on the Jewish male body, with circumcision perhaps the most loaded index of Jewish racial difference as sexual difference. But the Jew's body gave him away at every turn, from his stumbling gait to his singsong voice.[51] Freud's elaboration of the problem of sexual difference and its primacy cannot be understood apart from the scientific conceptions of Jewish racial difference in his day. Drawing on new vocabularies of medicine, Freud transcribed the hysterical signs of male Jewishness into the enigma of "Woman" and "femininity."[52] These attempts to deracinate psychoanalysis and close the door on the Jewish question were never fully successful, I'd argue, and they ghost psychoanalysis today, as theory and practice.

Much more could be said about psychoanalysis's Jewish question. My point in raising it here has to do with the long history of association in Western thought between both the "religious-spiritual" and "the feminine." If psychoanalysis has a lingering problem with both religion and spirituality, this may be because it continues to have a linked "woman problem" and "Jewish problem." Woman-Jew-religion: Within the binary logics of secular modernity, all three of these terms have been aligned with primitivism, irrationality, backwardness, bodily excess.

## RADICAL RECEPTIVITY AND THE CONTAMINATION OF THE VOICE

In North America, liberal Protestantism embraced psychology and psychiatry as a means of bringing out the spirit and remaking religion in the image of scientific progress.[53] This was to be a spirituality that fit both the modern Protestant and the modern secular self. As religious studies scholars Courtney Bender and Omar McRoberts helpfully summarize:

> The story of "spirituality" and its various settings, from psychology to hospital therapy, from the most down-at-the-heels excesses of popular therapeutic culture to its most elevated invocation in high-culture circles, is less one of religious organizations conceptualizing spirituality in the process of extending their authority into secular settings than one of

> secular settings drawing from and cultivating spiritual language for their own purposes. In many instances, the translation or de novo emergence of "spiritual" language has taken shape on the boundary between liberal religious and secular projects.[54]

Is this psychoanalysis as border project?

Here it is worth cocking our ears between couch and chair and learning from the horizontal listening of psychoanalysis. In one of his early papers on technique, "Recommendations to Physicians Practicing Psycho-Analysis" (1912),[55] Freud offers the would-be analyst instructions on how to hold in mind the vast amount of information conveyed by a single patient (let alone "six, eight, or even more") in the course of months and years of treatment, without "confusing" the details "with similar material produced by other patients under treatment simultaneously or previously."[56] The solution to this problem turns on a specialized technique of listening, which Freud twice describes as "simple," although in practice (including in Freud's, if his published case studies are to be entered as evidence) this technique seems anything but. It "consists simply in not directing one's notice to anything in particular and in maintaining the same 'evenly suspended attention' . . . in the face of all that one hears."[57] This "rule of giving equal notice to everything is the necessary counterpart to the demand made on the patient that he should communicate everything that occurs to him without criticism or selection." Freud continues:

> If the doctor behaves otherwise, he is throwing away most of the advantage which results from the patient's obeying the "fundamental rule of psychoanalysis." The rule for the doctor may be expressed: "He should withhold all conscious influences from his capacity to attend, and give himself over completely to his 'unconscious memory.'" Or, to put it purely in terms of technique: "He should simply listen, and not bother about whether he is keeping anything in mind."[58]

In the shuttle between the patient's free associations and the doctor's hovering ear, we are given a picture of two unconsciousnesses rising to meet the other without prejudgment of what is to be found. (It is this unconscious meeting between two unconsciousnesses that would later incline Freud not to write off telepathy out of hand.)[59]

In a further attempt to clarify the "simple" technique of "'evenly suspended attention,'" Freud directs the would-be analyst to turn himself into a telephone receiver. I am preserving the male pronouns of Freud's text so as to underscore the "feminizing" receptivity Freud assigns to the doctor as he listens for / to / from the other scene:[60]

> To put it in a formula: [the doctor] must turn his own unconscious like a receptive organ towards the transmitting unconscious of the patient. He must adjust himself to the patient as a telephone receiver is adjusted to the transmitting microphone. Just as the receiver conveys back into sound-waves the electric oscillations in the telephone line which were set up by sound waves, so the doctor's unconscious is able, from the derivatives of the unconscious which are communicated to him, to reconstruct that unconscious, which has determined the patient's free associations.[61]

There is much to arrest in this passage. First, there is the striking modernism of Freud's reference to the telephone.[62] This is all the more surprising given Freud's well-established ambivalence toward modern technology.[63]

Second, and paradoxically, the sonic reverberations Freud describes, along with the active passivity assigned to the receiver, cast the presumptively male physician in an older role, as a kind of spiritual medium, communing with the dead. This is an apt double image for a practice that explores how the past continues to haunt the present and shape the future. The psychoanalyst as medium also amplifies the gender crossing (usurpation?) performed in the exchange, for the great preponderance of spiritual mediums were women. As Ann Braude has shown, spiritualism was even a major vehicle for late-nineteenth- and early-twentieth-century U.S. feminism.[64] The doubling—spiritual medium / telephone receiver—may also be an instance when we can see psychoanalysis haunted by practices it left behind—namely, mesmerism, magnetism, and hypnosis[65]—and practices it disavowed: spiritualism. Avowing these discarded practices—and their religious resonances—may make psychoanalysis more able to move across cultural and geographic borders and risk its own weird and wild transformations in the process.

## TROUBLING TIME

I want to return to my earlier point about the multiple times of psychoanalysis to connect this more centrally to recent thinking about queer temporality. The fruitfulness of thinking queer temporality and psychoanalysis together is that both offer us resources for understanding the plural ways time coats, codes, and disciplines the body in secular modernity. This is complicated, because psychoanalysis *is* one of these disciplines—and not just because of the tick tick ticking of the clock during the analytic hour. To underscore: The secular aspirations of psychoanalysis—Freud's desire to distinguish it from *other* occult and spiritual practices—sometimes result in a tension in the ways psychoanalysis tells time. On the one hand, psychoanalysis quite frequently hews to a developmental imperative, in which not just the human organism, but the individual subject is supposed to mature along a set pathway: from A to B to C.

An individual may go off the rails, and often does; however, detours and disruptions prove the rule of time and telos. On the other hand, this chrononormativity is at profound odds with the capacity of psychoanalysis to make room for, and help *us* make room for, the coexistence of past and present in ways that confound secular time's forward march. This latter recognition—co-temporality—may lay down routes for the cultivation of counter-codes, ways of living and experiencing and telling time out of sync with the linear logics of what José Esteban Muñoz calls "straight time."[66] Here is even a potential meeting point between the temporal turn in queer theory and psychoanalysis as theory and clinical practice. As Carolyn Dinshaw argues in *How Soon Is Now? Medieval Texts, Amateur Readers, and the Queerness of Time* (2012), perhaps we need not choose so sharply between now and then, here and next—because "the now" contains a multiplicity of ways of being in, with, alongside, under, and over time.

Nevertheless, not all disruptions in time are equal. The commingling of past in present can be a bar to imagining and living out other possibilities—and all in the name of a better future. In the "cruel optimism" Lauren Berlant so urgently exposes,[67] past, present, and future fuse to produce a stall. As Dinshaw cautions with regard to living with and in the time of AIDS, there is nothing "inherently positive or revolutionary about the experience or condition of inhabiting multiple temporalities."[68] So, to take another powerful recent example: The rhetoric of "fetal personhood" and "fetal life" proffers the fetus as pure futurity,[69] unmoored from the constraints of being creatures *of* time, who live and change in time and depend on an array of others for sustenance and survival. The temporal logic of this rhetoric does not square with secular ways of narrating biological sequence. But part of the appeal of this language is precisely the way that it can abstract "life" from life.[70] Put otherwise, "straight time" need not be linear to get us. This is all the more reason for queer theory and psychoanalysis to keep working to speak to—and get—each other in time.[71] Getting each other in time might also involve reckoning with the feelings—of awe, wonder, ecstasy, as well as dis-ease, trembling, terror—that belong as much to the queer as to the religious.

## NOTES

1. Sigmund Freud, *The Future of an Illusion*, in *The Standard Edition of the Complete Psychological Works of Sigmund Freud* (hereafter *SE*), vol. 21, ed. James Strachey (London: Hogarth, Press, 1961), 42–43.
2. Ibid., 43.
3. This stark contrast between religion and reality (and the realities psychoanalysis can help us reckon with) depends on very particular understandings of religion

and of psychoanalysis, too. Freud correlates religion to fantasies of omnipotence revived in the adult when confronted with "the great forces of life." In this view of things all religions offer protection (false as it ultimately is) from the exigencies of existence by promising to take our cares away, if not in this world then in the next. But magical thinking of this kind is not the purview of all religion nor is magical thinking exclusive to religion. Art, technology, science, hyperrationalism: these too can function as forms of magical thinking. Moreover, far from a turning away from or denial of human dependence and interdependence, many religious/spiritual systems in fact urge us to attend to the ways in which we depend on others from before the beginning. For "great forces of life," see Freud, "Leonardo da Vinci and a Memory of Childhood," in *SE* 11:123. For a discussion of Freud on the moral resources that may come out of being helpless, see Adam Phillips, "Freud's Helplessness," in *The Joys of Secularism: Eleven Essays for How We Live Now*, ed. George Levine (Princeton, N.J.: Princeton University Press, 2011), 115–33, 236–37.

4. Freud, *Future of an Illusion*, 49,
5. In posing this question I am riffing off Carolyn Dinshaw's *How Soon Is Now? Medieval Texts, Amateur Readers, and the Queerness of Time* (Durham, N.C.: Duke University Press, 2012).
6. Diana Fuss, ed., *Pink Freud*, special issue of *GLQ: A Journal of Lesbian and Gay Studies* 2, no. 1 (1995).
7. Sigmund Freud, "Creative Writers and Day-Dreaming," in *SE* 9:150.
8. For the interaction between queer and feminist studies, on the one hand, and secular anxieties about "religion," on the other, see Ann Pellegrini, "Feeling Secular," *Women & Performance* 19, no. 2 (2009): 205–18.
9. Robert Orsi, "Snakes Alive: Religious Studies between Heaven and Earth," chapter 6 in *Between Heaven and Earth: The Religious Worlds People Make and the Scholars Who Study Them* (Princeton, N.J.: Princeton University Press, 2004), 177–204, 237–39.
10. Max Weber's 1918 Berlin lecture (first published in 1919) "Science as a Vocation" is the authoritative source for such an equation among disenchantment, modernity, and the decline of religion's power—except that his own view of the matter is far more ambivalent. Not only is it not clear that he thinks disenchantment has had only or even primarily ameliorative effects, but, more centrally, he connects disenchantment not to the decline of religion per se, but to the triumph of Christianity over a pagan world of plural divinities. It is also worth noting that the German term Weber uses is *Entzauberung*, which means the removal or elimination of magic. This is the decline that interested Weber, and it has a different connotation than its most common English translation, "enchantment." See Max Weber, "Science as a Vocation," *Max Weber: Essays in Sociology*, trans and ed. H. H. Gerth and C. Wright Mills (New York: Oxford University Press, 1946), 129–56.
11. Adam Phillips, "Introduction," *Wild Analysis* (London: Penguin Books, 2002), xx.
12. For an extended discussion of psychoanalysis as Foucauldian practice of freedom, see my "From No to Know: Charting the 'Space Between,'" in *Boundary Trouble: The Ethics of Psychoanalytic Intimacy in Relational Perspective*, ed. Charles Levin (New York: Routledge, in press).

13. Michel Foucault, "The Minimalist Self," in *Politics, Philosophy, Culture: Interviews and Other Writings, 1977–1984*, ed. Lawrence D. Kritzman (New York: Routledge, 1988), 14.
14. Freud famously described himself as a "Godless Jew" in a 1918 letter to his friend and long-time correspondent, the Christian pastor Oskar Pfister. This assertion, phrased in the form of two questions, "Quite by the way, why did none of the devout create psychoanalysis? Why did one have to wait for a completely godless Jew?" is the jumping-off point for Peter Gay's *A Godless Jew: Freud, Atheism, and the Making of Psychoanalysis* (New Haven, Conn.: Yale University Press, 1989). For Freud's household rule against the lighting of Sabbath candles—and the distress this caused his wife, Martha Bernays Freud—see Gay's *Freud: A Life for Our Time* (New York: W. W. Norton, 2006), 54, 600.
15. Geeta Patel, "Ghostly Appearances," in *Secularisms*, ed. Janet R. Jakobsen and Ann Pellegrini (Durham, N.C.: Duke University Press, 2008), 226–46.
16. Michel Foucault, *History of Sexuality, Volume I: An Introduction*, trans. Robert Hurley (New York: Vintage, 1980).
17. Michel Foucault, *History of Madness*, ed. Jean Khalfa, trans. Jonathan Murphy and Jean Khalfa (New York: Routledge, 2006).
18. Michel Foucault, *Madness and Civilization: A History of Insanity in the Age of Reason*, trans. Richard Howard (New York: Vintage Books, 1965).
19. Lynne Huffer, *Mad for Foucault: Rethinking the Foundations of Queer Theory* (New York: Columbia University Press, 2010), 159.
20. Paul B. Preciado, *Testo Junkie: Sex, Drugs, and Biopolitics in the Pharmacopornographic Era* (New York: Feminist Press, 2013).
21. Michel Foucault, *Security, Territory, Population: Lectures at the Collège de France, 1977–78*, ed. Michel Senellart, trans. Graham Burchell (New York: Palgrave Macmillan, 2007).
22. Ibid., 199.
23. Ibid.
24. Ibid.
25. Adam Phillips, *Unforbidden Pleasures* (London: Hamish Hamilton, 2015).
26. Michel Foucault, "Practicing Criticism," in *Politics, Philosophy, Culture*, ed. Kritzman, 156.
27. This paragraph condenses points made more extensively in the introduction to *Secularisms*, ed. Jakobsen and Pellegrini, esp. 1–6.
28. David E. Nye, *American Technological Sublime* (Cambridge, Mass.: MIT Press, 1994).
29. See David E. Nye, *Electrifying America: Social Meanings of New Technology, 1880–1940* (Cambridge, Mass.: MIT Press, 1990); and Carolyn Marvin, *When Old Technologies Were New: Thinking about Electric Communication in the Late Nineteenth Century* (Oxford: Oxford University Press, 1988).
30. The distances became still greater with the laying down of the transatlantic cable, in 1858; this precipitated the standardization of time internationally. See Eviatar Zerubavel, "The Standardization of Time: A Sociohistorical Perspective," *American Journal of Sociology* 88, no. 1 (1982): 12.

31. Ibid., 8, 10.
32. Mark Aldrich, *Death Rode the Rails: American Railroad Accidents and Safety, 1828–1965* (Baltimore: Johns Hopkins University Press, 2006).
33. Herbert L. Sussman, *Victorians and the Machine: The Literary Response to Technology* (Cambridge, Mass.: Harvard University Press, 1968).
34. Freud, *Beyond the Pleasure Principle*, in *SE* 18:12.
35. Nye, *Electrifying America*, 189.
36. Raymond Williams, *Marxism and Literature* (Oxford: Oxford University Press, 1977), 128–35.
37. Freud, *Civilization and Its Discontents*, in *SE* 21:88.
38. Elizabeth Freeman, *Time Binds: Queer Temporalities, Queer Histories* (Durham, N.C.: Duke University Press, 2010).
39. Freud introduces this concept in his 1918 essay "The Taboo of Virginity" and returns to it in *Group Psychology* (1921) and *Civilization and Its Discontents* (1930).
40. Sudhir Kakar, "Is Psychoanalysis also a Spiritual Discipline?" Unpublished paper presented at the annual meeting of Division 39, New York, April 2014.
41. Judith Butler, *Gender Trouble: Feminism and the Subversion of Identity* (New York: Routledge, 1990), 25.
42. Quoted in Gay, *Freud*, 445. For a beautiful reading of this exchange and of psychoanalysis as a kind of "teleplastic abduction"—bodies moved across time and space —see André Lepecki, "Teleplastic Abduction: Subjectivity in the Age of ART, or Delirium for Psychoanalysis: Commentary on Simon's 'Spoken Through Desire,'" *Studies in Gender and Sexuality* 14, no. 4 (2013): 300–308.
43. Personal communication.
44. Frederick Mark Gedicks, *The Rhetoric of Church and State: A Critical Analysis of Religion Clause Jurisprudence* (Durham, N.C.: Duke University Press, 1995), 116. Janet Jakobsen and I invoke Gedicks in our discussion of the meaning of government neutrality in the face of religious difference. See *Love the Sin: Sexual Regulation and the Limits of Religious Tolerance*, 2nd edition (Boston: Beacon Press, 2004), 110.
45. *Holt v. Hobbes* 574 U.S. (2015).
46. For an important Supreme Court case in which religious practices on the frontiers of Christianity were accorded free exercise protections, see *Church of Lukumi Babalu Aye v. City of Hialeah*, 508 U.S. 520 (1993), which concerned Santeria, a syncretic Afro-Caribbean religion. Available at http://www.oyez.org/cases/1990–1999/1992/1992_91_948 (accessed 8 November 2011).
47. Eliza Slavet, *Racial Fever: Freud and the Jewish Question* (New York: Fordham University Press, 2009), 156.
48. The relation of Freud's Jewishness and the role of anti-Semitism for the history and development of psychoanalysis continue to be sites of rich and contested study. Important texts in these debates include David Bakan, *Sigmund Freud and the Jewish Mystical Tradition* (Mineola, NY: Dover Books, 2004); Daniel Boyarin, *Unheroic Conduct: The Rise of Heterosexuality and the Invention of the Jewish Man* (Berkeley: University of California Press, 1997); Gay, *Godless Jew*; Jay Geller, *On Freud's Jewish Body: Mitigating Circumcisions* (New York: Fordham University Press, 2007); Sander

Gilman, *Freud, Race, and Gender* (New York: Routledge, 1993); Ann Pellegrini, *Performance Anxieties: Staging Psychoanalysis, Staging Race* ((New York: Routledge, 1997); Karen Starr and Lewis Aron, *A Psychotherapy for the People: Toward a Progressive Psychoanalysis* (New York: Routledge, 2013); and Yosef Hayim Yerushalmi, *Freud's Moses: Judaism Terminable and Interminable* (New Haven, Conn.: Yale University Press, 1993).

49. The term "thought-collective" is Ludwick Fleck's, quoted in Sander Gilman, *The Jew's Body* (New York: Routledge, 1991).
50. Ibid., 202.
51. Marjorie Garber offers a useful summary of some of these stereotypes. See *Vested Interests: Cross-Dressing and Cultural Anxiety* (New York: Routledge, 1992). For discussions of the Jewish foot and voice, see Gilman, *Jew's Body*.
52. I make this argument at greater length in *Performance Anxieties*.
53. See Christopher White, *Unsettled Minds: Psychology and the American Search for Spiritual Assurance, 1830–1940* (Berkeley: University of California Press, 2008); Pamela Klassen, *Spirits of Protestantism: Medicine, Healing, and Liberal Christianity* (Berkeley: University of California Press, 2011); and Heather R. White, *Reforming Sodom: Protestants and the Rise of Gay Rights* (Chapel Hill: University of North Carolina Press, 2015).
54. Courtney Bender and Omar McRoberts, "Mapping a Field: How and Why to Study Spirituality," Working Group on Spirituality, Political Engagement, and Public Life, SSRC Working Papers, October 2012. Available at http://blogs.ssrc.org/tif/wp-content/uploads/2010/05/Why-and-How-to-Study-Spirtuality.pdf.
55. In *SE* 12:109–20.
56. Ibid., 111.
57. Ibid., 111–12.
58. Ibid., 112.
59. Freud, "Psychoanalysis and Telepathy," in *SE* 18:175–93, esp. 184.
60. For the feminizing risk of this analogy, see Diana Fuss, with Joel Sanders, "Berggasse 19," in *The Sense of an Interior* (New York: Routledge, 2004), 93.
61. Freud, "Recommendations to Physicians Practicing Psycho-Analysis," in *SE* 12:115–16.
62. The references to literature and the arts that pepper Freud's body of work are hardly modernist; if anything, they tend to be fairly conservative in genre. Think, for example, of his caution against theater that goes too far in soliciting the suffering of its audience, in "Psychopathic Characters on the Stage," in *SE* 7:305–10 (1942 [1905 or 1906]) or his citation of literature and theater as particularly favorable representational forms through which readers and spectators might experience the necessary risk of death, in his 1915 essay "Thoughts for the Times on War and Death," in *SE* 14:275–300. Notable for its absence in this latter essay is any mention of film, despite the early circulation in Vienna of film (Austrian, U.S., and French).
63. As Thomas Elsaesser summarizes, "He did not like radio, he was shy of photography, he used the typewriter sparingly and preferred to compose in longhand, and he refused to have the telephone connected to his consulting room or his private

office." See Elsaesser, "Freud as Media Theorist: Mystic Writing-Pads and the Matter of Memory," *Screen* 50, no. 1 (2009): 105. Though this falls outside the focus of Elsaesser's essay, Freud's "shyness" about being photographed was intensified by the multiple disfiguring surgeries (thirty-three in total) for jaw cancer that hollowed out the right side of his face, took much of the hearing in his right ear (requiring him to shift his chair from one end of the couch to the other), and made speaking and eating excruciatingly painful during the final decade of his life. See Lydia Marinelli, "Smoking, Laughing, and the Compulsion to Film: On the Beginnings of Psychoanalytic Documentaries," *American Imago* 61 (2004): 35–58.

64. Ann Braude, *Radical Spirits: Spiritualism and Women's Rights in Nineteenth-Century America* (Bloomington: Indiana University Press, 2001).
65. For an indispensable history of these transformations, see Ann Taves, *Fits, Trances, and Visions: Experiencing Religion and Explaining Experience from Wesley to James* (Princeton, N.J.: Princeton University Press, 1999).
66. See José Esteban Muñoz, *Cruising Utopia: The Then and There of Queer Futurity* (New York: New York University Press, 2008).
67. Lauren Berlant, *Cruel Optimism* (Durham, N.C.: Duke University Press, 2011).
68. Dinshaw, *How Soon Is Now?* 34.
69. Melinda Cooper, *Life as Surplus: Biotechnology and Capitalism in the Neoliberal Era* (Seattle: University of Washington Press, 2008).
70. Khiara M. Bridges, "Capturing the Judiciary: *Carhart* and the Undue Burden Standard," *Wash. & Lee L. Rev.* 67 (2010): 915–84. Available at http://scholarlycommons.law.wlu.edu/wlulr/vol67/iss3/3.
71. For an extended discussion of the time of fetal life, see my "Preconceiving Life: Response to Gentile's 'Troubling Temporalities,'" *Studies in Gender and Sexuality* 16, no. 1 (2015): 49–55.

# More Than a Feeling: A Queer Notion of Survivance

LAUREL C. SCHNEIDER

*Survivance is greater than the right of a survivable name.*
—GERALD VIZENOR, *Survivance: Narratives of Native Presence*

New thinking in queer temporalities and affects outside of the (temporally, affectively charged) field of religion constitutes a challenge and invitation to stretch queer thinking in theology yet again, and further. Although feminist, womanist, process, and other theorists in religion and theology have been working around the fuzzy borders and stubborn impasses that fleshy experiences—bodies and histories of bodies—present, queerly inflected affect theory expands these moves into a complex materialism.[1] Affect theory's approach to embodiment in terms of the deeply constitutive dynamics of temporality, proximity, touch, and even elemental gravitation provides a conceptual framework that helpfully limits any intellectual tendency toward reductive or neglectful accounts of bodies by recentering corporeality in the domain of antinormative meaning making. It offers at least one kind of answer to Madhavi Menon's pointed question "What is the *particularity* of queerness?" by locating queerness in bodies that are always formed, normed, and productively failing to norm in relation to other bodies in specific times and places.[2]

As promising as affect theory's theoretical development for the study of queerness and religion is, I wonder if the very antinormativity demanded of queer theory in general sets up a prerequisite obedience in that theory to inherited categories of bodies and desires that allows them to be thought in distinction from each other (even as affect theory strives to overcome that inheritance) and in so doing reinscribes some of the very problems that it sets out to overturn. After all, affect theory has to argue for inseparability between semiosis and affects, and for assumptions of physical, mental, and environmental co-constituency.[3] Queer theory's obedience to antinormativity may foreclose ontological intuitions that cleave neither to normative nor to antinormative concerns. Ontology is often caricatured as the conceptual structure that makes normativity possible, a structure that ossifies fairy-light mobile affects into narrow and immovable rules. Although criticisms of ontology regnant in poststructuralism must be taken seriously, wholesale foreclosure of ontological intuitions may not serve queer theory's wider possibilities in religion. But to the extent that queer theory allies its name more or less strictly with antinormative impulses, such forays may end up meaning that the name "queer" is not queer enough. It is therefore possible though not inevitable that queer affect theory's powerful reformulation of the matter-thought relation may fall short of queering the stuff of religion if it does not also intend something more than queer theory's usual menu of oppositions to norms. As Robyn Wiegman and Elizabeth A. Wilson point out, "Nearly every queer theoretical itinerary of analysis that now matters is informed by the prevailing supposition that a critique of normativity marks the spot where *queer* and *theory* meet."[4] Admittedly, religions do chart the courses of normativity in almost every instance, and they bear the brunt of responsibility, directly or indirectly, for just about every repressive disposition that queer theories seek to illuminate, critique, or dismantle. So queer theory's antinormative itinerary of analysis is long and unfinished, as far as the religions are concerned. But religions also, in being religious, concern themselves with ontological matters—what they often call creation—and these matters, well, matter.

Having said that, the question that I raise here about affect theory's promise regarding a wider queer purview in religion and its vulnerability to unintended reinscriptions is not rooted in certainty but in lingering worries about how Christian ideologies and norms (about bodies, purities, and hopes) seem magically to reappear in even the most radical and promising of critiques, especially oppositional ones. This question mirrors others that I have begun to ask elsewhere regarding Christian theology's enthrallment to parochial ethnic categories of thought within which it constructs and reiterates problems it also seeks to overcome.[5] The promise of queer affect theory is partly its willingness to shed light on such heretofore discursive limits by venturing into the swirls of ontological waters, to entertain ideas of physics alongside queer notions of desire in ways that throw everything—planets, humans, metals, memories—into provocative question.[6] By doing so, queer affect theory sticks a toe out the door of cultural and textual theory and so stretches beyond, even if by just a hair, queer theory's usual concerns. Queer affect theory suggests a wider horizon for queer theoretical engagement and so expands the possibility of unusual discursive companions, especially in religion.

This essay is therefore a tentative, playful exercise in the question of queer theory's queerness in relation to the very religion that largely produced it. It is also a reflection on queer theory's own intellectual future and the (questionable) desirability of a survivable name. A survivable name is a matter of identity, and the question of its questionable desirability comes from the Anishinaabe literary theorist Gerald Vizenor. It's a good question, one he poses to native people who struggle to live beyond the ever static, ever erroneous "indian" that signifies imposed and imposter identities, identifications that name fictions and disallow sovereignties. In every possible ironic sense of the question, are the names—are identities—survivable? After reflecting more fully but by no means comprehensively on the relation between queer and Christian thought, I suggest that Vizenor's own notion of survivance beyond a survivable name offers, from outside of queer theory and the religion from whence it came, an ironic and helpful nuance that may help us reimagine a bit of queer theory's (hopeful) queerness.

## QUEERLY CHRISTIAN

Queer theory in the realm of religion is theory come back to its origins in Christianity, to its first antinormative battles. Thanks largely to Foucault, queer theory's relation to religion and to Christianity in particular is virtually inescapable. His development of the idea of technologies of the self directed early queer thinking toward the normative, formative, and performative "operations" through which bodies function in sexually disciplined and disciplining ways, and did so in direct relation to "Christian spirituality . . . of the late Roman Empire," not to mention the late medieval development of religious practices of confession.[7]

Queer theory via Foucault builds on a foundation focused on the intimate relation between lived practices, material effects, and the concomitant production of meaning and identity. This nascent queer concern with Christianity and sex in one of the putative founders of queer theory made plain the philosophical problem of bodies, materiality, and norms, all of which Judith Butler took up as key philosophical questions, ones that have described a major trajectory in later queer theory.[8] She wrestled with the status of bodies in relation to perceptions, norms, and ideologies as she sought to identify the ways that bodies both perform and reproduce cultural norms, and, following Foucault, how such performances work back on bodies to discipline and reproduce persons who recognize themselves as such (or as failing at such).

Since Foucault and Butler, queer theory arguably has struggled to think the incoherences of Christian/Cartesian dualisms to better illuminate the bodily effects of norms (as well as spaces of antinormative possibility). Indeed, Butler's *Bodies That Matter* was a specific rebuttal to critics who (mis) read her theory-founding *Gender Trouble* as an antimaterialist argument.[9] But the fact that the body (as sex, sexed, raced, and colonized) is—and remains—a question in queer theory indicates a certain philosophical pressure placed on that theory to presuppose a prior essential distinction between matter and thought, or bodies and performances. Foucault's impressive work to theorize biopower, for example, illustrates by its very synthesis a prior conceptual gulf he seeks to bridge.[10] And queer of color critiques resist any move in queer theory to make transparent the bodies of its inquiries and so "reap the dividends of whiteness."[11]

In answer to this challenge, queer affect theory offers a tool for imagining bodies complexly, for better understanding the material terms of sociality, change, and wide fields of normalization without dividing subjects and objects or agents and impotents. It goes a long way to healing the stubborn epistemological presupposition of divisible mind and matter that may yet dog queer and other constructivist theories grounded in the parochial ethnic field of western European philosophy. But accusing queer theory of showing the marks of its culturally specific epistemological heritage is hardly an insight, though certainly tendentious. It is possible to suggest that contemporary queer theory, especially recent forays into non-Western and nonwhite temporalities and materialities, has done much to think differently about the constitution of bodies ontologically and politically.[12] Whether such work answers Hiram Perez's challenge that in general "queer theory has exchanged too hastily the politics of identity for the politics of difference" in its attention to heterogenous affects remains to be seen.[13] The question of bodies remains; the need to assert their reality in the process of thinking about the gender-sex-race-colony assemblage remains precisely because the aftermath of colonialism so flattened the "human" into an abstract one-size-fits-all that even thinking whatever difference bodies make is a challenge. Affect theory gives material sophistication to experiential intuitions of deep relation in which bodies and socialities come into and out of being, which in turn drives queer theory beyond the old divisive terms of embodiment, particularly as those terms (body/spirit/matter/mind) show up in Christian writing.

But there is more than affect theory pushing on the conceptual frameworks at play in Christian thought here. Queer theorists of late have begun to follow physicists and are shaking time out of its quiet, supposed groove of impartiality. The supposed hum of time's little motor at the mechanical edge of (modern conceptions of) reality has begun to cough and sputter, throwing past and future into question. Or from a conventional eschatological standpoint, the malleable clay of time's substance resting in an omnipotent deity's hands, ready to be thrown and turned to a beatific (potted) end melts into vapor, a fantasy of dominance. Suddenly, time itself is a social, cultural, and religious fantasy, vulnerable to and structured by, among other things, heteronormativity.[14]

This is as it should be. Just as curious queer theory follows its own critical trajectories out of sexuality alone into considerations of political economy, homonationalism, and racialized heteropatriarchy, it reencounters religious horizons of meaning in the form of social temporal normativities, "right" and "wrong" times, teleological imaginations, and reproductive itineraries. Lee Edelman's queer challenge to conventional schemes of time, particularly indictments of linear time's service to Western heteronormative reproductive values and demands in both material and ideological terms by default (and by necessity) also challenge any self-avowed queer Christian theology wherein pasts, presents, and futures show up in questions of creation, incarnation, and eschatology. The closet door behind time's masquerade of neutrality swings open here to reveal its many intimate relations with norming power—including theologies that seek to overcome hetero- and homonormativities in their conceptions of divinity.

Although, as I have suggested, affect theory, queer temporality, and queer theories more generally tend to implicate theological questions—sometimes without meaning to—Christian thinkers who with seriousness take up these theories find their work inevitably changed by them. No theological position, however apologetic, can remain unmoved by the depth of criticism embedded in queer theory, affect-inflected or otherwise. Doing so, I suggest, requires attention not only to the particularities of each theoretical position, but also to the culturally rooted presuppositions that *eo ipso* they bring to bear on the question. But this is difficult to do when the culturally rooted presuppositions include popular, literary, and scientific assumptions about the essential separability of bodies and ideas, and when these presuppositions structure the horizons of philosophical reasoning at work in Christian thinking and its progeny.

Sara Ahmed's efforts to think queer orientations and embodiment in mutually constitutive formation challenge deeply embedded assumptions about the passive necessity of bodies and the ephemeral but meaningful accidents of desires and intentions.[15] The fact that so many upper-level college students struggle to understand her very clear prose indicates the distance affect theory has come to conceptualize bodies otherwise to philosophical convention. I do not mean to say that every difficult piece of writing is an innovation (what a laughable error that would be) but instead precisely that Ahmed does not write in an obtuse or difficult style. It is the unfamiliar way of thinking about everyday things that cause students to stumble.

Likewise, queer reimaginings of time encounter the resistance that conceptual unfamiliarity and underlying, if barely conscious, religious sentiment often inspire. Edelman's provocative rejection of the future and José Esteban Muñoz's notion of utopic failure, like Thomas Altizer's Nietzschean death of God, tend toward misunderstanding in first-time or secondhand readers. In each case these authors are rejecting a totalizing regime of thought in which only radical denial (or in Muñoz's case a moderate failure to succeed) breaks its hold. Or if its hold does not break, at least its grip is illuminated.[16] In any case, such arguments tend to leave, in the minds of students first encountering them, an imaginative blank. What? No future? God is *dead*? (Atheism seems preferable to that!) "We have to have hope!" so many students have cried. As if "hope" and "future" are synonyms.

For Edelman to equate futurity and Muñoz to equate success with heteronormativity seems at first blush to argue for the same nihilism that readers (still, stereotypically) see in death of God theologies. They are in fact reiterating that death, if such religious thought still rides incognito in "the logic of futurity." And it does. "No future," it seems, is the demise of all possibility, when quite the opposite is the case. Drawing the curtain back on the numbing symbol of the (white) Child and its "mechanistic" regime of reproductive obedience liberates, or so Edelman suggests, the human into the possibility of something "inhuman" and presumably more alive by virtue of slipping the leash of the logic of futurity.[17] We could say that possibility itself—the possibility of other, more life-inspiring possibilities—is what is at stake.

It has occurred to me that part of the conceptual difficulty in thinking these affective and temporal ideas in queer theory has something to do with the proximity of queer theory to the religious/philosophical soil from which it emerged and to which it returns as critic. Might an idea rooted in and intended for other worlds of discourse and culture provide roadside assistance without delaying or diminishing delivery to its intended audiences? Might a sideways look through another cultural presupposition about bodies and normativity contribute to this effort of reimagining? Perhaps. Gerald Vizenor's notion of "survivance," gleaned from his life and work as a native (Anishinaabe) philosopher may be just such a sideways look that offers more than mere cultural difference to the problem of queer bodies and futures. Indeed, there needs to be more than just difference, as Perez cautions.

Survivance is a "more" that, by virtue of its own cultural presuppositions, may help loosen the grip of some of the potentially more damaging ones still regnant in much of Christian thinking. It is the term that Vizenor uses to describe the innumerable and unnameable ways that native individuals and communities in North America become and are present in active resistance to the multiple romantic and ossifying renderings of Native American Indian people.[18]

> Survivance is a practice, not an ideology, dissimulation, or a theory. The theory is earned by interpretations, by the critical construal of survivance in creative literature, and by narratives of cause and natural reason. The discourse on literary and historical studies of survivance is a theory of irony.[19]

"Survivance" is an invented term, a mash-up of "survival" and "resistance" with a nod toward the French poststructuralists with whom Vizenor sometimes thinks. The reason that the term "survival" by itself, for Vizenor, is insufficient is that he sees it as a fundamentally tragic concept, which for him means that it is rooted in the romance and settler-colonial demand of reproducibility. Focused on the production of sameness, "survival" temporally freezes things such as identities, names, or traditions and in so doing misses a great deal: the living, tricky present, the surprising encounter, the life in the story retold, but that is never the same.

This conceptual assemblage of survival and resistance gives Vizenor a non-colonial way to think about native presence in a historical and narrative context that, to paraphrase Audre Lorde, never meant them to survive except as signifiers of absence, doomed to erasure in an eternally static and reproduced "Indian" facade—fabrications of settler imagination.[20] This mechanically reproductive logic of the past provocatively mirrors, I suggest, Edelman's equally mechanistic logic of futurity. "The indian," Vizenor claims, "was the accidental invention that became a bankable simulation; the word has no referent in tribal languages or cultures."[21] Declaring himself a postindian warrior, Vizenor freely uses the term "native" because for him it is not a name, not a narrow identity marked by capitalization, but an adjective that he uses to gesture toward the peoples of the American continent who despite so many odds still practice "an active sense of presence over absence, deracination, and oblivion."[22]

Because survivance refers to what he calls a nontragic resilience of living and changing presence in a people made absent even down to their name, there is an epistemological challenge in the concept to think differently about presence in temporal and ontological terms that run counter to the conventional, ossifying practices of identity survivability, or even of names. As in affect theory, other markers matter more. Against what he calls the closures of dominance, Vizenor wields his own cultural presuppositions of trickster hermeneutics and reversals of irony, chance, and humor—all of which he makes hallmarks of survivance. These markers of survivance show up in stories and in chance encounters between tribal people on city streets and in grocery parking lots. They matter, materialize, and unfold in the handed-down stories of resistance and everyday crafty reversals of everyday native people, and they form the epistemological basis of what Vizenor characterizes as "natural reason" and "native sovereignty."[23]

Native survivance is therefore not a biological claim, a matter of blood quantum, or tribal rolls. It is not an identity in the not-so-funhouse of American social and governmental politics, but he argues that survivance is "unmistakable in native stories, natural reason, remembrance, traditions, and customs and is clearly observable in narrative resistance and personal attributes, such as the native humanistic tease, vital irony, spirit, cast of mind, and moral courage."[24] There is a cultural horizon in Vizenor's work despite his relentless critique of things "indian," but that is the point of native survivance. It is the unnameable affective trace of specificity and encounter between actual people and their specific memories, *their* stories. It is not the surviving abstract (or absent) ubiquity of the falsely fabricated, generically broadcast (and romantically claimed) indian spirit.

One of the strengths of Vizenor's notion of survivance is that it does not constitute an attempt to abstract a quality of human existence out of the customs and traditions that make human persons specific and real to begin with. This is no generic theory of presence, or of reason. It is not another erasure of peoples whose real, embodied presences and cultures have been under assault for centuries.[25] It is a specifically North American, more specifically native, and quite possibly even more specifically Anishinaabe theory of presence and rationality that eschews the romance of identity, authenticity, and "last lines" in favor of chancy encounters, tricky reversals, and ironic movement. Among his many definitions of native survivance that circle around themes of presence and resistance, he also describes it as the "continuance of stories, not a mere reaction, however pertinent. Survivance" he argues, "is greater than the right of a survivable name."[26] It is this last description, I want to suggest, that may signal the "more" I am looking for in shifting the cultural presuppositions of Christian thought and so loosening the grip of the old dichotomies in its engagements with the work of queer theory working on the ontological edges of affect and temporality.

## BUT FIRST: AFFECT, TEMPORALITY, AND THAT PESKY DICHOTOMY

The recent surge of philosophical interest in ways of thinking—and especially feeling—that resist old mind-body dichotomies represents a welcome and slow turn in academic inquiry that has been a long time coming. The ontological emphasis in some affect, new materialist, and animacy theory is actually building some helpfully different epistemological ground for thinking outside of the binary structures that have so dominated Christian (and Western scientific) thought. I should not need to rehearse the dependence of new materialisms, affect theories, incarnational theological experimentation, posttheory, multiplicity theory, and so forth on earlier, mostly outsider, intellectual movements, though the reminder is usually helpful lest we forget that difficult work preceded and made possible our own. But for the purposes of this essay it is important to gesture broadly to that lineage: The turn to affect and to questions of temporality make sense in contemporary queer religious thinking as an unsurprising outcome of a prior turn to abjected desires (human and divine) in those discourses.[27] This is itself an unsurprising outcome of much earlier attendings to feminized and, at least in some analyses, dark bodies. This legacy is largely the reason that theorizing sociality as a structure of feeling requires attention to the matter of proximity, which in an older intellectual tradition is attention to the complexity of material context in the fight for full personhood.[28] As Ahmed beautifully puts it, it is best to "begin with the messiness of the experiential, the unfolding of bodies into worlds, and the drama of contingency, how we are touched by what we are near."[29] This is not so far from Vizenor's notion of survivance as a revolutionary claim to presence, is it? Or from Edelman's refusal of a coercively absent future? Or Muñoz's exuberant, albeit fleeting, failures to survive the norm?

Beginning with touching what we are near seems to me all to the good. It suggests that theory is catching up, with its truckloads of sophistication, to decades' old arguments and intuitions by old-timey black, white, Chicana, and other feminists, and even older-timey native "storiers," as Vizenor calls them. This is not to say that there is nothing new in the new queer theories, far from it. Affect theory particularly offers attention to the proximal ontology of feeling, *how* bodies and worlds are "unfolded" and brought into being by feeling. This is an important step substantially beyond the argument *that* bodies matter in personhood, that both persons and those denied personhood are shaped (or disfigured) by common feeling, a claim present in American letters at least since Frederick Douglass, who wielded the notion of "common feeling" to illustrate the cold violence of Christian slavery.[30] Feeling depends on proximity, and "fellow feeling" on the communicative mattering of shared times and spaces. Persons come into (and out of) being in entangled relations of affect, which is a more-than normativity. The excesses of feeling, the failures of normal feeling, animate queer energies and hint at (perhaps) possibilities of survivance.

The recent queer turn to temporality and questions of futurity also stands on older shoulders, as a mode of heteronormative expectation depends in part on Marxist and neo-Marxist materialist analyses of ideology as the constraining frame of possibility and expectation for the oppressed working and slave classes. The oppressive and alienating powers of dominant narratives of expectation (and, by the same token, the telling of histories) that curtail and manage horizons of possibility for everyone—but especially for marginalized communities—require critical exposure of the ideologies at play (what, following Mary Daly, we might call "the courage to see") and then, through revolutionary action, an unrelenting renunciation of them (or the "courage to sin").[31] Queer refusals of the heteronormative (Christian) future and its prosthetic (Christian) past by renouncing the future's most sacred trope is, in a heteronormative expanse, a refusal to be straight or to survive, a revolution in orientation and expectation.

So the turn to affect and temporality in queer thinking and theological construction is part of a wider and longer set of fleshy turns against the classed, raced, and heteronormatively gendered ideal citizen/subject. But is affect theory's corrective import toward social embodiment structured by feeling and queer renunciations of futurity still partially entrained to a trite, but resilient, dichotomy between flesh and spirit that does not disappear upon being named, despite all of the (now rather tired) complaints lodged against it by feminism? The answer is yes, if the religiously entrenched dualism of soul and body remains secure. It is also yes if the religiously entrenched and politically deployed future and past remain imaginative structures of a heteronormative and settler colonial spirit.

The liberation of queer sexualities from temporal narratives of both heteronormatively framed reproductivity *and* maturity is dependent on the death of dominant expectations for both. Time is therefore a conceptual problem for queer thought and queerly sexed persons because queerness, understood rather conventionally here as disordered or wrongful desire, nonreproductivity, and/or unconventional intimacy,[32] pins "queer" onto flesh and so onto an atemporality that opposes the future (the spirit of heteronormativity as the logic of futurity, that is) and of ordered genealogies (successful pasts). Childhood (not to be confused with the trope of The Child in Edelman) is also amenable to queering, its strange landscapes and atemporal flights illuminated by Katherine Bond Stockton.[33] Queerness as a kind of refusal to grow up, to remain native to lands uncolonized and to affects without productive ends all hints at possibilities foreclosed by heteronormativity.

In other words queerness, having to do with disordered sexual regimes, is a matter of bodily desires and as such, like all disordered desires, functions outside of and as a threat to the orderly progression (and reproduction) of normative desires and ordered hetero-futures. Affect theory's move to think more clearly the ontological role of desires and proximity in the formation of queer others has the potential to disrupt the old body-mind binary to the extent that it disregards any boundaries between body, place, space, matter, idea, and desire. Add to this the queer critique of heteronormative time, and queer theory becomes a powerful ontology of the present, eschewing the inevitable coercions and conformities that come with the abstractions of future orders, even beatific ones. But a powerful ontology of the present may reinscribe the binary of body and mind or flesh and spirit by ultimately accepting its terms, ceding futures and opting for an atemporal (and so still abstract!) body. As Muñoz argues, this is the problem with the "no futures" argument, and there may yet be queer futures imaginable in terms of failure that do not by necessity devolve into their opposite, namely a calculus of achievement that resuscitates the old chains of heteronormativity.[34]

Whether the queer move that recognizes and denounces the conservative servility of temporal schemes is able also to jump the tracks that have structured temporality in opposition to actual bodies to begin with, remains to be seen. Or, to put it another way and in the more expansive and challenging terms of survivance, whether this particular queer refusal to survive (into heteronormatively structured futures) can do more than resist, remains to be seen. Mere opposition to dominant norms is, as we know, not a departure, though it can be a gesture toward the need to think differently.

The messiness of experience pushes against the coercion of heteronormative regimes of expectation and, for queer affect theorists, becomes an avenue of thinking otherwise about what may be already otherwise for actual bodies in the drama of contingency. This resistance to temporally frozen futures is not so far removed from Vizenor's understanding of native survivance against the coercion of temporally frozen indian regimes of expectation. Perhaps there is enough resemblance here to make for an interesting transcultural conversation without conflating the contexts. Because these regimes of expectation (the future of the Child, eschatology, indianness) are at present so global, so relentlessly broadcast, virally reproduced, and so banal, it is understandable that radical alternatives become, in the crazy context of global capitalism, sanely moderate. Edelman gives us outright refusal of the future through affirmations of nonreproductivity coupled with precise and searing outrage over lynching as the cost of survival. Muñoz gives us utopic failures that reinvent jubilantly queer sociality without coercive survivability. And Vizenor gives us postindian/postidentity warriors whose sovereign presences refuse drab survival and recognizable names. Each of these approaches becomes a serious temporal exit strategy from survivability and the "dominance of closure."[35]

The benefit of these theoretical moves, especially to something that might be emerging as "queer theology" is immense. The challenges for queer Christian thinkers are ones of balance, translation, and revolution. Our work is recognizably *theological* in part by virtue of its fidelity to certain texts and storied traditions and in part by virtue of its ability to narrate stories of the present that somewhat and somehow create access to embedded (and emerging) notions of incarnate divinity.[36] It is queer at least to the extent that it recognizes and revolts against the ideological weight and coercive power of sexualized abjection.

Thus I suggest that queer Christian theology (that is worth reading, in my opinion) needs new, improved theories for the deconstruction of its own stubborn enmeshment in hardened, colonial dichotomies and the modern philosophies (and universities and missions) that were constructed in service to them.

The burgeoning and deepening chorus of queer theories and their attendant theoretical partners that privilege abjected, fleshy things can, when taken seriously at the most rigorous edges of thought, change the entire project of contemporary Christian thought, top to bottom (so to speak). Catherine Keller's work on entanglement and Mayra Rivera's work on corporeality and flesh indicate at least two directions that theology in this key can begin to go.[37]

## WE SEE THE PROBLEM, SO WHAT'S THE PROBLEM?

My general and ever-present hesitation about a stubborn remnant of modernity's dichotomous conceptualization of bodies and minds in even the most promising of theories comes from its ability to ride incognito in even the most adventurous of theological projects. It has a tricky and presumptive familiarity that quietly and easily can return queer efforts back into rehearsals of the same. To think queerly past—or better yet otherwise to—the Euro-Christian metaphysics of dualism requires first a recognition that queer rationality need not be constrained by that particular ethnic frame in order to be theoretically sound or theologically rigorous. Implied in this recognition of the narrow cultural presumptions that have dominated high theory (or systematics) in Christian theology is, second, a willingness to think theologically from quite different cultural frames, wherein the dualist constraints peculiar to the European heritage of thought already are—and always were—alien. Too much of Christian theology, including that written with queer intent, labors under the presumption that if it does not conform to European ethnic epistemological and forensic frameworks, it is neither properly theological or philosophical nor is it sufficiently persuasive.[38] Queer interventions in theology may be "decorative" or "contextual," perhaps, but not foundational to the whole task of theology from the ground up. As Vizenor points out, the "rules of evidence and precedent are selective by culture and tradition, and sanction judicial practices over native presence and survivance."[39]

The creative convergence of affect theory, queer temporal suspicions, and Christian theology points toward a revised ontological frame. The unfolding world is, in a move suggestive of process thought, an eventful story of deep relation and material sensitivity, but deprived of the temporal confidence that sanitary progressive schemes might induce. Human beings no longer own the realm of feeling and response, but participate in a far more "entangled" mesh of influence that includes the animacy of all things (like trees, elephants, or lead).[40] Nothing exists outside of this web of affective multiplicity, not concepts, not temporal schemes, not divinities.

But queer Christian theology is in danger of getting stuck or paralyzed in this web despite the many benefits and corrections that both affect theory and queer temporal suspicion offer to its musings on divinity, creation, desire, and purpose. The demand for completion is strong in theology, which is why binaries so often thrive and multiply there. The long-standing tendency in Christian thought toward comprehensive accounts—even ones named "queer"—militates against the most important insights and corrections that affect theory, queer temporal suspicion, and now survivance all offer, namely an ontology of always incomplete, promiscuous relation. Even the attempt to name creation in terms of such unbounded affective particularity and temporality misses the point, rises to an abstraction (of, for example, "multiplicity") that necessarily reduces relation and time to an apparently comprehensive and comprehensible story, even if it is a story of incompletion. Negativity becomes, again, the only approximation that protects the depth and breadth of affective relation and influence, just as it has long protected divinity, precisely because the theological demand for a finished story—for final words or what Vizenor calls the closures of dominance—is so heavy.[41] What would queer theology look like that does more than gesture—if appreciatively—toward the relational indecency of incomplete liaisons, partial affections, affectations, and nonreproductive pleasures? What would such queer theology look like that enacts these pleasures in its method and foundational concepts?[42]

## QUEER SURVIVANCE . . .

That question leads me to the deeper question of this essay: Is *queer theology* enough like *survivance* to be greater than the right of a survivable name? In his novel *Hotline Healers*, Vizenor's character Almost Browne announces that the "most romantic representations of natives are the advertisements of cultural dominance, not the natural sources of motion and sovereignty."[43] The advertisements of cultural dominance Almost refers to are all of the ways that "being indian" is a demand for ossification of an image, a stilling of a culture, a recording of a song. I borrow from Almost and suggest that the most romantic representations of Christian theology (including whatever we may call queer theology) are the advertisements of cultural dominance—the privileging of ethnic European sources and reasoning norms, the association of Christianity with sexual and reproductive surveillance, the passing of "religious freedom" laws. Not the "natural" (cf. Vizenor) sources of active queer incarnate presence over against the homogenized (romantic, married, assimilated, reproductive) survival of the lgbti/queer, which only turns out to be an absence anyway, like "indian."

Survivance, in the cadence of Vizenor's notion of native reason, runs otherwise to the closures of dominance. Like affect, it is a force of life in a passing glance, in a story told and retold, in a sense of humor that rejects tragedy or victimry. In Vizenor's hands it is undeniably native because what he is tracing is a particular—call it cultural—vivacity, animacy, and moral character that constitute the agency at work in native stories, stories that affectively assert themselves, get up and walk coyote-fashion around the dead plains of erasure, and change things—when they are told, that is. Vizenor, standing within a heritage of these stories, is seeking to heal his people through a remembering that is not nostalgia and an ironic engagement with the narratives of dominance that also get told, over and over ad nauseam, and so also walk around and change things. His point, in other words, is not to find a pure essence of native existence, but rather to trace a moving sovereignty that was never surrendered, that does not stay still, that laughs at the posers and the simulators even as it poses and simulates. "Hardly anyone ever asked my cousin what his stories might mean," Almost Browne's cousin muses. "Almost every native who hears stories knows that the meaning of one story is truly another story."[44]

The primary characteristics of survivance reflect an ethnic frame that eschews completion. This is a theory that does not fight with or against other theories because the point is not who or what is correct, but what other stories emerge out of the telling. The point is not to determine who is "right" but to learn from each story on its own terms. Edelman's "brilliant polemic" (as Muñoz praises it) is not a battlement to defend or batter. It is an illumination, a story with multiple lessons according to various tellings and retellings.

Survivance as a strategy means that the rules of engagement are different, the epistemology is rooted in insight rather than persuasion in order never to get caught in the mistake of assuming that things stay (or should stay) the same, including gods. This means that chance, the "shimmers of imagination," humor, irony, and attention to experience, especially experience of the world's presence, matter more than essential final words or doctrines.

> Native stories of survivance are prompted by natural reason, by a consciousness and sense of incontestable presence that arises from experiences in the natural world, by the turn of seasons, by sudden storms, by migration of cranes, by the ventures of tender lady's slippers, by chance of moths overnight, by unruly mosquitos, and by favor of spirits in the water, rimy sumac, wild rice, thunder in the ice, bear, beaver, and faces in the stone.[45]

I suggest that Vizenor's ethnic frame, predicated on attention to what breathes, moves, and blows around him is no more particular and parochial than the European, especially German and French, ethnic frames that have dominated contemporary Christian theology and its companion theories thus far. To suggest that Vizenor's notion of survivance might well serve emergent queer theologies is not to import, or steal, cultural property (well, Almost). It is to question what would be different in so-called queer Christian theologies if they attended first to traces of unsystematic and unsystematizable vitality, irony, chance, and proximal bodies in their own poses and simulations *as a basis for* theological construction and reflection.

Muñoz ruminates on Fred Herko's suicidal "jeté" out of a window as a utopic expression of aliveness. It is not a story of surviving with AIDS. It is not a story of resistance to the reality of AIDS. It is, quite possibly, a story of queer survivance.[46] Unsystematic vitality, irony, chance, and proximal bodies are no strangers to queer narratives and the well-loved stories and proud/shamed simulations of queer poses. These aspects of survivance may translate to something we accept for now as queerly theological (but not Queer Theology), and they are already at play in the making-present lives of sexual outsiders who remember to tell and retell stories of resistance, tricky resurrections, campy refusals, and brave failures. These folk understand the prison of names and the futility of holding still to identity as the alphabet of names grows and changes. The problem is that Christian theology, as yet, has few tools to address that experience and instead tends toward reassurances of stability in the form of metanarratives over against the funny, chancy, incarnational world of affect and temporally unstable presence.[47]

The parochial notion of survivance, I suggest, may help queer theology correct its own unacknowledged parochial epistemological tendencies by adding a culturally framed presupposition that does not look for closure or certainty and so need not fight rival theories on behalf of any other kind of closure or certainty. The element of surprise and the expectation of reversal seems necessary to a queer epistemology and ontology, not as an appropriation of native survivance, but as a kind of queer presence that acknowledges the cultural framework of its tutelage. Perhaps. I suggest that something like this assemblage of survival and resistance can add buoyancy to queer Christian theology precisely because there is (still) vivacity and resiliency in queer stories. They do get up, walk around, and change things. The name "queer" is less important than the vitality of life toward which it theoretically points. It is tempting to merely survive, to seek a permanent place in the rolls of approved identities. But I am after a queerness that is greater than the survivable name.

## NOTES

1. In theology, see especially Mayra Rivera's various works on corporeality, such as "A Labyrinth of Incarnations: The Social Materiality of Bodies," *Journal of the European Society of Women in Theological Research* 22 (2014): 187–98.
2. Madhavi Menon, "Universalism and Partition: A Queer Theory," *Differences: A Journal of Feminist Cultural Studies* 26, no. 1 (2015): 117. My own approach to—and appreciation for—affect theory most closely follows Sara Ahmed's development of it. See especially "Orientations Matter," in *New Materialisms: Ontology, Agency,*

*and Politics*, ed. Diana Coole and Samantha Frost (Durham, N.C.: Duke University Press, 2010), 234–57. Also Mel Chen has developed a fascinating claim of necessary and indivisible relation between the concept of animacy in linguistics and the materiality of cultural meaning in *Animacies: Biopolitics, Racial Mattering, and Queer Affect* (Durham, N.C.: Duke University Press, 2012), esp. "Queer Animation," 57–85.

3. As Margaret Wetherell points out, "'Affect theory' reflected an understandable desire for something different in social research—a desire to recognize the way the world moves us. It was exciting (and it was transgressive) to talk about bitterness, envy, joy and paranoia in the same breath as social and critical theory." Margaret Wetherell and David Beer, "The Future of Affect Theory: An Interview with Margaret Wetherell," *Theory, Culture & Society*, October 15, 2014. (http://theoryculturesociety.org/the-future-of-affect-theory-an-interview-with-margaret-wetherall/). Accessed October 19, 2015.
4. Robyn Wiegman and Elizabeth S. Wilson, "Antinormativity's Queer Conventions," *Differences: A Journal of Feminist Cultural Studies* 26, no. 1 (2015): 1.
5. I first identified this problem in the essay "Crib Notes from Bethlehem," in *Polydoxy: Theology of Multiplicity and Relation*, ed. Catherine Keller and Laurel C. Schneider (London: Routledge, 2010), 19–35.
6. Karen Barad is particularly interesting in this vein of thinking. Karen Barad, "Transmaterialities: Trans*/Matter/Realities and Queer Political Imaginings," *GLQ: A Journal of Lesbian and Gay Studies* 21, no. 2 (2015): 387–422.
7. Michel Foucault, *Technologies of the Self: A Seminar with Michel Foucault*, ed. Luther H. Martin, Huck Gutman, and Patrick H. Hutton (Amherst: University of Massachusetts Press, 1988), 21. For his discussion of practices of confession, see Michel Foucault, *History of Sexuality: An Introduction*, vol. 1, trans. Robert Hurley (New York: Random House 1978), 17–35.
8. Judith Butler, *Gender Trouble: Feminism and the Subversion of Identity* (New York: Routledge, 1990). Another trajectory, better described by Eve Kosofsky Sedgwick, begins less from philosophy's concerns with history and metaphysics via Foucault and more with literary constructions and norms. *Epistemology of the Closet* (Berkeley: University of California Press, 1990).
9. Judith Butler, *Bodies That Matter: On The Discursive Limits of "Sex"* (New York: Routledge, 1993).
10. Foucault, *History of Sexuality*, 135–51.
11. David L. Eng, Judith Halberstam, and José Esteban Muñoz, quoting contributor Hiram Perez in "Introduction: What's Queer about Queer Studies Now?" *Social Text* 23, no. 3–4 (2005): 12.
12. José Esteban Muñoz traces queer of color performances that deliberately create paradoxes of identity and in so doing illustrate both the malleability and stubbornness of body politics. *Disidentifications: Queers of Color and the Performance of Politics* (Minneapolis: University of Minnesota Press, 1999). Erica R. Edwards offers an example of queer of color literary analysis that thinks through the materiality of blackness and survival in the "interdependence of human and nonhuman life," especially through reflecting on the character of Esch in *Salvage the Bones* by

Jesmyn Ward. Edwards notes that "Esch" is truncated "flesh" and sounds like "sex" where Black women "work within and *athwart* the norm . . . the bodily labor of the imagination." Erica R. Edwards, "Sex after the Black Normal," *Differences: A Journal of Feminist Cultural Studies* 26, no. 1 (2015): 156–62.

13. Hiram Perez, "You Can Have My Brown Body and Eat It Too!" *Social Text* 23, no. 3–4 (2005): 187.
14. Queer reflections on time include Lee Edelman, *No Future: Queer Theory and the Death Drive* (Durham, N.C.: Duke University Press, 2004); Elizabeth Freeman, *Time Binds: Queer Temporalities, Queer Histories* (Durham, N.C.: Duke University Press, 2010); J. Jack Halberstam, *In a Queer Time and Place: Transgender Bodies, Subcultural Lives* (New York: New York University Press, 2005); Kathryn Bond Stockton, *The Queer Child, or Growing Sideways* (Durham, N.C.: Duke University Press, 2009).
15. Ahmed, "Orientations Matter," 2010.
16. Edelman, *No Future*; José Esteban Muñoz, *Cruising Utopia: The Then and There of Queer Futurity* (New York: New York University Press, 2009); Thomas J. J. Altizer and William Hamilton, *Radical Theology and the Death of God* (Indianapolis: Bobbs-Merrill, 1966).
17. Edelman, *No Future*, throughout, but these comments reflect especially 47–54.
18. The idea of survivance is one of Vizenor's defining concepts as a scholar. It appears many times across his work, and he has edited more than one volume that revolves around the concept. He cannot be accused of being too systematic: He defines it enough times and differently to make a single reference impossible. However, taking his theoretical essays, novels, and poetry together, a more or less consistent understanding of survivance as a more-than survival and not-just resistant mode of cultural production among native people who never were and never will be "Indians" but who live in complex relation to that stereotype. See especially chapters 1–4 in Gerald Vizenor, *Native Liberty: Natural Reason and Cultural Survivance* (Lincoln: University of Nebraska Press, 2009), 1–104.
19. Gerald Vizenor, ed., *Survivance: Narratives of Native Presence* (Lincoln: University of Nebraska Press, 2008), 11.
20. Audre Lorde, "A Litany for Survival," in *The Black Unicorn: Poems* (New York: Norton, 1978), 31–32.
21. Gerald Vizenor, *Manifest Manners: Narratives on Postindian Survivance* (Lincoln: University of Nebraska Press, 1999), 4.
22. Gerald Vizenor, *Hotline Healers: An Almost Browne Novel* (Middletown, Conn.: Wesleyan University Press, 1997), 11.
23. Vizenor, *Survivance*, 3–7; also Vizenor, *Native Liberty*, 159–78.
24. Vizenor, *Survivance*, 1.
25. For example, the explosion of "Cherokee grandmothers" in American self-descriptions in recent years is a matter of some humor and irony for Vizenor, but this phenomenon also represents for him "the absence of tribal realities . . . posing as the verities of certain cultural traditions." Vizenor, *Manifest Manners*, 17. Erasure of real presence happens on many levels, especially where romantic notions of tribal traditions and identities persist.

26. Vizenor, *Survivance*, 1.
27. Excellent examples of this kind of work can be found in Mary Daly, *Pure Lust: Elemental Feminist Philosophy* (Boston: Beacon Press, 1985), Mark Jordan, *The Invention of Sodomy in Christian Theology* (Chicago: University of Chicago Press, 1998), and Marcella Althaus-Reid, *Indecent Theology: Theological Perversions in Sex, Gender, and Politics* (London: Routledge, 2001).
28. For example, see Patricia T. Clough, "The Affective Turn: Political Economy, Biomedia, and Bodies," in *The Affect Theory Reader*, ed. Melissa Gregg and Gregory J. Seigworth (Durham, N.C.: Duke University Press, 2010), 208–28.
29. Sara Ahmed, "Happy Objects," in *The Affect Theory Reader*, ed. Melissa Gregg and Gregory J. Seigworth (Durham, N.C.: Duke University Press, 2010), 30.
30. Many of Douglass's speeches appeal to feeling as a means toward abolition, in particular toward recognizing that Black men, women, and children are human beings. He often expresses frustration with "convincing argument" although he is a brilliant practitioner of it. One of the best examples is his famous 1852 "5th of July" speech in Rochester, New York, in which, among many other glittering lines, he declares of the Christian church, that "these ministers make religion a cold and flinty-hearted thing, having neither principles of right action, nor bowels of compassion. They strip the love of God of its beauty, and leave the throng of religion a huge, horrible, repulsive form. It is a religion for oppressors, tyrants, man-stealers, and *thugs*." Frederick Douglass, "What to the Slave is the 4th of July? 1858," in *Great Speeches by African Americans* (New York: Dover, 2006), 28.
31. Mary Daly, "Sin Big," *New Yorker*, February 26 and March 4, 1996, 76–84. Daly first developed the concept of the courage to sin big in *Beyond God the Father: Toward a Philosophy of Women's Liberation* (Boston: Beacon Press, 1972).
32. See Chen, *Animacies*, 11.
33. Stockton. *The Queer Child*.
34. Muñoz, *Cruising Utopia*, 11 and 22. The vulnerability of queer theory to its own undoing is well theorized in part, for example, in the idea of queer settler colonialism (see Scott L. Morgenson, *The Spaces between Us: Queer Settler Colonialism and Indigenous Decolonization* [Durham, N.C.: Duke University Press, 2011]), or xenophobic homonormativity (see Jasbir Puar, *Terrorist Assemblages: Homonationalism in Queer Times* [Durham, N.C.: Duke University Press, 2007], among others). Note, however, that Puar accomplishes this in part by considering queer theories in relation to affect.
35. Vizenor, *Manifest Manners*, 14.
36. Although "queer fidelity" is a dubious notion (see Althaus-Reid, *Indecent Theology*), and one worthy of suspicion, its deployment here may serve also to undermine common dismissive glosses of Christian texts in queer thinking.
37. Catherine Keller, *Cloud of the Impossible: Negative Theology and Planetary Entanglement* (New York: Columbia University Press, 2014); Mayra Rivera, *Poetics of the Flesh* (Durham, N.C.: Duke University Press, 2015).
38. The argument that culture matters in the formulation of theological claims is by no means new, but slow to make its way into the rarefied realms of systematic

reasoning. Some scholars of ancient Christian texts have pointed very effectively to the cultural differences at play in ancient text production and interpretation as a means of decentering modern and postmodern conventions about Europe's own philosophical past, particularly when contemporary theologians try to characterize "the tradition" in monolithic or modernist terms. See, for example, Virginia Burrus, *Saving Shame: Martyrs, Saints, and Other Abject Subjects* (Philadelphia: University of Pennsylvania Press, 2007); see also Denise K. Buell, *Why This New Race: Ethnic Reasoning in Early Christianity* (New York: Columbia University Press, 2005).

39. Vizenor, *Survivance*, 3.
40. Chen's *Animacies* is particularly helpful in thinking queerly beyond the human.
41. Vizenor, *Manifest Manners*, 3.
42. Marcella Althaus-Reid has probably come closest to approximating the incomplete pleasures toward which I only gesture here. It is a great loss to queer theology that her own jubilant and outraged work was stopped by cancer. See *The Queer God* (New York: Routledge, 2004).
43. Vizenor, *Hotline Healers*, 5.
44. Ibid., 6.
45. Vizenor, *Survivance*, 11.
46. Muñoz, *Cruising Utopia*, 147–68.
47. A significant example of this dynamic is the demand in many "open and affirming" church bodies that queer relationships and erotic arrangements look just like straight ones. The whole move toward legalized gay marriage was predicated on this similitude. Queer sexualities and other nonconforming relationships (including heterosexual ones) are further stigmatized on behalf of a reproductive, heteronormative resurgence. And since federal recognition of same-sex marriage in the United States in 2015, businesses and educational institutions (such as Vanderbilt University) are requiring same sex couples to marry to receive domestic benefits. We might say therefore that former eras were much queerer than either decade of this millennium.

# Remember—When?

KARMEN MACKENDRICK

"Surely my memory is where you dwell," Augustine famously writes in his *Confessions*, addressing the puzzling, immaterial God for whom "there can be no question of place." We might hope to resolve the puzzle by replacing the "where" of memory with a "when," but chronologically, too, God turns out to be not quite placeable. Augustine argues that one way that we can be sure that we *remember* God is that we all seek the happiness God brings, even though we have not yet found it in this life: How else could we know about it?[1] It must be that we are haunted by this possibility of perfect joy, a joy that can be found only in the divine. God dwells in memory not as a datum learned and filed for recollection, but as one who has been found there since Augustine first thought to look. Always—and only—remembered. But when was before this always, such that we find it in recollection?

In *The Book of Resemblances*, the poet Edmond Jabès creates a fragment of rabbinic dialogue:

> Memory means the promise of a future. "Tell me what you remember, and I shall tell you who you will be," wrote Reb Horel, one of the imaginary rabbis. . . .
>
> "Can we remember a place where we have not been, a face we have not come near, an object we have never held?" Reb Zaoud asked Reb Bécri.
>
> "I well remember God," replied the latter.[2]

This passage is more overtly strange than Augustine's, but not altogether different in kind. We were never there, in "a place where we have not been"; there can be no question of (that) place, no sight of that distant face. This memory too is unplaceable, yet it is distinctly sensuous. Reb Bécri remembers it, and well—but from when? And how does that memory, from when we never were, of a place we have never been, of an untouched object, promise a future? When is *that*? This never-was, only remembered (or already forgotten), always promising, offers us a distinctly queer temporality, a time tangled up in happiness and God and the chance of some after to our exile.

The time of the God who dwells in memory is no simple past. It is not even the re-presentation of the past in the present again, in the manner of "ordinary" memories. It is something, I want to say, like a memory of futurity, memory as the promise of the future. And the ways in which divinity gives us this memory of the future, the God of happiness that Augustine and Reb Bécri both remember, is the God of strange time, of a wonderful though often frightening disruptiveness.

## MOURNING (SOME)WHERE

To make sense of this, we might helpfully think about other modes of memory that aren't quite ordinary, and that might be at work in recollection of a God. Surely one important option is that of mourning. Peter Homans has hypothesized that we mourn religion, broadly and culturally, and that our productive response to this mourning has included the development of both sociology and psychoanalysis.[3] Religious studies, too, can be analyzed as the product of religion's loss, a creative response to the rejection of religion and the mourning that accompanies it.[4]

Religious studies is not quite theology; to mourn religion is one thing, but do we also mourn God? At times, surely. Perhaps we find God only in memory just as we find in memory a childhood belief in the Easter Bunny, which was a lot of fun while we had it, but which we necessarily outgrew. Sometimes we mourn a very particular God. "I miss God who was my friend," says the narrator of Jeanette Winterson's *Oranges Are Not the Only Fruit*; "I miss the company of someone utterly loyal."[5] Though less eloquently, the poster RingoThe CraftySquid on the Reddit site *exchristian* expresses a similar loss: "I miss god. I miss the safety that came with god. . . . The love I had for god was *real*. I loved him with all my heart and more than I've ever loved a real person. Isn't that crazy? When I realized christianity was all BULLSHIT it hurt so bad. It's like he died. . . . I feel like I killed god. I feel like shit."[6]

Respondents to the post attempt reassurance, deny the reality of the emptiness as much as of the divine presence, assure Ringo of the rightness of the position that G/god is inexistent, and, not least, kindly insist that of course the writer has not killed anyone. One cannot kill what does not exist, what never existed.

An object we have never held.

Friedrich Nietzsche's madman, carrying a lantern in the morning like the cynic Diogenes, might well disagree with the Reddit respondents. "Where is

God?" the madman frantically demands and, receiving no answer from the laughing people he passes, answers himself, "We have killed him—you and I! We are all his murderers."[7] But Nietzsche's is not the triumphant cry that "new" atheisms often take it to be. Murder is a dangerous move, the madman knows; dangerous not because we have risked the wrath of a demanding divinity, but because we have wiped away the horizon and unchained the earth from the sun, all without even realizing it, with no consideration for the consequences.[8]

No horizon and no center, after we have rid ourselves of the circle without circumference whose center was everywhere. Though God may find no question of place, we thus decentered might mourn our own displacement, our sense of exile manifest from the tales of Eden through to contemporary diasporas. (And queerness, after all, is paradigmatically linked to a sense of displacement and the impossibility of being at home.) Often, as Nietzsche is aware, we quickly make substitute certainties, such as those of scientism, rather than dwell in discomfort. Perhaps in happiness we remember a place where we belonged and were not so ill at ease, but to which we cannot seem quite to return. For many, the exile is from a tangibly remembered home; for many others, home too is a place we have never been.

There is much to be said of mourning divinity, I think, and of exile as a mourning of home; and sometime I would like to do some of that saying, but for now I must note that Augustine and Reb Bécri are not mourning or are mourning in a complex combination with something closer to a hint of hope. The second seems more likely: Both are complex thinkers, and both acknowledge that what they remember is neither present nor locatable in a past. Still, where would that hope come from? When is happy? What kind of strange memory is this?

## WHOSE MELANCHOLY?

In a possibility closely related to mourning, hope could be entangled with melancholy, which refuses to acknowledge loss fully. In melancholy, as Freud describes it, the lost object (less clinically, the lost beloved) who would be grieved in mourning is instead introjected, made over into a part of oneself. Desire is transformed into identification. In his early work, Freud finds melancholy an unhelpful reaction; he argues that the loss is too little acknowledged (I haven't lost the beloved; here she is within me!) and the effects largely negative. "In grief the world becomes poor and empty," he writes; "in melancholia it is the ego itself."[9] The refusal of grief does not even save the world outside the ego, which, as Graziela Durante says, "seems to contract and lose itself."[10] In both mourning and melancholy, the world is impoverished—it is emptied out into a vast hollowness, or it contracts into a shriveled version of itself.

Augustine describes something like this after the death of a friend: "Everything on which I set my gaze was death. My home town became a torture to me; my father's house a strange world of unhappiness. . . . My eyes looked for him everywhere, and he was not there. I hated everything because they did not have him." But these problems are not entirely external; Augustine at the same time becomes a great problem to himself.[11]

This could be a response to happiness lost, but not to happiness hoped for: This memory holds no promise of a future. Augustine himself criticizes it for being too time-bound, for its failure to see the eternity in which time is gathered. It amazes him that life remains at all, "since he whom I had loved as if he would never die was dead."[12] But this mortality is the problem: "It is not adequate to get a grip on things that are transient," he tells himself.[13] This is more complex than it may seem; he advocates not ceasing to love what passes, but ceasing to expect it not to pass. One option to this is indifference; one is rejoicing at the passage into an expected afterlife; one is to love the transient incompletely by affirming only the eternal within it—and one is to accept that mourning will touch on our loves.

For all its misery, mourning does have one advantage over melancholy: It at least allows one to acknowledge attachments and then to dissolve them in favor of new loves. Melancholy seems to be a form of denial or refusal instead. However, as Judith Butler writes, "Where melancholy is the refusal of grief, it is also always the incorporation of loss."[14] Freud too moves from his early rejection of melancholia as counterproductive to a view of this incorporation as actually vital to the formation of the ego.[15] That is, he believes that melancholia can reach pathological levels, but it can also be part of a process that is not only "normal," but necessary: We are made in no small measure by our incorporation of those we have lost. In Butler's terms, the self "appears to be the sedimentation of those objects loved and lost, the archaeological remainder, as it were, of unresolved grief."[16] We "let go" of our desire for loved objects through identification or incorporation, but sorrow does not let go of us quite so casually.[17] "We always bear witness to a death we have survived," says another of Jabès's rabbis.[18]

The well-known complications that Butler introduces to the Freudian understanding will be relevant shortly. For now, I note that melancholy, too, has only some elements of the sort of memory that I am seeking to specify, though these elements are important. In Augustine's search for his memory-dwelling God, he finds that he has to turn within himself—seeking the divine in the world outside him is even counterproductive much of the time.[19] Moreover, as Amy Hollywood has pointed out, the imitation of Christ much practiced by Christian mystics has no small element of melancholic identification. This is perhaps one reason that it is so often sought through suffering.[20] That such melancholy takes on a redemptive aspect through this suffering might well strengthen our sense that God is "remembered" in melancholic introjection. But the aspect of *happiness* seems to elude us still; and the tantalizing sense of materiality, hinting from the rabbis' place and face and object, from the beauty in Augustine's world, likewise evades.[21] We have remembrance and sorrow and introjection, but not happiness, and not material things, and not the fullness of things that promises happiness among them. *Once and lost* is not *never and to come*, but neither is the memory of divinity purely projected expectation.

## A NEARLY LEGIBLE TRACE (SPECTERS OF MARKS)

So let us try again to work out a beginning. Those elusive hints of happiness may tell us something important. Memory, says Freud, works by traces, by something that remains or is left behind in the passage of the present. The mind lays down "permanent—though not unalterable" traces of the sensory, as memories.[22] It is not by chance that we write things down to help us remember them; the written trace is "a materialized portion of my mnemic apparatus."[23] Traces remain even when later input has rendered them illegible, Freud argues; there is a palimpsestic quality to remembrance.[24] Not only are some memories thereby a bit blurry, but many more are really layers, syncretions, or alterations—all modes of being strange and even unrecognizable, but something other than gone.

Paul Ricoeur takes the concept of trace as central to both history and memory, "and not only in the neurological sense. There are traces, of course, in the brain, . . . but also, there are emotional traces. . . . And then you have a third kind of trace, the documentary traces in our archives. Here you have a kind of public memory inscribed in a system of traces."[25] Traces are always at risk, both from loss and from palimpsestic overlay: What is remembered may be forgotten, smudged over, erased. As Martin Hägglund argues, "The trace of the past that is left for the future . . . can never be in itself, but is essentially exposed to that which may erase it." To exist at all, a mnemonic trace must exist as vulnerable. David Johnson points out, "Hägglund's elaboration of the temporal logic of the trace opens onto the logic of survival. Only what is mortal survives, lives on, always at risk of being destroyed, eradicated, forgotten. To survive means to live on exposed to the time of life, to mortality."[26] What is true of memory is true of us, too; we live only in the possibility of loss. This loss must accompany hope, but hope itself seems as yet to be out the picture. At most, it might subtly nuance our sorrow and fear.

To be purely remembered, to be found nowhere and nowhen else but in memory, would thus be to be especially vulnerable, at risk, always, of invisibility. What the trace signifies, says Ricoeur, is "the invisible, the nonvisible, the unvisible, the lost origin. Once more we hit upon the concept of loss."[27]

What is only remembered can only be traced: always, in some measure, lost, and vulnerable always to further losing. When the recalled is pure memory, then, it must be an original originally lost. In "the enigma of the mnemonic trace," Ricoeur claims, we find "the most hidden but most original meaning of the verb 'to remain' or 'to endure.'"[28] A moment's reflection drives home a strangeness that, while not Ricoeur's own intention, fits beautifully the remembered God: Think of an originary remaining, that which is, from the first, traced in memory; from the first, remaining from . . . when? Both present and future threaten it, yet the God found in mnemonic traces is precisely the one supposed, certainly by Augustine, to be uniquely free of the threat posed by futurity, to be outside of time such that it will never run out of time at all.

The trace, the sign of the now-absent past which is not only absent in the present, is left for the future. It is fragile: It may be destroyed. Augustine would argue that even undestroyed, it will likely remain unread. For him the whole world and for Jabès all of language bear traces of God. But this does not help us much unless we can catch some glimpse of what (in the world) a mnemonic trace is when what it traces is God, who, from the beginning, is (what) only remains. And the temptation not to read the possibilities that such a memory opens is immense, because possibility, for all its promise and temptation, is unsettling as well. The pure remembered *isn't*, quite, ever; yet it is always possible. As Catherine Keller writes, "One is tempted to swat away *the possible* because it is not *the probable* and relieve oneself of the vulnerability of hope."[29] Knowing the fragility of the trace, we might wish not to incorporate or mourn it, but to hurry up and erase it now, not let it continue to haunt us. We may be blowing out the light of the madman's lantern, wiping away the horizon with brisk forgetfulness, simply because vulnerability can be so nearly unbearable.

What is it, though, to encounter a trace, to see the threatened past in the present, if we do not ignore it? And what in the trace of divinity is otherwise than in most kinds of tracing (my own suspicion is that the otherwise is less in the sign than in the nature of the reading)? What, that is, allows us to sometimes read traces of the future? Undoubtedly some traces are clear, at least to those literate in their kind; we read them like words in a book, like wolf tracks in the desert, like the signatures of medicinal herbs. But if divinity were so easily read, not only would it not be read so seldom, but it would be—I know this is not really an argument—massively uninteresting. God must be an elusive trace, a barely there track, something we can mistake—and perhaps often do. And it will be a trace, I promise, that will lead us back to questions of melancholy entangled with desire, of mourning that enhances new creation.

Let us review quickly our options so far, and their limitations. Mourning gives us a sense of loss, of the receding or absent which we cannot cease to love, to desire. It has a deep effect on the sensory, as Augustine's world without his friend reveals. Melancholia includes introjection and a strange kind of persistence even of what is lost, but it too can empty out, even the melancholic self. Thinking memory as trace is a reminder of the fragility and the complication of all that survives, and of the importance of signs—of being able to read something other than what is directly given. Elusive still are the persistence of hope, especially the hope of happiness, and the strange never-givenness of the remembered, which is otherwise than what is lost. Or, I might say, what is elusive is the queerly sexy, the opening of the future that frightens. Heather Love writes, "Perverse, immature, sterile, and melancholic: even when they provoke fears about the future, [queers] somehow also recall the past."[30] I have not quite read this provocative recollection, not just yet. I must further complicate matters.

I can begin with a complication that is well known, Butler's reworking of Freud's theory of melancholic identification. Butler points out that some options for desire are culturally foreclosed, rendered unspeakable and impossible in advance,[31] even though "there is no necessary reason for identification to oppose desire, or for desire to be fueled through repudiation."[32] Such foreclosure serves to sustain tidy gender binaries by repudiating some (same sex) desires, eliminating them from the possible, declaring collective invulnerability to them. "The identification contains within it both the prohibition and the desire and so embodies the ungrieved loss of the homosexual cathexis."[33] One cannot even work through mourning and then transfer one's desire onto another same-sex figure; the desire itself is disallowed. To keep gender steady, boring, and unpanicked, what must be rejected is not just same-sex desire, but the *possibility* of such desire, and the speakability that might let it work its way in, leaving its traces in language.

Some desires must be not merely pushed out, doors slammed shut behind them, but *fore*-closed, never let in in the first place. Though Butler adds new details to Freud, she gives us as well a tidier account. For Freud, the possible returns with all the stubbornness of the repressed, and the foreclosed sometimes cracks open. For some, this slightest opening suffices to induce panic. For some, who need not always be others, it opens the joy of possibility, and vice versa. And the fore-closed can close up again, leaving only mnemonic traces. This melancholia is for what never was, what was never allowed to be or become. It is for a possible: what was not, to be sure, but *might have been*.

Butler refers to the outcome of this ungrieved loss as a haunting, "a love and a loss haunted by the specter of a certain unreality, a certain unthinkability, the double disavowal of 'I never loved her, and I never lost her,' uttered by a woman; the 'I never loved him, I never lost him,' uttered by a man."[34] We are haunted by what never was, by desire never felt, by the objects we were not permitted to desire to touch, the distant faces on which we refused to want to gaze. Yet they dwell in our memories, even as the discarded possibilities of happiness refused.

## THE NOW THAT WAS THE COULD BE

*Haunting* is a largely negative term, linked to loss and regret, or to our refusal to acknowledge history—for which reasons it has recently become strongly associated with queer theory.[35] But it may also be more neutrally described. Denise Buell writes of it as a "nonlinear temporality," a "form of memory transmission" that helps "communicate temporal intersectionality."[36] (Like the trace, read now from the past, vulnerable to the future.) Hauntings bring into the present, which seems so self-evident, an element of the uncertain: "Hauntings take place in the present but are untimely; as Derrida notes, one cannot know whence a specter arrives."[37] Where then did I find you, to be able to learn of you?[38] We are, nonetheless, responsible, even without being fully in control of the memorial work—accountable, without being altogether in charge. This is "memory work that is not simply in the control of the living interpreter." The responsibility, as Buell notes, is to respond.[39] It is a responsibility that we bear even without being able to control that to which we are responding.

Those things that haunt us hover not so much between memory and forgetting as between memory and unknowing: "As if you were, in short, exploring a past diverted from the course of your memory, but originally yours," as Jabès provocatively suggests—after which he adds, "Oblivion, too, is a pledge of the future."[40] If oblivion and memory both pledge, then the future must mutually pull at the past.

What haunts us may also be readings of the world that project our own desire. I think especially of the ways we are forever seeing those we loved in the faces, walks, or gestures of others, and how startling it is each time we realize that we are wrong. And yet it was a real trace; that *was* a reminder of her hair, of his voice—a reminder of presence by which absence is rendered vivid. What haunts us is a little unsure, a little uncanny. Importantly, Buell adds, the haunting is unknowable in its inclusions and in its effects: "A haunting always harbors the violence . . . that made it, and the . . . 'Utopian,' the potential for alternatives to present social structures and ethical relations."[41] More succinctly, "The hope haunts," writes Keller, keeping the future possible without determinism.[42] And haunting, as Avery Gordon argues, transfigures: "Haunting is a very particular way of knowing what has happened or is happening. Being haunted draws us affectively, sometimes against our will and always a bit magically, into the structure of feeling of a reality we come to experience, not as cold knowledge, but as transformative recognition."[43] Perhaps this *is not*, says what haunts us; but perhaps, and even now, it *could be*: We recognize transformation, even transfiguration, as the possibility of the world.

## AND THE POSSIBLE THAT COULD BE YET

This, I want to argue, is the temporality we have been looking for. Not even in the utopian alternatives, but in the potential itself. Haunting, which seems to have much in common with melancholy as both try to deny the very loss that they feel, so much in common with mourning as it fills the world with the lost, might also serve as their corrective, not to replace despair with hope, but to live in their stubborn intermingling.[44] If we are melancholic, as Butler argues, due to our foreclosed possibilities, then potential may be every bit as salvific as Christic torments. And haunting, rather than robbing the present of life and desire, as mourning and melancholy both may do, enriches and complicates it, grants us glimpses of what is missing in a manner at once evocatively tantalizing and achingly sad. What if what haunts us, though only remembered, is not something only lost? Might we be haunted by the may-be of the to-come?

This bears some elaboration. We know that we may be haunted by what we have lost. This is the clearest sense of the experience and of the word. We are rarely haunted by the absolutely impossible—by what physics or logic, say, render out of bounds for us (though it is conceivable that we might be in some fashion— thinking, for instance, "If only I could have bilocated!"). But the haunting that intrigues me here is that of what actually was-not, yet is known as what could have been. It is because of this haunting, I think, that we know that there is a could-be.

The haunting memory is neither denied nor incorporated melancholically. It is not forgotten, nor is it unseen, though it is made in the shadows and the almosts. We may misrecognize the thing—but not the trace of our desire. The ghost is remembered neither in pure sadness nor in identificational refusal; it is the presence of what is absent.

The potential for alternatives is potential itself—the realization that we are not locked into the actual, into what is. In fact, every haunting, somehow present yet not quite actual, somehow a trace that could be a trace of something else, is entangled in potentiality. It is a reminder that what is could be otherwise—whether because it was otherwise, once, or because, for a moment, we saw otherwise in it. We are haunted by a strange combination of those possibilities realized, which tell us that things really can become other than they have been, and those unrealized, which tell us that another otherness might yet be. It is particularly the latter that render us vulnerable to hope. Potentiality belongs to the not-yet, the nonactual, the future—the very time that threatens the trace. The trace that desire reads in the world, the trace that does not close it down but is its very opening, is that of the future:

the future, in which the trace is so much at risk. Possibility risks itself in the world. Better: Possibility is the world risking itself, taking the chance of something other.

Leaving aside for just a moment the complexity of this notion, I must acknowledge how fraught it is to evoke futurity at all: The attempt to guarantee "the future," as if it were not necessarily multiple and uncertain, can be evoked against queer desire and temporality.[45] Or the future might be, as it is for José Muñoz, itself the temporality of queerness, which "we can feel as the warm illumination of a horizon imbued with potentiality. . . . Queerness," he writes, "exists for us as an ideality that can be distilled from the past and used to imagine a future." We need this ideality because "the here and now is a prison house."[46]

The overlap of what I have tried to say with what Muñoz says is considerable. But for him the horizon, whether we feel it or not, whether we distill it from the past or not, can be glimpsed only rarely through the bars of the imprisoning present (especially through art). Although not more optimistic about the likelihood of these glimpses, I find through Jabès and Augustine a subtle difference in focus: The present is not rigid, and we do not hope for the future because now is so bad, but because the actual is such a limited sense of "is," because the possible is so vast *and so real*.

In fact, an uncertain otherwiseness and unknowability (a literal uncanniness) are distinguishing traits of the future.[47] Obviously, much depends on how we intend or understand futurity. An emphasis on the possible that is not-yet demands a future wholly unknowable. As Johnson glosses Derrida, "What or who comes remains necessarily undetermined as the condition of its coming. Thus the gift of the future is a monster, a promise, and as such both a chance and a threat, which explains why we must welcome, anticipate, and fear the gift."[48] Thus that which makes us seek a queer futurity, the hope of an explosion of possibility against the narrow straits of the present, must also risk the identities and alliances of those who seek. This is one of the dangerous sides of politics, that it must risk not only the present but also what makes it possible. When the bad things change, their butterfly wings may shift the identities even of those groups that have changed them. Yet as Jabès has Reb Makhaalim warn, "What is unchangeable is not eternal, but dead."[49] Queer identity is vulnerable, not just as all identity is, but especially so because it demands surviving.

The future is the tense of this, of any, possible. It promises, but no more than that. That is, it does not promise one thing or another, but is only the promising and is sustained only as promising (or, of course, threatening, but not as certain, seldom even as probable). Like memory, it is traced in the present, but in a manner even less certain than memory is—there are signs and hints, but they open in many directions. Our memories are haunted by what was. But they are also haunted by what has not been but could be, by the possible; we know, we have always known since we knew at all, that this that is might not be, might not have been. This is where both agony and happiness dwell, the possibilities both of having love and of losing it. Haunting is the half-memory, the occasional always-disappearing glimpse, the trace in the world. Divine haunting is the trace of pure promise, the opening: the promise given by the realization that there is something, rather than nothing; that something else and something more could yet come. In opening, only, are those things that cannot be within the closed: love, forgiveness, and even hope.

It is by possibility, by promise, that our time is haunted; it is promise, the promise of happiness, of home, that we remember. Jabès muses, "They said to themselves that the beginning was perhaps the innocent wager of a past nestled at the heart of a day to come: a past of mind and body—and God, its beginning."[50] The actuality of our time is haunted by its ontological beginning in the possible future; there is a will-be traced throughout it yet not contained within. We have never seen the future, never been there, never held it. It is fear of futurity in its utter unpredictability that makes us cling to the demands that it reproduce the present. It is desire that reaches forward to memory: The desire that reaches for happiness is far more of an epektasis than it is a satiable hunger. It is the very possible that holds happiness; it is foreclosure, advance refusal that cuts off possibility, that makes us melancholic or mournful or numb. The possible does not promise happiness, though: It only makes it possible. Or, more exactly, happiness itself is only promise; it is not a state of givenness and stasis. The divine in the world is the possible itself, an always promised that remains promising, unless we refuse its promise, unless it is closed. We may refuse to read it, but it haunts.

The temptation of foreclosure is pretty strong. The future, after all, is also terrifying. Who knows what might come? Destruction, as easily as utopia—more easily, it always seems. But if we allow queer haunting, possibility will not have been closed off in advance. The queer melancholy of Butler's theorizing is grounded in foreclosure, in what is taken away before it can be given, in the death of desire. The possible is fore-given; anything at all might unfold. This, in fact, is the sense of God that Nicholas of Cusa will develop out of his careful study of, among many others, Augustine—a God, as Keller emphasizes, that Cusa calls *posse ipsum*, the *possible itself*, the condition of any is-ness, the power and potential of being-otherwise.[51]

It is important, finally, that divine otherwiseness might unfold in the flesh. Augustine's is, for all of his struggles with the notion, an explicitly incarnated God; Jabès's God of the elegant abstractions of monotheism is no less remembered in place, in a face, in a tangible, holdable object. Sharon Betcher reminds us that at least for Christianity, flesh, such as that into which the word is made, must be a place of flux, which "differs with itself day to day," and "situates difference as preceding identity."[52] If difference precedes identity, to be is to be possibly otherwise. To accept flesh as a gift and a space of possibility is to face both the astonishing rewards of sensuousness and a perilous vulnerability. Possibility and loss do not come apart: The archaeology of unresolved grief is entangled in the opening of joy and hope. This possible haunting opens up the very self. It allows that both I and my desire may be—indeed, to some degree necessarily will be—otherwise than we are. Future panic includes loss of as-I-am, not only through development, but because we are vulnerable to what will come.

And yet this vulnerability and promise are divine. They echo in the double sense of a God through whom all is possible, and a possible through which the divine is explicated. It is a memory given to us by traces, in traces. It is a memory of what has never been: an originary remaining, never begun except as once-was, left to show us to-come. It is the trace of the future remaining. We are haunted by what could have been, to be sure, but also by what could yet be. We well remember. A God whom we remember well, remember as happiness—that which is purely desired—remember as face, place, object, and joy, gives us and is given as the possibilities that haunt the actual. The world as it is hints, tantalizes, and frightens with what it cannot quite show us, the world as it may be. The world as it was haunts us both with what has been and with what could have been; what we know of each was that it might have gone otherwise. If the remembered God is the nonforeclosure of the possible, is the possible, the open, the giving in the given, then all time is queer: always open to other than it is, as the very condition of its being.

## NOTES

1. Augustine, *Confessions*, trans. Henry Chadwick (Oxford: Oxford University Press, 1991), 10.25.36, 10.26.37, 10.20.29–33.
2. Edmond Jabès, *The Book of Resemblances*, vol. 3: *The Ineffaceable, the Unperceived*, trans. Rosmarie Waldrop (Middletown, Conn.: Wesleyan University Press, 1992), 79.
3. William B. Parsons, Diane Jonte-Pace, and Susan E. Henking, eds., "Mourning Religion: An Introduction," in *Mourning Religion* (Charlottesville: University of Virginia Press, 2008), 3.
4. Parsons, Jonte-Pace, and Henking, *Mourning Religion*, esp. 3–5. "The study of religion in the academy in both secular and religiously affiliated universities, represents a socially legitimated, institutionalized forum for the mourning of religion (or the melancholic response to the loss of religion) in contemporary culture," 5.
5. Jeanette Winterson, *Oranges Are Not the Only Fruit* (New York: Vintage Books, 1985), 165.

6. RingoTheCraftySquid, "I Miss God So Much," accessed at http://www.reddit.com/r/exchristian/comments/1ch3lj/i_miss_god_so_much/.
7. Friedrich Nietzsche, *The Gay Science*, trans. Walter Kaufmann (New York: Random House, 1991), §125.
8. Ibid.: "How were we able to drink up the sea? Who gave us the sponge to wipe away the horizon? What were we doing when we unchained the earth from its sun?"
9. Sigmund Freud, "Mourning and Melancholia," in *The Standard Edition of the Complete Psychological Works of Sigmund Freud*, ed. and trans. James Strachey, vol. 14 (London: Hogarth, 1957), 246.
10. Graziela Durante, "The Melancholy of Social Life: The Power of Loss in J. Butler," *Humana.Mente: Journal of Philosophical Studies* 12 (January 2010): 115.
11. Augustine, *Confessions*, 4.4.9.
12. Ibid., 4. 6.11.
13. Ibid., 4.10.15.
14. Judith Butler, "Melancholy Gender—Refused Identification," *Psychoanalytic Dialogues* 5, no. 2 (1995): 174.
15. Sigmund Freud, *The Ego and the Id*, 1923, trans. James Strachey (New York: W. W. Norton, 1990).
16. Butler, "Melancholy Gender," 167.
17. The interchanges that make us, as Butler also points out, keep us from being quite fully made, or finished; we are "undone by each other." Judith Butler, *Undoing Gender* (New York: Routledge, 2004), 19. I am grateful to Joe Marchal for this reference.
18. Jabès, *Book of Resemblances*, 60.
19. Not always: The case of beauty is a notable, if tricky, exception. But I have gone on about that in detail elsewhere, and shall for the purposes of this essay stick to the inward search.
20. Amy Hollywood, "Acute Melancholia," *Harvard Theological Review* 99, no. 4 (2006): 383: "The most striking feature of this pattern is its movement from external objects to their internalization by the devout person (the key component of melancholy for both medieval and modern theorists), and then their subsequent re-externalization in and on the body of the believer (the rendering visible of melancholic incorporation whereby the holy person becomes Christ to those around her)."
21. I would not wish to deny at all the ecstatic joys that can accompany pain. But happiness, for all its complexity, seems to me to have a subtly different relation to suffering, to demand suffering at a lower intensity than this ecstasy allows, even though we may speak of being "ecstatically happy." In any event, the sense that we are pulled by memory is experientially distinct from the ecstatic sense that we are broken out of selfhood.
22. Sigmund Freud, "A Note upon the Mystic Writing Pad," in *General Psychological Theory*, ed. Philip Rieff (New York: Touchstone, 2008), 208.
23. Ibid., 207.
24. Ibid., 210–11.

25. Paul Ricoeur and Peter Homans, "Afterword: Conversations on Freud, Memory, and Loss," in Parsons, Jonte-Pace, and Henking, *Mourning Religion*, 225.
26. David E. Johnson, "Time: For Borges," *New Centennial Review* 9, no. 1 (2009): 209–25, at 215 (citing Martin Hägglund, *Radical Atheism: Derrida and the Time of Life* [Stanford, Calif.: Stanford University Press, 2008], 18).
27. Ricoeur and Homans, "Afterword," 226.
28. Paul Ricoeur, *Memory, History, Forgetting*, trans. Kathleen Blamey and David Bellauer (Chicago: University of Chicago Press, 2009), 427.
29. Catherine Keller, *Cloud of the Impossible: Negative Theology and Planetary Entanglement* (New York: Columbia University Press, 2014), 282.
30. Heather Love, *Feeling Backward: Loss and the Politics of Queer History* (Cambridge, Mass.: Harvard University Press, 2007), 6.
31. Butler, "Melancholy Gender," 172: "When the prohibition against homosexuality is culturally pervasive, then the 'loss' of homosexual love is precipitated through a prohibition that is repeated and ritualized throughout the culture." See also Judith Butler, *The Psychic Life of Power: Theories in Subjection* (Stanford, Calif.: Stanford University Press, 1997), 185: "Social forms . . . have made certain kinds of loss ungrievable."
32. Butler, "Melancholy Gender," 179.
33. Ibid., 169.
34. Ibid.,171.
35. Carla Freccero's "Queer Spectrality," in her *Queer/Early/Modern* (Durham, N.C.: Duke University Press, 2006), has been especially influential.
36. Denise Kimber Buell, "Cyborg Memories: An Impure History of Jesus," *Biblical Interpretation* 18 (2010): 317.
37. Ibid., 337, citing Jacques Derrida, *Spectres of Marx: The State of the Debt, the Work of Mourning, and the New International*, trans. Peggy Kamuf (London: Routledge, 2006), 4–10.
38. Augustine, *Confessions*, 10.26.37.
39. Buell, "Cyborg Memories," 337.
40. Jabès, *Book of Resemblances*, 37.
41. Buell, "Cyborg Memories," 337, citing Avery Gordon, *Ghostly Matters: Haunting and the Sociological Imagination* (Minneapolis: University of Minnesota Press, 2008), 207.
42. Keller, *Cloud*, 2.
43. Gordon, *Ghostly Matters*, 8.
44. "Nor is the question how to cultivate hope in the face of despair, since such calls tend to demand the replacement of despair with hope. Rather, the question that faces us is how to make a future backward enough that even the most reluctant among us might want to live there." Love, *Feeling Backward*, 163.
45. See, paradigmatically, Lee Edelman, *No Future: Queer Theory and the Death Drive* (Durham, N.C.: Duke University Press, 2004).
46. José Esteban Muñoz, *Cruising Utopia: The Then and There of Queer Futurity* (New York: New York University Press, 2009), 1. I am indebted to Mary-Jane Rubenstein

for her helpful comments on this entire essay, but particularly for the gentleness with which she reminded me of my failure to invoke this important connection.

47. Norma Alarcón writes, "The drive behind the 'not yet/that's not it' position in [Chela] Sandoval's work is termed 'differential consciousness,' in [Audre] Lorde's work, 'difference,' and in [Jacques] Derrida's work *différance*." The divergence in the works "does not obviate their agreement on the 'not yet,' which points toward a future." Norma Alarcón, "Conjugating Subjects in the Age of Multiculturalism," in *Mapping Multiculturalism*, ed. Avery Gordon and Christopher Newfield (Minneapolis: University of Minnesota Press, 1996), 129 (cited in Juana Maria Rodriguez, "Queer Sociality and Other Sexual Fantasies," *GLQ* 17, no.: 2–3 [2011]: 333). Rodriguez adds, "Through an insistence on critique that nevertheless points to a 'not yet' of possibilities, refusal remains an operative mode of analysis that demands, rather than forecloses, futurity" (ibid.).

48. Johnson, "Time," 221, referring to Derrida, *Spectres*.

49. Jabès, *Book of Resemblances*, 88.

50. Ibid., 87.

51. See Keller, *Cloud*, 47–48, emphasizing *posse* as both power and potential. Citing Nicholas of Cusa, "On the Summit of Contemplation," in *Nicholas of Cusa: Selected Spiritual Writings*, ed. and trans. H. Lawrence Bond (New York: Paulist Press, 1997), 295.

52. Sharon V. Betcher, "Becoming Flesh of My Flesh: Feminist and Disability Theologies on the Edge of Posthumanist Discourse," *Journal of Feminist Studies in Religion* 26, no. 2 (2010): 111.

# *Response*: Queer Enfleshment

MARY-JANE RUBENSTEIN

On numerous occasions, I have had the chance to respond to Karmen MacKendrick's challenging and beautiful work, or to respond to her response to something I have written (often under the influence of her challenging and beautiful work). In the face of this complex and perennial entanglement, I admit to feeling both prideful and indulgent. Steeped in such sinful affect, I would like to think for a nonlinear moment within some of the possibilities MacKendrick's thinking opens, most recently in the preceding essay "Remember—When?" for something like a queer-incarnational apophasis.

Mashing up the inexhaustible *Confessions* of Saint Augustine with the rabbinical riot of Edmond Jabès, MacKendrick draws our attention to the oddball spatiality of a God who dwells in the placeless place of memory, both within and beyond the human self. The timing is off, too: God dwells both within and beyond us from "before" the beginning, and has therefore never yet been where God "is" when we go about remembering God. The God we remember is a God we haven't seen, whose traces are not particularly clear, who has never presented Godself, and whose presence therefore remains tantalizingly, frustratingly futural. Remembering God, we remember that which never was—for us, at least—and, in MacKendrick's words, "This never-was, only remembered (or already forgotten), always promising, offers us a distinctly queer temporality."

As modes of this queer temporality, MacKendrick offers the work of mourning, the mess of melancholia, and the hovering of haunting. In each of these modes, a past that never was—and as such one that always risks obliteration—opens out as possibility, specifically, as the possibility of a different kind of future. Here Nicholas of Cusa begins to rattle his chains: God may be *posse ipsum*, or possibility itself. This divine possibility entices MacKendrick, raveling her with Catherine Keller in an interdetermined effort to relate the nonrelational and enflesh the apophatic.[1] It is this "strange flesh" I would like briefly to pursue here, in order to ask, on the one hand, what is queer about this theological temporality and, on the other, what might be theological about queer temporality. These are effectively the same question posed from two different directions so that we might home in on the elusive figure of divine enfleshment.

In MacKendrick's rendering, the possible becomes a ghostly not-yet: a might-yet-be that haunts as a past-that-never-was to disturb a self-satisfied present. The possible is not here, not now, and as such remains possible, portending an undecidable terrain of transformation or devastation that has never been—and so is never quite—present. In its very gesture of negation, however, apophasis collides with the incarnate: "It is important," MacKendrick reminds us, "that divine otherwiseness might unfold in the flesh." Examples of this divine unfolding include the gift of the Torah, the memory of a temple, the memory of another temple, the infinite in the face of the other, and of course, for some, the Nazarene. But what is the mode of this enfleshment? Does it remain, well, modal? Granted the importance that divinity might fleshily unfold, is it also important that it does? Or that it has? Or that it will? Does the possible give way, in other words, to the actual? Or perhaps more subtly, might the possible—or does it, has it, will it—appear in and through the actual, and if so, in what kind of actual?

In an essay titled "Promiscuous Incarnation," Laurel Schneider suggests that the history of Christian thought is one of the "gradual and inexorable erosion" of its central profession.[2] The "good news," to put it bluntly, is that God has shown up, that divinity is right here in the flesh, that the kingdom—as Nietzsche reminds us with mounting frustration[3]—is not in some inaccessible realm, but "at hand." And yet the moment the councils and fathers acknowledge such enfleshment, they rein it back in: God is there, yes, but only "there": only in that one man, born to a girl in a barn in occupied Palestine, a perfect sacrifice for the whole world. So he lived for a while and then died for us all, even "us" in our not-yet-ness, and as such remains the only site—the only-ever site—of incarnation.

For Schneider, Christianity's recoiling from the incarnate is a function of the West's long-lived enchantment with abstract singularity and immutable oneness. By virtue of the nature of bodies, she argues, incarnation disrupts everything an imperial power might want from its God: "The coming to flesh of divinity disrupts the smooth otherness of the divine, its separateness from the changeable stuff of earth, its abhorrence of rot, its innocence of death, and its ignorance of life or desire."[4] Flesh, moreover, "is indiscriminate in its porous interconnection with everything,"[5] so insofar as divinity becomes flesh, it becomes the permanent disruption of godly abstraction and sovereign singularity. The scandal of particularity, then, is that the particular can't hold: The porosity of flesh means incarnation can only be promiscuous.

Glimpsing this danger, the very tradition that proclaims incarnation denies it in the same breath, producing theologies, liturgies, and ecclesiologies that "honor incarnation in terms of the body of Jesus but force actual bodies in the church, and outside of it, onto the bottom rungs of a tortured hierarchy of being."[6] In its predictable privileges of light over dark, male over female, solvent over unemployed, monogamous over promiscuous, and reproductive over perverse, this "tortured hierarchy" manages to undo all the work even a narrowly construed incarnation might have done, what with its small, despised, and colonized divinity, conceived by an unwed teenager.

Divinity *was supposed to have been* of and for the marginalized. What sort of queer temporality is that?

Faced with the never-was on the one hand and the incarnate on the other, I am reminded of José Muñoz's *Cruising Utopia*, which opens by appealing to the queer as a figure of radical alterity. "Queerness is not yet here," Muñoz begins; queerness, in fact, would be the tireless critique of the "here" in its unlivability for minoritarian subjects.[7] Queerness would be the tireless rejection of the here and now for the sake of a utopian future. Like MacKendrick, then, Muñoz appeals to a Derridean-inflected "hauntology as a powerful mechanism" for queer history and queer futures.[8] Attending as it does to the never-present and perennially disavowed, spectrality might help us listen for that which never quite *is*: the racially subordinated, the sexually marginalized, the racially sexualized, the economically invisible, the juridically unrecognizable.

Like ghosts, queer subjects *aren't*, quite. And yet of course they aren't *not*. Complicating our negativity, queer desires and practices do not exactly have the status of "never-was"; rather, they occupy all sorts of spookier dreamscape modalities like "almost was," or "would-have-been," or "no-longer conscious," or "was, -ish; you know, in a what-the-hell-was-that sort of way." For MacKendrick as for Muñoz, queerness is both not-yet and enfleshed, and this "both" makes the enfleshment fall irremediably short of a full-out, bells-and-whistles ontology. Or it exposes such ontologies as puffed-up, uninteresting, plodding . . . straight and minivanned.

It is this sort of queer enfleshment that Muñoz allows us to glimpse in his reading of Frank O'Hara's "Having a Coke with You."[9] For Muñoz, the poem testifies to a not-here, not-now that is also right in the middle of the ordinary: a "concrete utopia."[10] Nothing dramatic happens in this poem; there are no angels or trumpets or statues. In fact, the statues in particular seem ridiculous in the midst of mortal lovers walking, barely touching, breathing together before the dried paint and the chiseled stone, sharing a drink that more serious types would reject as too lowbrow, too corporate, or too corrosive of septic systems. Queer art, for Muñoz, performs a kind of "future in the present,"[11] enacting queer temporality in its fleeting actualization of a modest utopia. So we are not yet queer, and yet there it just was, *as* not-quite, in its odd apophatic enfleshment. Right there.

Incarnation has not yet been what it was. The kingdom is not what it is. The poor, perverse, and persecuted have yet to be what they already are, and yet somehow—we know this—divinity shows up where it is most denied, at the bottom ranks of that undead Great Chain. So to mourn the dead God is one thing. It is, in fact, to mourn one thing, which *was* back then and is no more and, yes, may be, but who would want him back? Enfleshment is different, I think. To be haunted by incarnation would be to live on the lookout for that which never really was, which calls all that is into question and remains in the realm of the possible, and which precisely *as* possible, in its promiscuous not-quiteness, just might be all over the place.

## NOTES

1. See Karmen MacKendrick, *Divine Enticement: Theological Seductions* (New York: Fordham University Press, 2012), 209, 17; Catherine Keller, *The Cloud of the Impossible: Negative Theology and Planetary Entanglement* (New York: Columbia University Press, 2014), 87–126.
2. Laurel C. Schneider, "Promiscuous Incarnation," in *The Embrace of Eros: Bodies, Desires, and Sexuality in Christianity*, ed. Margaret D. Kamitsuka (Minneapolis: Fortress Press, 2010), 232; cf. Laurel C. Schneider, *Beyond Monotheism: A Theology of Multiplicity* (New York: Routledge, 2008).
3. Friedrich Nietzsche, "The Anti-Christ," in *The Twilight of the Idols and the Anti-Christ; or, How to Philosophize with a Hammer*, ed. Michael Tanner (New York: Penguin, 1990), 153.
4. Schneider, "Promiscuous Incarnation," 232.
5. Ibid., 241–42.
6. Ibid., 232.
7. José Esteban Muñoz, *Cruising Utopia: The Then and There of Queer Futurity* (New York: New York University Press, 2009), 1, 27.
8. Ibid., 42.
9. Ibid., 5–9.
10. Ibid., 3.
11. Ibid., 49.

# In Search of Queer Theology Lost

MARK D. JORDAN

1

"Time-and-again [*longtemps*] we have endured, and today suffer still, a Victorian regime."[1] You recall the opening of Foucault's *History of Sexuality*. With its first word, the short book alludes to the beginning of Proust's *In Search of Lost Time*, that torrent of written memories about loves, their captivating intensities and evaporating fulfillments.

Foucault declares an interest in how languages applied to sexed bodies mark time while pretending to be timeless. *History of Sexuality* is not a history of sex, as you know, but a narrative of the invasive fictions that "explain" bodies in order to manage them from birth to death. Those fictions include both the theories of state-sponsored science and the slogans of sexual liberation. Foucault's opening page juxtaposes Proust's experiments in scribbling affect with the bombastic certainty of every political science of sex. Do I need to say that Foucault sides with Proust, writes with Proust?

*History of Sexuality 1* names other exemplars for its writing: There is Diderot's satire, *The Indiscreet Genitals*, and the eleven volumes of *My Secret Life*, recorded perhaps by Henry Spencer Ashbee, pedantic indexer of pornographic books.[2] Still Foucault begins and ends with Proust's writing of lost time.

How has the history of sexuality been lost? Foucault has already explained that it is now concealed by a self-righteous tale of liberation. It is lost more importantly just the way time is lost in Proust before "Marcel" begins to compose the narrative that ends with the resolve to write. Like unnarrated time, the history of sexuality waits in a sort of latency—ready to spring as involuntary memory, but even more to call out obscurely for authors.

2

Time and again I tried to put together the reading list for a course on queer theology, chiefly Christian. I added texts only to take them off. I begged recommendations, studied other course plans, even—I blush—even followed the pimping suggestions of Amazon. Still the reading list would not settle into the shape of a story.

I realized soon enough that I was trying to tell too many stories at once. I had a tale about the succession of *attitudes*: Some Christian theologians have moved in fifty years from mere toleration of same-sex desire to its ethical affirmation, then its "liberation," and finally its inclusion in the bright spectrum of identities. I also wanted to reconstruct the series of supposed *objects* in this theology: It has moved from homosexuals and inverts to homophiles and lesbians and gays to the mismatched elements of various acronyms like "LGBT," only to reach—at last—the queer, an object that claims dogmatically to be no object at all.

There was something more in my vacillation over the reading list: This very impulse to tell *stories* about queer theology. As if theological thinking about sex traced such simple plots of progress. As if it were possible to separate off the theological or religious from the rest of what we might as well call "queer life." As if the tentative establishment of queer theology as an academic subfield entailed that its progress could now be summarized and its prospects confidently predicted.

I could not settle the list because I secretly doubted that we had written enough queer theology to be summarizing its progress, much less tabulating its conclusions. I wanted to teach it not as achieved result, but as uncertain attempt. Or to go back over all the writing to ask, "What did we miss?"

Queer theology is not a trophy somehow mislaid. It is now "lost" as Proust's memories were in the moment before he tasted the prompting madeleine. The episodes, the claims, the passions of queer theology encircle us, waiting for us to recognize that we must learn to write.

## 3

I could say that queer theology is Christianity's long postponed encounter with all the specters of pleasure.

Or it is the effort to represent bodies that have been denied the right to show the creaturely gift of their sex.

Or it is Christianity having second thoughts about surrendering to modern biopower.

Or queer theology returns to the gospel prophecy of bodies subtracted from strategies of useful reproduction.

Or it refuses the gender binary in the no-name of an ungenderable God, who nonetheless begets.

Or it reminds its readers stubbornly that the erotic is more than a storefront in the mall of commodity fetishes.

Each of these descriptions by topic is true enough, yet taken together they tell less than half the story. They leave out the relation of topic to shape, of content to form. They neglect queer theology's very queer looks.

4

The revelation of an incarnate god demands that its believers honor form. So I can never separate the question, What might make Christian theology queer?, from the question, How does queer theology tell, persuade, move?

I am not looking for an approved list of genres to replace the guild-issued lists we already have. I hope instead for the recognition that queer theology must perform new "stylizations" (Foucault again).[3]

5

The obvious place to look for styles is in the arts and literature of "queer communities" (while putting pressure on both those words). Indeed, the most convincing queer theology written so far counts in its pedigree pulp novels, dirty pictures, criminal cabaret acts, the dance floor, the music festival, the gestures and costumes of a hundred fabulous liturgies.

6

I turn by habit to the queer forms lumped together as "camp."

Perhaps more successfully than the queer, camp refuses definition. If you try to define camp, you show that you do not understand the first thing about it. The first thing is that you cannot separate camp's form from its content. I turn back to Susan Sontag's much abused "Notes on Camp" because whatever she got wrong, she got the first thing right.[4]

Sontag records her notes in movements of numbered aphorisms, punctuated by quotations from Oscar Wilde. The citations of Wilde are one sort of camp gesture; the numbering, another. With the numbers, Sontag camps the genre of the manifesto. She connects it to the modernist collage or pastiche.[5] She follows camp in abandoning the ruses of continuity for the splice or jump, the surprising juxtaposition or constellation. These devices are also hallmarks of what we call artistic and literary "modernism." Sontag's piece makes clear that her introduction to camp was part of an education in modernism—and that both were undertaken within circles of sexual dissidents.

Sexual stigma is a curriculum that teaches the falsity of the most potent vocabularies. To dissent from societal judgments about what is shameful, filthy, diseased, or demonic is to yearn for another language, another itinerary of beauties. Camp is one way to make beauty from what others call ugly, to invent speech out of curses and spitting.

7

Refusing to define camp, Sontag resorts to lists of examples.[6] (Recalling a page in Borges, Foucault notes that some lists provoke laughter by unlikely juxtaposition.[7] Of course, other lists are like the shots of a sequence in film or the succession of movements in a dance.) I too have taken to jotting down lists of the anticipations of queer theology.

First on my lists I usually put Sontag's essay. Coy about religion, the piece displays queer pieties—not least in quoting Oscar Wilde as scripture. In her frequently misunderstood claim that camp is not political, Sontag criticizes the Left that promulgates theses and marches under slogans. To say that camp is not "political" means for Sontag that it fails at dogmatic seriousness, refusing moralized certainty.[8] She places camp instead next to serious art, the best practice of attention to the mysteries of the word.

Next I add to my lists something like Samuel Delany's "science fiction" novel, *Triton*.[9] In his heterotopic narrative, Delany locates the queer in the resolution to risk one's body on the torsion between any fixed linguistic categories and the art of sexed life. The best hope for flourishing on his imagined satellite is offered by artistic-religious groups that "stylize" bodies at the edges of speech. I love this novel, but I also use it to stand for the dozens of literary works that have imagined sexed bodies otherwise, not least in relation to religion. Instead of *Triton* I sometimes put *The Left Hand of Darkness* or *Bloodchild* or—reaching further back into other canons—Djuna Barnes's *Nightwood* and John Rechy's *City of Night* and William S. Burroughs's *Cities of the Red Night*.

My lists tend to run on, so let me mention only two other examples. One is Kiki and Herb's "Total Eclipse of the Heart," as recorded in Carnegie Hall.[10] Justin Bond in character as Kiki, lounge chanteuse, performs variations on a pop hit, comic by repetition and exaggeration, pierced by raw feeling. Kiki juxtaposes Bonnie Tyler's lyrics with other bits of text. At the beginning, there are lines from Pat Benatar. At the end, in a transport indistinguishable from ecstasy, Kiki quotes The Byrds' "Turn Turn Turn," Joni Mitchell's "You Turn Me On, I'm a Radio," and William Butler Yeats's "The Second Coming," only to end with the lung-shredding lines, "Kiki loves you, / Kiki needs you, / Kiki would die for you." Kiki is beautiful with the grotesque insistence of a virgin martyr or a crucified God. Camp pastiche as vicarious atonement—because it is, dear, it is.

My lists of anticipations of queer theology usually end with some pages from Marcella Althaus-Reid. Other authors come to mind, many of them contributors to this volume. But I think especially of Althaus-Reid, because I can see most clearly in her books the unhappy struggle to write queer theology within recognizably academic forms.

8

For Marcella Althaus-Reid, queer theology presents "the challenge of a theology where sexuality and loving relationships are not only important theological issues but experiences [that] un-shape Totalitarian Theology . . . while re-shaping the theologians."[11] So "queer Theology is . . . a first person theology: diasporic, self-disclosing, autobiographical and responsible for its own words."[12]

When Althaus-Reid says that queer theology is "self-disclosing" and "autobiographical," she does not mean that theologians should parade around in the latest identities (to measure time for a moment by the issuing of commodities). She held in suspicion the approved performances to which imperial powers assign the roles of noble savage or ransomed victim. She was alert to the frauds of earnest testimony. Althaus-Reid saw that some claims of testimony, some appeals to personal experience, evade the difficulty of writing human lives. No tableau vivant of coming out—however sincere—can capture an embodied life in a final representation. No matter how much my pulse races, how deeply I blush, how tearfully glad I feel in speaking at last (I have felt all that and more), "coming out" is not the final revelation of my inner truth. It is, at best, one move in a strategy of resistance. At worst, it is just another script distributed by biopower.

This is a hard truth. It is the beginning of queer theology. To refuse the metaphysics of identity is to reject the reduction of language that identities require. Socially assigned identities are positivist fictions attached to randomly abstracted human differences. We cling to the identities assigned to us in part to make sense of the suffering inflicted on us through them. To admit how much they are standard fictions, to admit how differently our differences could be valued and must be named—it can seem that we topple our lives from their foundations and abandon our martyred dead. But when it rejects both the metaphysics and the syntax of identity, queer theology discovers unsuspected life among the dead.

Queer theology cannot be just a matter of cheering on or cheering up certain identities. It begins in the refusal to take identities as the basic units for a literal description. The sharpest protest we can make against the fictions of biopower is to deny again and again that a human life can ever be identified.

9

Marcella Althaus-Reid hoped to write "[a] theology [that] understands that the dislocation of sexual constructions goes hand in hand with strategies for the dislocation of hegemonic political and economic agendas."[13] In order to reform political power, we have to dislocate "sexual constructions," which include the "idealism and romantic visions of femininity" still perpetuated by some feminism and the squirming reticence about sex in some liberation theology. If Althaus-Reid was less explicitly critical of LGBT theologies, she was not at all interested in so-called queer theologies that want to join the prevailing identity systems instead of undoing them. Never shy about words, Althaus-Reid says that queer theology must be a demonology. Its starting point is "the knowledge of rebellious spirits," of refused identity performances, so that it may "[accuse] the legal sacred order of being constructed and not natural."[14]

Althaus-Reid's reference to demonology is not just a fiery inversion of official creeds. It is another literary allusion. In Pierre Klossowski's *Bath of Diana*, the Demon is the intermediary power of simulation required both to represent and to conceal divinity for human eyes. It is the Demon who bares and covers the body of the goddess Diana when she is caught bathing by the hunter Actaeon.[15] With this term, Althaus-Reid reminds her readers that Klossowski is one of her writing partners.[16]

I could say that queer theology as demonology is an art for endowing gods with bodies that we then uncover through desire.

Or queer theology is a sentimental reeducation in divine beauties that we were earlier taught to despise.

It took Julian of Norwich decades to decipher the beauty of Christ's bleeding face once seen. She deciphered by rewriting.

## 10

Marcella Althaus-Reid is a complicated writer with many voices. We remember some more easily than others. We recall the lemon vendors or the drag-queen Guadalupes or the scandalous little girl who refused to kneel where she was supposed to at her first confession. We forget Althaus-Reid's voices on other pages, pages that cite Klossowski or the Marquis de Sade or Kathy Acker.

Althaus-Reid turns to experimental literature not despite her politics but in order to articulate her politics. She feels how deeply power is written into our languages and imaginations, how it overwrites our skin. She sees how much will be required to open even a little space for writing otherwise. So Althaus-Reid recalls difficult languages to interfere with power's familiar scripts. She practices "loving solidarity with ambiguity and . . . the inconceivable in itself."[17] She declares, "If Queer holiness has a characteristic, it may be its unrepresentability. . . . Holiness is always the holiness of the Other."[18]

I take these as Althaus-Reid's aspirations for her writing. Sometimes, on some pages, she writes into them. Then, on other pages, she falls back toward academic habit or appears to give in to demands that queer theology be immediately useful.

I do believe that writing theology is something more than the manipulation of texts fancied by the powerful. (Theology is not a parlor game for courtiers.) I also believe that writing theology is something more than dusting off forgotten curiosities. (Theology is not antiquing.) The queer theology I await wants to change the world by reshaping subjects in community. For that very reason, it can never consent to be a "progressive" version of Stalin's socialist realism: It cannot be reduced to cartoons of the party line, even if the line is "liberation."

## II

Every reader remembers Marcella Althaus-Reid's stories. Few readers notice the techniques of her large-scale narratives. Kathy Acker provides the clue here. She points a reader back to Bataille or Burroughs and sideways to the "New Narrative."

Directions for an experiment in reading: Take Althaus-Reid's comments on Acker not as academic exposition but as one writer appreciating another, one novelist acknowledging another's inspiration. Pair Althaus-Reid's use of Sade with Acker's. Notice that she shares with Acker techniques of cut-up, graphic depiction, apocalyptic periodization, hallucinogenic autobiography. Acker places herself in a line of writers that goes back to Delany and Burroughs, to queer science fiction and the Beat antinovel.[19] Put Althaus-Reid in that same lineage.

A second experiment: Read *Indecent Theology* and *Queer God* as examples of "New Narrative," that queer literary technique that wanted to unite high theory with erotic recollection and political advocacy. Its practitioners conceived an autobiography of "daydreams, nightdreams, the act of writing, the relationship to the reader, the meeting of flesh and culture, the self as collaboration, the self as disintegration, the gaps, inconsistencies and distortions, the enjambments of power, family, history and language."[20]

After repeating the experiments until they change your reading, go back to Althaus-Reid's expressed hope for a queer theology that would be "diasporic, self-disclosing, autobiographical and responsible for its own words."[21] To be responsible for queer words under the linguistic regime of biopower is to recognize the impossibility of literal self-reporting. Biopower owns the copyright on literal autobiography. It regulates in advance all reports certified as accurate. A queer self can only be "told" in dis-integrations, in-consistencies, language twisted around bodies until it rips. Queer theology needs the techniques of some "new narrative" because queer living will not fit into the acceptable narrative forms—into the little plots of "sexual hygiene" or "psychosexual maturity" or profitable domesticity.

12

If you cannot tell your own life, you certainly cannot tell divine action in it—or describe the divine image glimpsed through it. (The reverse is also true.) Yet so much of theology is written as if it were easier to describe God's essence than to give an account of a single evening's desires.

13

The task of narration would not be so urgent if queer theology were more fluent. Still a theology only recently allowed to speak has to exert itself to find a voice, its voice, in the middle of things. It cannot drowse in the contentment of commenting on the familiar texts, the established words—or wear itself out just in their critique. Critique in theology is a prelude to composition—which is not the same as "confession" or "construction" or "system" or even satisfying "story."

Where are Kierkegaard's pseudonyms now that we really need them? And what would it be to write *Queer Stages on Life's Way*?

14

I could say that "queer theology" has sometimes meant the peculiar game of trying to narrate the most elusive desires in the clumsiest genres—and then declaring victory.

15

Everything I have written so far is prologue to a (new) narrative I meant to write. In it, I would remember various incidents that promised some queer stylization of language around human bodies animated or undone by the divine.

On a spring evening in 1997, Gayle Rubin took me on a walking tour of the then remaining leather bars in the SoMa neighborhood of San Francisco. I undertook the pilgrimage—as, a boy, I walked the cobblestones up to the basilica of Our Lady of Zapopan. Gayle told memories attached to the buildings, block after block.

Above the Eucharistic table at MCC San Francisco on Eureka Street, a painting illustrated one of Harper's monologues from *Angels in America*, the one about souls floating up to repair the hole in the ozone layer. Some evenings when it came time to share the consecrated bread, I watched souls gather around the table. I am not talking about the painting.

There is a Japanese dance form, *butoh*, developed after the American occupation of Japan. At least one of its founders was a man most Americans then would have called "queer." The dance distorts every convention for beautiful movement. Its grotesque figures alternate precise stillness with convulsion or riot. I watched the old master, Kazuo Ohno, perform "Admiring La Argentina," his *hommage* to a tango queen. Is this drag or camp?, I wondered. Aren't those all too provincial categories for something more important and more obscure? When dancing, Ohno says, he holds hands with the dead.[22] What is the difference between camp and spirit-possession or an ancient oracle's trance?

One Sunday, I gathered with friends to celebrate a eucharist, that memorial prescribed on the eve of a death. We cut up the consecration narrative to share it out. A person of blurred gender chose the words, "Take, eat, this is my Body, which is given for you." *They* had a pack of cigarettes rolled up in one sleeve of *their* t-shirt. I had seen *them* wear that shirt while tending bar. I remembered Althaus-Reid saying, "There are many sexual dissenters whose theological community is made up of the gathering of those who go to gay bars with rosaries in their pockets."[23]

I heard a friend recall once again a legendary memorial service for a congregant who died of AIDS. The man left instructions that the service should end with all those present smashing his precious collection of Fiestaware. Because, my friend said, the losses are real. Because you have to summon your rage to get through some days. Because grand opera fancies mad scenes.

## 16

In my other narrative, having told these stories, I would say to you: Some of those things did not happen that way. Actually, given the limits of my writing, of our languages, not one of them happened *that way*.

What does it matter? The distinction between fact and fiction is too crude for theology, especially when we write it to resist the tidy certainties of this world's cruel powers.

## 17

I said that the episodes I meant to narrate "promised" queer theology. I was thinking that queer theology could rewrite them as protreptic, both exhortation and prophecy, that it could change their verbs from indicative to optative. I wanted to emphasize that writing memory is always imagining other lives and (sometimes) beginning to enact them.

Althaus-Reid says that queer arts and literatures offer a "necessary utopia," another place for recognizing queer holiness.[24] So I took something very like that string of episodes as a sufficient syllabus for my course.

18

Near the end of my other narrative, the one I meant to write, I would pursue questions like these: Once we've found queer theology, so far as it can be found in mortal time, what do we expect it to do for us?

Do we expect it to ease our lives (if only by explaining them), to excuse God's silence, to reform the world, to hasten the eschaton?

Then: How do you say what you're waiting for?

## A POSTSCRIPT, OR AFTER-WRITING

My essay really did start with reflection on my own difficulty in putting together a syllabus for a course titled "Queer Theology / Queer Religions." In the course, I wanted to return to the desires that had animated the project of queer theology—desires lost or frustrated by the rapid absorption of queer theology into academic business-as-usual but still awaiting enactment, if not fulfillment, in bolder writing.

One thing that struck me in trying to put together the syllabus was the prominence in queer theology of the genre of the anthology. Many of us had been writing short pieces: Our articles sketched programs or made promises or offered predictions for the future—and not the eschatological future, but the future of some as yet uncompleted masterwork. There are good excuses to be made for our writing that way. The project of "queer theology" is recent—the project, not the questions behind the project. The project is recent, the number of those able to join it few, the resources scant, the professional penalties still high, and so on.

The project of queer theology is also ambitious—perhaps fantastically ambitious. Its subject matter is both elusive and invested with the energies of the reigning powers. The topics treated in queer theology are protected by potent political magic, not least within "progressive" communities.

Still, having recited all the excuses, I found myself feeling that my own failure to write better resulted as well from my conceiving the writing wrongly. I was still using the wrong genres or pursuing the wrong compositional goals or simply misunderstanding what needed to be written.

So I returned to familiar problems with the phrase "queer theology." I recalled the endless multiplication of questions around the term "queer," which are only evaded when we tack it on to the impossible acronym, LGBTQ. I reviewed the troubles in the syntactic relation of "queer" to "theology": Is this theology done about queers, by queers, for queers, in order to produce queers for the first time? What is it supposed after all to do for anyone? Then I came to the term "theology."

The jolt supposed to be produced by speaking of queer theology is roughly like the jolt of saying "indecent theology" or "the queer God." It is the jolt of putting the stigmatized next to the holy. We are to imagine a stable or standard theology, a reigning orthodoxy, that is disrupted by the queer. But I am now more interested in the disruptions that run in the opposite direction. For example, I am interested in how liturgies with theological characters can move beyond the angry certainties of identity politics. I want to see whether the claim of even so tired a theological word as "mystery" or "apophasis" can still contest the flattening of human lives into sums of social identities. Most of all I hope that the enormous range of theological genres can remind us of the challenge in the composition we undertake.

In this essay, I press on the difficulty of description. Although theology is neither only nor mainly descriptive, description ought not to be taken for granted in it. Indeed, writing itself—the wager of composition—is typically forgotten in academic genres. We may worry about the length of our papers, their clarity or coherence. Rarely do we fret over how their language—on its many levels—works to produce its truth effects, much less its teaching or persuading.

The hope of queer theological writing is not only to produce less clichéd descriptions or more helpful evaluations—though we should be grateful for either. The hope is that we will be able to make pedagogical structures, text-schools, scripts for ethical performance, that enable someone to hear more than we know to say. I have spoken elsewhere of theological texts as scenes of instruction.[25] They teach not by reciting propositions or propounding rules or even marshaling arguments. They work instead by narrating teaching relations in a way that activates them. That is what I mean by scene of instruction. I could just as well have called theological texts drag acts: Theological writing is grace-drag or beatitude-drag or theiosis-drag. Theological writers lip-sync the announcements of angels or the colloquies of heaven in order to speak as their future selves.

Here, now, I am not sure that Christian theology knows as yet what to say about God or sex or gender, much less God-and-sex-and-gender. Still it may be able to make textual structures that provoke or evoke a character who might eventually learn a language useful in the future, on that "one day" in "another economy of bodies and pleasures."[26] My effort in this piece was to put together some pieces of a text-structure that could lead its readers—or rather its writer—toward the usage of future languages not audible now except as the silence of an empty stage cleared within certain texts.

Queer theology is not a field, much less a project ready for summary. It is a cue—a prompt for a writing exercise. The prompt can take different forms:

"Write as if Christianity or Judaism or Islam had got sexual relations mostly wrong."
"Write as if your best chance of glimpsing the divine is offered by the most stigmatized genders."
"Write as if all sexual identities were fleeting historical artifacts."

Choose your cue or conceive another. Remember that the point of the writing exercise is formal experimentation—the effort to find or invent the shape that could invoke a queer theology of the future.

## NOTES

1. Michel Foucault, *Histoire de la sexualité, 1: La volonté de savoir* (Paris: NRF / Gallimard, 1976), 9. I follow Richard Howard's proposal in rendering the Proustian *longtemps*. James Grieve offers instead "Time was." Both versions give crucial prominence to time.
2. Foucault, *Histoire de la sexualité 1*, 30–31 (Ashbee), 101–4 (Diderot).
3. For Foucault on "stylization," see Mark D. Jordan, *Convulsing Bodies: Religion and Resistance in Foucault* (Stanford, Calif.: Stanford University Press, 2015), 152–60.
4. Susan Sontag, "Notes on Camp," *Partisan Review* 31, no. 4 (1964): 515–30. I follow the corrected version in her *Against Interpretation and Other Essays* (New York: Farrar, Straus and Giroux, 1966), 275–92.
5. Ibid., 287, no. 36.
6. Ned Rorem reports that Sontag took many of the examples from the Parisian apartment of Elliott Stein, sometime collaborator of Kenneth Anger. See Ned Rorem, *Knowing When to Stop: A Memoir* (New York: Simon and Schuster, 1994), 470.
7. Michel Foucault, *Les mots et les choses: Une archéologie des sciences humaines* (Paris: Gallimard 1966), 7.
8. Compare Sontag, "Notes on Camp," 277, no. 2; with 288, no. 41; and 290, no. 51.
9. Samuel R. Delany, *Triton* (New York: Bantam Books, 1976), republished with a foreword by Kathy Acker as *Trouble on Triton: An Ambiguous Heterotopia* (Hanover, N.H.: Wesleyan University Press / University Press of New England, 1996).
10. Kiki and Herb, *Kiki & Herb Will Die for You at Carnegie Hall* (Die For You LLC / Evolver, 2005), disk 2, track 12.
11. Marcella Althaus-Reid, *The Queer God* (London: Routledge, 2003), 8. Compare the later remarks on not trying to improve theology only by "some addenda such as gender and sexual equality" (148).
12. Ibid., 8.
13. Marcella Althaus-Reid, *Indecent Theology: Theological Perversions in Sex, Gender, and Politics* (London: Routledge, 2000), 6.
14. Althaus-Reid, *Queer God*, 134. Compare the disruption of "citational processes" with regard to identity (139).
15. Pierre Klossowski, *Le bain de Diane* (Paris: J.-J. Pauvert, 1956).

16. See especially Althaus-Reid, *Queer God*, 63–75, but also throughout.
17. Althaus-Reid, *Queer God*, 138, in a passage on masturbation.
18. Ibid., 154.
19. See, for example, Acker, "Foreword," in Delany, *Trouble on Triton*, ix–xii.
20. Robert Glück, "Long Note on New Narrative," *Narrativity*, no. 1, https://www.sfsu.edu/~newlit/narrativity/issue_one/gluck.html.
21. Althaus-Reid, *Queer God*, 8.
22. For dancing with the dead, Kazuo Ohno, "Workshop Words," in Kazuo Ohno and Yoshito Ohno, *Kazuo Ohno's World from Without and Within*, trans. John Barrett (Middletown, Conn.: Wesleyan University Press, 2004), especially 267–69, 274–77, 279–81. On his performance of "Admiring La Argentina," see the remarks by Yoshito Ohno, 143–69.
23. Althaus-Reid, *Queer God*, 2.
24. Ibid., 153, for the phrase.
25. "Missing Scenes," *Harvard Divinity Bulletin* 38, no. 3–4 (2010): 58–67.
26. Foucault, *Histoire de la sexualité 1*, 211.

# *Response*: To Mark Jordan's "In Search of Queer Theology Lost"

CATHERINE KELLER

"In Search of Queer Theology Lost" opens by way of the opening of *The History of Sexuality I*, in which Foucault plays on the opening of Proust's *In Search of Lost Time*. So we should not be surprised when Mark Jordan lets us know, many pages later, that "everything I have written so far is prologue to a (new) narrative I meant to write." If his writing has been eluding his intention, queer theology, hey, theology tout court, may have to follow him on this prolegomenal peregrination. "Time-and-again."

Finding the way will be hard to distinguish from getting lost. We might get our bearings by asking: How did queer theology get lost when it has barely had a chance to find itself? For Mark Jordan the question folds into the bigger query: "How did the history of sexuality get lost?" Hidden, as Foucault contends, by its own "self-righteous tale of liberation"? But wasn't getting lost, going wayward, errant, always its best chance? Getting off the straight and narrow? If straight time—unilinear, teleological, or predictable even in its randomness—is the negative measure of queer time, what kind of aporetic temporality does Jordan's very search perform?

He does not romanticize lostness. But queer theology has such a short history that I did wince to read that it "has sometimes meant the peculiar game of trying to narrate the most elusive desires in the clumsiest genres—and then declaring victory." Perhaps every fresh burst of emancipatory discourse, and certainly those in theology, compensates for its vulnerability with some delusional proclamation of success. Yet queer theory as such, including its nascent theology, surely exists only in the *Wirkungsgeschichte* and the debt of Foucault, allergic to every triumphal identity. Of course no queer critique of LGBTQI subjectivities mirrors any other postidentitarianism. But I am reminded of feminist autocritique, as we (that includes me) keep working free of embarrassingly clunky essences of identity, fallacies of misplaced concreteness, phalluses of premature certainty, where ethical simplification sabotages not only the subject's complexity but its heterogeneous alliances. If for Foucault sexuality is lost by the "self-righteous tale of liberation," Jordan heads off that tale within queer theology itself. He offers critique as autodeconstruction, as loving struggle.

Still, I wonder: Mustn't we honor bits of actual progress that keep "progressive" politics possible? Just when is it that the due celebration of a fragile and difficult historic achievement, or the acknowledgment of a tormentingly hard-won step in an unfinished liberation, turns self-righteous? Aren't there explosions of rightness that have not and will not always already have morphed into the victory march? But when they do, their progress does indeed mark straight time.

Let me rephrase Jordan's first question: How is the "loss of the history of sexuality" correlated with the "loss of queer theology"? Sexuality in some historic form or another is really old, vastly predating the species. Queer theology remains really young, compared not only to a mammalian species but to other species of theology. And yet lost already? Is Jordan's writing of loss a way of *finding* what once was lost—a way less prone to the straight conversionism of amazing grace, but not lacking its own gracious maze?

Already in *The Invention of Sodomy*, Jordan has deftly exposed the intersection of the lost history of sexuality with the current emergence of queer theology. With his fierce respect for the textual archive, he tracks the historical production of "the sodomite" and then, only with the eleventh-century Peter Damien, of "sodomy," resulting from "long processes of thinning and condensing." "Sodomy," he concludes, "is not a name for a kind of human behavior, but for a failure of theologians."[1] This failure does not express the "queer art" but its successful Christian repression. Performing a theological genealogy Foucault would love (and in some really queer temporality surely does), Jordan's book offers theological history rather than historical theology. It never claims actually to be doing queer theology. But we might read it as prologue, if not prolegomena, not just for queer theology but for any theology that would cease to reproduce its own loss of sexuality.

This essay of Jordan's, differently from the book, is (re)activating the possibility of queer theology itself. The peculiar grace of its possibility gets enacted in the nonseparability of its *what* from its *how*. For queer theology "must perform new 'stylizations.'" One may be tempted to canonize certain passages of the essay as criteria for the dis- and re-orientation of all theological writing: "It cannot drowse in the contentment of commenting on the familiar texts, the established words—or wear itself out just in their critique. Critique in theology is a prelude to composition—which is not the same as 'confession' or 'construction' or 'system' or even satisfying 'story.'" *Composition*—suggestive of a work of art, of performance, or for that matter the materiality of a Whiteheadian concrescence—signifies the rendition of complexity.[2] God, of course, was classically simple, ontologically forbidden to be composite. The composite was firmly opposed by "the logic of the One."[3] Simplicity reigned in metaphysics and allowed convenient simplifications in practice. Hence "so much of theology is written as if it were easier to describe God's essence than to give an account of a single evening's desires." Jordan's apophatic anti-essentialism hints revealingly at the collusion between the simplifications of divine and of sexual identity.[4] And in its nuance it does not merely complicate; it practices a performativity that invites a new style of theological composition.

The specific stylization at play in the composition of Jordan's essay happens to be that which he identifies with Susan Sontag's camping of "the genre of the manifesto." If she does this by way of the "numbered aphorism," that is, with lists of pithy examples, let us note that the form of a list in itself interrupts the straight time of straight-ahead reason. Gaps between numbers take the place of steps in a linear argument unfolding in a homogenized temporality. But a list is hardly atemporal. Jordan's eighteen numbered aphorisms perform their own temporality: eventive juxtapositions, lists within lists, intimate micronarratives anticipatory of the narrative that (according to number 15) he would have written. His manifesto lists; it moves. Indeed, the verb "to list" manifests its own edgy motion, a nonlinear careening, as that of a ship "listing" to one side. Hence the old meaning of listing as bordering, inscribing a margin. But the word unveils a yet more revealing etymology, rooted in the Old English *lystan*: "to please, cause pleasure or desire, provoke longing," from the Proto-Germanic *lustijan*—which is the root of *lust*. In other words, the stylistic device of the list performs a lusty bit of the lost history of sex.

Number 3 on Jordan's list announces that "queer theology is Christianity's long postponed encounter with all the specters of pleasure." So does it not follow that the lostness of queer theology, far from being dismissible as the mere effect of a party line of liberation, signifies here its haunted embrace of lost pleasures? Presumably these specters of pleasure draw on the ghostly possibilities of desires historically disciplined, depressed, or thwarted. They may return only tinted with loss. But Jordan never sacrifices the glimmers of yet possible delight that bubble up desirously no matter what. Of course, to a theologian the encounter with that spectral plenum of pleasures does sound like Marcella Althaus-Reid's indecently polyamorous God. And what could the radical scriptural identification of God as love possibly signify but an infinite polyamory, spectral in its unending composition, holy, ghostly, eschatologically "long postponed," a queer communion of saints?

It seems only fair to fail to end with an answer. I can offer in return only a whole list of questions, anticipating answers that Mark Jordan will no doubt somehow somewhere already have given.

1. How do these long-lost lusts come coupled in queer time with grief for all that had been lost? When Jordan seductively lists those micronarratives he might have written, he writes that they promise "some queer stylization of language around human bodies animated or undone by the divine." I've elsewhere linked Judith Butler's sense of "coming undone" in grief with the medieval Beguine Hadewijch's "in the infinite."[5]

2. Does Jordan's queer theology—*s'il y en a*—allow not just for our animation and undoing "by the divine," but for a divinity animated and undone by us? By human bodies? Not just in one exceptional incarnation, but time-and-again? Polytemporally, polymorphically, perversely, polyamorously?

3. "Animated or undone": Might such animation also signal what Mel Chen means by the animacy of queer affect, flashing beyond anthropocentrism? In the convergences of queer theory, affect theory, and the "new materialism" can we learn a new way of composing ourselves across sexualities—indeed, across cultures, across species, across human and nonhuman force fields? Do new energies animate what Whitney Bauman calls, in his application of Althaus-Reid to ecotheology, "the polyamory of place"?[6] Do they do so in time—given the ravaging advance of climate change?

4. If the undoing of human bodies signals the fragility of flesh, mortal, earthbound, beside itself in lust or in loss, what deftly queer "stylization of language" might Jordan compose, for example, as christology? How might we through his lenses now recode the ancient symbols of incarnation, crucifixion, resurrection, body of Christ? For my part, and in a Jordanian spirit, I would try intercarnation, naked resistance, life beyond bounds, the entangled flesh of a new assemblage.

5. I presume that, for Jordan the theologian, undoing by the divine signifies also undoing of *language* about divinity. What, for instance, might be the queer potential of the apophatic unknowing and unsaying so relentlessly performed in the ancient tradition known as negative theology? I suspect there can be no cozy appropriation of Lee Edelman's "queer negativity" to the mystical negativity. Would Jordan list to a third space, critical of the homo- as well as heteronormative socialities, but only for the sake of unpredictable, apophatically ever still mysterious metamorphoses?

6. How shall we negotiate Jordan's delivery of queer theology as theology itself? Will its queerness avoid being erased, lost again—before it is quite found? And how will he articulate the bodily irreducibilities named, however clumsily, by the particular letters of a still unfolding alphabetic LGBTQI . . . ? What sexual practice, what social performance, would make one able to claim for one's own perspective the lost subject of queer theology? I would not so presume. Nor would I cease to worry that queer theology, recognized as theology itself, could again lose those listing letters, with their particular perfor-

mativities. Yet I imagine that in Jordan's delivery the queerness of theology, even when it unsays itself, will be somehow amplified, intensified, through-composed, by its divinely boundless network.

7. And what sort of human subject is embodied in the haunting multiplicity of a numbered aphorism, a the list? Here why not return to Proust: The Narrator observes in the third volume of *In Search of Lost Time*, "One finds, not oneself, but a succession of selves."[7] Not the self-same ego underlying straight time, not its linear unfolding, but a listing intermittence, an iteration of linked differences. Such a subjectivity gets done and undone in a succession of self-compositions. In such a queerly theological anthropology does the succession mark a process, not the progress of an isolate series or of isolable moments, but the intermittency of mutually entangled becomings? If so, its desirous ethos would surely take pleasure in an altered collectivity, a sociality that cannot be forced, imposed, or willed: "The queer theology I await wants to change the world by reshaping subjects in community."

## NOTES

1. Mark Jordan, *The Invention of Sodomy in Christian Theology* (Chicago: University of Chicago Press, 1998), 175.
2. For Whitehead each event is a bodily self-composition out of its world. Cf. Brian Massumi's rhythmic correlation of activity and composition, as he wires affect theory through Whitehead's concept of the connectively nonlinear temporality of event. Massumi, *Semblance and Event: Activist Philosophy and the Occurrent Arts* (Cambridge, Mass.: MIT Press, 2011), 8.
3. Surely, Laurel Schneider's critique of monotheism, which is already the composition of a divine multiplicity, performs a queerly companionable theology, itself artfully correlating its how with its what. Schneider, *Beyond Monotheism: A Theology of Multiplicity* (London: Routledge, 2008).
4. On the complexities, indeed the *complicatio*, of varieties of apophatic entanglement, see Catherine Keller, *Cloud of the Impossible: Negative Theology and Planetary Entanglement* (New York: Columbia University Press, 2014).
5. Keller discusses Judith Butler and Hadewijch in chapter 7, "Unsaying and Undoing: Judith Butler and the Ethics of Relational Ontology," in *Cloud of the Impossible*.
6. Whitney Bauman, *Religion and Ecology: Developing a Planetary Ethic* (New York: Columbia University Press, 2014). See especially chapter 6, "Developing Planetary Environmental Ethics: A Nomadic Polyamory of Place."
7. Roger Shattuck's translation of *"On ne se réalise que successivement"* in Marcel Proust, *À la recherche du temps perdu* (Paris: Grasset and Gallimard, 1913–27), III 380/v511. Shattuck, *Proust's Way: A Field Guide to* In Search of Lost Time (New York: W. W. Norton, 2000), 6.

# Afterword

ELIZABETH FREEMAN

In the Episcopal Church, there is a Sunday school curriculum called Godly Play. Based on Montessori principles, the curriculum involves an adult telling a Bible story, parable, or "liturgical action" story, using small figurines and symbolic objects to make the story pictorial and compelling to children ages three through ten. The very first story the children hear, "The Circle of the Church Year," is about time.[1]

"Time," the teller asks in this story. "What is time? Some people say that time is in a line, but I wonder what that would look like?" (26). The storyteller pulls a length of gold cord partway out from where it has been concealed in her hand. She goes on: "Time in a line. This is time in a line. Look at this. Here is the beginning. It is the newest part. It is just being born. It is brand new. Now look" (27). She pulls the cord all the way out until it drops to the floor: "Look. It is getting older. The part that was new is now getting old. I wonder how long time goes. Does it go forever? Could there ever be an ending?" (27). Then she picks up the two ends of the cord and looks at them: "The beginning that was so new at the beginning now is old. The ending is the new part now. We have a beginning that is like an ending and an ending that is like a beginning" (27).

Then, the miracle. The storyteller ties the two ends of the golden cord together: "Do you know what the Church did? They tied the ending that was like a beginning, and the beginning that was like an ending together, so we would always remember that for every ending there is a beginning and for every beginning there is an ending" (27). She places the gold cord around a circular puzzle set in a flat square board. The pieces of the puzzle are small colored wedges of different colors, set into a circular groove: a long run of green wedges, a run of purple, a white one with a star, a shorter run of green, a longer run of purple, a white one with a cross followed by six white ones, and a single red one.

The story goes on to tell the children that each wedge stands for a week in the year, and that time has colors: green for ordinary "growing" time and purple for "getting ready" times (Lent and Advent). The teller then points the three arrows toward the major feast days: white blocks for Christmas and Easter, and a red block for the singularity that is Pentecost. "Ouch—that's hot!" the storyteller says when she touches the red block.

Children begin attending Godly Play at the age of three. And having absorbed already that, as the story begins, "There is a time to get up in the morning. There is a time to go to bed. There is a time to go to school and a time to come home. There is a time to work, and there is a time to play," they are inculcated into the mysteries of liturgical time even before they can tell mechanical clock time (26). I didn't grow up Episcopalian, so this was not my childhood. I more or less followed my then-partner—who was in training to be an Episcopal deacon—into church as an adult, and started teaching Godly Play because it seemed just about my speed as far as absorbing scripture and theology went. But when I first started as a storyteller, I went around feeling secret glee that it was green time, or purple time, as if I partook in a rare form of temporal synaesthesia shared by only a few.

Of course, Christianity is full of strange temporalities. Is this time of colors, liturgical time, queer? Not, I suppose, if queer must have something to do with recognizably erotic embodiments and practices, as I've argued elsewhere without thinking about what might distinguish a secular form of eroticism from a religious one.[2] But one of the great things about living adjacent to Christianity for more than a decade—in it, but not fully of it, insofar as I admit that my beliefs remain stubbornly and sometimes agonizingly agnostic—is how much it has broadened my sense of the erotic beyond modern sexual taxonomies, beyond what is recognizably sexual in secular culture, and how much it has resonated with seemingly secular queer theories of the erotic, as so many of the authors in this collection seem to have known for far longer than I.

Part of this capacious eroticism involves living adjacent to, in dissonance with, or otherwise aslant of secular time, the time that sharply divides getting up from going to bed, going to school from coming home, working from playing. The synaesthesia of purple time is erotic insofar as it disposes bodies toward practices and forms of togetherness that are less than fully visible to secular culture. Within the strange temporalities of Christianity, bodies and desires are unbound from their proper places: I think here of Joseph Marchal's Corinthian women who experience change in terms of an unauthorized velocity; of James Hoke's dissidents whose relation to pleasure discombobulates Roman imperial time; of Cherríe Moraga's Chicanx Codex as described by Jacqueline M. Hidalgo, which disorients Judeo-Christian time even as it brings Chicanx subjects home; of Maia Kotrosits's "queer persistences" in the face of the theological impulse to get to the end of that golden cord; of Lot's wife looking and feeling backward, turning to salt as a way of bearing witness in Kent Brintnall's essay; of those death-driven queers tumbling off the cliff in Brock Perry's reading of Peter (and that's just the first half of this volume). These are bodies whose ways of living time warp, (dis)orient, stretch, transmogrify, splatter them into being/unbeing/form/nonform: The grammar of this sentence frustrates, as these bodies do not exist before the temporal twists that constitute them, nor does time exist separately as something they encounter.

With these bodies in mind, the queerest moment in that Godly Play story for me, then, is this: "Ouch—that's hot!" The children always giggle; the very littlest ones want to touch the red block. They want to meet this strange new time with their bodies, as the storyteller has done. We don't explain to them what Pentecost is at this point in the year, so the moment remains a mystery: Even the newest students probably know that Christmas is Jesus' birthday and possibly that Easter has something to do with his death, but they rarely know a thing about Pentecost (and anyway, Pentecost is slightly embarrassing to a lot of genteel Episcopalians). But they experience it vicariously and are prepared for it unknowingly, in the storyteller's gesture. You touch something holy, or it touches you, and your body responds with a sensation, and the sensation brings you closer to God: That's Pentecost, and that moment when red becomes hot is the wooden calendar's most charged moment of synaesthesia. And it appears as a moment of instantaneity, on a map of what otherwise represents time in lines, circles, and segments.

Mark Jordan writes movingly and beautifully, in this volume, of queer theology needing the techniques of a "new narrative," one that can surmount or displace the secular times of identity, of maturity, of profit—all these times of arrival. The circular time of the liturgical calendar is not particularly new, but its tangible qualities bring up important questions to me about theology. Must theology, queer or otherwise, always involve the linguistic? Insofar as logos is the word, I suppose it must. Yet what narrative structure can capture that flash, that mutually transformative meeting of object and body, which the little Pentecostal moment of the Godly Play story emblematizes? I can't pretend to be a theologian of Pentecost—perhaps there are things to say about why the touch of the Holy Spirit as wind and fire causes the disciples to speak in other languages, and why in modern Pentecostalism these tongues have become entirely theretofore unheard-of languages (are they, then, languages at all?)—but I can say that its appeal to me lies in the way it indexes the incarnational. The Pentecostal moment shows us the incarnational as the performative, thought in terms of gestures that do what they purport only to represent: I am touching this block, and that touch confirms its hotness. In this encounter, the incarnate becomes "promiscuous," as Laurel Schneider describes it elsewhere, for I, the toucher, am not God, but incarnation leaks in, somehow.[3] The block becomes, at least for the children, animated and sensate as it "burns" me. There is an incarnational impulse in this touch.

Or, to use Catherine Keller's term from this volume, in this gesture incarnation becomes *inter*carnational: I am making this block, whose hotness makes me touch it, hot, and its hotness is making me react, making me something else too. Is that what the Holy Spirit does, I ask, risking bad theology? That's what I think José Muñoz was getting at when he wrote of those glimpses of utopia in the dance club: those moments when we were (are still, José, I promise!) making, with our bodies, the worlds we need to live in, even as those worlds are clearly making us too, making us queer. And that makes me wonder: Must queer theology always involve not only language but also God? Is affect—that intensity felt when an experience passes from one body to another, transforming one or both—divine in and of itself, rather than merely evidence of the divine? Is it what divinity is? Michael Moon and Eve Sedgwick make a claim of this sort, describing divinity as "the precipitation of one's body" in fatness, or gender extravagance, or both.[4] And the time of this precipitation can certainly feel epiphanic and instantaneous, but is it always? Can it happen slowly, over time, through loving and careful inculcation?

Might that transfer of intensity or that precipitation of the body, on a small scale, at a slow pace, simply be called teaching? It is funny to think of the story of Pentecost as a story about teaching: The teacher (and I was brought up to think of Jesus only as a teacher, a mortal teacher, not the son of God) blows a mighty wind that touches the students, enlightens them in some way, and they begin to talk in ways they never have before, but not to one another. Some people can understand other people, but not everybody can understand everybody. Speaking (speaking theory?), the students sound merely drunk. They see visions, and they dream dreams, and that's the beginning of their own worldmaking. Is that, too, incarnational? Is that what the touch of the red block also emblematizes?

I, too, have been a student, most recently of this volume. Momentarily, I have experienced and/or been transformed into: a dog left out of Revelation (Eric Thomas), a practitioner of the contemplative (Brandy Daniels), bipolar time (Karen Bray), the possibility that all my radical thinking is absolutely in keeping with neoliberalism (Linn Marie Tonstad), the capacity of psychoanalysis to do highly religious things (Ann Pellegrini), hauntings of the yet-to-come (Karmen MacKendrick), the possibility that queer theory is theology and that queer theology is queer theory (Mary-Jane Rubenstein), and much more. Reading it as a mostly secular person with a keen sense that faith is a knowledge form and that queer is where the secular and the religious become indistinct, I have felt like my own Godly Play students, peering at things that alternately seem inscrutable and miraculously transparent. These writings have touched me, and I am different, but I can't say how by arriving at a fixed form that will allow me to represent myself to you right now. I can only say: Ouch—that's hot.

## NOTES

1. "Lesson 1: The Circle of the Church Year," in *The Complete Guide to Godly Play*, by Jerome Berryman, vol. 2 (New York: Morehouse Education Resources/Church Publishing, 2002), 23–33. Hereafter referred to by page number in the body of the essay.
2. Elizabeth Freeman, "Still After," *South Atlantic Quarterly* 106, no. 3 (2007): 495–500.
3. Laurel Schneider, "Promiscuous Incarnation," in *The Embrace of Eros: Bodies, Desires, and Sexuality in Christianity*, ed. Margaret Kamitsuka (Minneapolis: Fortress Press, 2010), 231–45.
4. Michael Moon and Eve Kosofsky Sedgwick, "Divinity: A Dossier, a Performance Piece, a Little-Understood Emotion" (1992), in Eve Kosofsky Sedgwick, *Tendencies* (Durham, N.C.: Duke University Press, 1993), 217. The full quote describes "the precipitation of one's body as a kind of cul-de-sac blockage or clot in the circulation of economic value," but I am not sure that I would limit the effect of this precipitation to blockage or its field of impact to the economic.

# ACKNOWLEDGMENTS

This volume had its origins in the proceedings of the fourteenth Transdisciplinary Theological Colloquium, also titled "Sexual Disorientations: Queer Temporalities, Affects, Theologies," and held at Drew Theological School in Madison, New Jersey, on September 26–28, 2014. The first Transdisciplinary Theological Colloquium, which took place in 2001, was the brainchild of Catherine Keller, George T. Cobb Professor of Constructive Theology at Drew, and Catherine has been a beatific guiding presence and sturdy supporting pillar behind and beneath every TTC since then, including "Sexual Disorientations." Crucial too was the unstinting support of Javier Viera, Dean of Drew Theological School.

The editors of this volume experienced TTC XIV and the preparation of this volume as an energizing collaboration. Kent Brintnall and Joseph Marchal appreciated the opportunity to be the first non-Drew folk ever to co-organize a TTC, in partnership with Catherine Keller and Stephen Moore. The editors also thank Lindsey Guy and Jimmy Hoke, two Drew PhD students, for capably and indefatigably attending to every practical aspect of the colloquium, ensuring that it ran smoothly from beginning to end.

In addition to the colloquium participants whose essays appear in this volume, an extensive cast of further participants—moderators, respondents, discussants, and student presenters—also enriched the program. They include Ellen Armour, Christy Cobb, Richard Coble, Rhiannon Graybill, Lynn Huber, Melanie Johnson-DeBaufre, Minenhle Nomalungelo Khumalo, Paige Rawson, Shelly Rambo, Sara Rosenau, Max Thornton, Terry Todd, Natalie Williams, and Lydia York.

Special gratitude is also due to Richard Morrison and Tom Lay, editorial director and acquisitions editor, respectively, at Fordham University Press, whose interest in the theme of TTC XIV extended to making the pilgrimage out to Drew to participate firsthand in the proceedings.

# CONTRIBUTORS

**KAREN BRAY** is an assistant professor of religion and philosophy and the director of religious studies and philosophy at Wesleyan College in Macon, Georgia. She earned her PhD in theological and philosophical studies in religion from Drew University in 2016 and her MDiv from Harvard Divinity School in 2010. Her research areas include continental philosophy of religion; feminist, critical disability, affect, critical race, queer, political, and decolonial theories and theologies; and secularism and the postsecular. She is particularly interested in exploring how secular institutions and cultures behave theologically. Dr. Bray's work has been published in the *American Journal of Theology and Philosophy*, the *Journal for Cultural and Religious Theory*, *Palgrave Communications*, and in volumes published by Fordham University Press and Palgrave Macmillan.

**KENT L. BRINTNALL** is an associate professor of religious studies and director of the graduate certificate in gender, sexuality, and women's studies at the University of North Carolina at Charlotte. He is the author of *Ecce Homo: The Male-Body-in-Pain as Redemptive Figure* (University of Chicago Press, 2011), coeditor, with Jeremy Biles, of *Negative Ecstasies: Georges Bataille and the Study of Religion* (Fordham University Press, 2015), and editor of *Embodied Religion* (Macmillan, 2016). He is currently working on a project on the intractability of violence that stages a conversation among Leo Bersani, Georges Bataille, Lee Edelman, and Jean Laplanche.

**BRANDY DANIELS** is a PhD candidate in theological studies at Vanderbilt University. Her research focuses on theological anthropology and practices of formation, exploring intersections between constructive theologies and feminist and queer theories to better understand and envision accounts of faithful Christian identity and community amid difference. She has an MDiv and an

MA in comparative literature from Duke University. She is currently a faculty fellow at McCormick Theological Seminary and is preparing for ordination in the Disciples of Christ (Christian Church).

ELIZABETH FREEMAN is a professor of English at the University of California, Davis, and coeditor of *GLQ: A Journal of Lesbian and Gay Studies*. She has published two books with Duke University Press, *The Wedding Complex: Forms of Belonging in Modern American Culture* (2002) and *Time Binds: Queer Temporalities, Queer Histories* (2010).

JACQUELINE M. HIDALGO is an assistant professor of Latina/o studies and religion at Williams College in Massachusetts. She is the author of *Revelation in Aztlán: Scripture, Utopias, and the Chicano Movement* (Palgrave Macmillan, 2016), which examines the Chican@ civil rights movement as an intervention into hemispherically American legacies and interpretations of the Book of Revelation.

JAMES N. HOKE is Visiting Assistant Professor of Religion at Luther College. He received his Ph.D. in New Testament and Early Christianity at Drew University in 2017. Drawing from Greco-Roman, Jewish, and early Christian materials, James's research reconstructs conversations within the earliest assemblies of Christ-followers and shows how they manifest and contribute to contemporary queer, feminist, and affect theories.

MARK D. JORDAN is the Mellon Professor of Christian Thought and a professor of studies of women, gender, and sexuality at Harvard University. His books include *Moral Formation in the Summa of Thomas Aquinas* (Fordham University Press, 2016), *Convulsing Bodies: Religion and Resistance in Foucault* (Stanford University Press, 2014) and *Recruiting Young Love: How Christians Talk about Homosexuality* (University of Chicago Press, 2011).

CATHERINE KELLER is George T. Cobb Professor of Constructive Theology at Drew University Theological School and Graduate Division of Religion. In her teaching, lecturing, and writing, she develops the relational potential of a theology of becoming. Her books reconfigure ancient symbols of divinity for the sake of planetary conviviality—a life together, across vast webs of difference. Thriving in the interplay of ecological and gender politics, of process cosmology, poststructuralist philosophy and religious pluralism, her work is both deconstructive and constructive in strategy. Her most recent book, *Cloud of the Impossible: Negative Theology and Planetary Entanglements* (Columbia University Press, 2014), explores the relation of mystical unknowing, material indeterminacy, and ontological interdependence.

MAIA KOTROSITS is an assistant professor of religion at Denison University. Her research finds points of contact between ancient Christian / diaspora Jewish literature and contemporary cultural studies, queer and feminist theories. Surfacing themes of violence, belonging, and collective experiences of pain and loss, she finds connections and disjunctions between the ancient world and some worlds of the present. She has co-written books on the ancient Coptic poem *The Thunder: Perfect Mind* as well as on the Gospel of Mark. Her book *Rethinking Early Christian Identity: Affect, Violence, and Belonging* (Fortress Press, 2015) is a reexamination of the centrality of the designation "Christian" in the doing of what is called early Christian history, and a set of proposals for how to understand some New Testament and affiliated literature without it.

KARMEN MACKENDRICK is a professor in the philosophy department at Le Moyne College (Syracuse, New York). Her work centers on and returns to a small cluster of interests: desire, language, flesh, and time, especially in their various and paradoxical entanglements. Recent works include *The Matter of Voice: Sensual Soundings* (2016), *Divine Enticement* (2013), *Seducing Augustine*, with Virginia Burrus and Mark Jordan (2010), and *Fragmentation and Memory* (2008), all from Fordham University Press.

JOSEPH A. MARCHAL is an associate professor of religious studies and affiliated faculty in women's and gender studies at Ball State University. His work explores, combines, and elaborates aspects of feminist, postcolonial, and queer approaches, crossing between biblical studies and critical theories of interpretation, the ancient world and its many, very contemporary echoes and impacts. He is the author of *Philippians: Historical Problems, Hierarchical Visions, and Hysterical Anxieties* (Sheffield Phoenix, 2014); *The Politics of Heaven: Women, Gender, and Empire in the Study of Paul* (Fortress, 2008); and *Hierarchy, Unity, and Imitation: A Feminist Rhetorical Analysis of Power Dynamics in Paul's Letter to the Philippians* (Society of Biblical Literature, 2006). He is also the editor of *The People beside Paul: The Philippian Assembly and History from Below* (SBL, 2015) and *Studying Paul's Letters: Contemporary Perspectives and Methods* (Fortress, 2012). He is currently working on a book focused on queer approaches to the strangely gendered figures echoing behind and after Paul's letters.

STEPHEN D. MOORE is Edmund S. Janes Professor of New Testament Studies at Drew University Theological School and Graduate Division of Religion.

His many books include *God's Gym: Divine Male Bodies of the Bible* (Routledge, 1996), *God's Beauty Parlor: And Other Queer Spaces in and around the Bible* (Stanford University Press, 2001), *The Bible in Theory: Critical and Postcritical Essays* (Society of Biblical Literature, 2010), *The Invention of the Biblical Scholar: A Critical Manifesto* (with Yvonne Sherwood; Fortress Press, 2011), *Untold Tales from the Book of Revelation: Sex and Gender, Empire and Ecology* (SBL Press, 2014), and *Gospel Jesuses and Other Nonhumans: Biblical Criticism Post-Poststructuralism* (SBL Press, forthcoming).

ANN PELLEGRINI is a professor of performance studies (Tisch School of the Arts) and social and cultural analysis (Faculty of Arts & Sciences) at New York University, where she also directs the center for the study of gender and sexuality. Her books are *Performance Anxieties: Staging Psychoanalysis, Staging Race* (Routledge, 1997), *Love the Sin: Sexual Regulation and the Limits of Religious Tolerance*, coauthored with Janet R. Jakobsen (New York University Press, 2003), *Queer Theory and the Jewish Question*, coedited with Daniel Boyarin and Daniel Itzkovitz (Columbia University Press, 2003), *Securalisms*, coedited with Janet R. Jakobsen (Duke University Press, 2008), and *"You Can Tell Just by Looking" and 20 Other Myths about LGBT Life and People*, coauthored with Michael Bronski and Michael Amico (Beacon Press, 2013). She also coedits the Sexual Cultures book series at New York University Press with Tavia Nyong'o and Joshua Takano Chambers-Letson. She enjoys psychoanalysis and show tunes, and began the respecialization program at the Institute for Psychoanalytic Training and Research (IPTAR) in New York City in September 2014.

BROCK PERRY is a PhD candidate in theological and philosophical studies in religion at Drew University. He holds an MA from Chicago Theological Seminary and a graduate certificate in public health from the Indiana University School of Medicine. Drawing on theology, continental philosophy, cultural studies, and critical theory, his scholarship focuses primarily on the history of Western Christianity, the history and theories of secularization, political theology, and queer studies in religion.

MARY-JANE RUBENSTEIN is a professor of religion at Wesleyan University; core faculty in the Feminist, Gender, and Sexuality Studies Program; and affiliated faculty in the Science and Society Program. Her research interests include continental philosophy, theology, gender and sexuality studies, and the history and philosophy of cosmology. She is the author of *Strange Wonder: The Closure of Metaphysics and the Opening of Awe* (2010) and *Worlds without End: The Many Lives of the Multiverse* (2014), both from Columbia University Press.

LAUREL C. SCHNEIDER is a professor of religious studies and women's and gender studies at Vanderbilt University, where she teaches courses in Christian theology, queer and gender theories, and Native American religious traditions. She is the author of *Beyond Monotheism: A Theology of Multiplicity* (Routledge, 2008) and *Re-imagining the Divine* (Pilgrim, 1999) along with numerous articles and anthology chapters that variously work at the intersections of theology with queer, race, postcolonial, and feminist theories. She also coedited, with Stephen G. Ray Jr., *Awake to the Moment: An Introduction to Theology* (Westminster John Knox Press, 2016), and with Catherine Keller, *Polydoxy: Theologies of Multiplicity and Relation* (Routledge, 2010). She is currently at work on two books, one titled "Promiscuous Incarnation" and the other, untitled as yet, on Native American philosophy and Christian ontology.

ERIC A. THOMAS is a PhD candidate in New Testament and early Christianity at Drew University. His research focuses on the intersection of Africana studies and queer theory as a site for biblical interpretation, with an emphasis on meaning making with LGBTQ faith communities and allies. He is a graduate of the Interdenominational Theological Center (ITC) and serves as the director of Christian education at the First Presbyterian Church of Brooklyn, New York. His essay "Tales from the Crypt: A Same Gender Loving (SGL) Reading of Mark 5:1–20—Backwards" was published in the *Journal of the ITC*.

LINN MARIE TONSTAD is an assistant professor of systematic theology at Yale Divinity School. She is a constructive theologian working at the intersection of systematic theology with feminist and queer theory. She is the author of *God and Difference: The Trinity, Sexuality, and the Transformation of Finitude* (Routledge, 2015), which explores the limitations of contemporary Trinitarian theology from a queer and feminist perspective, as well as several articles on Trinitarian theology and theological method. Her next project will treat anthropology and ecclesiology in conversation with recent debates about queer temporality.

# INDEX

## TRANSDISCIPLINARY THEOLOGICAL COLLOQUIA

Laurel Kearns and Catherine Keller, eds., *Ecospirit: Religions and Philosophies for the Earth.*

Virginia Burrus and Catherine Keller, eds., *Toward a Theology of Eros: Transfiguring Passion at the Limits of Discipline.*

Ada María Isasi-Díaz and Eduardo Mendieta, eds., *Decolonizing Epistemologies: Latina/o Theology and Philosophy.*

Stephen D. Moore and Mayra Rivera, eds., *Planetary Loves: Spivak, Postcoloniality, and Theology.*

Chris Boesel and Catherine Keller, eds., *Apophatic Bodies: Negative Theology, Incarnation, and Relationality.*

Chris Boesel and S. Wesley Ariarajah, eds., *Divine Multiplicity: Trinities, Diversities, and the Nature of Relation.*

Stephen D. Moore, ed., *Divinanimality: Animal Theory, Creaturely Theology.* Foreword by Laurel Kearns.

Melanie Johnson-DeBaufre, Catherine Keller, and Elias Ortega-Aponte, eds., *Common Goods: Economy, Ecology, and Political Theology.*

Catherine Keller and Mary-Jane Rubenstein, eds., *Entangled Worlds: Religion, Science, and New Materialisms.*

Kent L. Brintnall, Joseph A. Marchal, and Stephen D. Moore, eds., *Sexual Disorientations: Queer Temporalities, Affects, Theologies.*